Icelanders in North America

ICELANDERS
IN NORTH AMERICA

THE FIRST SETTLERS

JONAS THOR

UNIVERSITY OF MANITOBA PRESS

University of Manitoba Press
Winnipeg, Manitoba R3T 2N2
Canada
www.umanitoba.ca/uofmpress
Printed in Canada.

Cover Design: Kirk Warren
Text Design: Karen Armstrong and Sharon Caseburg
Cover photograph: Icelandic Immigrants Crossing the Atlantic Ocean (Þjóðminjasafn Íslands)

Canadian Cataloguing in Publication Data

National Library of Canada Cataloguing in Publication Data

Jónas Þór, 1949-
  Icelanders in North America : the first settlers / Jonas Thor.

  Includes bibliographical references and index.
  ISBN 0-88755-661-2

  1. Icelanders--North America--History. 2. Iceland--Emigration and
immigration--History--19th century. I. Title.
E49.2.I3J66 2002   971'.0043961   C2002-911113-7

The University of Manitoba Press gratefully acknowledges the financial support for its publication program provided by the Government of Canada through the Book Publishing Industry Development Program (BPIDP); the Canada Council for the Arts; the Manitoba Arts Council; and the Manitoba Department of Culture, Heritage and Tourism.

Publication of this book has been made possible by the support of the Icelandic Literature and Language fund of the Department of Icelandic, University of Manitoba, and of Dr. T. Kenneth Thorlakson.

To my family

Contents

List of Maps and Photographs

Map of Iceland / 6

Maps and Photographs Following Page 94
Reykjavík, c. 1870
Akureyri, c. 1886
Immigrants Crossing the Atlantic
Oddur Magnusson on Washington Island, 1873
Pall Thorlaksson
Jon Bjarnason
Gudmundur Gudmundsson, 1931
Steamship *Ontario*
"Icelandic Castle"
Sigtryggur Jonasson and Pall Johannsson, 1874
Women at spinning wheel
Map of Ontario settlements
Map of upper midwestern settlements

Maps and Photographs Following Page 162
Map of Manitoba and Saskatchewan settlements
Map of Alberta and West Coast settlements
Icelandic woodcarving
Stephansson home and family, 1907
Petur Asmundsson, 1905
O.G. Arngrimsson
O.G. Anderson's store, c. 1915
Steamship *Manitoba*, 1875
Vidir School, c. 1915
Sigurdsson's general store, c. 1915
Icelandic River post office, 1907
Winnipeg, c. 1890s
Steep Rock, Manitoba, c. 1916-1917
Brailing salmon, Point Roberts, c. 1898
West Point Roberts, c. 1890s
Point Roberts school class, c. 1914

Acknowledgements

First and foremost I would like to thank the Government of Iceland for funding my research and writing. This book has been published with their assistance. Special thanks to Einar Benediktsson and Atli Ásmundsson, to whom I could always turn for assistance and advice. I am greatly indebted to Professor Gerald Friesen at the University of Manitoba, who read and edited the manuscript in the preliminary stages and whose help during the entire process of writing was invaluable. I owe thanks to one of Iceland's leading historians, Jón Þ. Þór, who co-wrote the segment on nineteenth-century Iceland. Thanks to another Icelandic scholar, Viðar Hreinsson, for sharing important material and valuable information on the Shawano County settlement. I would like to thank Skarphéðinn B. Steinarsson in Reykjavík, Iceland, for his patience and understanding through the years.

Special thanks to David Carr of the University of Manitoba Press, who from the beginning was encouraging and understanding. I also would like to express my gratitude to Pat Sanders, for her editing, to Sharon Caseburg, assistant editor, and to Weldon Hiebert, for producing maps.

I owe much to many others for the production of this work. My wife, Anna Bára, not only stood by me through the entire process, but also was invaluable in proofreading and indexing. I wish to thank especially Baldvin and Margaret Juliusson, formerly of Regina, Saskatchewan, Dale Amundson and Dr. Ken Thorlakson in Winnipeg, Arleen Wagner in Fisher, and John Bergson in Duluth, Minnesota, John Sand in Blaine, and Pauline Dehaan at Point Roberts, Washington, John Bjarnason in White Rock, BC, and Jón Ólafur Þórsteinsson in Reykjavík, Iceland.

The publishers would like to thank the following people for their valuable and willing assistance in locating photographs: Frank Josephson, Daren Gislason, and Ray Olafson of Minneota; Hannes M. Andersen of Washington Island, Arlene Wagner of Fisher; Dee Anna Grimsrud of the Wisconsin Historical Society; and Sigrid Johnson, Icelandic Collection, University of Manitoba.

Icelanders in North America

Introduction

During the nineteenth century, Iceland experienced great societal changes, as economic, political, and cultural developments throughout the century eventually resulted in the migration of thousands of Icelanders to the New World.

The Romantic movement that swept across Europe in the first half of the century, demanding freedom of thought, press, and conscience, had a significant impact on intellectual life and social thought in Iceland. The contemporary literature expressed strong feelings, and stressed patriotic sentiment tinged with emotionalism. It demanded freedom from foreign intellectual influence and foreign dominion, and called for a new emphasis on nationalism. A new periodical, *Fjölnir,* championed slogans such as "We will all be Icelanders," "We will protect our language and nationality," and, finally, "We will have Althing at Thingvellir." (The last referred to the love of historical traditions; Althing had been founded at Thingvellir in 930, making it the oldest parliament in the world.) Poets sang of the beauty of Iceland, its natural splendour and its titanic, mythological grandeur. At the same time, the new literature called on the people to fight foreign influence.

The reawakening of the old national spirit, the Romantic love of country, and the pride in ancient traditions raised the self-esteem of the Icelandic people, but many adverse conditions during the period eventually created an environment where romanticism was replaced by realism. There was little headway in the struggle for independence from the Danes, volcanic eruptions greatly damaged the limited arable land in parts of the country, and unusually cold winters forced a large number of farmers in certain regions to abandon their farms. Critical and often negative realists pointed to the darker side of life in Iceland, the poverty and poor economic conditions, and eventually, many people opted for migration.

From 1870 to 1914 there was continous emigration from Iceland to America. Those years have always been referred to by the Icelanders as the Emigration Period, probably because never before or since has there been emigration on such a large scale from the country. Conditions in North America often had no effect on the number of Icelanders choosing to leave their homeland. For example, despite the financial crises in New York in the early 1870s, which resulted in tremendous unemployment in the succeeding years, two large groups of Icelanders arrived in North America in 1873 and 1874.

In the period from 1906 to 1914, there was a clear drop in the annual number of emigrants from Iceland to North America. Signs of economic growth in Iceland, as well as positive results in the struggle for independence, resulted in a decreasing interest in emigration. The outbreak of World War I may not have completely ended the migration from Iceland, but after 1914 it became insignificant and by that year, the major Icelandic settlements in North America had been established. This book examines the founding of numerous Icelandic settlements in the US and Canada until 1914. Several were eventually abandoned, but others flourished almost from the beginning.

Although just a small portion of the Icelandic emigrants had reached North America by the 1870s, this first decade of Icelandic migration to the New World was significant, because it was then that the dream of establishing a homogenous Icelandic colony was born and ended. Immigrants in America sought freedom for various reasons, many wishing to settle exclusively because of religious reasons. To this day, such groups exist in the US and Canada. But most Icelanders dreamed of their all-Icelandic colony for ethnic reasons. None of them left Iceland fearing a loss of their religion, but most worried about their Icelandic heritage. How Icelandic could they remain in the New World?

The struggle to accept their role in the North American community took place in the 1870s. It was a struggle that brought about controversies and eventually disunion. The settlers from Iceland did not carry much with them from their homeland, which made their adjustments to American society difficult. The vast difference between their own country, where only ten percent of the land was arable and around one percent was cultivated, and the enormous prairies of North America, where most Icelanders eventually settled, was overwhelming. Their agricultural knowledge was limited to raising stock; any type of grain growing was new to them. This inexperience in North American agricultural ways is clearly reflected in their choice of settlement sites in the 1870s. For example, the heaths of Nova Scotia in 1875 offered plenty of grass but nothing else grew there, and to this day no attempts have been made to cultivate that area.

Coming to America and insisting on an exclusive settlement site also meant the immigrants would manage all their own religious and cultural affairs. Their own direct involvement in the nineteenth-century State Church of Iceland was minimal, and all education was in the hands of the state, as well. Inexperienced in such affairs, the Icelanders had different opinions as to how to participate in the New World's church and state. Some argued that in North America they should accept North American systems and mores, while others insisted their religious institutions be based on the Icelandic system. To the latter group, the construction of religious and cultural life in an exclusive Icelandic settlement had to be purely Icelandic in nature.

In the 1870s there was no reconciliation among these dissenting factions, and a religious controversy that began in 1874 eventually ended the dream of an Icelandic colony at the close of the decade. Gradually, however, this approach to settlement changed. Wherever the Icelandic immigrants chose to assimilate and live mixed with other ethnic groups, their adjustment to North American ways was faster and smoother. Such was the case, for example, in Minnesota, North Dakota, rural Manitoba after 1880, and Saskatchewan.

A gradual assimilation took place, but the continuous immigration from Iceland and the dedication of the pioneers ensured the transplantation of Icelandic heritage. This was most evident in the tremendous quantity of material published in Icelandic throughout the continent during the settlement period. In addition, thousands of unpublished letters, autobiographies, and articles have surfaced in recent years, both in North America and Iceland.

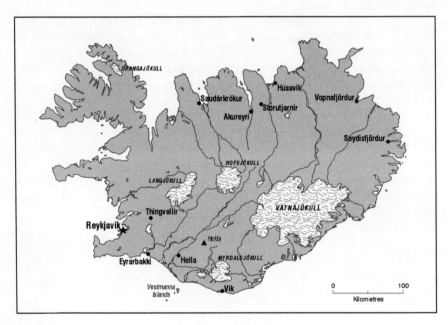

Iceland

1

Nineteenth-Century Iceland: Early Migration

In the history of Iceland, the nineteenth century is often considered to be a period of almost uninterrupted economic and demographic progress, an age of renaissance and revival when the Icelanders began to regain their national self-confidence, and the long struggle for independence from Denmark commenced. However, during most of that century, life was still difficult in Iceland, and during the last three decades, almost 12,000 Icelanders opted to leave their homeland and emigrate to North America. The reasons for this exodus, by far the biggest in Icelandic history, are many and complex, and can be understood best through an examination of the general development of Icelandic society.

The eighteenth century was undoubtedly the most difficult period in the history of the Icelandic people. In 1707 a smallpox epidemic wiped out nearly one-third of the population, and the century ended with worse natural disasters caused by volcanic eruptions in southern Iceland. In 1785, the population was at an historic low of 40,623. In addition, the climate was unusually harsh during much of the 1700s; and the Danish trade monopoly was unfavourable to the Icelanders, and despite reform attempts, the two main industries, fishing and livestock farming, stagnated.

The Napoleonic Wars at the beginning of the nineteenth century prevented normal communication with Denmark, severely damaging export of Icelandic products and import of necessary items such as cereals. To make commerce worse,

Denmark suffered a crisis of inflation, which eventually resulted in a bank crash
in which many Icelandic officials were affected. The Bishop in Reykjavík, for
example, who received his salary in Danish currency, went bankrupt.

Slowly, conditions began to improve during the mid-nineteenth century. The
climate was relatively favourable from 1820 to 1860; average temperatures rose
to approximately 3.2° to 3.3°C, compared to 2.7° to 2.9°C during the last quarter
of the 1700s. Trade improved, as did fishing and farming. As a result, a population growth occurred.

Population in Iceland 1801-1901

Censuses	Total Population	Annual Increase
1801	47,240	......
1835	56,035	0.50
1840	57,094	0.33
1845	58,558	0.51
1850	59,157	0.24
1855	64,603	1.57
1860	66,987	0.73
1870	69,763	0.41
1880	72,445	0.38
1890	70,927	-0.21
1901	78,470	0.92

Source: *Hagskinna* (Reykjavík1997), 49.

The population increase was significant; it probably was the first time since the
Middle Ages that a prolonged population growth could be recorded in Iceland. The
relatively slow population growth during the 1860s and 1870s, and the decrease in
population during the 1880s, were, to a great extent, caused by emigration. Demographic growth was also hampered by a high mortality rate, especially among infants and young people.

Since the Middle Ages, the economy of Iceland had been almost exclusively
based on fishing and livestock farming. Farming was the most important occupation in the north, east, and south, and fishing was predominant in coastal regions
in the southwest and the northwest.

Farming in Iceland was traditionally on single farms, which were often located at a considerable distance from each other. The farming villages or communal farming known in parts of Europe were unheard of in Iceland. Icelanders
concentrated on rearing livestock, mostly sheep, cattle, and horses. Sheep were
raised for production of meat, milk, and wool, cattle were raised for milk, and
horses were used for transportation. All grain had to be imported, and cultivation
of potatoes and other vegetables was still on a very small scale. Farming was
thus primarily aimed at producing food for domestic consumption, and wool and

hides for clothing. However, there was always some export of knitwear and other woollen products. Salted meat was also exported. These exports were vital for farmers, especially in the northern and eastern regions.

The pattern of habitation in the Icelandic countryside changed little from around 1500 until the early twentieth century. Farms were scattered all along the coast-line, the lowlands, and often deep into the valleys. Clusters of huts and small dwellings were built close to the main fishing stations. But, despite the absence of significant changes, the countryside was far from being static. Most of the main farms were populated throughout the period (1500 to 1900), but occupation of many smaller and more peripheral farms, mostly held by tenants, was less stable. In periods of epidemics or prolonged harsh climate, when many people died of disease or hunger, tenants of smaller farms either died or abandoned their farms, because the land could not sustain them. On occasion, they moved to settle on bigger and more productive farms, when such opportunities were available.

During good periods, the opposite happened. The population grew; young people married and started families. These new families would obtain possession of abandoned farms, often in places where farming was possible only in the best years. This frequently occurred in the 1800s.

In 1800, the number of occupied farms in Iceland was 5309, rising steadily to 6264 in 1872. However, the growing population could no longer be sustained through traditional farming methods and the countryside became overpopulated. In order to overcome the problem, young people began to settle in peripheral areas, especially in the northern and eastern regions where they ventured into the mountains, places no one had ever attempted to settle before.

While the climate remained favourable, such settlements managed to subsist, but during the 1870s and 1880s, this changed, due to severely cold spells, which often lasted well into the summer. To make matters worse, a volcanic eruption began in 1875, spreading layers of ash and poisonous gases over large, vulner-able regions, on which the livelihood of many farmers depended. This forced settlers in the remote parts off their land and back into the lowlands. However, in the lowlands, there was nothing available for them. Not only was every inch of arable land used, but farmers were ridding themselves of labourers, rather than adding new ones. The small towns and villages offered no prospects and some even turned away new settlers. Displaced farmers had two choices: either to break up their families, who then would be scattered onto farms, sometimes in different regions; or to emigrate from Iceland to America. Most chose the latter.

The farmers were joined by peasants and tenants. The leasing of lots or small farms had been a common practice, but the land was usually of poor quality, able to sustain only a few animals. The possibility of improving conditions on such farms was extremely limited, and when the climate was unfavourable, these farms were hardest hit.

The majority of emigrants, therefore, consisted of displaced farmers with families, tenants on tiny plots of land, and farmhands who knew their future in Iceland was anything but bright. Most of these people were very poor, but they were courageous, used to hard work, and willing to take a risk if it offered a chance of a better future.

Fishing, the other main occupation in Iceland, was more prosperous. By tradition, fishing was mostly centred around the south and west coast of the island, all the way northwest. Icelanders fished from rowing boats in three main seasons—winter, spring, and fall—and the hand-line was the most common fishing equipment. During the winter season, men lived at the fishing stations close to the fishing grounds. Many of the stations were permanently populated, but at others, men lived in primitive huts only during the season. Fishermen came to the fishing stations from practically all parts of the country, often having to travel great distances in the middle of winter. Most of them were registered farmhands, peasants, or tenants (Icelandic law demanded that every person be registered at a farm). Many of these fishermen fished on behalf of their master or landowner, handing over most of their catch to him as the season ended.

Before 1800, most of the catch was dried for domestic consumption (some sixty percent of the total catch in 1750), but the rest was exported to Denmark. At the end of the eighteenth century, production of salted fish was introduced in Iceland and, simultaneously, new markets opened up in the Mediterranean. This created new possibilities for expansion and the result was increased rowing-boat operation. Around 1800, the use of decked fishing vessels commenced, at first in the southwest and from the posts in the Westfjords.

The operation of decked vessels gradually led to the emergence of fishing towns and villages and, shortly after 1870, when the curing and exporting of salted fish gained momentum, some of these villages grew rapidly. The inhabitants of the growing villages and towns saw little cause to emigrate from Iceland except, in rare cases, for political reasons. However, most of the towns and villages were too small to accommodate the additional increase in population.

The nineteenth century was a period of political revival in Iceland. Due to civil strife from 1200 to 1262, the Icelandic nation had surrendered its freedom to Norway in 1262. The Union of Kalmar in 1397 between Norway, Sweden, and Denmark brought Iceland under Danish rule. This had little adverse effect in the country until 1602, when the Danish government granted a trade monopoly to merchants in Copenhagen, Helsingfors, and Malmö. Unscrupulous foreign trade monopolies during the seventeenth and eighteenth centuries, along with adversities wrought by the elements, had a severe negative impact on the nation. However, the movement for independence from Denmark began around 1830, and the 1830s and 1840s were a period of growing national self-confidence, enthusiasm, and optimism. These were times when many people believed that increased autonomy and political reform were just around the corner. The Althing was restored as an advisory parliament in 1843. In 1851, a convention was organized in Reykjavík for the purpose of writing a new constitution for Iceland. Many Icelanders hoped it would result in enhanced political independence. However, the convention failed to achieve its purpose, and all the issues concerning the union with Denmark remained unsolved. In 1871, the Danish government tried to force matters by imposing an act on the status of Iceland within the Danish monarchy, which stated that Iceland was an inalienable part of the Danish Crown.

This caused widespread anger in Iceland, which was only partly abated by the introduction of a new constitution in 1874, giving the Althing legislative and financial powers. Many people remained dissatisfied with the gradual reforms in both health and education. Most felt these systems were ineffective and that change was being introduced too slowly, especially in the case of political reforms.

Farming in Iceland had very limited possibilities for sustaining a growing population. As the climate worsened and natural disasters struck in the 1870s and 1880s, many people were left with little option but to emigrate. The majority of emigrants came from the predominantly farming areas of the northern and eastern regions. Fewer emigrants originated from the southwestern and western parts of the country, mainly because economic conditions were better there and these regions were not as hard-hit by climatic deterioration and natural disasters.

Many young Icelandic students in Copenhagen were greatly influenced by the intellectual movements that swept across Europe. For example, both Rationalism and Romanticism were brought to Iceland from Copenhagen. New religious trends, such as Lutheranism in the middle of the sixteenth century, had also reached Icelandic shores via the University of Copenhagen.

Three hundred years later, in 1851, two young Icelandic students heard, for the first time, the message of a Mormon preacher in Copenhagen. Gudmundur Gudmundsson and Thorarinn Haflidason were both from the Vestmanna Islands, a group of small islands just south of the mainland. Both young men decided to adopt this new faith. After receiving training in Copenhagen, they were sent to Iceland as missionaries and chose to begin their work in their home in the Vestmanna Islands. Their mission was not only to introduce the new faith, but also to speak about the Mormon State in America. Their efforts were met with suspicion, even hostility. Certain aspects of the new faith contradicted what was taught in the Icelandic Lutheran State Church; for example, many Icelanders could not accept polygamy.

Young Haflidason unfortunately accidentally drowned near the islands in 1852. His friend Gudmundsson continued the missionary work alone until a Danish missionary joined him in Iceland. Although they both worked diligently at their mission, only a handful of Icelanders was converted. Nonetheless, they were responsible for the first Icelandic emigration to North America. Late in the summer of 1855, three people began the long journey from Iceland to Utah: Samuel Bjarnason, his wife Margret, and their friend, Helga Jonsdottir.[1]

After consulting with people in Salt Lake City, Bjarnason decided to head for Spanish Fork, where a group of Danish converts had settled. The leader of the

Mormon movement in Utah, Brigham Young, thought that since Denmark and Iceland were politically linked, a joint settlement of Danes and Icelanders would work. Bjarnason selected an area in the southeastern part of Spanish Fork and was granted 160 acres of farmland. He is, therefore, the first Icelandic settler in America.

Margret, his wife, apparently welcomed the new challenge and took an active part in her husband's enterprise. Together, they built a productive farm and, as time went by, added both land and livestock to their farming. Bjarnason became a wealthy farmer with several wives and many children, and lived on his farm until his death in 1890. Two of his sons followed in his footsteps and became successful at raising sheep.

While Bjarnason and his companions were approaching their destination, a young Icelander by the name of Thordur Didriksson was aboard a train from New York, heading to Alton, a small place near St. Louis. With him on the same train was Gudmundur Gudmundsson, the man who had originally brought the Mormon faith to Iceland in 1852.

The two men left Liverpool, England, in early January of 1856 and had a most dreadful crossing. Everyone aboard the ship became ill and fifty people died. After spending some time in New York, they caught the train for Alton. Here, after considerable effort, they found work but the heat in May and June was unbearable to them. Late in June, one of the Mormon elders brought them the news that soon they were to travel up the Missouri River to Omaha, to join a large group of immigrants destined for Salt Lake City. The trip upriver took nine days and they spent three weeks in Omaha while the final preparations for the last leg of their long journey were made.

In early August, this large group of 220 people began the journey from Omaha to Utah. The carts were pulled by two of the men while two women pushed. Children walked ahead of the group. They had travelled almost 100 kilometres into the desert when people began to get sick. An ox was slaughtered every night and the meat distributed among the travellers. Many years later, Didriksson recalled his suppers on that trip. He never got enough meat but, to compensate for this shortage, he stayed up late and boiled parts of the hide, which he then ate. This had been a custom in early Iceland during days of famine and, he claimed, kept him alive. For a few days he had to pull his cart alone, due to the illness of his companions.[2]

After three months, the group finally reached Salt Lake City. Didriksson moved to Spanish Fork, where he claimed 150 acres of land and started farming. He met and married Helga Jonsdottir, who had been in the first group from Iceland. She lived to be ninety-three years of age and died 27 September 1905. As was the norm, Didriksson had other wives and, with them, six children.

Didriksson was an intelligent man and a poet. He was skilled in woodcarving and a good blacksmith, was well liked and respected. During his days in Utah, he was considered one of the leaders of the Icelandic settlement in Spanish Fork. Many a newcomer spent several days at his home before finding a place to homestead. Didriksson was a religious man and around 1880 he travelled back to Iceland to resume the missionary work that had been started nearly thirty years earlier.[3] Gudmundsson never lived in the Icelandic community. He married a Danish woman, became a jeweller, and settled in Lehi.

Another group from Iceland arrived the following year. Led by Loftur Jonsson, the group of eight left Iceland in the fall of 1856 and arrived in Spanish Fork in the spring of 1857. Jonsson claimed land in the area and eventually became one of the wealthiest men in the district. He and Samuel Bjarnason went back to Iceland for some mission work. Jonsson was married to Gudrun Halldorsdottir when he emigrated from Iceland in 1856, but on his return to America in 1874, he brought with him a second wife, Halldora Arnadottir, whom he had married during his short stay in Iceland. Shortly after his return, Jonsson met his untimely death in Spanish Fork.

Jon Jonsson and his wife, Anna Gudlaugsdottir, also settled in Spanish Fork in 1857 and lived to an old age on the same farm. Jonsson had a second wife and eight children, four by each wife. He is the only Icelander known to have been involved in the struggle between the Mormons and the Aboriginal people. He brought his family with him to Sanpete County, where he served as guard. His sister, Gudrun, accompanied him across the Atlantic and died in the US at the age of ninety on 28 September 1916. Another single female, Vigdis Bjornsdottir, aged thirty, was in this group, and she settled in Utah. In 1860, she married an Englishman, William Holt. She was a midwife and served in her community for decades. Magnus Bjarnason, his wife, Thuridur Magnusdottir, and a friend, Gudny Erasmusdottir, completed Loftur Jonsson's group.[4]

The last Icelandic Mormons to settle in Utah before 1860 were Ragnhildur Hansen and her young daughter. Ragnhildur and her husband Benedikt had made it together to Omaha, Nebraska, where she gave birth. She continued to Utah but her husband died en route. As a single mother with a newborn child, she had a difficult time at the beginning of her life as a Mormon. She named her little girl Maria. Much later, in Levan, Utah, then a married woman, Maria became known as Mrs. Mary Hansen Sherwood. She was the only living Icelandic pioneer in 1938, when a monument commemorating Icelandic settlement in Utah was unveiled.[5]

This early migration from Iceland to Utah came to an end in 1860. During the next ten years, no emigration from Iceland to America took place, but during the last thirty years of the century, the small settlement in Spanish Fork, Utah, received some additional Icelanders.

These Icelandic pioneers in Utah experienced hard times in the beginning. None of them spoke much English, although both Gudmundsson and Didriksson knew some Danish, which obviously helped in relations with their Danish neighbours. Their unfamiliarity with the American soil and climate created hardships initially, and their pride in their heritage was often scoffed at, especially their determination to dress in Icelandic clothes. However, this first Icelandic settlement had one major advantage over all other Icelandic settlements in North America for years to come. The Icelanders in Utah belonged to a large group of immigrants of various ethnic backgrounds, who were all of the same religion. They benefitted immediately from others' experiences. They learned new, different agricultural methods, and how to prepare food, construct houses, and make clothes. They wanted to preserve as much of their Icelandic background as possible, but primarily they had come to Utah as Mormons to become part of a religious haven. They did not intend to establish an exclusively Icelandic colony, and they accepted that one day their mother tongue would no longer be spoken in their community. To them, however, that did not necessarily signify the end of Icelandic heritage in their community. On the contrary, their pride in their background was most important. To this day, evidence of their heritage can be found in Spanish Fork.

In 1860, the tiny Icelandic settlement in Spanish Fork consisted of sixteen individuals. No increase in their number from Iceland took place until 1874. During the 1860s, as Bjarnason and Jonsson and the others acquainted themselves with the North American soil and climate, in Iceland the talk about emigration increased considerably. Iceland was no longer as isolated as it had been for centuries. More ships from Europe and America traded in the country, and news of great opportunities in the New World reached the ears of young and able Icelanders. The Icelandic community was changing also as a result of increasing traffic in rural areas. Small trading posts had developed through the years and, around them, small villages, which became centres of information for farmers bringing their products to the market.

Thousands of young people from the Scandinavian countries, from Ireland, Great Britain, Germany, and other European countries, had opted for the opportunities in America. Icelandic students in Denmark and elsewhere, as well as travelling individuals, witnessed the migration movement sweeping across Europe. Publications, both Icelandic and foreign, discussed the issue, comparing the situation in Iceland with that of other countries where young, energetic people did not have much hope for improved conditions. America, by contrast, became the land of freedom and of opportunities.

In the late 1850s and early 1860s, people in northeast Iceland discussed possible emigration to several places.[6] Severely cold winters had destroyed livestock and left the ground frozen throughout the summer. Unable to make hay, farmers in those areas had no alternative but to abandon their farms. The steady increase in population in certain regions meant that many farms became too small to sustain the growing number of people.

Icelanders in the northeast began to consider emigration to Greenland, because it is the closest country and an settlement had been established there by Eric the Red in the tenth century. Several meetings were held about Greenland. At one meeting, a respected farmer named Einar Asmundsson, in a single speech, persuaded everyone in attendance to abandon all plans of emigration from one cold country to another even colder. He had researched possible places to establish an exclusive colony and had concluded that Brazil would be best suited for such a venture.[7] An organization was formed to plan and prepare for the long journey to Brazil. This was probably when the first idea of an exclusive Icelandic colony was formed. Later, this dream of an exclusive settlement was expressed by Icelanders all over North America, but its organization was never planned. Those familiar with settlements in America in the 1860s had undoubtedly heard of German or Norwegian settlements, but little information was available on how those settlements functioned.

The discussions on emigration from Iceland to Brazil led to the departure of Kristjan Gudmundsson, who sailed for Copenhagen in 1861. His plans were to continue from there to Brazil. Such a journey was expensive and young Gudmundsson needed money. He worked in Copenhagen for a little more than two years before leaving on 14 February 1863. After spending forty-four days at sea, the ship docked in Rio de Janeiro. He settled in the city and, as time went by, made a name for himself as a hotel owner and carpenter. His letters to his parents showed a positive appreciation of living conditions in his new homeland and he encouraged them to join him. Parts of his letters were published in Icelandic weeklies and contributed to the general discussions on emigration. His last letter, dated 24 February 1873, stated that everything was now ready for the arrival of his parents and their children. The family made it to Curitiba City in the state of Paranagua in March of 1874, but waiting for them there was the sad news that their son had died of yellow fever the month before.[8]

The organization in northeast Iceland that promoted emigration to Brazil sent four young men to explore possible sites in the new country. They left Akureyri in the north of Iceland in 1863, five months after Kristjan Gudmundsson had sailed from Copenhagen to Rio. After spending some time in Denmark, they left for Brazil on 4 July 1863, and reached their destination, Joinville on Serra de Mar, on 26 October of the same year. Their instructions were to concentrate on investigating regions in southern Brazil, but after considerable exploration they returned to Joinville without any prospects. They all found work and were content but they sent letters home discouraging people from emigrating to Brazil until a permanent settlement site had been found.[9] In Iceland, however, many farmers sold all their property, livestock, land, and buildings, and waited for a ship to transport them from Iceland. They expected to go first to Denmark, like the others, but then to proceed to Brazil. Gradually, a list of future emigrants to Brazil grew and by 1865, 150 people had signed up.

In the 1860s, there were no regular sailings from Iceland, so anyone interested in travelling needed to find a vacant spot on one of the merchant ships. None of them was large enough to transport both a full cargo and a large group of people. Einar Asmundsson attempted to solve this problem by finding a ship that would take his people to Denmark. He discussed this with Brazilian government agents in Denmark, but he never received confirmation from Copenhagen. Finally, in 1871, a letter from one of the Icelanders in Brazil reached Akureyri, stating that the Brazilian government promised everyone under forty-five years of age a free passage from Hamburg, Germany, to Curitiba City in Brazil.[10]

The list of willing participants in the Brazilian venture grew fast once this news spread, but the same problem remained: no ship was available in the country to take future Icelandic Brazilians to Copenhagen or, preferably, Hamburg. The situation did not change, despite a renewed offer from Brazil. This time the government was willing to pay the entire fare from Iceland to Brazil. In 1873, almost 500 people had put their name on the list from northeastern Iceland and sixty-five in the south also expressed keen interest.

In spite of all the efforts to find a vessel or accommodation on other ships, only thirty-five people managed to secure a spot on merchant ships destined for Copenhagen. From there they sailed to Germany, and on 10 October 1873, they left for Brazil, arriving in Curitiba City on 8 January 1874. This was the only organized group from Iceland that emigrated to Brazil. By 1874 most people in Iceland had their eyes on Canada or the United States.[11]

The small number of Icelanders in Brazil never organized their dream colony, but scattered in different directions in and near Curitiba City. Relations with their motherland were difficult, due to the great distance. Only one person ever returned to Iceland, while another, Magnus Gudmundsson Isfeld, who was the most successful Icelander in Brazil, moved to Canada. He and his family settled near Mozart, Saskatchewan, in 1905.[12]

Early discussions in Iceland about emigration to America generally involved only those people seriously contemplating such a move. No one believed that the desire to emigrate from Iceland would become so widespread. As Einar Asmundsson got his organization going and articles on the emigration issue became more numerous in Icelandic periodicals, opposition to the idea of emigration arose. Those opposing migration suggested that such a move amounted to betrayal of the independence movement in the country.

This sentiment had an effect on anyone planning a move to America, especially when emigration became more general and the voices of the opposition grew louder. Most emigrants determined to remain as Icelandic as possible on foreign soil, which explains the desire of so many to seek an exclusive Icelandic colony. It mattered almost as much to many of the migrants to be able to speak their mother tongue and maintain Icelandic traditions and culture, as to create a better life for themselves.

Were the Icelanders any different in this respect from emigrants from other cultures? One obvious difference is the size of population. Compared to other European nations, the Icelanders were like one big family. In rural Iceland or in the small seaside villages, everyone knew one another well, and in many instances, relatives lived close to each other in the same district. A decision to abandon one's homeland, to leave those remaining to struggle on for independence, and to sacrifice one's native language and culture was, to many people, an unforgivable crime. This often led to bitter family strife or angry neighbourhood quarrels. Good neighbours became bad and families were split up. In the big

European cities, where people of different ethnic backgrounds occupied all ranks of society, it is unlikely that bonds existed similar to those among families and friends in rural Iceland or in the fishing villages. An Irish or German family may have emigrated from the homeland without much fuss, but no one could leave Iceland unnoticed. It was hard enough to leave, but to do so with the ill will of family and friends was heartbreaking.

Most of the Icelandic emigrants were peasants, the poorest of Icelandic society, but by no means an ignorant and illiterate lot. Far from it. All of them were literate and had received an elementary education similar to that of other young people in the country. The most highly regarded Icelandic poet in America, Stephan G. Stephansson, was one of these early emigrants. They were individuals, however, who had little if any means of improving their situation in Iceland. Farming in Iceland had become stagnant and the demand for farm products had decreased, although the demand for fish and fish products grew steadily. Yet, a move from a predominantly farming society to one based on fishing occurred only gradually. In fact, changes in the structure of society were extremely slow, undoubtedly as a result of Iceland's lacking the powers of government in its internal affairs.

The economic and social progress during the nineteenth century, slow as it was, had given young people confidence in the future, which the young people 100 years earlier had lacked. Their predecessors in the eighteenth century would not have considered emigration, had such an idea been presented to them, because their knowledge of the world was so limited. But 100 years later, their descendants were ready to face the challenge awaiting them in America, and although they did not leave their homeland celebrating, they knew that on the other side of the Atlantic Ocean was the opportunity to improve their lives. Most of them knew they might never see their island again, but that made them all the more determined to preserve what they could of their heritage in their new, foreign environment.

Statistics show that in the beginning of the emigration period, most of these Icelandic emigrants were young couples with children. During the first decade, from 1870 to 1880, 2857 individuals left Iceland for North America. Of these, 1894 were children, teenagers, and adults under the age of thirty. Four hundred and forty were between the ages of thirty and forty. This ratio did not change much throughout the entire emigration period of 1870 to 1914.[13]

Coincidence played a role in the decision of four young men to migrate to Wisconsin in 1870. A Danish store clerk named William Wickmann, who had worked in Iceland for ten years, had a sister in Milwaukee, whom he visited in the fall of 1865. Wickmann first went to work in Reykjavík, but later he moved to the trading post in the village of Eyrarbakki on the south coast. His employer, Gudmundur Thorgrimsen, a merchant, was interested in prospects in America. Wickmann corresponded with him and described as best he could what he had experienced in America. Among other things, he mentioned the fish in Lake Michigan, which he said were both abundant and large. People of different ethnic backgrounds fished immense quantities and Wickmann saw no reason why Icelandic immigrants could not also.

In addition to Wickmann's letters, Thorgrimsen gathered information from every source he could find. Foreign traders who frequented his store were bombarded with questions. If Einar Asmundsson could gather information on Brazil in the early 1860s, then Thorgrimsen surely must have had little difficulty in getting more on America. He also had a few assistants who were just as interested in America. One of them, Jon Gislason, had inherited some money from his father and was financially well prepared for emigration.[14] He read Wickmann's letters with keen interest. Although no evidence exists of his correspondence with Wickmann, it is likely he was in contact because Wickmann prepared for his arrival in Wisconsin and awaited him in Milwaukee in the fall of 1870.

Thorgrimsen apparently supported emigration from Iceland and his views on the issue may well reflect the general opinion of men of means and authority at the time. Another of the four migrants, Gudmundur Gudmundsson, was from a well-to-do family in the south and had made a good name for himself as a foreman of a fishing boat in Eyrarbakki. He had been at sea since the age of nineteen but now, at thirty, he was ready for a change. He was a frequent visitor in Thorgrimsen's store and took active part in discussions on America. Like Gislason, he read Wickmann's letters and decided to try his luck in America. Another of the group, Arni Gudmundsson, was a carpenter by trade, originally from Reykjavík, but had joined the staff at Thorgrimsen's store in the late 1860s. Finally, the fourth emigrant, Jon Einarsson, had been an assistant for three years to Iceland's chief medical doctor on his exhausting trips around the country.[15]

All four of these men seem to have had better opportunities in Iceland than most young men at the time. Gislason had inherited his father's money; Gudmundur Gudmundsson was a successful foreman with a bright future; Arni Gudmundsson was a trained carpenter and held a respectable position at Thorgrimsen's; and Einarsson was assisting a doctor on his travels around Iceland. None of them was married with children, nor were they struggling farmers. In short, their situation in Iceland could hardly have been the reason they chose to emigrate. Their decision reflects the spirit that was evident in so many European countries, where young people dreamed of a fresh start and the freedom to make their own decisions and take chances. Milwaukee became their destination, probably as a result of their correspondence with Wickmann. In the next few years, most Icelandic emigrants followed suit and went to Wisconsin.

They left Eyrarbakki for Reykjavík on 12 May 1870. After spending a few days in the city, they sailed for Copenhagen. During their short stay in Reykjavík, many people attempted to change their minds. People in those times had most amazing ideas about the New World. They pointed out that letters could not be sent from America without being censored. How the Americans were to read and understand the Icelandic language was never explained. One man was told that if he escaped the cannibals, he would most certainly be made a slave. These warnings did little to change the minds of the four young men, however.

They spent four days in Copenhagen and used the time to explore the city and visit some of their countrymen. On 3 June, they crossed the North Sea to Hull, England, and took the train to Liverpool. The Allan Line *Atlantis* carried them across the Atlantic Ocean, docking in Quebec City, Canada, on 19 June. The journey from Quebec to Milwaukee was long and tiring, but they arrived in Milwaukee on 27 June 1870.

William Wickmann was there to greet them. He had prepared for their arrival by finding a place on a fishing boat for Gudmundsson, Einarsson, and Arni Gudmundsson. Jon Gislason was the only one who had brought some money and did not need to work immediately. He and Wickmann had agreed to invest and they spent the rest of the summer looking for something of interest. After some deliberations they concluded that land on Washington Island was a good prospect. In 1870, about fifty Danes resided in the Detroit Harbor region of the island, which probably explains Wickmann's interest.

The island is in the northwest part of Lake Michigan, separated from the mainland by the Port la Mort. The island is basically one solid rock but covered with soil and, in 1870, it was heavily treed. Several farmers of different nationalities had bought land there and were already breaking it. Fishermen had had their summer camps out by Washington Harbor for a number of years. They chopped down the trees around their huts for firewood, but used the best pine for their barrels, in which fish was salted. Wickmann and Gislason jointly bought wooded land, in the Detroit Harbor area, from a Civil War veteran: a sixty-one-acre homestead with 1500 feet of harbour frontage.[16] They immediately began clearing it, just as they saw the other farmers do. They built a hut and, as the years went by, cleared more and more land and increased the number of livestock. The original hut was replaced with a log house, which later was moved to make way for a wooden home.

Wickmann and Gislason made a dock to load their products, both fish and farm. In 1873, they divided their property, Gislason keeping most of the farmland and the buildings, while Wickmann got the coastal part. The others, who had spent most of their time fishing and had arrived on the island in the fall, were then ready to invest. Gudmundur Gudmundsson started farming but, after a year, he sold his property, bought another lot by the coast, and, for the rest of his life, fished just as successfully as he had done back in Iceland.

Arni Gudmundsson worked at carpentry and fishing on the island, while Jon Einarsson kept to fishing.[17] As 1870 came to an end, the first four Icelandic settlers in America (not including the Utah settlers) had had a positive start in the New World. They had the good fortune of knowing and trusting someone who already had had the opportunity to examine prospects in the United States. Wickmann had not exaggerated in his descriptions, and already had made necessary preparations prior to the arrival of the four immigrants. For example, he had secured room and board in Milwaukee, fishing opportunities for the three, and, last but not least, he had made plans for himself and Gislason to explore certain investments. In his letters to Thorgrimsen, he had emphasized the significance of the fishing in Lake Michigan and strongly recommended it to the future emigrants. It was an occupation familiar to most young men in Iceland, even though the type of fish and the fishing methods were different.

It is important to note from this successful venture that they had no plans to establish an exclusive Icelandic colony. They settled on the island where people of other nationalities already had made their homes, knowing that dealings with the "foreigners" would be inevitable. Neither did they insist on forcing their own religion or culture on others. They recognized that living with people of other nationalities in America was their future and that sharing knowledge and heritage would be beneficial. This does not mean that they were any less Icelandic at heart than those who arrived later, determined to find a site for the Icelandic dream settlement, but it was clear to them that they would become part of a new nation in the making.

When Einar Asmundsson was planning the settlement in Brazil, he knew Brazil wanted and needed young people. As the most desirable immigrants, they were offered free transportation. He appears to have been selective in his choice of the first emigrants. It was his belief that young, able men were needed to prepare a settlement site for others. The four young Icelanders who made their homes on Washington Island seemed to have shared similar views. They were single and had good experience in different fields. It was their conviction that only young, energetic people would be successful in America. Consequently, they became concerned when the news reached them in early 1871 that Johannes Magnusson, his wife Gudny, and their four-year-old daughter were making plans to emigrate to the island. Both Magnusson and his wife were middle-aged, in their forties.[18] They were poor and spoke neither English nor any other foreign language. The Icelandic pioneers on Washington Island felt they would have a most difficult time, as the life of a pioneer was very demanding.

Another man, Einar Bjarnason, a merchant in Reykjavík, also moved to Washington Island in the early part of 1871. Accompanying him to America were two of his children. His wife, Helga, arrived a year later with their other children.[19]

Jon Gislason and the others already on the island worried that people emigrated without proper plans. The four of them had had work as soon as they had arrived in America and, in fact, everything they needed had been arranged before their arrival. Although they had not been long in America, they knew how difficult the life of the pioneer could be, building a house, clearing land, and preparing soil. Most settlers had to work at these things in their spare time; they had to make a living away from their farm because they would have arrived with very little money. Paid work on the island was scarce and physically demanding.

Back in Iceland, friends and relatives eagerly awaited news of the progress of the young men in America. The first letter from Washington Island, printed in *Norðanfari,* one of Iceland's leading newspapers, was written on 8 March 1872 by Gudmundur Gudmundsson.

> The weather has been quite good although at times it became very cold but the last three days have passed without any frost. It is the general belief here that this signifies the end of winter and that the sun will now melt the snow but it takes very little time once the temperature rises.
>
> I have spent the last four days here out on the ice fishing and have caught fifty, which I have already sold for almost $7.00. People come here to buy fish and give four cents for the pound. There are quite a few fishermen here nearby. They bring with them small huts but will soon leave, as the ice will break any day.
>
> Time for the saga of Johannes. He came to us and found work at chopping firewood, which turned out to be very hard for him at first but working with us helped as he gradually got the knack of it. His wife also earned some money working as a housemaid. He stayed with us well into the winter but then we found [room] for him and his family in the house of a widower. They can stay in the house this summer without having to pay high rent, as the owner will go someplace off the island for work. Johannes is supposed to seed the field, which is not big by the way his wife Gudny can actually manage it while he earns some money working the fields for others.
>
> This winter he earned some $1.00-1.50 a day for chopping wood. He only needed 30 cents per day for the three of them. He says he is not yet used to pancakes and syrup, bacon and beans, fried meat and potatoes and white bread. In addition, he dislikes all the coffee but it is quite customary here to drink some 12-14 cups—a cup is always refilled almost immediately after one drinks up. This is the simplest of food in these parts but Johannes misses the milk the most. Some people, Germans and Norwegians mostly, have a bite to eat up to five times a day. The sort of food Johannes is buying is normally what one gets during hard times but you can see from the prices I mentioned above whether it's very expensive to live here or not.
>
> However, this place is one of the best for anybody poor to come to as one can live off the land and fish in the lake. I dare say that the most idle man in Iceland, someone who may have several children does not have to work all that much to survive. His wife could work the field while he fishes in the lake. There is plenty of fish, just off shore, which is good to eat. But the fish we sell, white-fish and trout is caught further out.... [20]

Johannes Magnusson and his family later moved to Lincoln County, Minnesota, where he died at the age of seventy-one on 7 November 1898. Gudny outlived her husband and died in the same place on 7 December 1911 at the age of eighty-six. Despite a shaky start, they both came to terms with the new environment and eventually adjusted well.[21]

Gudmundsson's letter seems encouraging to prospective immigrants in his discussion of the possibilities in farming and fishing. His intentions, however, were not to encourage emigration but rather to give the reader an idea what life on the island was really like. Einar Bjarnason had to be away from his family for a year and found the work hard to manage in the beginning. Future immigrants should have learned from this letter that if they had little or no extra money, they needed work, and most of it was hard labour. Also, most available work was quite different from what men might have been accustomed to in Iceland. They would need to learn new techniques in every field and, to acquire proper skills, would have to work with experienced people. Bjarnason became better at chopping wood after he had worked with others. Unfortunately, many people arrived later in America from Iceland without work, and ignored offers of working with experienced farmers, which would have made their start in America much better.

During the next three years, several people from Iceland settled on Washington Island, most of them friends or relatives of the early settlers. Some of them moved away, but two women stayed. Agusta Einarsdottir married Jon Gislason in 1877 and they were blessed with ten children. The other was Gudrun Ingvarsdottir, who married Gudmundur Gudmundsson in 1875. They had five children.

These two families and Arni Gudmundsson, who never married, made up the nucleus of the small Icelandic community on Washington Island for many years. Arni Gudmundsson stayed on the island until 1880, when he moved for two years to Andaton County, Iowa. He returned to the island, bought land, and lived in prosperity until his death, just after the turn of the century.

Jon Einarsson married an Irish woman, Irene Guinan. They moved to Milwaukee in 1877, by which time Einarsson had become ill with a disease that eventually led to his death. He never had any children.

Jon Gislason was undoubtedly the most successful of the four. He invested wisely and bought the district's general store in 1884, which he managed until his old age. As evidence of his success, he paid the highest income tax on the island for many years and became quite wealthy. He was elected on the county council and was chair of the local school board for many years. He was also Justice of the Peace.[22]

The four pioneers from Iceland on Washington Island seemed to be successful from the very beginning. Other than Jon Einarsson's illness and untimely death, their story is one of success and steady progress. Before they moved to America, they received good advice and knew what their possibilities were. They wasted little time on speculation about settlement sites. They made every effort to adjust to a new and different way of life. Their intention was primarily to create a better life for themselves and they succeeded.

They settled among people of other ethnic background and did not attempt to isolate themselves from such people on the island. On the contrary, they took part in all developments, such as building roads, drilling for water, and constructing schools. They spoke Icelandic in their homes and in the company of other Icelanders, but used English in their dealings with others.

In Iceland, hundreds of people discussed emigration to America, pointing at the small Icelandic community on Washington Island as proof of success. However, many people did not learn from the valuable experience the four first migrants gained on the island, which they described in letters published in Iceland. Instead, the majority of future immigrants from Iceland chose a different approach, often with unfortunate consequences. Most of these people made Milwaukee in Wisconsin their first destination.

2
Migration to Milwaukee

Gudmundur Thorgrimsen at Eyrarbakki had been involved in the first emigration to America from Iceland in the 1870s. He was still involved in 1872 as he prepared his own son, Hans, for the long journey to America. Led by Pall Thorlaksson, a group of seventeen left Eyrarbakki on 13 June and travelled to Liverpool, England. Thorlaksson was to play a very important role in the history of Icelandic immigrants in North America during the next ten years.

Thorlaksson was born on 13 November 1849 in the north of Iceland. His father, Thorlakur Jonsson, was then a store clerk, but two years later he moved to Storutjarnir, where he began farming. Pall received the usual education at home during his childhood and was a diligent student. He was sent to Reykjavík for further education, and graduated from the Latin School in the spring of 1871.[1]

He had considered philology at the University of Copenhagen in Denmark, encouraged by Dr. Jon Hjaltalin. Dr. Hjaltalin was the same medical doctor whom Jon Einarsson had escorted on his travels. The fact that these two young men, who both emigrated from Iceland to America, were connected in some sense to Dr. Hjaltalin is perhaps evidence of the general opinion of senior Icelandic officials that the future for young and promising Icelanders was greater in America than in Iceland.

During his last winter at the Latin School, Thorlaksson took a course in Hebrew. Attending the same course was a young pastor by the name of Jon Bjarnason.

They became close friends. Certainly, they did not know that in a few years they would become opponents, each leading a group of Icelandic settlers in America who held different views on an important settlement issue.

During the early winter of 1870-1871, Thorlakur Jonsson wrote to his son in Reykjavík and asked if he could be persuaded to alter his plans and sail for America instead of Copenhagen. If he was not against the idea, Jonsson encouraged him to discuss the matter with Dr. Hjaltalin. Jonsson admitted that during the previous few years, he had been opposed to the idea of emigration, but Thorgrimsen at Eyrarbakki had changed his mind. Young Thorlaksson was taken by surprise, but, after discussing the possibilities with Dr. Hjaltalin, he determined to emigrate to the United States.[2] He moved to his parents' home at Storutjarnir in the fall of 1871 and spent the winter preparing young students for higher education at the Latin School in Reykjavík. He also taught English to a few people who, like himself, had decided to emigrate to America.

In the spring of 1872, Pall Thorlaksson, his brother Haraldur, and Arni Sveinbjornsson packed their gear, saddled their horses, and went south to Eyrarbakki, on their way to Wisconsin. These three young men had several things in common with the four who went to Wisconsin. Except Haraldur, they were single, and all were in good standing in Iceland. They surely must have been considered an important part of the future for the Icelandic nation, yet they chose to emigrate. They had the support of influential men, and they either had money themselves to pay for the costly journey, or had the financial support of parents or other benefactors. Many Icelanders may have dreamed about emigration to America, but most knew they were unable to meet the expenses.

In Eyrarbakki, Gudmundur Thorgrimsen told the travellers from the north that his own son, Hans, would be accompanying them to America. At the same time, he supposedly announced the engagement of his daughter to Pall Thorlaksson.[3] Joining them at Eyrarbakki was a group of thirteen people from the southern regions.[4]

The group ready to depart from Eyrarbakki consisted mostly of young, single individuals from well-respected families. For example, Arni Gudmundsson was the son of the magistrate at Eyrarbakki; Stefan O. Stephensen's father, Thorvaldur Stephensen, was a merchant in Reykjavík; and Olafur Gudmundsson Johnson was the son of a senior official in the Church of Iceland. One woman, Gudrun Ingvarsdottir, was joining her husband-to-be, Gudmundur Gudmundsson, who was already on Washington Island. A married couple from the Reykjavík area brought their two daughters, aged six and three. Finally, Jakob Palsson, a graduate from the Latin School in Reykjavík in 1866, who had studied medicine, also travelled to Milwaukee, where he found work in his field. Unfortunately, he died of tuberculosis on 26 January 1874.[5]

From Eyrarbakki the group went to Liverpool, England, and boarded a ship on 2 July, reaching Halifax, Nova Scotia, in Canada on the 11th. They were in Quebec City on the 15th, from where they travelled by train to Wisconsin. Most of them continued to Washington Island. Some took up permanent residence but others returned to the mainland, looking for different kinds of work.

The brothers, Pall and Haraldur, Haraldur's wife Maria, and Jakob Palsson settled in Milwaukee and soon found work. Haraldur was hired by a carpenter and had a difficult time initially because he spoke little English. His pay was $1.25 per day. Pall found work in a lumberyard and, in a letter to his father dated 8 September 1872, he claimed he found the work easy and physically not too demanding.[6] He worked ten hours a day, but nine on Saturdays. At first they rented rooms and bought food from a Danish store clerk named Kreyser. He was formerly of Eyrarbakki, where Pall Thorlaksson had first made his acquaintance. Later, however, they rented a house in the city for $5.00 per month. It was a large house and by the end of September, five more Icelanders had moved in with them.

The household was organized: Pall Thorlaksson was the leader and handled all the finances. Maria, his sister-in-law, managed the kitchen and all other domestic affairs. She was paid $4.00 a week for her work, and each tenant paid $3.00 a week for room and board, to cover Maria's salary, the rent, and food supplies.[7] One wrote home that "still we have better meals on the average than any government official in Iceland I can think of.... From this you can see that living expenses here are not as high as people in Iceland generally insist."[8]

While this group had been making final preparations at Eyrarbakki, three men had left Akureyri aboard a Norwegian freighter bound for Christiansand in Norway. These were Johannes Arngrimsson, who later played a role in the emigration of his fellow countrymen to Nova Scotia, Canada; Jon Halldorsson, who later led an Icelandic delegation that explored regions in Nebraska in search of an area large enough for a big Icelandic settlement; and Jonas Jonsson, who had been involved in the Brazilian movement in the northeast of Iceland. (In the Icelandic community in the United States, he later became known as "Omaha Jonas," and was the first Icelander known to have settled in Chicago, in 1880. Later he moved to Winnipeg, Canada, where he produced and sold washing liquid he called O.K. Cleaner.)

From Norway, these three men sailed to Liverpool, and on 11 July they left aboard the steamer *Oceanic* and arrived in New York on the 21st. They reached their final destination in Milwaukee on the 25th. Their original plan was to go to Washington Island, but the Danish consul in Milwaukee persuaded them to reconsider their plans. They were told that the Icelandic settlers on the island were not doing very well. This was partly true, as none of them had cleared all their land and some had yet to harvest the first crop. This was not surprising, as the summer of 1872 was only their second on the island. However, other Danes in Milwaukee shared this view, which was rather discouraging to the three Icelanders, and they decided to remain in the city.

Shortly after their arrival, they met Thorlaksson, and in September, Arngrimsson and Halldorsson had moved in and joined the Thorlakssons' household. In a letter published in the weekly *Norðanfari* in Iceland in September 1872, Halldorsson stated that in addition to the $3.00 a week, they all had to pay $7.00 each for the purchase of furniture: "It is truly amazing to see what kind of furniture we have got for the money we spent. In Iceland we would not have been able to buy half of what we have bought here at such low prices."[9]

The interest in emigration from Iceland to America was growing and widespread, and people gathered information from whatever source they could. In 1872, no organization had been established in Iceland to assist people to emigrate. Instead, people made their plans alone. One such individual was Sigtryggur Jonasson, who, late in the summer, travelled on his own to Canada. He arrived in Quebec City on 12 September and was the first Icelander to choose Canada as his future homeland in America. Jonasson was to become one of the leaders of the Canadian Icelandic settlers.

The last person to emigrate from Iceland in 1872 was Einar Thorlacius. His first place of residence in America was Boston, where he lived for two years. He moved to Minnesota and later to the Gardar settlement in Dakota. Two of his sons, Hallgrimur in 1873 and Eggert in 1889, moved to America and settled in Dakota.[10]

By late 1872, there was much talk of emigration from Iceland but nothing indicated the mass migration that was to occur in the years to come. Knowledge of North America was still limited, but as more information on America reached Iceland, general curiosity regarding the possibilities began to push aside the ignorance. The few thousand Icelanders who emigrated in the next few years might well have done so without the encouraging reports received from America. But gradually it became clear that emigration to America was not at all as risky as had been the general assumption, especially among the peasants.

Pall Thorlaksson was determined to further his studies in America. Shortly after his arrival in Milwaukee, he became acquainted with U.V. Koren, a Norwegian pastor. Koren invited Thorlaksson to join him on trips to different Norwegian communities in Wisconsin. A new world opened up to Thorlaksson as he learned how the Norwegians had settled and organized their churches, schools, and communities. He met several Norwegian pastors on his travels and these connections led to his registration at Concordia University in St. Louis, Missouri, in the late fall of 1872. At that time, the Norwegian Synod in the United States, to which Thorlaksson's Norwegian friends belonged, had not yet founded its own theological seminary. Their students were therefore sent to Concordia, the educational centre of the German Missouri Synod.

Although Thorlaksson applied himself to his studies for the next three years, he continued to correspond with friends and family in Iceland, and with his fellow countrymen in America. Anyone who voluntarily starts a new life in another country is bound to describe his new environment on a positive note. First, he may have left his homeland against the wishes of his family and friends, and thus would want to prove to them that his decision was correct. Any report written under such circumstances will not necessarily reflect the true picture. Second, he may have had everyone's support and therefore no reason to exaggerate. He is actually expected to be highly critical and observant in his reports, as others may depend on his words when making decisions on emigration. This individual makes every effort to state the positive but at the same time carefully accounts for the negative.

The early Icelandic immigrants in North America had the support of their family and friends, and their letters most often reflected careful observations. No one did this as well as Thorlaksson. His reports always contained realistic attitudes and observations. He avoided exaggeration and remarks that might misrepresent the New World to his countrymen in Iceland. Instead, he cautioned Icelandic people against rushing away from their country, insisting that emigration should not be taken lightly. In a letter written at Concordia, 23 January 1873, and addressed to the editor of *Norðanfari,* he described his views on immigration in general, but also the achievements of the Norwegian settlers.

> I understand that many or more than a few of my countrymen are planning to immigrate here. When I contemplate this, many questions come to mind as my thoughts wander back to Iceland. The first one is whether living here is in all reality better than in Iceland. I cannot help saying that such a question is in many respects irrelevant and at the same time hard to answer. The reason I say it is irrelevant is probably based on the fact that I personally have adjusted to local circumstances and from my own standpoint I feel it is almost impossible to compare them to those in Iceland, considering both the land itself, the economy and last but not least the politics.
>
> But everyone knows that the beauty is always in the eyes of the beholder so if I were to answer that question for everyone I would need their eyes. What one likes is often distasteful to others. One dresses in rags and is quite content even though his financial situation allows for more costly attire, while another sacrifices everything he has for fine appearance. Some do not mind living in an earth-house while others could not take that. Some do not mind simple meals all the time while others demand a three course meal each time they consume food.
>
> I say to you: Come here, it is better here. You say: No it is better where I am. Both of us speak the truth so who is to judge? The good becomes bad and the bad becomes good. The sensible thing to do in this situation is to give an example—a true narrative from which people can draw their own conclusions.
>
> Whenever nations, communities or families are faced with major decisions, which may alter the course of life, people naturally take sides for or against. Many of those in favor of immigration to this place and those already making plans, more than anyone else only want to hear the good news but are less interested in anything negative. And then, there are those strongly opposed to emigration to America. These look for anything negative, true or false, in order to support their theory that emigration is not the solution of any domestic problems. Furthermore, there are some, who know absolutely nothing but are the loudest.
>
> There are some, who do consider the situation to a certain point and create their own, often utterly false conception. These maintain the people here either live in luxury, without having to make any effort or that the poverty is such that

meals consist of a few potatoes only. Nonsense! Some oppose these "foolish wanderings" for the sole reason only that all able men will emigrate from Iceland while only poor, idle peasants will remain behind. If it befalls that many will emigrate from Iceland who is to say that life for those left behind will deteriorate?

It is quite remarkable that Norway remains just the same despite the mass migration to America during the last thirty years. The Norwegians here claim that soon there will be just as many of them in America as back in Norway. During this short period it is quite amazing to witness what the Norwegian immigrants have accomplished. Gradually they have developed Norwegian communities, have formed congregations, built churches, established elementary schools and founded Lutheran synods. They even have built their own Latin School, which cost $87,000. They, themselves, have paid for it all.

What does this tell us? That these people are industrious and energetic? Yes. Anything else? ... the field produces nothing without the work of the farmer. If he does not work the field, there will be no crop. If he does not work his fields and care for it, it matters little how often he seeds, there will not be any crop. Although the soil here is fertile it needs tending to and only then will it produce. This simple fact encourages the farmer to be industrious. No one here survives on idleness! Those, if any, who think they can immigrate without planning to work should stay home....

It is best for anyone coming here, especially Icelanders, not to rush ahead and immediately attempt to start their own farming. It makes more sense to spend some time adjusting, learning new ways, not be too greedy or selfish because that is harmful. . . .

Everyone immigrating here realizes the importance of knowing the language of this nation. Apart from English, German is quite common and both Danish and Norwegian are useful too. Actually, here one finds most languages of the world, but our blessed Icelandic is, of course, the least spoken.

It is not unrealistic to assume that if we Icelanders immigrate here and establish an Icelandic community, then we might in due course increase in number, strengthen our financial situation. Gradually become more noticeable as a part of this nation—and become active participants in the making of history with all our good qualities. But the site for such a colony is not easily found especially when unity in the future is considered.

Many will undoubtedly maintain that this immigration will only result in the loss of our language—that it will split us up as an ethnic group and as time goes by we will be swallowed up by other, much larger and more dominant ethnic groups. This may well happen, but in my mind, it does not have to because there will always be a community in Iceland as long as there will be something more than just glaciers, lava fields and desert sands. The arable parts of the land will be used to the maximum by people even though migration may continue for a while. And then I expect the Icelanders here to be able to protect their language as long as they have their own publications, teachers and pastors, like the Norwegians. And in addition, communication with the homeland will always be maintained....[11]

This letter addresses several concerns of the people in Iceland regarding emigration to America. Obviously annoyed with the ignorance about America in his homeland, Thorlaksson emphasized the importance of correct information. It irritated him to hear ridiculous or misinformed statements. He carefully avoided taking sides, but admitted that he was quite content himself. At the same time, he made it clear that others in his position might not be.

In his attempts to provide the reader with a true picture of possibilities in America, he used the experience of Norwegian settlers, which obviously impressed him. He recommended that the Icelanders should take their time in establishing themselves in America and learn new agricultural ways before attempting to start their own farming. This suggestion, made in earnest and quite logical, was later one of the reasons for a bitter debate. As he wrote this letter, and later, when he expressed the same views either orally or in ink, he did not know that in doing so he started a controversy among the early Icelandic immigrants in North America. This controversy resulted in a complete division among the settlers in New Iceland, Canada, in 1879.

To this point all Icelandic immigrants in America had been able to find work and were adjusting to a new way of life. A small Icelandic community had been established on Washington Island and Thorlaksson hinted in his letters that an Icelandic colony could become a reality. Otherwise, the idea of an exclusive Icelandic settlement in North America had not yet dominated discussions in Iceland on migration.

Letters from America to Iceland were generally optimistic. People had work, and shelter over their heads, and appeared on their way to better times. However, as the months of 1873 went by, the tone in these letters gradually changed. The New York bank crash late in 1872 resulted in widespread unemployment throughout North America in 1873. However, in Iceland, more people than ever before were planning their emigration to America.

At Storutjarnir on 24 January 1873, Thorlakur Jonsson called a meeting to address the emigration issue. Forty people attended. An agent in Reykjavík named Gudmundur Lambertsen had published a questionnaire in *Norðanfari*, asking anyone interested in emigration to America to respond. Lambertsen was an agent for a shipping company in England called Allan Brothers & Co. Line. If enough participants were found, a steamer would be sent to Iceland from Scotland to transport people to Great Britain. At the meeting, an organization was formed to plan the emigration from Iceland to America. Thorlakur Jonsson was elected chair. The meeting was adjourned with the agreement that the main reason for emigration from Iceland was the reluctance of the Danish government to grant the Icelandic people any of their civil rights and privileges as a separate nation.[12]

The fact that an Icelandic organization had been established to address emigration shows how general the interest had become. The involvement of Thorlakur Jonsson may well indicate that ever since he suggested emigration to his son Pall, he expected a growing interest. The need for an organization was obvious.

In the past, the main obstacle, aside from lack of money, had been the unavailability of transportation from Iceland to Great Britain. An organization would have a better chance in securing transportation than would a few individuals.

The new organization was apparently to operate only in Iceland. No plans were made for its involvement in finding settlement sites in North America. Had Thorlakur Jonsson known that the day before his meeting, his son Pall Thorlaksson had written and warned people in Iceland against rushing the migration, he might have cancelled the meeting or approached the issue differently. Despite Pall Thorlaksson's letter and others of similar note, Jonsson never appeared to have altered his plans. It seems as if his organization held itself responsible for getting everyone who was interested in migration out of the country as soon as possible. News from America described the steadily increasing unemployment, yet the organization never changed its course. Never was it suggested that all migration to America from Iceland should be postponed until economic conditions there improved.

There were no sudden changes for the worse in general conditions in Iceland. No volcanic eruption, earthquake, or destructive plague forced people to abandon their homeland. However, conditions had been bad in the last few years, especially in the northeast. Winters had been long and cold, and summers wet. Poverty was increasing and Danish authorities showed no signs of granting the Icelandic people any additional rights. Once an organization presented the opportunity to emigrate from Iceland, many people immediately signed up. The presence of agents for British shipping lines was also encouraging. Letters of caution from America, published in Icelandic periodicals, could not prevent people from leaving.

Another meeting in the north of Iceland was held 22 February 1873 in Akureyri. Its main purpose originally was to discuss trade within Iceland and demands for a new constitution. Emigration from Iceland to America was also on the agenda. The meeting was well attended and discussions lively. Three men were elected to tour the country and discuss trade, the new constitution, and emigration at local meetings. Thorlakur Jonsson was chosen to handle the migration issues at those meetings. He was given the authority to register all Icelanders interested in emigration that year and to negotiate the fare with the agent of the Allan Line, Mr. Lambertsen of Reykjavík, or any other agent there who would offer transportation to America for a reasonable price.[13]

They began their journey in early March and visited many places throughout the country. Thorlakur Jonsson was back home at Storutjarnir on 9 May. It is not known how many people signed up for emigration from Iceland during his travels, but he apparently met many supporters of migration as well as those opposed. Those opposed to emigration from Iceland still firmly believed that all descriptions from the States were false. Even when Jonsson produced a letter from his own son, some people insisted that his handwriting had been copied and that Thorlaksson never had written it. While in Reykjavík, the committee members met with numerous influential individuals who expressed their concerns over the general situation in the country, especially the lack of progress. Some felt that emigration to America was much too risky for the average Icelander, and others regarded emigrants and everyone contemplating emigration as traitors.

Meanwhile, tension was mounting in the north. Two men, Olafur Olafsson and Pall Magnusson, had been elected spokesmen for people in favour of emigration to America in the Eyjafjord disdrict. Magnusson had worked very hard at finding and arranging for a ship to come to Akureyri from Scotland to transport the emigrants.

Meetings were called 23 May in Eyjafjord and 30 May at Storutjarnir. A message had reached the leaders of the organization in the north from Reykjavík, stating that the ship was due in Akureyri in June. Both meetings were adjourned with the same message to all in attendance: Go home, sell or dispose of all your belongings that you cannot take with you to America, and be ready for the ship in Akureyri.[14]

While this was taking place, eleven people left Iceland on a ship to Norway. Among them were Skuli Magnusson, who launched the search for a site in Nebraska and later settled in Duluth, Minnesota; Sigurjon Sveinsson, who was one of the first Icelandic settlers in Dakota and a pioneer in the Gardar district; and Sigurdur Kristofersson, who was involved in the settlement of New Iceland and later the first Icelander to leave New Iceland for the Argyle district in Manitoba.

Although sailing eastward to Norway from Iceland was in the opposite direction of their final destination in America, it was the only choice these eleven people had, as they wanted to make it to Milwaukee in time for all the summer work normally available in the rural communities. They reached New York from Norway on 25 June, and went early the next morning to Castle Garden, where they secured a passage to Milwaukee, and reached their final destination on 4 July.

Sigurjon Sveinsson later wrote that they all were fortunate enough to find work in Milwaukee. He spent the rest of the summer working by the docks, but as harvest time grew closer, he and a few others decided to try their luck in the farming communities. Their tour around the countryside was short but quite eventful. Most farmers took them for beggars or thieves, and they spent the nights under open skies, suffering from the biting bugs.

Later in the fall, when they had gathered their strength, they left Milwaukee again, this time heading for the woods. Twelve of them travelled together, finding work at chopping wood. They were paid $1.00 for each load. This kind of work was new to them all; the axe was not a tool frequently used back home in Iceland. However, they gradually learned and soon picked up speed.[15]

Other small groups and individuals made their way across the Atlantic Ocean that summer. Just as the group of eleven men was making final preparations in the north of Iceland, twenty people from the eastern regions of the island arrived in Philadelphia on the morning of 29 May. Little else is known about their journey except that it appears that some of them had previously planned to go to Brazil. Once they were in Denmark, something or someone changed their minds.

Instead of proceeding to Hamburg and from there to Brazil, they caught a ship for America. This group went to Milwaukee and in a short while scattered all over Wisconsin, finding work at different places. Later, most of them found their way into the various Icelandic settlements that were founded in the next few years. One farmer, Gunnlaugur Petursson, was in this group. He became the first Icelander to settle in Minnesota, where a small Icelandic community developed.

A third group is known to have reached Milwaukee on 4 June. Only four men have been accounted for in this group. Torfi Bjarnason spent several years in America before he returned to Iceland, where he later established an agricultural school. His brother Larus settled in Nebraska. Gudmundur Gudmundsson made attempts in different parts of America before settling down permanently on the west coast. William W. Thomsen, a Danish shopkeeper from Reykjavík, was with the group. He had few dealings with the Icelanders once they reached America, but he was known to have lived in Nebraska for a while and later in Utah.[16]

A single individual travelled secretly to America in the late summer. This was Jon Olafsson, a poet and editor from Reykjavík who had attacked Danish authorities in his writings. Faced with criminal charges, fines, even a prison sentence, he fled to America. Olafsson had the support of many prominent Icelanders who pleaded his case in Iceland during his stay of two years in America. Although he came to the United States as a fugitive, he soon made his presence felt and was involved in the growing Icelandic community in America.

Reverend Jon Bjarnason and his wife, Lara Gudjonsen, also arrived in America late in the summer of 1873. He became one of the most influential leaders in the North American Icelandic community until his death in 1914. He had registered in the Latin School in Reykjavík in 1861, almost sixteen years of age, inexperienced, extremely sensitive, but talented and thirsting for knowledge. The spirit in the Latin School in Reykjavík was not to his liking but it was worse at the Theological Seminary, which he entered immediately following his graduation. What he disliked most was the lack of enthusiasm among the students, whom he felt almost detested diligent students.[17] Nonetheless, he completed his studies with praiseworthy results and was ordained immediately upon graduation in 1869. For a year he was assistant pastor to his father, who was not well. He then returned to Reykjavík where he married his fiancée on his birthday, 15 November 1870. They spent the next three years in Reykjavík, where he taught part-time at the Latin School and the elementary school but, in addition, instructed young students in foreign languages at his home. Bjarnason always considered these positions as temporary; twice he applied for vacant benefices but was turned down on both occasions.

It may seem strange that such an excellent student and devoted pastor was not immediately offered a benefice, especially since in many places pastors were known for neglecting their duties. But he had never shied away from speaking his mind. His disappointment with the Theological Seminary was well known to church authorities and, in the absence of definite proof, one suspects his criticism of the seminary as well as of the state church is to blame for his failure to obtain a position within the church.

During the winter of 1872-1873, Bjarnason corresponded with his friend Pall Thorlaksson. These letters clearly show Thorlaksson's appreciation of the Norwegian Synod and its leaders. It appears that Bjarnason asked in one of these letters for information on church life in the United States and in a letter he received 20 March 1873, Thorlaksson briefly discussed the Norwegian Synod. He emphasized that if Bjarnason wanted to come to America and serve as pastor, he should attend Concordia University for a year or so in order to understand the differences between the Church of Iceland and the Norwegian Synod. Thorlaksson pointed out that Bjarnason would undoubtedly be offered a post within the synod following his training at Concordia.[18]

However, Bjarnason was not easily persuaded. Letters from Thorlaksson on 10 May and 17 July of 1873 show that Bjarnason was having difficulty making up his mind. It is hard to tell what actually kept him from going. It may have been his father's illness or the hope of securing a permanent post within the Icelandic Church. Finally, late in August, he made up his mind to go and on 5 September, he sailed for Quebec City. He travelled to Milwaukee, where he spent some time among his fellow countrymen before heading south to St. Louis. Bjarnason left Iceland half-heartedly, not ready to go to America and accept a new way of life, including church life. This may explain his position in the controversies he became engaged in during the next six years.

Upon Bjarnason's arrival, Thorlaksson again suggested he attend Concordia University, but he never did. Instead, he was considered for a teaching post at Decorah, Iowa, where the Norwegian Synod had recently established a Latin School. Decorah was becoming the theological centre of the Norwegian Synod. The annual conference of the synod was scheduled there for January 1874, and Bjarnason was invited to attend a special meeting where his future within the synod would be decided. After a three-week period of confusion and indecision in St. Louis, the Bjarnasons travelled north to Decorah, where they were met by U.V. Koren, who was one of the most influential leaders of the synod.

Gradually, a new world opened up for Bjarnason. He saw active churches all around him, living faith, and extensive social functions controlled by these churches. This was the independent church, free from any interference by the state. This world was very much to his liking and he became increasingly convinced that the organization of the Icelandic Church was based on unsound administrative principles, including the lack of participation by common people in its administration. It was his conviction that this absence accounted for the declining effect of the church on the people of Iceland.

However, as he began to discuss religious matters with Norwegian pastors, he recognized he could not accept the fundamentalism in the doctrines of the Norwegian Synod. In his correspondence with Icelandic friends early in 1874, he frequently touched upon this matter. In a letter to his former instructor in Reykjavík, Helgi Halfdanarson, dated 15 January, he wrote:

> When my views are condemned, especially those which I know for sure are also yours, I feel I am wrongly accused. I would very much like to hear your point of view, and by all means do not hesitate to find fault with me if you think I am mistaken. My intention is and has been, at whatever cost, neither to deny my own conviction nor consider it wrong what I have accepted as right after careful deliberation. I hate all religious debates and I have no intention to deal with the Synod if I am not left in peace. I still dislike it but things may improve.... If not, then I must leave....[19]

At the conference in January 1874, it was agreed to offer Bjarnason a teaching post at Decorah, which he happily accepted. Since his arrival at Decorah in late 1873, he had instructed two of Koren's sons in languages and must have done well. Koren later stated he had been most impressed with their progress. Bjarnason's first term of teaching was a success and, as a result, he was invited to stay on. In the summer of 1874, he travelled to Milwaukee to meet with many of his compatriots.

Despite this positive record, Bjarnason seems to have come into conflict with both the Norwegian and the German Missouri synods immediately upon his arrival in America. Both were immensely powerful religious bodies, which had been founded on American soil and therefore also represented American religious practice. Bjarnason was impressed with the independent churches but could not accept their doctrines. He attempted to transfer the doctrines of his Icelandic religious convictions into an independent Icelandic Church in America. The origins of a bitter religious and ethnic controversy can be traced to his opposition to the synods.

In 1873 at Akureyri, in the north of Iceland, 200 people had been gathered since June to wait for transportation from Iceland to Great Britain. Many of them had sold all their valuables, such as livestock and farm equipment. As weeks went by, a few people began to lose faith in the enterprise. Some became convinced they had been betrayed by the agent in Reykjavík. At one of the frequent meetings, three men were elected as leaders for the group to solve the transportation problem. Discussions at these meetings gradually led to the conviction that it would be most beneficial for all migrants to stick together in America and to settle in an Icelandic colony. People had different opinions on future settlement sites. A few mentioned Nova Scotia; others had heard of the Canadian interior, which at that time probably meant regions in Ontario. The fact that such places were mentioned shows that more information on possible settlement sites in North America had reached Iceland. Sigtryggur Jonasson, the sole Icelandic immigrant in Canada at this point, was partly responsible for this, as he had written to friends in Iceland

and mentioned possibilities in Canada, although not any particular places. The organization led by Thorlakur Jonsson at Storutjarnir in January 1873 was responsible only for arrangements made in Iceland regarding transportation all the way to America. No serious attempts to secure a large enough area for such a settlement were ever made by anyone in Iceland.

Quite a few of those people waiting for transportation in Akureyri had committed to travel to Milwaukee. Pall Thorlaksson, convinced that Icelandic immigrants needed to learn North American agricultural methods, had found work for them on Norwegian farms in Wisconsin. However, the majority decided to go to Ontario in Canada, as news had just reached Iceland that there was land available and plenty of work to be found.

The ship they all had been waiting for finally appeared in August, six weeks late. Its appearance stunned onlookers: it had been primarily used for transportation of livestock and was already half-full of Icelandic horses to be exported to Scotland. It bore the respectable name *Queen*. Agent Lambertsen was aboard, much to the delight of all those who felt the strong urge to express their frustration and anger about the long period of wait and uncertainty. An obvious lack of communication had led the agent to believe that the number of people going was considerably smaller. So, in order to benefit the most from the trip to Scotland, he had agreed to transport the horses as well, since the Icelandic horse was in demand abroad.

Time was suddenly short. The uncertainty in the past few weeks had prevented many people from selling their livestock and other properties but now men disposed of everything they had. Some were unable to sell and gave their animals to friends or family to sell as soon as possible. But not everyone was going. Examination of the ship revealed awful conditions of the quarters allotted to the passengers: one individual decided not to go as "the horses have better quarters than we do."[20] And there was not room for 200 people.

A meeting was called in haste to discuss the deplorable conditions of the ship and how to determine who would go. A committee was chosen to determine the list of passengers. It was certainly not an enviable position to be in and committee members had their share of verbal abuse once the list was completed. The method of choosing is unknown but those who could prove they had sold their properties and had waited since late May or early June received preference. Many of these people had nothing but some clothing, books, and other valuables, while others had yet to sell some of their belongings.

The *Queen* finally left Akureyri on 5 August carrying 157 people. Forty had been left behind. Two families turned down the offer of sailing as they could not accept the conditions aboard. Others gladly took their places.

There is little doubt that this group, the largest to emigrate from Iceland in the early 1870s, had the worst departure. Not only had they been idle in Akureyri for weeks, but they had had to tolerate the degrading remarks from their countrymen who were opposed to emigration from Iceland. The emigrants were labelled traitors, and accused of betraying their homeland and their people in the bitter struggle for independence. They were constantly reminded of the fact that once the *Queen* left the harbour, all of them ceased to be Icelanders, not having any right to ever refer to Iceland as their homeland again. Never before in the young history of emigration from Iceland had any individual been faced with such accusations. But as a result, this group became all the more determined to remain as Icelandic in America as they could. They hoped there would be an area in America large enough for them all to settle together and where the exclusive Icelandic colony would develop.

The group sailing out of Eyjafjord to Scotland placed the dream of the Icelandic colony as a top priority, believing at the same time that their standard of living would improve. However, this attitude, noble and courageous as it was, became a burden for most of these people in the years ahead. The constant search for a colony site, the uncertain future, the travelling from one place to another, prevented these immigrants from having a good start in America.

It was just before noon, 8 August, that the ship docked on the Shetland Islands, where thirty horses were put ashore. The *Queen* left that same afternoon for Aberdeen in Scotland,where all the remaining horses were put ashore. After a short stop, the vessel sailed onwards to Granton, from where all the Icelanders travelled by train to Glasgow. On Tuesday, 12 August, the group boarded the *Manitoban of Glasgow*, which made a stop in Liverpool before heading west for America. Many people of different nationalities boarded the ship in Liverpool—Danes, Norwegians, Swedes, Germans, French, and, of course, British. Liverpool was the biggest city the Icelanders had ever seen and the number of ships in the harbour amazed them.

Finally on 14 August, the *Manitoban* left Liverpool for Quebec in Canada. The Icelandic immigrants were generally satisfied with everything aboard, although some complained about the lack of food variety. The atmosphere on the ship gave the Icelanders an early indication of what to expect in America. Numerous languages were spoken, and passengers wore different clothing and followed different customs. The Icelanders did not mingle much with others because language was a barrier, but, as they bumped into people getting their food or walked past a group on deck, they began to realize that these people would share with them their new homeland. The crossing of the Atlantic Ocean was uneventful, but a few people became seasick again and one Icelandic infant passed away.

It was close to six in the morning on 25 August when the ship docked in the harbour of Quebec City. The immigrants from Iceland, some of whom had waited up to two months in Akureyri, had made it all the way to America in just over twenty days. But reaching this vast continent was not the end of their journey; it was just the first step. For most of them, especially those opting to stay in Canada, several years would pass before they settled down permanently.[21]

News of a large group in the north of Iceland preparing for emigration to America had reached Pall Thorlaksson in St. Louis. At first he heard that 500 people had signed up and were ready to emigrate from Iceland. Three men responsible for this large group wrote to Thorlaksson and asked him to find a convenient colony site. It is not known who the three individuals making this request were, but there was only one organization in Iceland responsible for emigration from Iceland. Thorlakur Jonsson at Storutjarnir was on the committee and it is therefore possible he was one of the three. His son quickly declined the request. First, he pointed out that he was totally lacking in expert knowledge of the qualities of North American farmlands. Second, he believed that once they were in America, Icelandic farmers needed, first and foremost, experience and practice in North American agriculture. Finally, it was his conviction that most of the emigrants from Iceland could not afford to buy land and the expensive equipment such transactions inevitably entailed. Therefore, he suggested that the Icelandic immigrants should spend some time at the outset on Norwegian farms throughout Wisconsin in order to learn new skills in work and language. He pointed out that the Norwegian pioneers had, after they first arrived, spent considerable time on "Yankee" farms and benefitted greatly from that experience. The reasons Thorlaksson gave for his refusal to comply with the request from Iceland are valid and testify to his intelligence. Even though he was accused later of having suggested that Icelanders blend into Norwegian settlements in Wisconsin, it is doubtful if his decision and advice really reflect any such thoughts. Accusations of this kind were usually based on his involvement with the Norwegian Synod. Thorlaksson then communicated with the chair of the Norwegian Synod, asking if Norwegian farmers could house Icelandic immigrants who were expected to arrive in the summer. This request was immediately granted.

Thorlaksson travelled to Milwaukee and spent some time with his brother Haraldur. Here he waited for further information regarding the arrival of the group. He used his time in Wisconsin to contact pastors in order to find out how many immigrants each congregation could accommodate. Four responded quickly to his request, stating that between them they could accommodate forty families and a few individuals, if needed. Just as he received this positive answer, he also learned that the large group expected from Iceland totalled 200 people and that they would be in Quebec, Canada, no later than mid-August.

On 12 August, a message reached the Thorlakssons' household in Milwaukee from Glasgow via Montreal. It stated that 150 Icelanders would be leaving the city (Glasgow) that day, destined for Quebec. Thorlaksson was asked to be there to meet his countrymen no later than 22 August. He responded immediately and expressed his willingness to comply with the request, asking at the same time for a return ticket for himself and an authorization to act on behalf of the Allan Line Company in transporting a group of Icelanders from Quebec to Milwaukee. He got both. He left Milwaukee in the evening of 17 August, crossing Lake Michigan to Grand Haven, and reached Quebec City in the evening of the 20th. Five days later, the *Manitoban of Glasgow* docked with 600 passengers aboard.

Thorlaksson immediately ran down to the harbour, asking in all directions if there were any Icelanders aboard. It was not until he shouted out loud in Icelandic whether there were any such people aboard that he heard his answer. A faint *já* ("yes") reached his ears and soon he was in the middle of a throng of his countrymen. Everyone was in good health and most pleased with having reached America at last.

Thorlaksson called the leaders of the group aside and told them of the preparations that had been made in Wisconsin. They, in turn, informed him that everyone but fifty had committed to travel to Muskoka district in Ontario, northwest of Toronto. Canadian authorities had promised them temporary housing, free land, and some other benefits. Apparently, a Canadian government agent aboard the *Manitoban* had made the offer to all the passengers during the voyage across the Atlantic Ocean. The Canadian offer also included free transportation to Muskoka but, in accepting, the Icelanders committed to working their land for at least three months. After that they were free to go wherever they wanted, even south to the United States. It was understandable that so many opted for Canada. Many of them had no money left for any additional train fare, so their choice was obvious. The fact that they were committed to work their land for only three months was also encouraging. However, Thorlaksson made it very clear to them that he could not guarantee that the Norwegian offer still stood after that period. He then turned his attention to the agents of the Allan Line in Quebec and asked for the Milwaukee fare for those joining him. He was given the fare for most people; a few people were forced to buy tickets again as their receipts, written in Akureyri, were not accepted.

All the Icelanders boarded the same train for Toronto. They stopped briefly the next morning, 26 August, in Montreal, long enough for refreshments such as toast and tea. The immigrants from Iceland observed with excitement the settled land on both sides of the tracks all the way to Kingston, noting a thick forest behind the farms. Near the small town of Coburg, one of the Icelandic women gave birth to a boy, the first Icelandic child born in Canada since emigration from Iceland to America had begun. He was given the name Jon, son of Kristinn Olafsson and his wife Katrin. The family remained behind in Coburg while the mother recovered but soon after they continued their journey south to Milwaukee.[22] The train continued to Toronto, arriving at eight in the morning of 27 August. Here, those going to Muskoka left the train and spent two days in the city.

Those going to Milwaukee continued south to Sarnia. They arrived in the evening and spent the night aboard the train. In the morning they crossed the St. Clair River to Port Huron, Michigan. Luggage was examined and the small amount of ten cents collected from each family before they were allowed to continue. They travelled onwards to the Milwaukee Junction where they stepped off the Grand Trunk and awaited the arrival of the westbound Express from Detroit.

At 6:00 a.m. the next morning, the train made an unexpected stop in the middle of the woods when a broken axle caused a delay. This resulted in a major train accident—the Detroit Express was rear-ended by a westbound freight train. Two women and a child died, none of whom was Icelandic. However, seven Icelandic immigrants were injured, among them the poet Stefan Gudmundsson, later better known as Stephan G. Stephansson. The accident caused a delay until 4:00 p.m., but none of the injured Icelanders had to be hospitalized and they all continued to Grand Haven. All the injured passengers received a written guarantee from the railway company that all cost incurred as a result of the accident would be covered by the company.

In Milwaukee, Thorlaksson consulted a lawyer about what kind of compensation the injured people could request. He was instructed to wait to see how well the company looked after the people while they were recovering. If the care was adequate, then there would not be a case against the company. Thorlaksson then visited the office of the company in Milwaukee and was pleased with his reception. He was given two options to present to his countrymen: one was to settle the case immediately and come to an agreement on a certain amount, after which they would not have any claim against the company. The second choice was that the company would pay for their room and board, medication, and other treatments until they were fully recovered. Everyone in question opted for the second alternative and spent some time in Milwaukee. As all but one had sustained minor injuries, they settled their cases in a matter of a few weeks. Eirikur Hjalmarsson had a badly bruised foot that would not heal properly. He was still in Milwaukee in the middle of October, tended to by Dr. Martin, whose assistant had been no other than young Jakob Palsson, who had immigrated in 1872. Young Palsson was not doing well at that time in October, as he was hospitalized with tuberculosis.

Thorlaksson escorted his people into the countryside 150 kilometres west of Milwaukee, where they were met by some Norwegians who had agreed to accommodate them for the next few months. On 18 October, Thorlaksson wrote to *Norðanfari*, describing the train accident, his dealings with the railway company, and his journey out into the Norwegian rural community along with his countrymen. He concluded with these words:

> Even though I know these Norwegians, who have so kindly accepted these Icelandic families, it will not surprise me to hear that my countrymen may not appreciate everything right away. Not knowing the language will be a problem to begin with. Other Icelandic families are staying with Norwegians, also a few single men but I have yet to hear from these people. This to me seems a much better arrangement than had they decided to stay in Milwaukee. A Norwegian pastor in Wisconsin just wrote to tell me that three Icelandic families in his congregation are quite content. I have heard nothing from the Icelanders in Ontario. Some 135 Icelanders have arrived in Milwaukee this summer. . . .[23]

One of the people arriving in Milwaukee that summer was Torfi Bjarnason. He was probably the only Icelander at the time to have some knowledge of North American farming, and he seemed to have had an Icelandic settlement in mind, though in the United States, not Canada. Torfi Bjarnason and his brother Larus travelled from Milwaukee to Nebraska to search for a good area along the Burlington-Missouri Line. Sections of the area were available with a ten-year mortgage, which was interest-free during the first five years. The brothers decided that the district, which was isolated, nearly forty kilometres from the railway, was too far from other settlements. Instead, Torfi bought a farm near a small town called Salt Hill, ten kilometres south of Lincoln and ninety kilometres west of the Missouri River, which separates Nebraska and Iowa.

Torfi and Larus spent the rest of the summer working the land, ploughing about thirty acres. Torfi Bjarnason became the first Icelandic farmer in Nebraska, but he didn't stay long. For some reason he decided to return to Milwaukee late in the fall and went home to Iceland. He never returned to America, but his brother found work for the winter on a neighbouring farm and looked after Torfi's estate at the same time.[24]

The year 1873 had been busy for Icelandic emigration to America: 323 people in total, compared to forty in 1872. The early pioneers appeared to have had little problem adjusting to their new homeland and accepting their role in the making of a new nation, a nation consisting of ethnic groups from all over the world. Everyone in America had made the same sacrifice; they had left their motherland but brought their culture and traditions. They were prepared to contribute to the multicultural American nation and at the same time were eager to draw from it what would be beneficial to their new way of life.

The large group from Iceland in 1873 had problems with this adjustment. Most of them wanted to remain Icelandic at all costs, constantly recalling the remarks of people in Akureyri prior to their departure. It had become their conviction that the only way to succeed was to establish an exclusive Icelandic colony somewhere in North America. For years, this belief prevented most of them from making progress in their new environment because they devoted their efforts to the search for a colony site.

By the end of 1873, the Icelandic immigrants in North America were divided into three different groups, according to their views on settlements. Thorlaksson was the undisputed leader of those who felt they needed some experience in farming before they started their own. He had the support of the powerful Norwegian Synod, which was willing to assist the Icelanders in this matter. It was his conviction that anyone settling in the United States had to adjust to a new way of life, although, in his opinion, that did not mean sacrificing one's mother tongue or ethnic background. After a period on a Norwegian farm, these Icelanders could settle together and create an Icelandic community. Most of the United States consisted of communities dominated by one ethnic group.

Many people agreed with Thorlaksson, among them Stephan G. Stephansson. Stephansson has long been considered the prime example of an Icelandic immigrant in America who never forgot his motherland, nor lost the ability to converse in his native language. He is also considered one of Iceland's greatest poets, even though he lived most of his life in North America. Yet he never lived in an exclusive Icelandic community and never seemed to have had such a dream.

The second group, which is associated with Reverend Jon Bjarnason, came into conflict with American religious organizations. The Norwegian Synod was an American institution, not a replica of the Church of Norway. Bjarnason felt that any contact with a foreign body would slow the process of establishing the Icelandic colony. He therefore opposed his friend's proposals. The poet and editor Jon Olafsson likewise had not moved to America to search for ways of improving his own life. He was a fugitive who had fled the Danish authorities and was not about to become American. As these two men were both influential, one representing the Church of Iceland and the other an active member of the independence movement, people listened to their arguments.

In the last group were those immigrants who went their own way from the minute they set foot on North American soil. All those who arrived during the first three years of the decade had assimilated into American society right away. Through the entire immigration period, there were always several people every year who vanished. Sometimes they were never heard from again, but more often they surfaced later in one of the Icelandic communities in the United States or Canada.

3
The Mood in Milwaukee: Search for a US Settlement Site

By January 1874, many Icelandic immigrants in America had found their way to Milwaukee. Unemployment was high throughout North America on both sides of the border. Most of the immigrants had no means of buying land and equipment. They came to Milwaukee looking for support and advice from other Icelanders. Thorlaksson had organized a collection of funds among a few Norwegian congregations in Wisconsin and, through his efforts, money was provided for necessities for the Icelandic immigrants in Milwaukee and also for many in Ontario.[1] The widespread economic crisis affected the Icelanders in Milwaukee and the voices of those demanding an Icelandic settlement grew louder. They were convinced that such an enterprise was the only way out of Milwaukee and their miserable living conditions.

Cautious men like Thorlaksson had warned his countrymen in letters published in Icelandic periodicals. He had also suggested that they accept the Norwegian offer of work on farms until they were ready to start their own. His message was clear: accept a different way of life and the fact that you will become American, then you will be successful. He never said that such assimilation would have to result in the loss of Icelandic heritage. He repeatedly pointed to the Norwegian experience, maintaining that they had accepted new ways, yet preserved from their heritage what they needed. Norwegian settlers had been in America for more than thirty years and still their language was spoken in every community; Norwegian schools and churches had been organized; and there were several publications of various kinds in Norwegian.

There is little doubt that the poor economic situation in North America during these early months of 1874 made most of the Icelanders in Milwaukee more determined to stick together. Had employment been plentiful, as it was during the first three years of immigration, people would have scattered in the beginning, and the adjustments to America would have been considerably easier and more pleasant. Almost all their predecessors had found work and were able to save money. But in Milwaukee the mood was different—it was one of hopelessness and despair.

Rev. Jon Bjarnason and Jon Olafsson, the poet and editor, corresponded regularly during this time. Bjarnason was at his teaching post in Decorah, and Olafsson resided in North Cape, Wisconsin. Their own situation was different in one major aspect: neither of them had come to America as keen immigrants. Both had emigrated somewhat against their will. Olafsson was a fugitive and Bjarnason was unhappy with his rejection by the Church of Iceland. Neither accepted Thorlaksson's point of view regarding the preparations of Icelandic immigrants on Norwegian farms. Consequently, as leaders of the discontented group in Milwaukee, they discouraged their people from accepting American ways. In fact, they warned against foreign influences such as those of the Norwegian Synod. For example, in a letter to Bjarnason, Olafsson said that the Norwegian Synod shrank from nothing to entice Icelandic immigrants into the synod, and that Thorlaksson and his father were "humble slaves of the Synod," constantly plotting to deceive their fellow-countrymen. He also claimed that the idea of Icelanders spending time on Norwegian farms before obtaining their own land was the synod's way of forcing its "bigotry" upon them.[2]

Late in 1873, Jon Olafsson wrote Bjarnason that he was planning to visit Milwaukee in early 1874 in order to meet with his countrymen. He intended to found an Icelandic organization that would concentrate on the search for a colony site. Though no such organization was born during his visit to Milwaukee, he met Olafur Olafsson from Espiholl, in the north of Iceland. "This man is endowed with intelligence and qualities of leadership,"[3] he stated later. Olafur Olafsson shared the opinions of the poet and Bjarnason. He informed Jon Olafsson that he led a group of Icelanders who intended to explore other regions in Nebraska in the spring.

Under the leadership of Olafur Olafsson, the first Icelandic association in America was established in the spring of 1874, and a general meeting was called. Among those attending was Thorlaksson. The meeting resolved to send a delegation to explore regions along the Burlington-Missouri line, both in Iowa and Nebraska. Thorlaksson, on the other hand, suggested that Wisconsin be thoroughly explored before attempts were made elsewhere. His presence at the meeting indicates that he was not opposed to the idea of an Icelandic settlement.

After careful preparations, delegates left Milwaukee on 5 May 1874 and arrived in Chicago that same day. They purchased tickets to Lincoln, Nebraska, from the Burlington-Missouri Line Co., which owned most of the land they intended to examine. Each delegate paid $25.00, which allowed them to stop over on the way wherever they wanted. The amount also was considered as part of a down payment on company land.

They left Chicago 6 May and arrived in Burlington, Iowa, early the next morning, where they found a land agency and studied maps of the area. They proceeded to Villisca, a small village, and then ten kilometres northeast of the village to explore available land, of which each acre was priced at $11.00 to $17.00. However, they concluded this land was too high and dry. After spending a day in Villisca, they continued on 8 May, arriving at the Missouri River the same day. "There was a huge steamer on the river onto which two cars were pulled. People sat still in both. The steamer then crossed the river and on the other side the cars were pulled ashore off the vessel. It was quite interesting to sail across a river still sitting on a train!" Sigfus Magnusson wrote to *Norðanfari*.[4]

They were delayed in Plattsmouth, a small town west of the Missouri River where the La Platte River enters it. They continued along the west bank all the way to Lincoln, where they stayed until 12 May, waiting for a letter from Larus Bjarnason. They visited Salt Hill and examined Torfi Bjarnason's farm, noticing that his fields had been seeded, then proceeded on foot to Firth, a small town where they spent the night. They located Bjarnason on a nearby farm, where he still had work. They spent two days in his company, using the time to explore regions. And finally, they found land to their liking and invested. Each of them bought land six kilometres from the Firth railway station and thirty kilometres from Lincoln.

They wrote a report to the Milwaukee organization, describing all the areas they explored and the land they had bought. According to the agreement of the general meeting in Milwaukee, Olafur Olafsson was supposed to join them as soon as they had found a suitable area. However, he never did, probably because their report stated there was not enough land available in Iowa for all the members of the organization. Nor was there an area large enough in Nebraska for an exclusive settlement. Still, they pointed out that they could all settle in the same area, close to one another, and learn the language and farming methods of their foreign neighbours. They might even find work on established farms where they could earn some money. This last suggestion of the report is very much in harmony with Thorlaksson's advice.

The two new settlers in Nebraska, Sigfus Magnusson and Jon Halldorsson, found work and temporary housing with some German farmers. Both had about ten acres of land ploughed, paying $2.50 per acre. Magnusson was hired for a seven-month period for $18.00 per month. In his June 1874 letters he stated that it was unfortunate the Germans only spoke Low German while he attempted to use English, but he hoped that communication would improve. He claimed that the area where he and Halldorsson had purchased land was beautiful and the air warmer than in Wisconsin. He concluded by saying that the water in Nebraska certainly tasted much better.[5] In Milwaukee, his report was well received, and many people decided to try to find work for a year and then move to Nebraska to settle. However, for the next three years, grasshoppers caused tremendous damage in Nebraska and nearby states as well as on the Canadian prairie. This forced the people in Milwaukee to reconsider their plans. Only three Icelandic settlers remained in Nebraska during the next winter and their number did not increase until three years later. Although nothing ever came of the original settlement plan, Icelandic immigrants were found in Nebraska for years thereafter.[6]

Meanwhile, Icelandic immigrants who had spent the winter on Norwegian farms were becoming increasingly restless. Those especially who had been independent farmers in Iceland found it very strange, even difficult, to be in the employment of others, not to mention foreigners. They contacted Thorlaksson, asking if he would assist them in finding a settlement site in Wisconsin. This he was willing to do, and in mid-July a meeting in Milwaukee decided he would seek assistance from Norwegian friends in the search for a settlement site. Early in the fall an area in Shawano County had been investigated and approved. Soon, twelve Icelandic settlers arrived on the site, selected and claimed land, and began the initial task of building huts. This was not a problem as there was building material all around them.[7] The area was heavily treed, but broken up by rivers and lakes. By now, all the settlers had some experience with the axe, and found work chopping wood during the winter. Thorlaksson's willingness, after refusing a year earlier, was probably due to the desperate need of his countrymen. Another reason for his change of heart could be that these people had followed his suggestion and had worked for some time on Norwegian farms, and he may have considered them much better prepared for their own farming.

Both Reverend Bjarnason and Jon Olafsson opposed the founding of this new settlement in Wisconsin. They felt, as did many others, that a future Icelandic settlement in Wisconsin was out of the question.[8] In the beginning, Thorlaksson had high hopes for the Wisconsin settlement but felt his compatriots needed outside help. He had returned to his studies in St. Louis and on 9 October he wrote to Professor Rasmus B. Anderson at University of Wisconsin in Madison asking for advice and whether the State of Wisconsin would assist his countrymen in getting established in Shawano. Anderson apparently was willing to help because Thorlaksson responded in a letter, 20 November:

> I am very glad to hear that you will be so kind as to apply to the Legislature of Wisconsin in January next for some public aid to the pioneer settlers from the poor Iceland, who are going to lay the foundation stone for a mighty building consisting of perhaps thousands of "Sagamen" in the State of Wisconsin. Certainly now is the time for making some attempts towards the promotion of the Icelandic immigration to Wisconsin. Just at this time it is a great, but still quite undecided question among the Icelandic immigrants, where to settle when they

have crossed the Atlantic Ocean; now the American people seem to be opening their eyes as to the merits of poor Iceland concerning the discovery of their "glorious" country; now is the time to make an appeal to their generosity—e.g. if the State of Wisconsin was willing to make an appropriation of some 100 dollars for the benefit of an Icelandic settlement in Shawano County.[9]

It seems clear that Thorlaksson believed that all his compatriots emigrating to America could settle in Wisconsin. It is not clear what happened next, but in a postcard to Professor Anderson, dated 15 January 1875 and written in St. Louis, Thorlaksson stated that the Icelanders themselves should sign a petition to present to authorities in Wisconsin. He suggested that Professor Anderson not spend more time on the issue. Rev. Bjarnason and Jon Olafsson both were also close friends of Professor Anderson, and Rev. Bjarnason actually moved to Madison, so perhaps, because Bjarnason was opposed to any Wisconsin settlement, he may have persuaded Professor Anderson to reconsider Thorlaksson's request. It is unclear how Thorlaksson envisioned a large Icelandic settlement in Shawano but there is little doubt that he wanted the best for his countrymen in America, and was motivated by the accomplishments in the US. He was being educated as a future pastor for the Norwegian Synod, which at that time was mostly confined to Wisconsin and Iowa. Therefore, he may have felt that if he was to serve his countrymen, there had to be an Icelandic settlement in Wisconsin. These are speculations but important to make in order to better understand the bitter controversy that was beginning among the Icelandic setters in the United States and later spread to Canada.

But those people wanting to leave Wisconsin and still looking for a suitable site soon made other suggestions and recommendations. Jon Olafsson had not been idle since his arrival in America. Patriotic as he was, he felt that the Icelandic immigrants should stop at nothing in their efforts to establish an Icelandic colony somewhere in America. A keen politician himself, he consulted with important people and sought their advice. Many scoffed at his suggestion of an exclusive Icelandic settlement, but a few listened. One was a lawyer in New York, named Marston Niles. He mentioned Alaska to Olafsson and suggested that the Icelanders would get all the support they needed to establish a colony there. Apparently impressed with Olafsson, Niles promised his full support to the Icelandic immigrants, not only in the Alaska project but also in any attempt to settle in the midwest. They agreed to focus on Alaska.

The United States had bought Alaska from Russia in 1867. An expedition had explored regions and compiled information about Alaska in 1869. A report by Lieutenant W.H. Dal, entitled "Alaska and its Resources," had been published in Boston in 1870, and Olafur Olafsson and Jon Olafsson found a copy in May of 1874. They studied it thoroughly and came to the same conclusion: Alaska was the right place for the Icelandic settlement in America. It was their understanding from the report that conditions there were, in many ways, similar to those in Iceland.

Olafur Olafsson, who was highly respected and considered by many the ideal leader, appears to have been easily influenced when it came to choosing a settlement site. During his life in America he contemplated more sites and settled in more places than most other immigrants. His excitement over the Alaska project explains his absence from Nebraska later that summer.

Having obtained all the information he could find on Alaska, Jon Olafsson called a general meeting in early July. He suggested that a delegation of three travel to Alaska for the purpose of exploring certain areas and securing land if it was found suitable for the Icelandic colony. He offered his services to those the meeting would elect and stated that he would try, with the help of Marston Niles in New York, to arrange for the cheapest possible transportation. The meeting elected Jon Olafsson, Olafur Olafsson, and Arni Sigvaldason. Jon Olafsson left Milwaukee on 10 July and travelled to New York, where he met with Marston Niles and Professor Hjalmar Hjort Boyesen, a Norwegian scholar lecturing at Columbia University. Both had considerable interest in Alaska and were aware of the Icelandic settlement dream.[10] It remains a mystery why Niles and Professor Boyesen had an interest in the Alaska project. Was it humanitarian, was there a chance for considerable personal financial gains, or was the reason political? At the time, authorities in the United States had not really decided what to do with Alaska, but the Democrats constantly blamed the Republicans for wasting money on Alaska.

Olafsson stayed in New York until 26 July and frequently met with Niles and at times also Professor Boyesen. He wrote a good deal about the Alaska project. He corresponded regularly with Reverend Bjarnason, now visiting in Milwaukee, and also Professor Fiske at Cornell University in Ithaca, who had an interest in Iceland and all matters concerning the nation. Just before Olafsson departed, Niles promised he would arrange for financial support for the planned exploration of Alaska and possibly also the transportation.

The year 1874 marked the passage of 1000 years since the beginning of settlement in Iceland. A national festival was planned 2 August at Thingvellir, probably the most historic site in Iceland, to commemorate this significant date. The King of Denmark had agreed to grant a new constitution to the Icelandic people that year, which was to be officially presented to the nation on 2 August.

Jon Olafsson had expressed his opinion in letters to Reverend Bjarnason during the winter of 1873-1874 that it was the duty of every Icelander, wherever he might reside, to take part in that celebration. His organization in Milwaukee was not only to concentrate on the search for a settlement site, but also to prepare an Icelandic celebration in Milwaukee on 2 August.

Jon Olafsson went to Milwaukee, met several Icelanders, and presented his idea regarding the organization and probably also the celebration. On 27 June he wrote to Bjarnason and urged him to come to Milwaukee as soon as possible because Thorlaksson was expected there any day, and, said Olafsson, "he may interfere with the festival plans...."[11] He gave no reasons for his objections to Thorlaksson's participation but a probable explanation is the latter's involvement with the Norwegian Synod. However, Thorlaksson was not as much of a problem as Olafsson expected and preparations went smoothly.

The first Icelandic festival committee ever assembled in America consisted of three women and three men. Elected in late July were Reverend Bjarnason and his wife, Lara, who had arrived in Milwaukee in mid-July, Olafur Olafsson and his wife, Olof Jonsdottir, and her sister Jakobina, Sigurjona Laxdal, and Thorlaksson. They emphasized that one of the purposes of the festival was to raise spirits among the Icelandic immigrants in Wisconsin and unite people to plan for the Icelandic settlement in America.

Jon Olafsson was away in New York when the committee was put together, which explains his absence and perhaps also Thorlaksson's presence. Olafsson may have opposed his nomination. On the other hand, Thorlaksson's presence on the committee strengthened efforts to unite all the Icelanders. Thorlaksson contacted his Norwegian friends in Milwaukee and was offered the use of one of their churches. This must have been hard for Reverend Bjarnason and Jon Olafsson to accept. By this use of the Norwegian church, the Norwegian Synod indirectly became part of the celebration.

Shortly after 12:00 p.m. on 2 August, between sixty and seventy people gathered in the church and heard the first Icelandic religious service delivered in North America. The festival committee had asked Reverend Bjarnason to base his sermon on the same text as had been prescribed for the celebration in Iceland. The first verse of Psalm 90 was the same verse that the Reverend Matthias Jochumsson in Iceland selected as the basis for a song, which he wrote specially for the celebration at Thingvellir. Today, this song is the Icelandic national anthem, sung to the music composed by Sveinbjorn Sveinbjornsson.

Bjarnason discussed the thousand years of hardship and struggle, despite which the Icelanders had always preserved their language and culture. He emphasized that it was the moral duty of all those present to do the same. He said:

> I hope and wish that the few Icelanders who have gathered here to listen to the first Icelandic sermon on this foreign soil will never forget their faith although fate has brought them here away from Iceland. I cannot imagine any of you forgetting your motherland or ever losing your love of the only nation you have ever known until recently. We are not here to forget our duties to the only nation the Lord has linked us with. Whoever forgets his motherland or pretends to have no obligations to preserve his ethnic background, which is of a religious nature for the simple reason he now lives on foreign soil has also forgotten God. It is a short step and quickly taken: you abandon your religion, then you also abandon your ethnic background.[12]

Bjarnason's message was clear. He warned his countrymen against joining any foreign religious group, stressing that ethnic background and religion cannot be separated. The implication was to stay away from the Norwegian Synod. He obviously worried that any contact with the synod would not only turn the

Icelanders away from the doctrines of the Icelandic State Church, but would also threaten the establishment of the Icelandic colony. Naturally, the very essence of such a settlement was the Icelandic heritage. It was Bjarnason's conviction that faith had always protected the Icelandic nation during times of crisis and this faith was firmly rooted. It could not be destroyed as a result of emigration to America.

Following the service, people gathered outside the church and formed a parade, led by two men, both wearing Icelandic national costumes. Wearing traditional costumes had gained popularity in the second half of the century among young students and served to awaken national spirit and pride in cultural traditions. Both leaders carried flags: one, the Star Spangled Banner, and the other, a blue flag onto which a picture of the Icelandic falcon was imprinted. In 1874, Iceland did not yet have an official flag. Behind these two leaders marched all the others, first all men and women wearing costumes, then other adults, and finally teenagers and children.

This small but remarkable parade slowly wound through the streets of Milwaukee. A Swedish man had agreed to provide beverages at a reasonable price and, according to Reverend Bjarnason's report on the events of the day, later published in Iceland, everyone became merry and enjoyed the hot afternoon. A platform had been built and the two flags raised on each side.

To begin the official program, Jon Olafsson addressed the gathering. In his toast to Iceland, he concentrated on the struggle for independence, both in the past and present, and discussed the visit of the Danish king to the millennial celebration. He mentioned the new constitution, which, in his opinion, was but one small step towards complete independence. He warned that more than ever before, the Icelandic nation needed to seize every opportunity for freedom. The crowd reacted to his speech with loud cheers, which were followed by a few Icelandic songs.

Olafur Olafsson spoke next and gave a toast to the Icelanders in America, both those already there and also future immigrants. He pointed out that emigration from Iceland had just begun but hoped that those Icelanders settling in America would always live in harmony. "Nothing matters more than cooperation and mutual respect," he concluded.

Thorlaksson chose to speak in Norwegian and briefly discussed prospects in the New World, mainly in the United States. He ended his address by thanking the few Norwegians in the audience for all their help on behalf of the Icelandic immigrants. He urged the Icelanders to make every effort to work with and learn from Norwegian settlers in America, to whom they were so closely related. A Norwegian pastor by the name of Gelmuyden rose and thanked Thorlaksson for his kind words, and wished the Icelanders good fortune in their new country.

Thorlaksson's speech received a mixed reaction. The people present considered the festival a means to unite their compatriots in their search for a permanent settlement site and to boost their spirits. Although Thorlaksson had not suggested anything different in his speech, he had spoken in Norwegian, emphasizing close working and living relations with Norwegian settlers. To Bjarnason, Jon Olafsson, and Olafur Olafsson, any relations with the Norwegians were a threat to the future Icelandic settlement. Bjarnason saw the need to respond.

He instructed his countrymen to make every effort in their new country to preserve their language. He acknowledged the need to learn English but stated that it was the holy duty of every Icelander neither to forget his mother tongue, nor mix with it foreign slang, which "our cousins, the Norwegians, are so guilty of. They have even changed their own names or adopted entirely different ones, which they use in the English speaking community, but switch to their own, Christian Norwegian names back in their Norwegian environment. The reason it is so done is to make it easier for the English speaking majority."[13]

Jon Olafsson completed the official program by mentioning the names of two friends of Iceland: Professor Rasmus B. Anderson at University of Wisconsin, and Professor Willard Fiske at Cornell University. Through their work, these two had introduced Icelandic culture to Americans. Both had been invited to the festival but neither was able to attend.

Bjarnason stated in his report that "everyone left in a good mood and more optimistic about the future."[14] He did not mention the emerging debate between the leaders. Bjarnason's summary statement can be interpreted in two ways: first, he may have meant that the plan to unite all Icelanders had worked and that he had succeeded in convincing everyone not to follow Thorlaksson's advice, which was to work with the Norwegians. Or, he may have meant that those attending had had a pleasant afternoon, putting aside the uncertain future for a while.

Everyone must have enjoyed themselves at this first Icelandic celebration in America. Social events of this nature were not a daily occurrence in Iceland. In fact, it is almost certain that only a few people had ever attended such a gathering. Their journey to America had been difficult and their time on foreign soil had been one of uncertainty. Less than seventy people attended, but more than 350 Icelanders had emigrated to North America by the time the festival took place.

Before everyone left, an Icelandic organization was formed. The main objectives of the Icelandic Association of North America were: first, to preserve and strengthen Icelandic sentiment in North America; second, to maintain strong bonds with the motherland; and, third, to organize the search for a permanent settlement site.[15] Jon Olafsson introduced the Alaska project to the crowd and produced a petition he had written and addressed to the president of the United States, Ulysses Grant. Forty-three adults signed the petition, although not Thorlaksson. The petition requested that the United States sponsor an expedition of three Icelandic explorers to Alaska, where they would spend three weeks investigating the suitability of Kodiak Island and other nearby areas as the future colony for the Icelandic immigrants. The petition pointed out that the 70,000 people living in Iceland had been faced with a steadily deteriorating climate in the second half of the century, and that many of them were considering emigration. Abortive attempts to find settlement sites were also mentioned, and Alaska was hailed as the ideal place for the Icelanders in the United States. The petition made clear the plight of the Icelandic immigrants in the United States: it was so serious that, if decisive measures were not immediately taken, Canada would soon become a major attraction for them. Moreover, the petition stated that if the three explorers approved of conditions in Alaska, two of them would stay behind while the third, Jon Olafsson, would return to Washington to give a detailed report on the entire expedition. The three explorers would take the frigate *Plymouth* from San Francisco to Alaska, and, in the case of positive results, Jon Olafsson would return on the same ship.

At a meeting of twenty-two Icelanders in Milwaukee in late June, Jon Olafsson, Olafur Olafsson, and Arni Sigvaldason had been elected to travel to Alaska, but, since then, Sigvaldason's situation had changed. He was replaced by Pall Bjornsson. Convinced that a solution had now been found, not only for Icelandic immigrants in North America but for all Icelanders, Jon Olafsson wrote with extraordinary enthusiasm that "the purpose is to settle a vast area where all Icelanders could live, where they could multiply, preserve their language and nationality. Here they would establish an Icelandic State as part of the United States, Iceland should be depopulated but established again, free and reborn in Alaska."[16] Alaska was to be the new home of all Icelanders, even those thousands still living in Iceland. It is doubtful if either Bjarnason or Olafur Olafsson were as enthusiastic about the project as the poet.

The new organization elected Bjarnason as chair and Jon Olafsson as secretary. Its first and probably only meeting concluded the festival in Milwaukee. However, its objectives became the basis for other Icelandic organizations, such as the Icelandic Festival of Manitoba and the Icelandic National League.

Thorlaksson left Milwaukee shortly after the celebration and went to Shawano County. He attended a meeting to which representatives of all settlements in the area were invited. With the support of a Norwegian friend, Reverend Homme, and a German man, Reverend Dicks, both Lutheran pastors in northern Wisconsin, he got the approval of the meeting to secure all available land in Shawano County for Icelandic settlers at half-price. No settler was allowed to buy more than eighty acres. One-tenth was to be down payment; the rest would be paid over ten years with seven percent interest. In those days the price per acre in Shawano was just around $1.00. This meant that for the Icelanders each farm of eighty acres was around $40.00 and the farmer would put down $4.00. The annual payment was then the same $4.00 plus interest until the land had been paid in full.[17] This was more like a present than a business transaction, but it was known that the soil in many parts was poor, which probably explains why the land had not been claimed by anyone else. Most of Wisconsin had already been settled by mid-1874. The meeting also agreed that all the land north of Lake

Shawano, which was useless for seeding, should become available to those Icelandic farmers specializing in raising sheep.

However, the area was not large enough for a major settlement, and not many settlers accepted the offer. Only a few people were added to the population in the next few years. Those who settled in Shawano, men such as Stephan G. Stephansson and Thorlakur Jonsson, remained content and stayed on despite the founding of New Iceland in Canada in 1875.

Three areas attracted the Alaska explorers: Kodiak Island, Cooks Bay, and the Aleutian peninsula. The three delegates left Milwaukee on 30 August for Chicago, and then went to New York to complete necessary paperwork. They then returned to Chicago and proceeded to Omaha and Ogden before reaching San Francisco on 10 September, where the *Plymouth* awaited them. They spent twenty-four days at sea before they saw land, and an additional week before finally docking at Fort Nicholas in Cooks Bay.

The Icelanders spent three weeks exploring, taking notes, and writing a report to their compatriots. Jon Olafsson then boarded the *Plymouth* again and returned to New York, while Olafur Olafsson and Pall Bjornsson prepared for a winter in St. Paul on Kodiak Island. The winter was hard, and despite their best possible preparations, both men suffered from shortage of food and exposure to the bitterly cold winter. The experience proved too much for them and by the time they returned to Milwaukee in the early summer of 1875, they agreed that Alaska was not the place for the Icelandic colony.

Meanwhile, Jon Olafsson arrived in New York and, before the end of 1874, he had completed his report to the US government. In it, he strongly recommended an Icelandic settlement in Alaska and asked for financial support for launching the project. He pointed out the great distance of travelling and the astronomically high cost of transportation. He said, "It is our conviction that Kodiak Island is better suited for the Icelandic people than any other land we know on earth. . . ."[18] He discussed places in Canada and the United States where Icelanders had attempted to settle or were considering as settlement sites, but, he continued:

> the climate is most important. The Icelanders are not used to extreme heats and are therefore ill prepared for hard toil under such circumstances. In so doing they are actually risking their lives. But in all places discussed above, summer heat is overwhelming. . . . The most suitable lands are not those where everything burns in summer and freezes in winter. . . . Nearly all, actually all ethnic groups immigrating to America, except for the Icelanders, are accustomed to working the fields. Therefore all of them look for areas suitable for that kind of farming. Such lands are plentiful in the east and will be settled during years to come. Consequently, these people have no reason to look as far west as Alaska. The area is available to the Icelanders who can settle there alone, at least for a while. If they choose to settle there it will be up to them to decide if they stay

there alone or accept other ethnic groups. The law enables them to keep other ethnic groups away if they so desire.

If they settle the land they can claim legislative power since no other settlements are there.

Apart from some native people, who have no rights as US citizens, nobody lives in Alaska. Once the legislative power is in the hands of the Icelanders, they will make Icelandic the official language of the State. They will have the right to make it the law that no one can vote as a citizen of the State unless he has proper command of the Icelandic language. This would force every "foreigner" who settles in Alaska to learn the language, accept their ethnicity as his own and thus become an Icelander. Land for schools and other educational institutions would be donated just as in all other States but all those can be purely of Icelandic nature. Immigrants would be supported but only Icelandic immigrants would be offered financial assistance in order to encourage them to settle. In brief, it is entirely up to them to settle and organize this new, free State. No other country offers a comparable opportunity. . . .[19]

Jon Olafsson expected the Icelanders in Alaska to increase in number and that their position in America would gradually be strengthened. In 300 years, he expected, there would be 100 million Icelanders in North America and their domain would stretch from Hudson Bay to the Pacific and possibly well into the northern States.

He went to Washington, DC, to find a member of Congress to present his case. But his project never was introduced. Most sources claim that members of Congress spent all their efforts at the time on the question of pensions for soldiers who fought in the Civil War.[20] Jon Olafsson appears to have been ill-prepared for his visit and anticipated a much more favourable reception. Perhaps his anticipation is understandable. Ever since he first heard from Marston Niles in New York, he was under the impression that Niles had contacts inside the government and Congress. After all, Niles had arranged for the transportation to Alaska and financial support of the exploration. It may well be that Niles was under the same impression.

The US government had been heavily criticized for "wasting" so much money on Alaska. When the Alaska project was first proposed, it appeared to be a golden opportunity for the government to impress the sceptics by supporting the founding of a permanent settlement in the area. The *New York Evening Post* said: "The Icelanders are certainly a very desirable class of people to add to our population, and we believe that their presence in Alaska will greatly aid in turning that district, which hitherto has been a rather costly appendage of the United States, into a profitable possession."[21] But interest in the project was gone by the time Jon Olafsson appeared in Washington with his report. Two reasons seem logical as an explanation: first, it was against US policy to assist ethnic groups to establish their own exclusive settlements, as Jon Olafsson wanted. Second, the cost of transporting all the Icelanders to Alaska would be too much. The government could not politically afford any additional expenditure concerning Alaska. General interest among Icelandic immigrants in America in the Alaska project also was small. Of the seventy people attending the Milwaukee celebration, only forty-two signed the petition to President Grant. Jon Olafsson undoubtedly began to realize that his dream would never materialize. The lack of interest in the project, both in America and Iceland, gradually became clear and his heart no longer seemed in it. During his period in Washington, he wrote much poetry that reflects his dedication to Iceland. He had come to America in an emergency and, despite being absent from Iceland, he never stopped fighting for independence of his nation. His Alaska dream involved all Icelanders, the entire nation, not just the few hundred already in America.[22]

In early 1875, when it became clear that there would not be an Alaska settlement, all hopes of establishing a large Icelandic settlement in the United States seem to have died. Those who were still attracted to that idea turned their attention to Canada. However, those who preferred the States and the settlement process advocated by Thorlaksson looked to Minnesota as the new site of interest.

The Icelanders selected an area in the southwest of Minnesota. Although they settled in three counties, some distance apart, everyone referred to the area as the Icelandic settlement in Minnesota. The district is a little less than 250 kilometres southeast of Minneapolis and the town of Minneota was in the centre of the colony. This was not an exclusive Icelandic settlement, however, as both Norwegians and British-Americans were numerous. Marshall, about twenty-five kilometres east of Minneota, also became home for a few Icelanders. Northeast of Minneota, twenty-two kilometres away, was the so-called Eastern Settlement, which spreads out into both Lyon and Yellow Medicine counties. Most Icelanders settled in Lyon County. West of Minneota is the Western Settlement, or the Lincoln County Settlement.

The first Icelandic settler in Minnesota was Gunnlaugur Petursson. He emigrated from Iceland to America in 1873 after managing his family's farm since 1857. Once he was in America, Petursson followed Thorlaksson's advice and worked on a Norwegian farm in Iowa County, Wisconsin, for a year and a half. In the early part of 1875, many Norwegian settlers in Wisconsin began to move west into Minnesota and in May of that year, Petursson and his family joined a group heading for the southwest of Minnesota. His small wagon was pulled by a team of oxen. After three weeks of travelling, he arrived in Lyon County. He spent some time exploring the area and examining the soil before selecting a site by the Yellow Medicine River, about twelve kilometres northeast of Minneota. He called his place Hakonarstadir, the name of his birthplace and family farm in Iceland. In 1925, when the Icelanders in Minnesota celebrated fifty years of settlement, they chose Hakonarstadir as the location for the event.[23]

In 1876, a few other Icelanders moved to Lyon County from Wisconsin and settled near Hakonarstadir. Among them were Sigmundur Jonatansson, Gudmundur Henry Gudmundsson, Eirikur H. Bergmann, and Kristinn Olafsson.

The latter two later settled in the Icelandic colony in Dakota. In the fall of 1876, Arngrimur Jonsson arrived from Iceland.[24]

In the next few years, there was a steady stream of Icelandic settlers to Minnesota, most of them settling in Lyon County. These settlers either came straight from Iceland or from other parts of America. It was not until several years later, after 1880, that Icelanders in Canada became attracted to the Minnesota settlement. But settlers of other ethnic backgrounds also came in large numbers into the area and claimed land. By 1878, all free government land had been accounted for and the Icelandic immigrants turned their attention to Lincoln County. In the spring of 1878, several of them had already claimed land there. In August 1878, seven families arrived from Vopnafjordur in the east of Iceland. The following year a few more people moved into the young Lincoln County settlement, direct from Iceland.

The land claimed in Minnesota by these Icelandic pioneers was ideal for mixed farming. Those who had gained experience on Norwegian farms were successful in working the fields, and they all raised cattle. The area was the midwest plains, fertile soil with few trees to slow down the process of breaking the land. However, the absence of building material forced many a pioneer to dig out a basement and roof it with wood and turf.

Although they were living in a predominantly American community, the Icelandic settlers soon began to discuss what they, as an ethnic group, needed to do in order to preserve their language and heritage. An organization had been formed before the settlement was five years old to promote literature and improve general knowledge among the Icelanders in the colony. It is noteworthy that a strong emphasis was placed on reading material on America, their new homeland. The organization was also to arrange for a cemetery and for regular prayer meetings.

Soon, similar organizations had been founded in other Icelandic communities in Minnesota. The one in Lincoln was later divided into two, the Progress Society and the Reading Society. The former concentrated on developments that often involved all ethnic groups in the community, such as constructing roads or building schools. The latter grew quickly and was instrumental in the promotion of Icelandic sentiment in Minnesota for many years.[25]

The Minnesota settlement was a success from the beginning. This colony was perhaps the best example of Thorlaksson's plan. The first pioneers had worked on Norwegian farms, and in turn shared their expertise with those directly arrived from Iceland. The Icelandic organizations had two main objectives: first, to preserve Icelandic heritage in the area; and second, to educate the settlers from Iceland in matters concerning American society.

The Icelandic settlers in Minnesota accepted that they were part of the young American nation, but they didn't shy away from their duties to their motherland or heritage. This Minnesota settlement must be considered one of the most successful Icelandic colonies in North America. To this day, there are indications they preserved Icelandic heritage as well as maintained strong bonds with Iceland.

At the same time, the pioneers and their descendents have contributed in numerous ways to American society.

Pall Thorlaksson graduated from Concordia, St. Louis, in the spring of 1875, and was ordained later that summer. In the fall, he visited the settlement in Shawano County where he eventually founded the first Icelandic Lutheran congregation in North America. He settled in the colony with his sister, Gudrun Jakobina, as his housekeeper. He also succeeded his friend, Rev. Homme at the Bethel Lutheran Church in Shawano, serving the Green Valley Scandinavian Congregation from 1875 to 1879. One of his clerical duties in Shawano was to perform the service for the marriage of Stephan G. Stephansson, his friend, to Helga Jonsdottir in 1878.

The settlers in Shawano had joined the Icelandic Association, which had been founded in Milwaukee on 2 August 1874. However, they became disappointed in the organization during the late summer and fall of 1875, when no news of the association's activities had reached Shawano. It became apparent that the elected committee was not functioning as had been expected, and a meeting was called at Thorlaksson's home on 14 November.

On the agenda were the Icelandic Association and its bylaws. People agreed that the Shawano members of the association should not pay their annual dues until the completion of the properly advertised annual meeting, at which the present committee would either be re-elected or replaced by a new one. The present committee's secretary, Jon Olafsson, had returned to Iceland. The meeting also agreed that the bylaws of the association should be amended to clarify the use of funds collected through annual dues. Finally, it was suggested that the association decide whether and how to recompense its elected committee members.

The resolutions of the Shawano meeting are noteworthy. The settlers in the region had become members of the association in good faith. Jon Olafsson, who had been instrumental in the founding of the organization, had left America. His enthusiasm was missing on the committee and, consequently, it was inactive. The meeting appointed Thorlakur Jonsson as the Shawano representative of the association. His first assignment was to write the chair of the committee, Reverend Bjarnason, in Madison to express the concerns of the members in Shawano. Jonsson was instructed to call another meeting in the colony upon the receipt of Bjarnason's response.

In December, Jonsson wrote to Bjarnason and added a register, which included information regarding approximately forty members of the association, all of whom gave their home address at Pulcifer P.O., Shawano County, Wis. The register was extremely thorough in comparison to other documents in existence from those times. It reflects one vital purpose of the association, which was to record the name and a brief account of every Icelandic settler, just as church registers had done in Iceland and which were an Icelandic custom. Every Christian and maiden name was given, also place of birth, and most often the name of farms, county, and district, as well as date of birth. Minutes of the 2 August meeting in Milwaukee do not exist, so it is impossible to state whether the intent was that every chapter of the association would keep similar records of their membership. Thorlaksson had attended that meeting and his father must have consulted with him before engaging in this documentation. Jonsson's register can be considered the first Icelandic census in an Icelandic community in America.[26]

By the end of 1875, seven families were listed as settlers in the community. In addition, there were nine single adults and seventeen children. In the following year, two more families moved into the region and several others came as guests for a period or worked for a year or two. This continued until 1880, when most of them left the area for the new settlement in Dakota. The population of the settlement always remained relatively low, as the area would not support a large community.

It was here in the woods of Shawano County that the young poet, Stephan G. Stephansson, wrote so much of his love poetry to his future wife, Helga. She produced this after her husband's death and in 1930 it was published in Winnipeg.

Emigration from Iceland to Utah had ended in 1860. In the spring of 1871, one person, Halldora Samuelsdottir Bjarnason, travelled from Copenhagen, Denmark, to Spanish Fork, Utah. In 1872, Loftur Jonson and another Mormon missionary arrived in Iceland from Utah, for the purpose of spreading the Mormon faith. They spent most of their time and energy in the south of the island and had some success. Their initiative led to the beginning of emigration from Iceland to Utah, which continued until 1892. Those who settled in Utah during these twenty years, 1872 to 1892, and came to Spanish Fork, did not have the same option to obtain free land as did their predecessors in the 1850s. Most of the newcomers tried to buy land in the surrounding areas, but resided in the town where they earned their living.

By 1877, people who had landed in Canada and were not content began to look south of the border for good prospects. Icelandic missionaries from Utah were sent to Winnipeg to meet with their countrymen and introduce the Mormon faith to them. There were a few willing listeners. One of them was Jakob Baldvin Jonsson, who arrived in Spanish Fork from Winnipeg on 8 August 1877. Jakob Baldvin lived in Spanish Fork until 1885, then moved to Castle Valley, where he bought 160 acres of land. He became one of the first settlers in the region and farmed successfully for fifteen years before he was forced to abandon his farm as a result of polluted soil. He bought land eight kilometres farther south, where he lived another nine years before returning to Spanish Fork. He married four women and remained a very devoted Mormon all his life. He travelled to Canada twice as a missionary and visited Iceland on two occasions.

In 1877, Sveinn Thordarson emigrated from the Vestmanna Islands to Spanish Fork. Here he and his wife, Helga Arnadottir, lived for a little more than ten years before moving to Castle Valley, where Thordarson farmed for the rest of his life.

Their son Jon was a highly ranked member of the Mormon Church and went to Iceland to do missionary work shortly after 1900.

Jon Thorgeirsson is the lone Icelander known to have emigrated to Utah in 1878. He was from the south of Iceland and had gone to the Vestmanna Islands as a young man. He went to New York in the mid-1870s, where he found a place aboard a freighter. Apparently, he sailed to South America and into the Pacific Ocean but later settled on the west coast of the United States. He arrived in Utah from California and became a shepherd. He married Gudrun Jonsdottir in 1886 but they were later divorced. Thorgeirsson was an avid reader and collected books. He also was a good writer and for numerous years contributed articles to the Icelandic weeklies published in Winnipeg.

Jon Eyvindsson and his wife, Vigdis Jonsdottir, emigrated from Iceland in 1879 and lived in Spanish Fork for twenty years, but then moved north to Alberta in Canada.[27]

The small but steady immigration of Icelanders to Utah obviously strengthened the Icelandic community in the sense that the language continued to be spoken, but this was, in one major respect, a different Icelandic community: this group of Icelanders had accepted a new faith and was but a small part of a powerful, American religious body.

Three Icelanders had remained in Nebraska during the winter of 1874-1875. When Olafur Olafsson returned from Alaska in the spring, he considered joining a group of a few Icelanders contemplating settlement in Nebraska. However, before any such move was made, news reached Wisconsin from Canada that an exploration party was on the way to the Red River Settlement to find a settlement site in Manitoba. One immigrant from Wisconsin joined the party and everyone decided to wait to hear the outcome of the expedition.

Jon Halldorsson was one of the settlers in Nebraska. He heard of the exploration in Canada but had no plans to leave. However, a grasshopper plague during the summer of 1875 left him in doubt. He managed to harvest eighty bushels of wheat, later recorded as the first Icelandic harvest in Nebraska. Grasshoppers were regular visitors in Nebraska during the next few years, destroying crops in the area and forcing many newcomers to leave. The stream of people east was suddenly just as heavy as it had been west a few years before. The farms of Torfi Bjarnason and Sigfus Magnusson again became the property of the railway company, as did many other farms. Cultivated land with some reasonable buildings, homes, and barns now could be leased at a low price and those who struggled through the hard times were later rewarded with some excellent crops, enabling them to purchase the land and pay in full in a short while. The Icelanders did not buy land to any degree until 1879, when Larus Bjarnason, Jon K. Halldorsson, and his two brothers, Pall and Sigurdur, purchased several farms.[28] The number of Icelandic settlers in Nebraska was never large and interest in the state declined following the grasshopper years. Only a few settlers arrived in the 1880s and, after that, no Icelander is known to have moved to Nebraska.

During the period from 1870 to 1880, there were three Icelandic settlements in the United States. The small settlement on Washington Island was on solid ground; everyone in Shawano was content; and the Minnesota colony was flourishing. Still, many Icelanders were waiting for news on the site for the exclusive Icelandic settlement. And in the second half of the summer, several Icelanders in Wisconsin, led by Olafur Olafsson, began to make plans to join the large number of Icelanders crossing the Big Lakes on their way down the Red River through Winnipeg to New Iceland.

4

Early Settlement Attempts in Canada

Sigtryggur Jonasson, the first Icelander to consider Canada as a future homeland, was born 8 February 1822. He was brought up on a farm, and his childhood was not different from the ordinary life of children throughout rural Iceland, except that he received the little education offered at the time from one of the best teachers in the north of Iceland.[1] At the age of twelve, Jonasson was placed under the supervision of Petur Hafstein, a senior magistrate at Modruvellir about fifteen kilometres northwest of Akureyri.

The home of a senior magistrate was a busy place, not only because of official business but also because people visited from all ranks of society. Representatives of the Danish king or the state church, farmers from far and wide, as well as vagrants, would frequently visit Modruvellir for various reasons. They brought news not only from different parts of Iceland but also from abroad.

Jonasson had yet another opportunity to broaden his horizon because of the library at Modruvellir. The magistrate received all Icelandic publications, such as weeklies and quarterlies, as well as books. Publications on foreign matters were also available, so Jonasson could become acquainted with politics in different countries. He read books on law and studied different forms of governments. Jonasson favoured the British form of government, which later led to his decision to settle in Canada rather than the United States. His interest began to focus on the New World, and in the early 1870s, when people in the north seriously contemplated emigration, he decided to go.

Late in the summer of 1872, he left Iceland for America. He knew of the Thorlakssons and their plans to travel to Milwaukee that summer. However, he chose to travel alone. It is interesting to note that he ignored the plans of his compatriots, which might indicate that he had already decided to settle in Canada. One source has it that while crossing the Atlantic Ocean from England to Quebec, he was urged by a British traveller to settle in Canada rather than in the States. Jonasson stated later that he discussed prospects in Canada with foreigners during his voyage and that Ontario had been strongly recommended as a place of great opportunities.

After a short stay in Quebec, he headed for Toronto and onwards to London, Ontario, where he worked for three weeks for a construction company until it went out of business, forcing him seek his fortune elsewhere. In St. Thomas, he found work with a railway company until the consequences of the New York bank crash reached Ontario. Reluctantly, he travelled to a small place called Bismark, about fifty kilometres west, where he found work at a sawmill in December of 1872. He kept this job until the spring, when he entered a partnership with a Canadian businessman selling railroad ties. By the fall Jonasson had saved about $1100.00, but continued his partnership until the spring of 1874. By that time a few Icelanders in the town of Rosseau in Muskoka, Ontario, were contemplating a search for a permanent settlement site in Ontario and he decided to become involved.[2]

Jonasson had spent almost two years in Canada and had become familiar with Canadian society. His business venture had brought him into contact with some influential government officials. These connections resulted in his being asked by the Ontario government to travel to Quebec in the summer of 1874 to meet those compatriots due to arrive from Iceland, and to persuade them to settle in Ontario. They all had signed the following declaration aboard the vessel: "We the passengers by the *S.S. St. Patrick* to Quebec whose names are given in the foregoing list do hereby declare our intention of proceeding to the Dominion of Canada and settling there, such of us are married, declaring for our wives and children who accompany us and in witness thereof we do affix our signatures to the same, having had explained to us in our own language the meaning of what we are signing." This appointment marked the beginning of Jonasson's involvement as a government agent with Icelandic settlers in Canada.

Of the first large group emigrating from Iceland in 1873, 115 people had signed a similar agreement that they would settle in Ontario. These people had travelled to Toronto from Quebec with the rest of the group, which then left for Milwaukee with Thorlaksson. After spending three days in Toronto, the Ontario group continued their journey on the morning of 29 August, and travelled by train and horse-drawn wagon until Gravenhurst, where they spent the night. They had reached Lake Muskoka, which they crossed aboard a steamer the following day, arriving in Rosseau, a small town north of the lake. The crossing had taken all day and so they spent the night aboard the steamer.

Early next morning, on 31 August, a government agent, J.G. Best, and members of the town council greeted them. The plans of this group of Icelanders had been forwarded from Toronto, reaching Rosseau long before the people arrived. The immigrants were immediately transferred to the Immigration Hall, where they were offered bread, bacon, syrup, and tea. The hall was too small for all of them, so the men spent the nights out in the woods while women and children slept inside.[3]

The government provided food during the first three days. The immigrants were welcome to stay in the hall as long as they chose, but most men went looking for work in neighbouring communities, often leaving their wives and children behind for some time. Work was scarce in the fall and gradually families moved away, many travelling south to Wisconsin where Thorlaksson was able to accommodate most of them on Norwegian farms. By early winter, only eight families and a few individuals were left.

All the land around the lake and in the vicinity of the town had been claimed, but agents suggested an available site thirty kilometres north of Rosseau. Three men travelled north and explored the area for a few days, but returned disappointed. It is not known why the Icelanders chose not to settle there, but later, Danish, Norwegian, and Swedish immigrants successfully settled the entire area.[4] Perhaps the Icelandic explorers lacked the skills and knowledge necessary to select a suitable colony site. They tended to concentrate on sheep and cattle farming, and fishing, rather than examining the soil for grain growing.

Another area was available, about ten kilometres east of Rosseau. Four Icelanders and one government agent explored the heavily wooded area. This time, they approved of the land. To the best of their knowledge, the soil was fertile and the site was not far from the town. The explorers decided to settle there, provided the government would guarantee to build a road from the town to the site. After two weeks, the government agreed, and several people obtained sections of land. Others, however, did not have the means to begin farming. A government agent found work for every male at a nearby sawmill but this was temporary employment, chopping firewood during a six-week period just before Christmas, for seventy-five cents per cord. At that rate, putting money aside to begin farming was out of the question.

The situation in Rosseau echoed Thorlaksson's warning to emigrants that if there was not enough money to start farming immediately upon arrival, and if work was scarce, then people should not emigrate. The only other option he could offer was a short-term stay on established Norwegian farms, but that opportunity was not available in and around Rosseau. Those who could, attempted to start on their own. However, their selection of land was made in haste and without careful examination. In a letter published in *Norðanfari* in Iceland, Vigfus Sigurdson described the difficult situation but predicted improvements:

> Improvement is in sight, as soon we will receive financial support from the Government. Our responsibility is to clear the woods for the road, which is to reach the Icelandic settlement. We have been promised $45.00 per mile but part of that will be in the form of supplies. The Government already has sent us food, coffee, sugar and tea at the going rate in Toronto. However, the Government covers the cost of transporting these supplies to us. This work will not last too long as the distance is only some three miles and we have almost completed the first. It has also become obvious to us all that this is far from being any quality job as we only average some 50 cents per day, still lacking all skills in chopping wood. However we are learning and improving and by working at it day after day will benefit us in the long run. This is comparable to mowing back home in Iceland ... that takes time to master.[5]

The winter of 1873-1874 turned out to be difficult for many in Rosseau. Sigurdson wrote in another letter a year later, published in *Norðanfari*:

> It would have been very difficult to survive for the poorest of us last year during the unemployment period in the winter if it had not been for the assistance of Benedikt Jonsson Bardal who was able to lend everyone in need a small amount of money. Also, an unexpected help reached us from Thorlaksson in Wisconsin but he had organized the collection of funds among Norwegian immigrants in the States. Some of this collection was sent to us. He has been most helpful in more ways than this and we all are greatly indebted to him.[6]

The only families that actually moved onto the settlement site in the fall of 1873 were those of Baldvin Helgason and David Davidsson. Together, they purchased 200 acres of land for $150.00. Included in the price was a house built by the previous owner. The house, which measured just over four metres by five metres, stood in a clearing in the woods and they named it Lundur. Helgason and Davidsson bought some animals and were able to make hay. They moved to the site in late October.[7]

At that time, work on clearing the woods for the road had not begun, but a path had been selected and trees along both sides of it marked. This was quite helpful, as the two wives and nine children began their journey up to the site on foot. On occasion the group was forced to climb over rocks. In most places, however, the journey was easy as no shrubs or brush could survive in the shaded, moist ground underneath the huge trees that blocked out all sunlight during the summer months. They reached their destination in one day, arriving at Lundur late in the evening. The men, on the other hand, took all their belongings in a rowboat along the lake and up the river until they had reached the vicinity of Lundur. Occasionally, they had to go ashore and carry both luggage and boat past waterfalls or rapids. They reached the log house a little later than the women and children, but had covered nearly twice the distance. It was a crowded house that first winter for the two families who shared the available space, and often other Icelanders visited and stayed for some time.

Two single men, Jakob Lindal and Bjarni Sveinbjornsson, built a small hut in order to spend the winter. They were the first Icelanders to build a dwelling in Canada, although Helgason and Davidsson were the first landowners. A little over two kilometres separated these two Icelandic pioneer homes in the wilderness of Ontario. These four men assumed the responsibility of clearing the ground across their property for the planned road. Others working in the woods during the winter benefitted from having the two homes in the area, as it gradually became more strenuous to walk the distance to and from Rosseau daily, especially during the heavy snow of winter.

Late in February 1874, when the snow was deepest and the frost most severe, the task of clearing the road from the town, a distance of about fifteen kilometres, was completed. The immigrants were tired and losing interest in the work, which was physically very demanding and offered little reward. Those who had secured land the previous fall began to clear it, but others gave up once they discovered their selection turned out to be too rocky and too hard to clear. Some abandoned their land after they heard of a more desirable region available around Nipissing and Parry Sound. This area also offered excellent fishing lakes and was not nearly as heavily treed. Parry Sound in 1873 was a tiny village, perhaps a little bigger than Akureyri in the north of Iceland. But a year later, thirty new houses were built and Parry Sound was growing. Those who went there intended to wait for a group of Icelandic immigrants expected to arrive in Ontario straight from Iceland in the summer of 1874. But that group did not arrive in Canada until late in the fall, so the search for a colony site never took place. By the late winter of 1874, only three Icelandic individuals were still residing in the Immigration Hall in Rosseau.[8]

The high unemployment, low wages, and lack of work were a great disappointment to the Icelanders in 1873. On the train from Quebec, they had been promised plenty of work to carry them through a difficult period until they could settle down on the free land that awaited them. But either this information was false or the circumstances in Ontario had worsened. Also, due to their limited knowledge of English, it is quite possible that Icelandic immigrants often misunderstood those offers.

Muskoka was supposed to be the site for an Icelandic colony, and most families and individuals went to Rosseau firmly convinced they would succeed in their efforts to establish a permanent settlement. The majority of those who went there maintained that the settlement could have worked, had the land been suitable for their needs and had there been more work available. It must be remembered that most of them reached Canada without any extra funds and, since the transportation to Ontario and land were free, they naturally grabbed this opportunity. They declined Thorlaksson's offer to join him and his group heading for Milwaukee on the grounds that they could not afford the fare. Plenty of work was what they needed before they even could think of breaking the land and starting on their own.

Anyone with some means left Rosseau soon after it became apparent that work was limited. Many chose to travel south to Milwaukee. Among those travelling together in one group were Olafur Olafsson, Fridjon Fridriksson, Jon Thordarson, and Jakob Eyfjord. Also in this group were two brothers, Skuli and Halldor Arnason.[9] Both Olafsson and Fridriksson became much involved in Icelandic affairs in North America. Olafsson, for example, travelled to Alaska in 1875 along with Jon Olafsson. Fridriksson was the first Icelander to build a log house in New Iceland in October of 1875.

Those who remained behind scattered over Ontario in search of work. A few went to Toronto, among them several young women, but none of these people had much luck. The men were unable to find any lasting jobs in the city and the women became discontented with the long hours and strenuous work of being housemaids. A few Icelanders travelled northeast into the woods, where they expected to find plenty of work in the lumber industry, and a group of seventeen went to Parry Sound, where work for at least six weeks had been guaranteed, but within sixteen days all were laid off.

Aboard the ship carrying them across the Atlantic Ocean, the immigrants had signed a document pledging to remain in Canada at least for three months. In return, they were offered free transportation to Rosseau and their own choice of land, which they must break and work, also for at least three months. At the end of the term they could abandon their land and travel wherever they wanted. Work was supposedly plentiful in Ontario. The agent(s) making this offer knew of the immigrants' poor financial situation and the urgent need for most of them to begin work in order to save money before they could even think of starting their own farm. When the Icelanders later found out that there was little or no work available, some of them believed they had been tricked. Some wrote letters of warning to Iceland, stating that promises made to future immigrants by so-called government agents should not be jumped at without some careful consideration. Such letters published in Iceland gradually resulted in increasing suspicion and those people opposed to emigration now insisted they had proof of broken promises. However, agents must have been working in accordance with official policies without realizing how different the employment situation had become. Neither the provincial nor the federal government could have benefitted from hundreds of unemployed, non-English-speaking immigrants in search for work.

Those who managed to start farming struggled on. Muskoka was flat and heavily wooded, the forests often so thick that the sky above was barely visible through the branches. In occasional clearings, settlers managed to make enough hay for their animals before they completed the task of clearing their lands. However, the soil was too soggy in places for growing grain. Yet, there were also benefits: lakes and rivers were everywhere, so there was no lack of water, and the vegetation offered numerous edible items, such as wild berries. As the settlers chopped down trees and bushes, they recalled the barren heaths and treeless valleys of Iceland— how the old homeland could use some of the plants that impeded their progress here.

By the fall of 1873, most Icelandic settlers in Muskoka agreed that establishing a large colony in the area was not realistic, because the wood clearing was too time-consuming.[10] However, a few were determined to make it work and refused to listen to speculation about better conditions elsewhere in Ontario. Baldvin Helgason and his wife Soffia became the heart and soul of the small Icelandic community in Cardwell municipality. He named his farm Baldurshagi. David Davidsson remained on his farm, Lundur. Others in the community were Jakob Lindal at Fagri-Hvammur, Bjarni Sveinbjornsson at Bjarnastadir, Thorsteinn Hallgrimsson at Laufas, Brynjolfur Jonsson at Hals, and, finally, Anton Kristjansson at Hlid. Naming their homesteads was an attempt to retain their Icelandic customs. In some cases they used the name of a farm they had in Iceland, but a few settlers named theirs in accord with the surroundings; Lundur, for example, means "clearing in the woods."

A well-known writer and poet, Helga, daughter of Baldvin Helgason, better known as Undina as a writer, described her childhood in the colony:

I have often read in books and other publications how the groups from home [Iceland] suffered at first upon arrival. However, most of them were met by someone, a relative or a friend, who had been here in America for some time. We were the exception—the first group settling in Canada.

I have no words to describe the misery and pain we suffered in the beginning. I often think how grateful we would have been if someone had been there to assist us. Everything we needed to buy was sold to us at a double rate. An apple pie, cut in six even pieces was sold to us for 25 cents each slice. My father bought a cow for $65.00 but the going rate was between $25-30.00 as we found out later. He bought a stove for $60.00 while others bought identical ones for $30.00. We just could not understand this attitude of the locals.

All of us spoke some English as we had received instruction during our last few months, back home in Iceland. We even began to think that our prices were doubled because people knew that father was better off than the others. He soon ran out, however, as he lent most of his money to his compatriots many of whom were flat broke. At one point we even began to think that the people of Rosseau had plotted against father and picked him out for whatever reason. And we were partly right.

Many years later one of my girlfriends explained to me and gave me the reason even though the people of Rosseau who knew insisted it be kept a secret forever. Somehow the English-speaking majority in the town had learned that father was the brother of the King of Denmark and that he had argued with His Majesty to such an extent that he was forced to leave Denmark in disguise. He had gone to Liverpool and aboard a ship for America decided that he could easily pass for an Icelandic immigrant! We all burst out laughing as she told us the story explaining at the time that the whole story was fiction. But here is the irony—she refused to believe us. She said she could not understand why we would not admit it now as so many years had passed, insisting that she would never tell anyone that we now knew that all of them knew. It mattered little how we tried to convince her, she even insisted that she had been warned that we would never admit that father was a brother of a king.[11]

In 1874, two single men from Iceland arrived in the colony. Arni Jonsson had come to live with his cousin, Baldvin Helgason. He stayed at Baldurshagi a little over three years but then returned to Iceland, never to go back to America. Bæring Hallgrimsson, brother of Thorsteinn at Laufas, was the other. He lived in the colony until 1881, when he moved to North Dakota.

Due to the small number of Icelandic settlers in the community, an Icelandic organization was not founded for many years (a reading society was established in 1888). But people used every opportunity to get together. Birthdays and the christening of newborns were always reasons for a gathering. Baldvin Helgason arranged for prayer meetings and the singing of psalms on Sundays, even though he did not have any religious training. Everyone, both permanent residents and visiting labourers near Baldurshagi, would gather there every Sunday for the "Holy Hour." Helgason performed other religious duties, such as burials and christenings, and he was often called to sickbeds in order to comfort suffering people.

The settlers in Cardwell soon realized how ill-prepared they were for a new life in a completely foreign environment, but they never hesitated to ask for help and guidance. An Irish farmer by the name of Case had homesteaded next to the Helgasons. He was married and had two half-grown daughters. Speaking of his neighbour years later, Helgason stated that Mr. Case may not have been a rich man, but he had a heart of gold. The Cases taught the Helgasons how to seed and plant, how to care properly for their fields and fences, how to cut potatoes in half before seeding, and many more important things necessary for every pioneer to know. Helgason learned how to recognize the maple tree, and the process of making syrup and sugar. He became quite successful, selling, at one stage, about 200 pounds of sugar for fifteen cents a pound.

Mrs. Case taught Soffia how to make soap from fat and ash, but making hats from dried wheat and barley straws was perhaps the most significant thing Soffia learned from her neighbour. Such hats became a necessity in the hot summer days, as protection both from the rays of the sun and from bugs. Young Helga learned the trade from her mother and later, when she moved to Dakota, taught Icelandic women in that settlement. Among her students was Gudbjorg, mother of the poet Stephan G. Stephansson.[12]

Like so many other middle-aged immigrants from Iceland, Baldvin Helgason became restless in Cardwell. During the Icelandic settlement period in North America, from 1870 to 1914, many of the men over forty years of age moved about, having found it difficult to settle down permanently. It was as if the move from Iceland was more disturbing than they had expected. In Helgason's case, his wife's illness may have contributed to his decision to move from Muskoka. Soffia had enjoyed the pioneer years in the colony but became seriously ill and never recovered. She was moved to Winnipeg in 1880, where she later died in 1902. Her husband bought land that year in the new Icelandic settlement in Dakota, but sold it a few years later and moved to nearby Mountain. He returned to Canada and settled in Selkirk, Manitoba, for some time before moving again across the border to Crookston, Minnesota, and then from there to the coast. In 1905 he died in Warrington, Oregon.

The Icelandic settlement in Dakota (now North Dakota) was launched in 1880 and apparently was much more attractive to the Icelanders in Ontario than New Iceland ever was. It is quite possible that Soffia's illness and Helgason's departure from the Cardwell colony caused the other settlers to contemplate a move. By late 1881 most of the pioneers in the colony had sold their homesteads and moved to Dakota. However, nearly all the Icelandic homesteads in Cardwell remained in the hands of Icelandic immigrants as newly arrived settlers bought the properties. This way the colony remained predominantly Icelandic for years.

Asgeir V. Baldvinsson, son of Baldvin Helgason, moved to Dakota in 1881 and managed a store in Hallson for a few years, but then returned to Cardwell. In 1886, he bought Lundur from David Davidsson, who moved to Dakota that same year. Baldvinsson farmed at Lundur but also managed the post office in the community. He had requested permission from the authorities to use the Icelandic name Hekla for his office, naming it after the famous volcano. His wish was granted but, much to his dismay, the authorities spelled it wrong. The official document referred to Hekkla P.O. Thinking it would be a simple matter to correct, Baldvinsson pointed out the error. But much to his amazement and despite his strong protest, the spelling was not corrected, and so the name of this very first Icelandic post office has been misspelled ever since.[13]

Asgeir Baldvinsson managed his post office for twenty years and became firmly established in the district. However, in 1908 he and his wife, Katrin Gisladottir, moved to Alberta and settled just west of Edmonton along with a few other Icelanders.

Although the settlement in Cardwell always remained a small Icelandic community, it left its mark in the Muskoka district. Those people who replaced the pioneers established a reading society, which gradually built up a good collection of Icelandic books. Most of the immigrants led a very active religious life, remaining faithful to the doctrines they knew from the old country. They never had the good fortune to have an Icelandic pastor in the community but they attended a Lutheran church. Despite several initial setbacks, this first Icelandic settlement in Canada became successful, even though all the original settlers moved on. Once land had been broken and the pioneers had worked it sufficiently, it turned out to be good land and, indeed, is still in use. Many of the farms remained in Icelandic families for generations.

Sigtryggur Jonasson remained convinced that immigrants from Iceland had a bright future in Ontario. In the fall of 1874, he travelled to Quebec City to meet a large group of Icelanders. This group arrived on 23 September and were met by two Icelandic agents—Jonasson, representing Ontario, and Johannes Arngrimsson, representing the Nova Scotia government. The Icelanders had left their homeland aboard the *St. Patrick,* on 10 September, heading straight for Quebec City. Everyone in the group had decided to settle in Canada and to follow Jonasson to Ontario.

Once ashore in Quebec, the new arrivals were escorted to the Immigration Hall, and then, late in the evening, took a train to Montreal. There, they were offered a hot meal before continuing to Toronto on 25 September. They spent the following two weeks in the Ontario capital, waiting for the construction of log cabins in Kinmount, about 160 kilometres northeast of Toronto.[14] The group of 375 people, most of whom came from the northern regions of Iceland, originally was expected in Canada some time in mid-summer. Preparations had been made for accommodation on Canadian farms where work was available during harvest time. This would have been beneficial for the immigrants, because they could have earned some money and gained valuable experience in Canadian agricultural methods. But since they arrived late in the fall, the decision was made to accommodate as many single women as possible as housemaids, and to keep all single men who could find jobs in Toronto. But other single men and all families were to be transported to the small town of Kinmount for the winter, where work on the railway was available. The initial plan was for these immigrants to earn some money at the railway during the winter but to homestead in the surrounding area in the following spring.

The Ontario government had negotiated with a railway company near Kinmount to construct temporary log houses near the town for all the Icelandic immigrants. Six houses were built. Four were about twenty-one metres long and six metres wide, while the other two were ten metres long and six metres wide. Ten stoves, which the Icelanders were expected to pay for eventually, had been purchased and placed in these buildings. The large group was divided in two, the first departing from Toronto by train on 9 October at 8:00 a.m. They travelled 140 kilometres on the Nipissing railway to a village called Cobakonk, where everyone had a hearty meal before the preparations were made for the final leg of the journey, about twenty-two kilometres in horse-drawn wagons. Women and children and the most important belongings were placed on the wagons, while the men and youth walked. It was dusk when the first wagons finally pulled out. The journey in the dark was anything but pleasant. The road was bumpy and muddy due to a recent rainfall. However, this group was more fortunate than the second, which arrived three days later on a bitterly cold evening. The evening of 9 October was quite warm but on the 12th it was bitterly cold. Many blamed several deaths of infants that night on the cold weather.[15]

Once in Kinmount, people were led to the cabins where food awaited them. Although these cabins were new, the arrangement was most inconvenient. The government agents who had arranged for the construction of these buildings had the impression that a community kitchen would suit the Icelandic immigrants. They expected the Icelanders to share in the cost and take turns in preparing meals, but such an arrangement was foreign to the people. Families wanted to prepare their own meals and, in addition, the cost was most often covered by those who were financially secure, causing tension in the group.

Almost from the first day, sickness increased steadily and many died. Sigtryggur Jonasson wrote in *Norðanfari* that many people had arrived sick in Quebec after the voyage across the Atlantic.[16] More became ill during the train ride to Toronto, and despite medical assistance from Canadian doctors, including medicine for the most needy, the ill people did not improve. The death rate among children was high. Several sources claim that all children two years of age and younger had died. One of the immigrants, Simon Simonarson, stated in a letter that "in Kinmount, almost thirty children died and a few adults (ten?), all older men."[17] He stated that he worked despite poor health, earning $1.00 a day initially. But by early January of 1875, his wage dropped to ninety cents. This was not a steady job, as heavy snow made the construction of railroads difficult. All the labourers could do was to prepare the ground, dig through hills, fill in crevices, and blow up boulders. This type of labour was unfamiliar to the Icelanders. They had a difficult time learning to use new equipment, and foremen often complained about slow progress. However, as their work improved, the comments made by the Canadian foremen changed and degrading remarks were replaced by compliments. Nevertheless, because the work was poorly rewarded and at times scarce, many of the newcomers began to look elsewhere. Several scattered in Ontario, while others went south to the United States where they had friends or relatives.

Sigtryggur Jonasson saw that job opportunities were few and in mid-January he travelled to Toronto to look for better-paid work for his compatriots. He had some success but it was not long before the situation worsened again. Companies simply ran out of funds and, one by one, the Icelanders were laid off. It soon became obvious to all that the future in the Kinmount area was bleak. The railway work was unstable and poorly paid, and many families were living near starvation in the overcrowded cabins.

These people, who had determined in Akureyri to make every effort to establish an exclusive Icelandic colony, saw their dream collapsing. The land was too rough and all the best areas in the province, in the south and east, had been settled. The Icelanders found themselves in the situation they dreaded most, being forced to scatter in order to survive. But just as confusion and general discontent were destroying the spirit in the Kinmount camp, a "foreigner" arrived, one who played a significant part in the history of the Icelanders in Canada.

John Taylor was born in Barbados in the West Indies in 1812, where his father, an Englishman, was stationed in the military. Theology had been his chosen subject but he was never ordained. He taught high school in Kingston, Ontario, for some time and later opened up a retail store in Peterborough. As it turned out, business was not his field. He sold his store in 1865, entered the British-Canadian Bible Society, and was working in Dysart Municipality in Haliburton district, sixty-four kilometres north of Kinmount, with his wife and two stepdaughters.

He learned of the Icelanders in Kinmount from his niece Carrie, who had met a few of them in the early summer of 1874. Carrie soon discovered that these settlers from Iceland were far from satisfied with their situation. Taylor's curiosity was aroused and he met Sigtryggur Jonasson in the fall, who introduced him to the Icelanders. Taylor was appalled by the housing and living conditions, and immediately persuaded the railway company, who was responsible for the construction of the cabins, to erect two more houses.[18]

Sigtryggur Jonasson had discouraged people in Iceland from emigration to America at this time. He maintained that the high unemployment rate in North America left many Icelanders struggling. Second, he claimed that the site for a permanent Icelandic settlement in America had not yet been discovered. He pointed out the disagreement within the group, some favouring Nova Scotia, others Ontario, or the American interest or Alaska. It was his conviction that future immigrants should wait until those already in America were established. By the spring of 1875, Jonasson had abandoned all plans of developing a big Icelandic settlement in Ontario.

No ship was sent to Iceland in 1875 for emigration purposes. However, fifty-nine people found their way across the Atlantic, some going to Canada and others to the States. These people were able to secure a place on merchant ships heading to Denmark or Great Britain and thence from English ports to America. By the end of 1875, 813 Icelanders had immigrated to America, fairly evenly divided between Canada and the United States.

Age of Immigrants in North America, 1875

0-4	99	30-34	68
5-9	96	35-39	58
10-14	78	40-44	61
15-19	62	45-49	36
20-24	128	50-up	33
25-29	94		

Source: Kristinsson, *Vesturfaraskrá 1870-1914*, Table 2.

Most of the Icelandic emigrants to America consisted of young people with children. Approximately 250 were under thirty years old and presumably could not find a place to start their own farming in Iceland. There were 273 children, fourteen years or younger, who had emigrated with their parents or relatives. A number had died by the end of 1875, mostly in Kinmount, but the exact figure is unknown.

The Icelandic representative for the Nova Scotia government, Johannes Arngrimsson, had been in Quebec City to meet the group from Iceland in the fall of 1874. Shortly after they had arrived in Kinmount, Arngrimsson appeared with a new offer. He was a compelling speaker and influenced those who heard him describe the "excellent" qualities of the site allotted to future Icelandic immigrants in Nova Scotia. Each settler was to have 100 acres of land, one acre of which would be cleared, a log cabin furnished with a stove, necessary kitchen utensils, and one year's supply of food for the entire family. Last, but not least, each settler was to receive a government grant of $11.00. The district selected for the Icelandic settlement was on the so-called Mooseland Heights, eighty kilometres from Halifax.[19] An offer like this, made to people with little or no means, was the most generous any group of Icelanders in America had received and it is little wonder that some families and single men decided eventually to move east. Johannes Arngrimsson returned to Halifax later in the fall, along with a few single men who chose to spend the winter in Nova Scotia. The others, almost eighty people, decided to leave Ontario the following spring.

The Mooseland area is on the slopes of an elevated, heavily wooded area with thick moss covering the ground. There was little likelihood of cultivating the land, which covered about sixteen kilometres in length from east to west, and was located sixty-four kilometres from the railway and fifty kilometres from the Atlantic Ocean. Icelandic migration to Nova Scotia began in the late fall of 1874, but settlement in Mooseland commenced in the spring of 1875. People arrived in the colony in the next few years, some directly from Iceland and others from other parts of Canada and even the United States. By around 1880, it is estimated that 200 people had settled in Nova Scotia.

The settlers had a steady job during the first two years, building the road through the colony. With the government's grant, most led a reasonable life. The agents continued to claim that the land would be ideal for cultivation and that once the road had been built, this community would not be isolated. Although most of the Icelanders kept their road-building jobs, everyone used whatever time was available to clear land. This was extremely hard and time-consuming work for inexperienced settlers from forest-free Iceland. Helgi Olsen, whose father, Olafur Olafsson, settled in Mooseland, recalled the difficulties the pioneers in Nova Scotia encountered:

> Father and his brother had adjoining plots of land and went to work at once cutting trees. To hew the logs into shape and raise them into place in buildings was no light work. The clearing of the land was an extremely strenuous chore, without any previous experience in cutting trees, grubbing around the roots or

pulling out stumps by oxen or horses—it was a never ending back-breaking job. The settlers, however, most willingly helped each other.[20]

As time went by and attempts to cultivate the land failed, the settlers began to realize that the area was not suitable for any kind of farming. The settlers had also been told of freshwater fishing and game hunting in the area, but neither turned out to be true. The agent Johannes Arngrimsson's involvement in the selection of the site in Nova Scotia is unclear, but he was a government agent for some time. He had married an English woman, moved to Halifax from Milwaukee, and changed his name to John Anderson.

Speculators who benefitted from the settlement of the Mooseland area have most often been blamed for the Nova Scotia mistake. Government agents who handled the matter appeared sincerely convinced that the land was of good quality. There is no doubt that the Nova Scotia government had been wrongly informed about the area—the government poured money into this project during the first year and a half. Once it was clear that a mistake had been made and that no settlement would ever flourish on the chosen land, all financial support stopped. Instead of the promised twenty-five houses, the government built nineteen. Young, single men did not waste much time in the colony. Some worked in mining for a while but most went to the town of Lockeport, where fishing was the big industry.

It is puzzling that so many people went to Nova Scotia, especially those from Kinmount, as they should have known that the land had not been approved by Sigtryggur Jonasson, who had visited the area in the fall of 1874. Neither had John Taylor anything positive to say about the site, and he had lived in Halifax and knew most parts of Nova Scotia. It is hard to believe that neither Jonasson nor Taylor spoke out against the move east because much was at stake for each family. However, the offer that was made was tempting and Arngrimsson very persuasive.

The actual number of people living in Mooseland at its peak was slightly over 100, but the total number of Icelandic immigrants residing throughout Nova Scotia climbed to just over 200 in 1880. Those who attempted to farm cleared several acres of their land, built fences around it, and seeded grass among the tree stumps and rocks. Some managed to make hay for a year or two but, eventually, livestock grazed the entire area.

Another evidence of the government's sincere effort to support the settlers was the construction of a school in the centre of the colony. As soon as the building was completed, the settlers decided to name the colony Markland (the name used by Leifur the Lucky centuries before) and to arrange for religious assemblies every Sunday. A non-Icelandic teacher was hired by the government to handle the education of the children, with English being the main subject. Apparently, the teacher was an Englishman, a very strict and determined fellow, who made remarkable progress with his students.[21] The settlers never had the opportunity to hire an Icelandic pastor to serve them. But in Lunenburg County, about 250 kilometres southwest of Mooseland Heights, was a German colony. They were Lutherans like the Icelanders, and once the news reached them that the Icelanders were without a pastor, German clergymen began to visit Markland. A young pastor by the name of David Luther Roth, who was ordained in 1876, attended to the religious needs of the settlers in Markland. Later he became a well-known author, best known for his book *Acadia and the Acadians*. Another pastor, Reverend C.E. Crossmann, also visited and served in the Icelandic community. These two men travelled the 250 kilometres and worked in the colony without ever demanding a penny for their effort. They visited twice a year, in the spring and fall. They held religious services in English, christened babies, confirmed youth, and married couples. But the funerals were in the hands of an Icelander, Brynjolfur Brynjolfsson, who, in many respects, can be considered the leader of the community.

Rev. Roth established a congregation in the settlement but general activity was scant, probably because Icelanders did not have a strong tradition of participation in the church. However, religious services were always well attended, and even Scottish immigrants from the nearby Museland colony were often present. But Rev. Roth did more for the community. He even organized a committee to maintain peace and order in the colony. Most of the Icelanders found this somewhat amusing, as none of them was accustomed to violence of any kind and disorderly conduct was never a problem. This committee never needed to meet.

The settlers had no knowledge of how to dispose of all the wood suddenly available. Many simply burnt everything, but soon the idea of sawmills was born. They decided to build two, one by the Tangier River on the east side, and the other by a stream in the west. The plan was to process lumber for construction. The enthusiastic settlers built dams, constructed the sawmill, and invested in machinery. Rev. Roth, learning of this positive enterprise, started a collection in his own community and raised $100.00, which he brought to the Icelanders. He also arranged for the transportation of food, seeds, and clothing from Lunenburg to Tangier, from where it was transported to the settlement.

Once the news reached Iceland that a colony had been established on the east coast of Canada, many Icelanders became interested. There is little doubt that more would have emigrated to Markland had the Nova Scotia government not cut its support in the second year of settlement, after it became obvious that this settlement was going to be too costly. It had been the understanding of many settlers that the offer stood indefinitely, and they had sent encouraging letters to Iceland to friends and relatives who had considered emigration to Markland. It has been estimated that in 1876, when 752 people arrived in Quebec City from Iceland, approximately 400 had bought transportation all the way to Markland. But the Nova Scotia government was not ready for this large number of settlers and refused to accept them. It must be pointed out that agents both in Iceland and Scotland had been instructed to inform these people of the government's decision. One immigrant wrote:

On the way up the St. Lawrence River, one government agent representing Nova
Scotia boarded the ship discouraging people from going there. He was accompanied by Olafur Brynjolfsson, who had resided in the Markland colony for
some time. He brought little good news to us and said that the situation in Nova
Scotia was bad—high unemployment and poor fishing. He brought with him a
letter signed by ten Icelanders who all encouraged us to stay away from Nova
Scotia.[22]

Before any Icelanders came to Nova Scotia, the size of their future settlement
had been determined, but in early 1877 its size had been cut considerably. This
decision resulted in more isolation than had been anticipated, which meant that
transportation to and from the colony was very difficult. The road across the colony
from Musquodoboit to the small mining town of Tangier was completed but the
Icelanders were now about sixty-five kilometres away from the nearest railway.
Had the government kept its original promise, this distance would have been only
about six kilometres.

Despite setbacks and constant hardship, the Icelandic colony survived for seven
years. Its isolation explains to a degree the complete absence of Icelanders from
all official capacities; nor were they involved in cultural or spiritual affairs. They
kept very much to themselves—neighbours who were of different ethnic backgrounds never had any reason to accuse the Icelanders of trespassing or unfriendly
conduct. On the contrary, it was noted that the Icelanders were extremely diligent, worked their land as if possessed, and were optimistic. The atmosphere in
the colony was generally good, everyone willing and eager to lend a hand if
someone was in need.

Life in the colony resembled that of rural Iceland in many ways. Some livestock
was brought in and fish was imported from the seaports. The women learned how
to cultivate the small patches between the tree stumps and grew some vegetables.
These and eggs were then traded for groceries in the stores. The easterly winds
brought in familiar rain off the Atlantic Ocean and the weather was, in general,
more similar to that of Iceland than in any other Icelandic community in America.

Although the pioneers in Markland later abandoned their settlement and moved
elsewhere in America, they all took with them valuable experiences. They had
learned that they needed to look after their religious lives themselves, establish
congregations, hire a pastor, and build churches. In Iceland the state had provided the pastor and built the church, and the only involvement of most people
had been attending religious services. Another significant experience in Markland
was the education of children, and the first school built solely for Icelandic immigrants. Also, the government sent some gardeners and experienced farmers to
the settlement to teach the settlers how to clear the land. The shallow soil was a
problem. Once an area had been cleared of trees, shrubs, and other vegetation,
and roots and stumps pulled out of the ground, there was no soil to till. Less than
a metre beneath the surface was either solid rock or thick layers of gravel, which

prevented the growing of grain. Instead, grass was grown, which yielded some hay, and eventually the land was used for grazing livestock.

The Icelandic settlers naturally learned of other Icelandic settlement attempts, including the hard times in New Iceland and in the new colony in Dakota. But around 1880, when the news of the Winnipeg boom reached Markland and the prediction was that the west offered a great future, most settlers in Markland moved out. The construction of the sawmills, then well underway, stopped, and farmers began to sell their animals for next to nothing in the Musquodoboit valley.

They got a much better price for their hay during the winter of 1881. A delegate was sent to Halifax to obtain from government officials legal rights for the Icelanders to sell their homesteads. And although everyone knew that the Icelanders who had received their lands free were now seriously contemplating a move west to the prairie regions and intended to sell their farms, nothing was ever done by authorities to obstruct the move. The farmlands in Markland were of little value, and the houses were sold at a low price, mostly for the wood. Brynjolfur Brynjolfsson, who, with the help of his full-grown sons, was able to work his land best, received only $300.00 for his property. But the average settler who sold everything he could most often had to accept a promissory note and never received full payment. Most of the settlers left just as they had arrived, with little or no money. By the late summer or early fall of 1881, most people had gone. Those who still remained left Markland in the following spring.

Although Markland was abandoned by Icelandic immigrants and no other group moved into the territory, this settlement has lived on in an impressive literature. One of the most significant Icelandic writers in America, Johann Magnus Bjarnason, was raised in the colony and experienced the tough teaching methods and discipline of Mr. Alexander Wilson. In his novel *Eiríkur Hanson*, he tells of the pioneer days in Markland. He also wrote numerous articles on the subject for newspapers and magazines. Another settler, Gudbrandur Erlendsson, wrote his memoirs, entitled *Markland*.

Although no Icelanders remained in the settlement, a few stayed in Nova Scotia, men who had married non-Icelanders. One family who left Markland moved to Lockeport, and one young woman, Sigridur Thorsteinsdottir, married a Canadian, Porter Taylor.

5

New Iceland: The First Year

In the spring of 1875, several Icelanders in Kinmount, Ontario, still lived in the houses built by the railway company the previous fall. Many had left the area in search of employment and a large group had gone to Nova Scotia. Shortly after their departure, Sigtryggur Jonasson and others in Kinmount concluded that land for an exclusive Icelandic settlement was not available in Ontario. About the same time, people in the United States received word from the two Alaska explorers, dismissing the idea of an Icelandic settlement there. Hundreds of people on both sides of the border were therefore left in confusion.

News of fertile soil in the Red River regions began to spread east and several settlers moved west from Ontario. In 1874, 1500 Mennonites moved from Russia to the young province of Manitoba and settled south of Winnipeg.[1] The Mennonites had sent their agricultural experts ahead of them to examine possibilities in Canada and to negotiate with Canadian authorities. After exploring regions in eastern Canada, they selected the district in Manitoba, believing that the fertile soil of the prairie was the best they had found. The Canadian government granted them the area they requested. Soon they had adjusted to the extremes of the prairie climate and acres upon acres had been cultivated. These people knew how to grow grain, and the Icelanders who arrived a year later could have benefitted immensely from the experience of the Mennonites.

The Icelanders in Ontario heard descriptions of the Red River Valley and the prairies. What caught their attention more than discussions about the fertility of the soil was the climate. Men spoke of bitterly cold winters, much colder than any region of Iceland, and the extreme heat of summer. There were also some conflicts with Aboriginal and Métis peoples, but, nevertheless, the two leaders, Sigtryggur Jonasson and John Taylor, began to talk about the possible move of all Icelandic immigrants in North America to a large area in the west. Taylor travelled in early June to Ottawa to meet with government officials. He requested financial support for a delegation to travel to the Red River Valley, which government officials approved, on the condition that he would lead the expedition. The additional delegates were to be selected at a general meeting by the Icelandic immigrants in Ontario.[2]

The meeting was held in Kinmount on 30 June, and John Taylor, Sigtryggur Jonasson, and Einar Jonsson were appointed to make the journey. Two others, Skafti Arason and Kristjan Jonsson, joined the party, both offering to pay their own expenses. Arason and Jonsson decided to leave immediately and went through Toronto to Milwaukee, where they were joined by a delegate from the Wisconsin Icelanders, Sigurdur Kristofersson. His inclusion signifies the interest of American Icelanders in the Red River Valley expedition. They travelled by train via St. Paul to Duluth and then onwards across Minnesota to Moorhead. John Taylor wrote, concerning the inclusion of additional members, that "as the same interest is felt by them [the Wisconsin settlers] in the proposed Icelandic settlement in Manitoba, I received them into our party, trusting that the additional expenses would not be objected to by the Department."[3]

John Taylor, Sigtryggur Jonasson, and Einar Jonsson left Kinmount on 2 July, met with the others in Moorhead, and travelled by steamboat down the Red River, reaching Winnipeg Friday, 16 July. This party of six, representing Icelandic immigrants both in Canada and the United States, was not impressed with what they saw. This was the summer of the disastrous grasshopper plague, the same that hit Nebraska and prevented an addition to that very small Icelandic community. Twice before, from 1818 to 1820 and 1865 to 1868, the area had been struck by these devastating visitors. The following report from an eyewitness of an earlier plague had appeared in the *Winnipeg Tribune*: "The grasshopper plague was the most terrible experience. When these flying myriads crossed Winnipeg, the sun disappeared. They were loaded upon wagons on Main Street and were dumped on the riverbank in windrows five feet high."[4]

As far as the explorers could see, nothing grew anywhere. Only the dark, almost black prairie was visible. They examined an area just west of Winnipeg where all vegetation in the vicinity had been destroyed by the grasshoppers. The immediate area surrounding Winnipeg was too small for a settlement of the size these Icelanders were considering, nor was it as secluded as they wanted. Another area further west, flat and treeless, was unsuitable as well, because most of the settlers were more interested in raising livestock than growing grain.

This decision was probably the biggest mistake made by Icelanders in North America. The site offered some of the best wheat-growing lands in the world. It is noteworthy that in the next few decades, Icelanders tended to avoid the flat, open, treeless prairies, but selected areas where hay was available around sloughs or in lowlands. Raising cattle was always a higher priority for them than the production of crops. Another reason they ignored this site was their ever-present dream of a large, exclusive Icelandic settlement. In their opinion, the flat, open prairie would never offer the required isolation.

The west coast of Lake Winnipeg presented another option. The area in question was north of the province in the North-West Territories. Both Taylor and Jonasson were hesitant, but, when they were told of fertile lands west of the lake and that the lake was teeming with fish of various types, they decided to explore the area. The party of six was provided with a Hudson's Bay Company York boat and three guides, and on 20 July they left Winnipeg. They examined the coastal regions and noticed immediately that there was no sign of grasshoppers. In their opinion, this area was much more attractive than any of the sites they had considered in Ontario, or that they had seen in Manitoba. Eventually, all agreed that this was where they wanted to settle.[5]

In their report to the Dominion government and in their appeal to all Icelanders in North America, the explorers strongly recommended the site on the western shore of Lake Winnipeg, which they called New Iceland. They gave the following reasons for their recommendation:

1. There was ample timber for construction of houses.
2. There was plenty of hay for the animals and the soil on the higher lands appeared fertile and good for growing grain.
3. The lake was teeming with such fish as whitefish, pickerel, goldeye, jackfish, and sturgeon.
4. The woods offered wild game, mostly moose but also wildfowl such as ducks, geese, and partridge.
5. Strawberries, raspberries, and currants grew in abundance along the banks of the Whitemud River.
6. There was no sign of grasshoppers.
7. The weather during the day had been bright and sunny but the nights cool.
8. The lake and the Red River provided transportation year-round to Crossing (now Selkirk), by water in summer but on ice in winter.
9. The area was large enough and unpopulated except for a few Aboriginal people north of the river. [6]

The explorers judged by the best of their ability and from the little experience they had, but even John Taylor did not anticipate the problems the settlers would have in cutting trees or cultivating the land. But time was getting short if a move was to be made this year. The group turned back in good spirits and at Crossing they wired Ottawa to have the land they had chosen reserved for the Icelandic immigrants. A positive reply reached them that same day. However, the actual Order-in-Council setting out the reserved area was not issued until October 1875.[7]

In Winnipeg, it was decided that the original and official group of three, John Taylor, Sigtryggur Jonasson, and Einar Jonsson, would travel back to Kinmount and Ottawa. Furthermore, once the settlers in Kinmount had been prepared for the journey to New Iceland, Sigtryggur Jonasson would go to Iceland and prepare prospective emigrants for the move to the settlement. In the meantime, John Taylor was to guide the Kinmount immigrants and other Icelanders in Ontario to the new settlement. The other three, Skafti Arason, Sigurdur Kristofersson, and Kristjan Jonsson, stayed behind and found work on the Canadian Pacific Railway line that was being pushed to Crossing. Some of the settlers who arrived later in the year complained bitterly about their decision to work on the railway line, as in Kinmount it had been the general belief that they were making hay in the colony for those who planned to bring livestock.[8]

In August John Taylor returned to Kinmount and gave a verbal account to the excited settlers. But, as everyone knew that such a move would be costly and most of them would never make it without financial assistance, John Taylor and Sigtryggur Jonasson travelled to Ottawa, where they prepared a report and requested a grant sufficient to transport the immigrants to their destination and to pay for the most urgent necessities during their first winter in the colony.

The report was well received but there were problems with the grant. John Taylor and Sigtryggur Jonasson were able to meet with Prime Minister Alexander Mackenzie, who was sympathetic, but the problem was that government policy was to assist immigrants coming to Canada, and there was no provision for grants to assist immigrants to move from one province to another.

Luckily, Governor General Lord Dufferin intervened. In 1856 he had visited Iceland and his regard for the people almost approached affection, which is borne out by the book he wrote shortly afterwards, *Letters from High Latitudes*. In this work he emphasized the sincerity of the Icelandic people and pointed out that in Iceland, crime, theft, and cruelty were non-existent, and that there were no prisons, gallows, army, or police. He strongly recommended every possible assistance to the Icelanders. Also, the settlement site was then part of the North-West Territories, which the Dominion government wanted settled. The grant was provided.

Once the matter had been resolved, Sigtryggur Jonasson began to encourage Icelanders in Ontario to join the move. The vision of New Iceland spread rapidly, not only in Ontario but also in the States. The urgency was such in Ontario that the few who had put in a crop on leased land left before harvest time. Those who had livestock such as cows sold them immediately at half-price. Everyone in the Kinmount area, men who had worked on farms for as little as ten cents a day, and women who picked berries and received twenty cents per bucket, was to travel west.[9]

Sigtryggur Jonasson and John Taylor had decided that everyone going to New Iceland must be in Toronto before 24 September. From there Taylor would lead the group to the settlement site with Fridjon Fridriksson as interpreter. Jonasson then went to Iceland where, on behalf of the Canadian government, he was to prepare future immigrants for Canada. At that time, many people desperately wanted to emigrate from Iceland, following tremendous volcanic eruptions in the Dyngju mountains earlier that year.

Most of the people in Ontario arrived in Toronto on 21 September and stayed at the same Immigration Hall as the previous year. On 25 September a group of 270 people left Toronto aboard the Grand Trunk train, arriving the same day in Sarnia, a small town on the east side of Lake Huron. Early the next morning they climbed aboard the steamer *Ontario*, which was already overcrowded with the passengers alone, but in addition with domestic animals such as cattle, horses, pigs, sheep, and poultry as well as luggage. All available space, both on deck and below, was completely packed with trunks and boxes. The people squeezed in-between or sat uncomfortably on top of their luggage, unable to move about.

In the town of Sault Ste. Marie the steamer went through the locks before continuing across Lake Superior, and reached Duluth in Minnesota five days later. The Icelanders stepped off the ship in the evening on 30 September and celebrated the end of their miserable voyage. A group of thirteen people from Wisconsin awaited them in Duluth, led by Olafur Olafsson, the same man who had explored regions in Alaska and who also had contemplated a move to Nebraska.

The group departed from Duluth the next morning on the Northern Pacific towards the Red River, and spent the next three nights in the town of Glyndon just east of Moorhead, in a much-too-small warehouse. That Sunday, Taylor gathered the people in a railway roundhouse for a church service. He selected the twentieth verse in Chapter 23 of the Book of Exodus as the text for his sermon: "Behold I send an angel before thee to keep thee in the way, and to bring thee into the place, which I have prepared."[10] Fridjon Fridriksson stood by his side and translated. In the course of his sermon, Taylor said he was convinced that the Lord had chosen him to lead the Icelanders into this large, unknown land. It was later reported that after the service, one of the immigrants had remarked that Taylor considered himself a chosen leader like Moses, and then added, "and who knows, perhaps he is."[11] The mood of the group was optimistic and in the evening there was dancing in the roundhouse to accordion music.

Another source states that the religious service was conducted in a dairy plant or a cheese factory where milk was available in unlimited quantity at a low price. The Icelandic travellers had not had the opportunity to drink much milk since arriving in America. Never before had the factory's managers seen adults as well as children drinking so much milk.[12]

The group continued their train journey early next morning to Fisher's Landing on the Red River, just south of Grand Forks in Dakota (now North Dakota), where they again spent an uncomfortable night. The following day, all boarded the *International,* an old sternwheeler, which was making its last journey downriver to Winnipeg.

Two barges were fastened together and then tied to *International*, and many of the passengers slept in the open during the trip to Winnipeg. The sailing took many days, because the boat with its two barges repeatedly went aground on reefs of sediment and sand. Late in the afternoon of 11 October, the boat finally reached the mouth of the Assiniboine River in Winnipeg. During that trip, Olafur Olafsson is said to have suggested that the first Icelandic village built in New Iceland be called Gimli, which means "Paradise." The Reverend Fridrik J. Bergmann gave the following report on the first impressions the Icelanders made in Winnipeg:

> Word had passed on to the north that many Icelanders were expected from the south. A large crowd had gathered at the river to get a look at these Icelanders. Some pretended to know all about them even though they had not seen any. Some rushed aboard the ship and the barges and impatiently asked: "Where are the Icelanders? Show us some Icelanders." John Taylor obviously was the man to answer. He pointed to the people on the ship and said: "These are Icelanders. There you can see them." But people did not believe him. They had expected to see totally different people. "We know what the Icelanders look like," they said, "they are short of stature, about four feet high, rather stout and sturdy, long jet-black hair, a good deal like Eskimos! These are not Icelanders, they are white people." John Taylor was at a loss what to do but said with a grin, which was his custom: "I met these people down east in Ontario. They had arrived there from Iceland shortly before. Down there no one doubted they were Icelanders, and here I am with them fully confident that they are genuine Icelanders. But of course you may believe what you like."[13]

The *Manitoba Free Press*, on the other hand, held different views. In an article dated 12 October 1875, it stated:

> They are a smart-looking, intelligent, and excellent people and a most valuable acquisition to the population of our province. Their Icelandic experience supplemented with some experience in our mode of life, is quite sufficient to give them that peculiar offhand manner of overcoming obstacles, and an energy of character which will ensure their success here.

The Plaindealer of Dakota said on the same day, "The Icelanders that went down on the last trip of the *International* are the best and neatest appearing batch of immigrants that have gone down river into Manitoba this season."

Sources differ as to how many Icelanders were in this first group but if 270 left Toronto and thirteen joined in Duluth, then 283 people probably arrived in Winnipeg.[14] The people were taken to the Immigration Hall, where they stayed during their stop in Winnipeg. Generally, everyone felt that the worst was over. The long, miserable journeys and terrible housing conditions were things of the past. Ahead was a short trip on Lake Winnipeg into a bright future. None of them could have anticipated that what they had experienced in Canada so far was nothing in comparison to what lay ahead in the next four years. While they waited, several men landed a job unloading the *International* and the barges, for which they were paid $3.00 per day, the highest pay any of them had ever received in North America.

Winnipeg did not impress the newcomers at all. They thought only a few buildings were noteworthy and the streets and buildings seemed too planned. The streets were uneven and became muddy in rain, and on the sidewalks there were two boards side by side, along which pedestrians inched their way. But Fort Garry, the headquarters of the Hudson's Bay Company, attracted their attention, with its solid limestone walls and towers on each corner.

As the days passed, people realized some of their plans would have to be altered; for example, there was no hay waiting for them on the site. In fact, no preparations for their arrival had been made. New Iceland awaited them just as the advanced party had left it earlier in the summer. No one in Winnipeg knew anything about the nature of the journey downriver to Lake Winnipeg and north to the mouth of the Whitemud River. Plans to buy cattle had to be abandoned and now it became a matter of urgency to obtain provisions sufficient to last until spring. The thought of no milk in the settlement throughout the entire winter, which the people knew would be difficult, made the outlook bleak.

A proposal that women and children remain in the Immigration Hall in Winnipeg until the men had completed building houses in the colony was rejected as people realized that navigation would soon be closed and that the men would be unable to return until after freeze-up. It was then suggested that women and children remain in the hall until spring, but that was also ruled out because the hall was unfit for winter quarters. There was no alternative: women and children would have to go with the men.

John Taylor decided that all single men and women, even teenagers, should remain in Winnipeg and find employment during the winter. This would mean fewer mouths to feed and require less housing space. A few families attempted to find accommodation in the city but only one succeeded: Bjorn K. Skagfjord, his wife, who was ill, and three sons remained in Winnipeg. The settlers were given two options: they either travelled with the group to New Iceland, claimed land, and settled, whatever the outcome might be; or they stayed behind and paid their own way later to the colony site. The second choice meant exclusion from the government grant.

The next problem to solve was the question of transportation. A steam-tug that plied between Winnipeg and Crossing could have taken people and goods in relays to the mouth of the Red River, which would have meant that people would have waited in the open air until the last trip was made. But once the owners of the steam-tug quoted their price, this problem was resolved. The ferry service would cost the settlers $1200.00, which was far beyond their ability to pay.

However, they soon discovered an alternative. Some flat-bottomed boats or scows normally used for the transportation of lumber were available at a reasonable price. They were over nine metres in length, almost five metres wide, two metres deep, and partly covered. Each one could carry between thirty and forty people with their belongings. The settlers bought six of the scows, and tied them together in three sets of two scows. An addition of one York boat completed the fleet. This flotilla docked by the moorings at the foot of Notre Dame Avenue and the settlers began packing and preparing for a year in the colony. Supplies to last to Christmas had to be purchased, but they believed that travel on sledges either to Selkirk or Winnipeg would be possible around Christmas time. Food, tools, stoves, and material for net-making were among the necessities. At that time, Winnipeg was on the outskirts of the settled Dominion and, due to the grasshopper plague, agricultural products sold at a high price. A sack of flour (forty-four kilograms), for example, sold for $7.00 late in the fall.

The food purchased was of poor quality, which had disastrous consequences. Some of it was spoiled and other items had little nutritious value. The pemmican, of which they bought large quantities, was old, bad-tasting, and poorly made. The beans were wormy, the wheat and flour, stale. John Taylor had asked the merchants in Winnipeg to provide supplies that would last until Christmas for more than 200 people. The little food bought by the settlers themselves was of much better quality. The government grant made the purchasing of supplies and tools possible, but many immigrants started the journey downriver in poor clothes because they were unable to buy new ones.[15]

On 17 October, under clear, calm skies, the excited group boarded the scows. Stefan Eyolfson later described those moments:

> It was late in the afternoon and I stood on the riverbank. John Taylor was there also watching the people busy getting ready. I looked north as that was our direction. I thought I spotted some darkness in the distance and said to Taylor: "It certainly is dark out there up north." Taylor turned towards me, remained silent for a while but then said: "The sky is beautiful and I do not see where you can spot darkness but is it possible that you are loosing your nerve? If such is the case you can stay behind just as I have said and encouraged people in your position to do." "I am going," I replied. I may have been mistaken but I had a hunch something would not go right.[16]

John Taylor, his wife, two stepdaughters, his brother William Taylor and his family, and Everett Parsonage, John Taylor's right-hand man, were the only foreigners aboard this flotilla. They were in the first scow along with numerous Icelanders under the direction of Parsonage. Sources differ about the total number of passengers, but about 200 to 235 people made the trip, and another fifty to eighty stayed behind in Winnipeg.

The rapids of St. Andrews are thirty-two kilometres north of Winnipeg and the flotilla reached them the following day. Since it was Sunday, John Taylor ordered the scows to be moored, and he preached a sermon. At the end of the service he announced that the Hudson's Bay Company steamer, *Colville*, would be waiting at the mouth of the river to tow the scows to the Whitemud River. Many people chose to walk along the riverbank as the scows went down the rapids, which was just as well, as one set of scows got stuck on the boulders that reached up above the surface in numerous places. No one was hurt but it took a long time to get the scow floating again. When the *Colville* appeared, the scows were tied in a single file to each other and to the steamer. The *Colville* then pulled the lot, a total length of ninety metres, out onto the lake. One scow was damaged when the *Colville*'s propellor struck it, and it was pulled half-full of water for the rest of the journey.

It was Friday, 22 October when the steamer cast anchor by Willow Point, about six kilometres southeast of present-day Gimli. The flotilla was about 1500 metres away from shore. Southeasterly winds had picked up quickly and the captain would not go closer to land, fearing the water was too shallow for his steamer. The only option for the settlers was to use their York boat to pull the scows ashore. Some say the entire fleet was pulled ashore in one trip but others claim it took several turns before all the scows had reached the shore. They were fortunate to have the wind at their back. The landing place was on the south side of Willow Point in a somewhat sheltered bay. The settlers spent that first night aboard the scows.[17]

The immigrants who stayed behind in Winnipeg looked for work. Most of the young women found work as housemaids at salaries between $4.00 to $8.00. The expression "young women" is perhaps misleading, as in some cases the girls were only fourteen. Most of the families who hired them made every effort to make these frightened, non-English-speaking maids as comfortable as possible. In many instances, the families attempted to teach them English. One girl recalled how her mistress would sit her down for an hour every day for some English lessons. Others were less fortunate. Some girls simply ran away, risking everything because their situations had become unbearable, although only one Icelandic girl is known to have been sentenced in a Manitoba court for vagrancy. Generally, however, these girls fared well. Most of them had families in New Iceland whom they supported as best they could, often sending the money they earned to their parents. As the years went by, some left for New Iceland and others married, some to non-Icelandic men.[18]

The single men and boys left behind in Winnipeg did not have much work to choose from this first winter. The loading and unloading of boats on the Red River was the best they could hope for in the fall, as most of the transportation to and from the United States was via the Red. The pay was twenty cents per hour. Some men were employed on construction work and others dug sewers in the city. This was done with pick and shovel, back-breaking work. Others worked in sawmills, and many a poem describing the hardships and misery of the sawmill worker was written.

Although only one family and a small group of individuals had remained in Winnipeg after the others went downriver to the colony, this arrangement marked the beginning of Icelandic settlement in the city. None of these people had the means to purchase a home during the few months that remained in 1875, but eventually they established themselves in Winnipeg, which today is the capital of Icelandic people in North America.

In the new colony, the settlers began to explore the surrounding area. Some went north to present-day Gimli; in their opinion this site was ideal, due to the thick poplar forest that covered most of the land all the way down to the water. In some places, one could not walk along the beach because of the trees. Because of the ample building material, this was an excellent site for the construction of houses. The settlers spent the first few days in transporting all the belongings to Gimli and in the construction of the first house. This was to be the storage shed for all the supplies bought in Winnipeg. Building the shed took a long time, as most of the men were inexperienced with chopping trees and woodwork in general.

The first home constructed was that of Fridjon Fridriksson, who assisted Taylor in managing the government grant. The building was divided in two: one half was to be his home, and the other was the warehouse for supplies such as food and tools. While the other houses were being built, many people were forced to continue sleeping aboard the scows, unprotected against the frost. The water around the scows was soon frozen solid and the bottoms of the scows also became icy overnight. However, as work progressed and houses were completed, the boats were dismantled and the wood used for fuel in the homes or for building small fishing vessels.

Other settlers were provided with tents similar to those used by the Aboriginal people, which John Taylor had borrowed from the Hudson's Bay Company. Most of the tents were torn and in poor condition, and they offered little shelter against the wind. As temperatures began to drop, many people were taken ill.

Shortly after their arrival, the men began to fish in the lake, using nets they had brought from Iceland or that they had acquired since their arrival in America. But freshwater fishing in central Canada was totally different from fishing in Iceland and here they either placed the nets much too close to land or the nets were the wrong size of mesh. All they caught in the beginning was driftwood or trash. John Taylor announced that whoever caught the first fish would win $5.00, and when the first catch, a goldeye, was brought ashore, there was general rejoicing and a large crowd gathered around the lucky fisherman to see what the fish looked like.[19] Although the lake and fish were unfamiliar, gradually, luck changed, and before long, fish was a regular meal in the small Icelandic community. However, just as the settlers had come to terms with fishing in the lake, the ice set in. It was late in October and it has often been claimed that never since was ice visible on the lake this early. The ice kept breaking up and then freezing again, making travel very treacherous until late November. The settlers made attempts to fish through the ice on the bay in front of Gimli but no one had ever tried this method of fishing before. The nets were placed under the ice in water much too shallow and, as the ice thickened, the floats froze to the ice and could not be lifted. Fishing through the ice was minimal this first winter. The cold also caused men to abandon their fishing attempts because most of them did not have warm clothing. The temperature on the ice in the beginning of December often measured -40°C.[20]

This first winter in the Icelandic colony by Lake Winnipeg is said to have been one of the longest and coldest to hit the area in many years, but the previous winter had been worse in Winnipeg. January of 1875 was one of the coldest ever recorded. Most settlers were poorly dressed for such severe cold. They wore rubber boots or rubber shoes, and although many possessed some woollen sweaters, socks, mittens, and hats, they still lacked protection against the wind.[21]

Unfamiliar with the construction of Canadian wooden houses, the Icelanders relied on their experience from home. Icelandic folk architecture had its roots in Norwegian forms. Individual long houses were used for special and separate functions, such as for sleeping, cooking, or meetings. By the fourteenth century, timber in Iceland became scarce, forcing the inhabitants to construct new types of houses where the separation of functions into isolated buildings was modified. The individual and spacious long houses were replaced by subterranean groups of houses, leaving each function in much smaller units. Growing prosperity in the nineteenth century resulted in improved housing. Icelandic homes then consisted of five or six small, grass-roofed buildings, which were separated by walls mostly made of sod. Each served a certain purpose: one was used for a porch, another for guests, one for storage, and another for the kitchen. Usually there was also a smithy and a dairy room. At the back of each row of houses, and connected by a long passage, was the so-called *badstofa*, originally a bathhouse but later combining the bedroom, living room, and dining room.

Once the storage hut had been completed at Gimli, cabins for the people were under construction. These log houses were neither large nor stately, often measuring only three and a half by three and a half metres, but some were three and a half by five. The walls were purposely low and surmounted by rafters, which were then covered with grass. The walls at the corners were connected with a saddle-notched joint, which the settlers had learned to make from a government survey team that had accompanied them down the Red River. Doors were very low; in some cases so low that adults crawled on their hands and knees to enter. Some houses had small, fixed windows; others had none. In the beginning, time and effort were not wasted on the floors. Some had floors of wood from the flat-bottomed scows, but most houses had floors of flat stones or hard ground. Despite the small size of the cabins, often two or three families shared one building, which included a stove as the only heater. These cabins, built in such haste and despair on frozen ground, offered very limited protection from the winter cold. Had the thick forest not almost surrounded most sheds, offering considerable shelter from the winds, living inside probably would have been impossible. These were not proper log cabins, but shelters made of unfinished logs. If the logs were not straight and gaps developed between them, clay or moss was used as filling.

Simon Simonarson described the shed he and a friend hastily built after he had spent two weeks in one of the tents, recovering from illness due to improper meals, fatigue, and lack of sleep. During the first week of November, they began their task. Apparently, most people had claimed lots down by the lake around the supply shed, so, forced to seek an area outside the developing village, Simonarson went southward. They built a cabin, which measured three and a half metres by three and a half, and used logs as thick as they could carry. A person could barely stand upright inside. The roof was flat, covered with moss, grass, and twigs. Clay filled every crack or hole in the wall. They worked hard and moved in with their families on 6 November, even though the shanty was not quite completed. Simonarson's house had a single door on the east wall and one small window on each side of the door. Inside, there was room for two beds made of wood, which were placed up against the walls, and the stove stood in the centre. Compared to the miserable conditions in the worn tent, this was first rate.[22]

John Taylor's plan was to have everyone involved in the construction of sheds. Once the sick or weak had a roof over their heads, everyone was to cooperate until all the people were in a shed. Thirty stoves had been brought down from Winnipeg, which limited the number of sheds. No one could survive the winter in an unheated building. However, John Taylor didn't fully understand the Icelandic character. Many settlers, like Simonarson, for example, built their own shed, gracefully turning down offers of help. The settlers' lack of enthusiasm for Taylor's plan did not mean a lack of interest in the well-being of their neighbours. The Rev. Fridrik J. Bergmann wrote in 1908 about the reaction of people to Taylor's idea:

> Men were content with just about anything this first fall as long as they had a roof over their heads. But as it was supposed to be a communal effort and the task quite extensive it progressed ever so slow that it became a problem. Many pulled out in order to escape the strenuous labor. It became so bad that many sensible men agreed that this project would never be completed if the same system were maintained. Fridjon Fridriksson was asked to inform Mr. Taylor who had a very hard time understanding the problem. He had strong faith in the Icelandic people and found this attitude towards communal work hard to comprehend. In the end he yielded and agreed that every settler should start his own shed immediately. Once this decision had been made progress soon became visible and it was not long until everyone was in a shed.[23]

It is quite possible that there was some resentment towards Taylor. Immediately upon arrival in the colony, he had put up a tent for himself and his family, which many insisted was the only tent in one piece loaned to the settlers by the Hudson's Bay Company. At least, he was the only person using these tents who was pleased with them. Later, he had a large house, a storey and a half, erected for himself. It was to be a temporary headquarters of sorts. It had double walls, the space between being filled with clay, but it proved just as cold as single-wall houses, because clay is a conductor of heat. The use of hay or dried moss would have made all the difference and the settlers would have discovered the laws of insulation. Many settlers worked at the construction of this house for weeks, earning $1.25 a day, but received payment in the form of food supplies. Taylor later stated that the building had cost him $600.00. He lived in it for a year or two or until it began to collapse. It was later used as a cowshed. A few of the settlers copied this style of construction and also built double-wall houses using clay as insulation between the walls. Their houses were naturally just as bad as Taylor's.[24]

Once the ice on the lake was solid enough, freighting with oxen began. One team of oxen for each sleigh hauled tools and clothing as well as food to the site. But since hay was not available in the colony or anywhere on the route from Winnipeg, each sleigh had to carry a hay supply that lasted the round trip for the oxen. Valuable space on every sleigh was thus lost.

By mid-December, supplies in the colony were getting short. John Taylor travelled to Winnipeg to make arrangements for more, but only two small teams of oxen showed up in the colony with some necessities by the end of the month. "The shortage of food was such by Christmas that one family only had a few breadcrumbs on Christmas Eve,"[25] wrote Gudlaugur Magnusson. It should be remembered that in Iceland, Christmas Eve is the holiest part of the Christmas celebrations. Magnusson shared Simonarson's opinion of Mr. Taylor, whom they respected for his religious devotion and kindness to all, but they believed he lacked foresight and the ability to lead.

Shortly after construction work in the colony was completed, three men, Stefan Eyjolfson, Paul Johnson, and Everett Parsonage, the only one with some hunting experience, were sent out into the woods in search of wild game, of which the explorers had maintained there was plenty. They travelled north along the coast to Black Island, just northeast of the island of Mikley (now Hecla Island), where they came across tracks of moose but failed to hunt down a single animal. They discovered later during this trip that the herd had been slaughtered by a previous hunter. The hunters continued north on the east side of the lake, crossed over, and came back on the west side. Travelling had become increasingly difficult due to heavy snow, and although they finally spotted game about forty kilometres west of the lake, they could not close in on the animals and returned on Christmas Eve to the colony empty-handed.[26] The disappointment in the colony was understandably great. Thoughts of past celebrations in Iceland, with memories of smoked lamb, homemade bread, and puddings, made the shortage of food in the colony all the more disappointing. However, the settlers planned a celebration on New Year's Eve on the ice in front of Gimli. As can be expected on 31 December in that part of Canada, the night was cold but clear. Men had spent several days immediately after Christmas, gathering dried wood for a bonfire, which was lit shortly before midnight. The significance of the bonfire lit just before midnight is the burning of anything bad that might have affected people during the year just ending, and preventing anything of that nature from being transferred over into the new year. These fires are, to this day, common throughout Iceland on New Year's Eve.

Just before midnight, the Old Year suddenly appeared right on the ice. It was represented by a decrepit old man with a long grey beard made of rabbit fur. He wore a large white smock and had on a two-foot-high hat made from tarpaper. He joked and mingled with the crowd, hobbling with the support of a cane. He had a bottle and a glass from which he drank an imaginary drink. From an improvised platform he delivered a farewell speech and then vanished into the darkness in the west. Just as people lost sight of him, they heard singing from the east. The New Year appeared, dressed in the bright clothes of youth, accompanied by twelve spirits. Six of these were in white, representing the six months of winter every year, and the other six, representing summer, wore green. The New Year delivered greetings, and then there was singing and dancing around the fire. When the celebration was over, John Taylor invited everyone who had participated in the entertainment to his home for refreshments.[27]

Despite the miserable conditions in the colony, spiritual and cultural life were not neglected. John Taylor continued religious services on Sundays, with Fridjon Fridriksson standing by his side, translating every word of his sermon. The matter of education was on the minds of everyone from the beginning. By Christmas a school for the children had been organized in temporary quarters. The primary purpose of the new school was to teach English. In Carrie Taylor, niece of John Taylor, the Icelanders had an excellent teacher.[28] She taught not only English, but also subjects related to Canada. Apparently she also became a good student, as she was one of the first non-Icelandic-speaking persons in America known to have learned the Icelandic language. She became interested in more than the language of Iceland: in February of 1877 she married Sigurdur Kristofersson, who was one of the explorers who chose the colony site.

During the first months of settlement in New Iceland, a committee was formed to govern the young community. On 5 January, a meeting elected Olafur Olafsson, the Alaska explorer, Fridjon Fridriksson, translator of Taylor's sermons, Jakob Jonsson, Johannes Magnusson, and John Taylor. This committee was responsible for the administration of all communal undertakings in the colony as well as the government loan, which was to assist the settlers in getting started but was generally spent during the first two years for necessities.[29] The committee was also to look into the matter of a pastor for the colony. John Taylor was not an ordained pastor and although he had done well in tending to the religious needs of the settlers, his preaching was in English and his message was often foreign, as well. Fridjon Fridriksson had corresponded regularly with the Rev. Jon Bjarnason and suggested he move to Canada to serve his countrymen in an Icelandic colony.

In a letter dated 14 November 1874, mailed in Toronto, Fridriksson responded to Bjarnason's request for information on Icelanders in Canada. He pointed out their need for an Icelandic pastor, whose duties, among other things, would be to instruct children in the same way as pastors had done in the old country. He concluded his letter by asking if Bjarnason could be persuaded to become a pastor in Canada. This was not a formal call, merely an enquiry. On 29 December 1874, Fridriksson raised the issue again in a postcard. This time he was more specific and suggested that Bjarnason, if he accepted the job, would settle among his countrymen in Kinmount. This showed that the question of having an Icelandic pastor was a matter of concern. Fridriksson wrote:

> Tonight I had the honor of meeting the Reverend Smithett from Lindsey and another pastor serving in Kinmount. Their business was to inquire what I last heard from you regarding the future pastorate among Icelanders in Kinmount. Mr. Smithett maintained he wrote to you about a week ago but had not yet received any reply; he will explain the terms offered to you. If you feel the need for an assistant he insists that suitable arrangements can be made. Please respond to Rev. Smithett's letter as soon as possible but do not decline any advantageous post until a definite proposal has been made to you.[30]

Rev. Bjarnason turned down the position in Kinmount in a postcard dated 4 January 1875. He gave no explanation but probably was aware of the difficulties the settlers in Ontario were having. He was between jobs, having given up his teaching position at Decorah, and, in the summer of 1875, he moved to Madison. He moved to Chicago in January of 1876, where he became employed at a Scandinavian paper, *Scandinaven*.

Fridriksson apparently wrote to Bjarnason some time in early 1876 from New Iceland again. Bjarnason's work at the paper in Chicago was demanding and prevented him from regular correspondence with his friends in America, but his wife, Lara Bjarnason, responded to letters and postcards on his behalf. On 1 May 1876, Fridriksson replied to a note from her in which she claimed that during the winter she had hoped to be able to persuade her husband to become a pastor in the new settlement, but he still was not ready. Bjarnason then terminated his job in Chicago and moved to Minneapolis, becoming the editor of the Norwegian paper *Budstikken*.[31]

Although these Icelandic settlers had no experience in organizing a settlement and their pioneer work was just beginning, they wanted a newspaper. In Iceland, newspapers had always played an important role in the lives of the people. News of whatever kind became the major topic of discussions in every home and wherever people met. This hunger for news had been manifest in every Icelandic generation since the days of settlement and the development of the oral tradition, and in the colony, men facing a late winter of starvation nevertheless discussed the possibilities of a newspaper. In early 1876, Jon Gudmundsson started a paper, which was entirely handwritten. He was not in a position to make extra copies, but either visited homes and read his paper out to the families, or organized a gathering at which he read to a crowd. He called his newspaper *Þjóðólfur*, the name of one of Iceland's leading newspapers published in Reykjavík. He made three handwritten issues, none of which has survived. The content of the paper is unknown but, aside from comments on local concerns, it probably contained news from Iceland and Icelandic immigrants elsewhere in North America because mail had been brought to the colony by that time.

The health of the settlers in the colony became an issue of concern. Since their arrival, many settlers had suffered from illness. Cold dwellings, improper nutrition, and exhaustion due to the extensive travel contributed to the lasting sickness. During the winter, several people passed away. Shortly after Christmas, life became a struggle for food. Fishing through the ice was disappointing and supplies became short. Skafti Arason stated in his records that he and Sigurdur Kristofersson had only managed to catch sixty fish in four nets throughout December, and no catch at all was made during January, February, and March. By the end of January, the only food items available for distribution were tea, some bacon, pemmican, wheat flour, nuts, and grains of wheat, which the Icelanders ground in the coffee-mills they had brought with them from Iceland. But there were supplies of tobacco to last for a long time. In March, more flour, bacon, and sugar were brought in from Winnipeg, as well as a few pairs of shoes and tools for gardening. No transportation of supplies to the colony took place in April, as roads up to the settlement were too muddy. However, ice remained on the lake until 20 May, and by the end of March and during the spring, a number of people walked to Crossing or Winnipeg in search of employment. Food shortages became serious in April and men resolved to eat the wheat that was intended for seeding in the spring. However, after 20 April, fishing increased and remained good throughout the summer. Slowly the general health in the colony improved.

Most single men and several married ones left the settlement in late winter or early spring to obtain employment. Only a few attempted to seed. Stefan Eyjolfsson had seven acres about five kilometres west of Gimli, where he seeded wheat. His crop failed completely, mostly due to inadequate preparation. Others fared no better. The situation in the small community in the early summer of 1876 was discouraging. The settlers from Ontario and those who came from the States had been under the impression that livestock would be purchased in the Red River community and that there would be plenty of hay available in the colony. None of them expected to spend a whole winter in freezing conditions without milk or sufficient food. Stefan Eyjolfsson stated in his recollections that the promise of the availability of cows had made the difference in people's decisions to abandon the little they had in Ontario for the new colony. He was adamant that many families, especially those with young children, would never have moved had it not been for the guarantee that there would be fresh milk. Eyjolfsson stated that thirty-six people died in the late winter and early spring, most of them of scurvy. One farmer lost seven of his nine children. By early April, a few more than 100 people remained in the colony, all the others having left to look for work. Of those left behind, a third, mostly children and sickly adults, passed away.[32]

The fact that so many people had left the colony in the spring indicates they had little faith in prospects there. They were not willing to stay on and work at improvements. The woods had to be cleared, the land broken and seeded, and if they were going to raise livestock they needed to make hay. Improvements on the cabins were necessary, roads or paths had to be built, and the fishing industry developed. A leader was needed, someone to assume responsibility and unite the people in the effort of making the settlement work.

Despite this disastrous first winter, several settlers wrote home in the spring and summer, praising the colony site and the fact that they owned their own land, on which they were going to built a great future. Such letters encouraged friends and relatives to immigrate to New Iceland.

Reykjavík, c. 1870, was a small village at the time with a population of 2000. (Þjóðminjasafn Íslands)

Akureyri, c. 1886, was the largest village in northern Iceland. The many Danish flags in the photograph indicate the extent of Danish influence. Iceland did not have her own flag at the time. (Þjóðminjasafn Íslands)

Icelandic immigrants crossing the Atlantic Ocean. (Þjóðminjasafn Íslands)

Oddur Magnusson, seen here on Washington Island in the summer of 1873, emigrated from eastern Iceland that year at the age of twenty. He was one of several young, single men from Iceland who spent some time in the 1870s on Washington Island. (Washington Island Farm Museum, Inc.)

Reverend Pall Thorlaksson was born in Iceland 13 November 1849. He died in his home in Mountain, North Dakota, 11 March 1882. (Provincial Archives of Manitoba)

Reverend Jon Bjarnason, who first served as minister in New Iceland in 1877. (Provincial Archives of Manitoba, N11460)

Gudmundur Gudmundsson was born in Iceland 8 July 1840 and emigrated in 1870. He was one of the founders of the Icelandic colony on Washington Island and lived there most of his life. This picture was taken in 1931, four years before his death. (Wisconsin Historical Society, Whi-4042)

The steamship *Ontario*, 1874, which transported immigrants across the Great Lakes. (Lake Superior Marine Museum, Duluth, Minnesota)

This "Icelandic Castle" was built by Icelandic immigrants on Washington Island in 1875 to shelter newcomers from Iceland until they had built their own homes. (Washington Island Farm Museum, Inc.)

Sigtryggur Jonasson and Pall Johannsson in Toronto, 1874. Jonasson, who emigrated from Iceland in 1872, was the first Icelander to settle in Canada. He became an agent for the government and is often referred to as the "Father of New Iceland." Johannsson, often Colonel Paul Johnson, arrived in Quebec 6 October 1873. He moved to New Iceland with the first group in October 1875, and, later, lived in Pembina, Akra, and Mountain in North Dakota. (Provincial Archives of Manitoba, New Iceland Collection, 493)

Women at spinning wheel. (Fred Hultebrand History in Pictures Collection, North Dakota State University, Fargo, North Dakota)

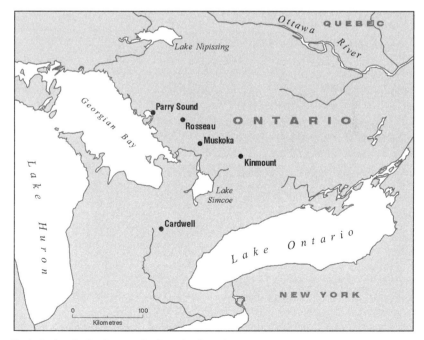

Early Icelandic Settlements in Ontario, Canada.

Early Icelandic Settlements in the Upper Midwestern United States.

6

New Iceland: Growing Population, Increasing Hardship

The area between Lake Winnipeg and Lake Manitoba is referred to as the Interlake. It has been inhabited for at least 6000 years. Aboriginal peoples from central parts of North America travelled north into the region in search of game when the ice retreated after the last Ice Age. The absence of major river systems and the low, marshy nature of large portions of the land meant only a small population could be sustained. Consequently, the fur-trading companies that entered the area in the eighteenth and nineteenth centuries considered the region of little significance. Only the Hudson's Bay Company bothered constructing a trading post at the mouth of the Icelandic (Whitemud) River in 1804, which was abandoned after a few years. The Canadian and the British scientific exploring expeditions, led by H.Y. Hind and Captain John Palliser in 1857, investigated the possibilities of agricultural settlements in the Canadian west. These explorations included the west banks of Lake Winnipeg. Although they noted the abundant timber resources and limestone cliffs on Hecla Island, they believed the agricultural potential of the Interlake was less than in other parts of Manitoba.[1]

The settlers in New Iceland were in an area that the exploration party of 1875 had not thoroughly examined. This district was south of their original destination, by the Icelandic River. Perhaps if the settlers had reached the river, the first winter might have been easier. However, because of the time of year the settlers arrived, and because no preparations had been made for housing, livestock, and haymaking, it is unlikely the river location would have made a difference. Sigtryggur Jonasson and John Taylor were responsible for rushing the people into this ill-prepared and highly questionable settlement. The size of the region, the isolation, and the ample timber and fishing opportunities had convinced them that the experiment would work. On paper, it looked very promising, especially with the support of the Dominion government. But no plans were made to organize the settlement. For example, who was to determine how land was claimed? Who was going to assist the future farmers in learning ways of seeding, tending the fields, and harvesting?

Most settlers had selected their lots by the end of December, but only four had erected cabins on their homesteads. The ancient Icelandic custom was upheld and each farm or homestead was given an Icelandic name. Just as it had been traditionally in Iceland, the name of each farm or homestead was used in distinguishing among families. For example, Sigtryggur Jonasson called his place Modruvellir and was referred to as Jonasson at Modruvellir. The competition for claiming land next to Gimli and along the lake was fierce. New Iceland had not been surveyed. Only Range 4 in Township 18, which is the southernmost part of the colony, had been surveyed. But once the lake froze, the settlers themselves surveyed the coastline from Boundary Creek north to Gimli, and another twenty kilometres further north to Arnes. While this was not an official survey, it guaranteed each settler an approximation of his homestead. The government survey team was expected the following year. No one examined the soil, nor was any attempt made, due to the lateness of the year, to explore areas further inland. Consequently, many settlers were later forced off their land, as it turned out to be much too marshy, sandy, or rocky.[2]

In Iceland, people followed the adventures of their countrymen in America. Letters from the immigrants were read and often referred to or published in Icelandic weeklies. Since his emigration to Canada in 1872, Sigtryggur Jonasson had been cautious in his statements regarding possibilities in Canada for an Icelandic settlement. The economic crisis in North America and the high unemployment rate convinced him that Icelanders should wait to see how those already in America would manage before emigrating themselves. But after his meeting with the prime minister in Ottawa, in the late summer of 1875, his tone changed. Convinced that the site for the Icelandic colony had been discovered, he travelled to Iceland, arriving in December of that year.

Earlier in the fall, William C. Krieger, the general agent of the Canadian government for the Scandinavian countries, had also arrived in Iceland, as well as two other agents, both Icelandic. Johannes Arngrimsson and Johann Straumfjord, representing the government of Nova Scotia, were unaware of their compatriots' difficulties in Markland and of the government's conviction that the site granted the Icelanders there would never flourish. They continued to recruit people. Many Icelanders favoured going to the Atlantic coast, as opposed to the wilderness of midwest Canada. It is estimated that between 400 and 500 people had decided on Markland. Once the Nova Scotia government heard of these plans, it hastened to order her agents to discourage the Icelanders. Meanwhile, Jonasson and Krieger described the new site in the District of Keewatin and the support of the Dominion government.

An increasing number of people in Iceland were ready to emigrate. In 1875, a volcanic eruption in the Dyngju mountains in east-central Iceland had forced hundreds of people off their land, as ashes and pumice, in many places as thick as ten centimetres, covered a large area. The destruction of arable land was devastating and many young people gave up hope of finding a possible farm site. Little progress had been made in the struggle for independence and neither farming nor fishing offered sufficient opportunities. There were no other significant industries.

When Sigtryggur Jonasson toured parts of Iceland, lauding the colony site in Keewatin, he did not know that hunger and cold threatened the lives of those already in New Iceland, nor was he aware of the fact that early in April most able men had left the settlement to find work instead of seeking to make their colony self-sufficient. He recruited approximately 800 people, mostly from the western and northern regions.[3] Although Jonasson was not aware of the gravity of the situation in New Iceland, he had spent three years in Canada and was the first Icelander who returned to Iceland as an agent for the Canadian government. He not only spoke from his own personal experience, but also could explain the government's plans regarding immigration in the next few years. Previously, letters from immigrants in America published in the weeklies had been the only source of information. Although they were useful, they left many questions unanswered. A common question concerned the status of Icelandic immigrants in the young Canadian society; others concerned religion and education, and, of course, employment.

The increasing flow of information to Iceland from North America resulted in more general discussions on emigration, but people remained divided. Icelandic publications also differed in their views on the issue. Some published articles and letters by immigrants in America without much comment. Others criticized the emigrants, often stressing their unfortunate position within the Icelandic society. "Only the poor and idle are emigrating," was a typical comment and, as people gathered in Akureyri, at Husavik, or Vopnafjordur, reports published in the weeklies often drew a picture of emigrants, poorly clad, gathered in a drunken state in any coffee shop or restaurant that would have them, sleeping in the streets, wasting days, weeks, or even months waiting for a ship to carry them to America.[4]

There were times when the ships were delayed and emigrants had gathered at ports shortly before the advertised departure date. As an example, in 1873, the ship expected to leave Akureyri in early July did not leave until September. Many of the settlers had only enough money for the fare to Quebec and were thus unable to pay for room and board while they waited for their ship. Many had no other choice but to wander the streets and sleep outdoors, although hardly any could afford to be in a drunken state.

The first group to leave for America in 1876 consisted mostly of people from the west and north of Iceland. One weekly source, *Fréttir frá Íslandi* (*News from Iceland*), stated that close to 800 people had been aboard the *Verona*, which left Akureyri on Sunday, 2 July.[5] Sigtryggur Jonasson was aboard as a tour guide. It was noted that during the voyage to Scotland, people were served Icelandic food, much to the delight of everyone. The *Verona* docked at Granton on 6 July, where all the passengers and their belongings were put ashore before the steamer returned to Iceland for another group waiting on the east coast. John Dyker, a Canadian immigration agent who prepared their papers, said of this Icelandic group of emigrants:

> I consider, from their appearance and demeanor, they were one of the finest lots
> of immigrants which have ever left Europe; just the people for a new country,
> very simple in their requirements and remarkably abstemious ... they were very
> highly thought of while passing through Scotland. Favorable notices respecting
> them appeared in the leading Scottish papers.[6]

The group at Granton was transported to Glasgow, where they waited a few days for the Allan Line steamer *Austria*. They departed 11 July and arrived safely at Quebec on the 22nd. The next morning the group was on a west-bound train, arriving in Toronto on 24 July. After spending a few days in the city, the group was divided in two before boarding trains for Collingwood and Sarnia. From there they travelled aboard steamers across Lake Huron and Lake Superior. The two groups were united in Duluth, Tuesday night, 1 August, where they spent the following day. They then boarded a train to Fisher's Landing (now Fisher), a small town in Minnesota by the Red River about twenty kilometres southeast of Grand Forks. On 5 August the group started their journey downriver aboard a steamer that reached Winnipeg in the evening of Tuesday, 8 August.

The Immigration Hall was much too small for a group of this size, so many people were transported downriver to the colony on the scows originally intended for their belongings only. All those who could afford to, purchased a cow. One person bought three; those who could not afford one, bought in company with others. Jon Jonsson from Mæri paid $20.00 for his share, and his partner paid the remaining $10.00. Two men were selected to drive the herd to Gimli.

Most of the travellers left Winnipeg on 13 August, voyaging the Red towards Gimli. Several individuals and a few couples stayed behind. All their belongings had been placed on six scows, and the people used rowboats provided by the Canadian government. Travelling on land was next to impossible because no roads had been built. The flotilla passed Crossing on the 16th and reached the mouth of the river the following day, where all the scows and most of the belongings were left while the people continued on towards Gimli. Northerly winds slowed them to such a degree that they did not reach Gimli until Sunday, 20 August. It had taken them exactly seven weeks to cover the distance from Iceland to Gimli. The new settlers spent the remainder of August in transporting their belongings from the mouth of the Red River to Gimli.[7]

Jon from Mæri reported that once they were in Gimli, little assistance was available because there were few men in the colony. The women and children appeared extremely tired and hungry. Little or no improvements had been made to the log cabins and the newcomers were forced to spend the night outdoors, using bedcovers for tents. While men examined the colony site, women lit up the stoves that had been purchased in Winnipeg, and experimented with baking. Jon from Mæri wrote:

> Many had bought stoves and other kitchen utensils in Winnipeg. But most could not afford anything and depended on the financial support from the Government. The baking of bread was similar in every instance—flat-bread was kneaded and made from the flour bought in Winnipeg and baked on the lids of the stoves. This flour was first rate, much better than what later arrived as part of the government supplies.[8]

At Seydisfjordur on the east coast of Iceland that July, 400 people were making themselves comfortable aboard the *Verona*. A young theologian named Halldor Briem was their interpreter. The group arrived in Granton after four days at sea and departed from Glasgow on 20 July. During the sailing up the St. Lawrence River to Quebec City, Olafur Brynjolfsson from Markland, Nova Scotia, boarded the *Verona* (he had also visited the previous group). He announced that the government of Nova Scotia regretted it was unable to assist the Icelandic settlers in any manner and urged them all to move west to New Iceland.

The group left Quebec City by train, arriving in Montreal around noon, 1 August. In Toronto the following day, they met a few of their fellow countrymen who had been in America since 1873-1874. Men stayed up late to discuss prospects in America and the economic and political scene in Iceland. The next evening, 3 August, the train left Toronto for Collingwood, where a steamer carried the people across the Great Lakes. The vessel was overcrowded and many people had to sleep outside on haystacks near sheep, horses, and other domestic animals. Several people became ill from drinking the water aboard the ship.

On Monday night, 7 August, the group arrived in Duluth. The next evening, their train from Duluth came to a final halt, but no one in the group knew where they were. The conductor of the train had not informed Briem as to where the Icelanders were supposed to disembark. The people spent that night aboard the train. At daybreak they saw that a thick forest surrounded them. Luckily, a young man approached them, and Briem asked him if they were anywhere near the Red River. The youth pointed at the forest and said that on the other side of the trees was the small town of Fisher's Landing. A steamer was expected later that day from Winnipeg to fetch the settlers.

Four days later the group left Fisher's Landing for Winnipeg. On Thursday morning, 17 August, they arrived in Winnipeg and then continued downriver two days. Some people stopped at the south end of the colony, while others travelled to Gimli.[9]

This second group from Iceland made the journey in much less time than did the first one, mostly because they did not have to wait long for transportation during the entire voyage. These two groups of immigrants arrived almost simultaneously in New Iceland and, therefore, have always been referred to as the large group of 1876. There was a third group that left Iceland that year. The last one, nineteen people from the south of Iceland, left Reykjavík in mid-summer. Guided by Olafur Gudmundsson from the Eyrarbakki group of 1872, they arrived in New Iceland a little later in the fall.

This was the largest Icelandic emigration to America in one year, but sources differ considerably as to the exact number. However, a study of 1190 new immigrants that year reveals the following division according to age groups:

Age of New Immigrants, 1876

Age	Number
0-4	198
5-9	152
10-14	128
15-19	78
20-24	119
25-29	104
30-34	104
35-39	86
40-44	113
45-49	53
50-54	33
55-59	22

Source: Kristinsson, *Vesturfaraskrá 1870-1914,* Table 2.

There were, in addition, twenty-six people sixty years of age and older. These figures show that the majority of immigrants were young; almost 900 are thirty-four years old or under, and almost 200 children were under the age of four.

The summer of 1876 was very unfavourable for the settlers in New Iceland. Making hay was difficult because of heavy rain and because most able men were away. Those settlers left behind in the colony did not have animals who needed hay. The number of cows was far from sufficient, and each animal had to be shared by four or five families. The cows were a great disappointment during the summer; bugs in the woods constantly harassed them, which resulted in less milk than the settlers needed.

Travelling on land was impossible because roads or paths had yet to be made. Instead, settlers took the scows apart and used the lumber to build smaller vessels on which they travelled along the coast. Clearly, the colony was far from ready for the large group and, understandably, most newcomers were disappointed, not only with the reception they received from their compatriots but also with the general state of the settlement. Sigtryggur Jonasson, who was responsible for bringing the people of 1876, had painted a bright picture of the area that, he claimed, was ideal for an exclusive Icelandic settlement. But Jonasson may have expected too much from the 1875 group. Construction of houses was not yet underway in August of 1876, when he led his group to the site. Little land had been cleared and haymaking was minimal.

The large group had arrived, but not without casualties. Many of the settlers were ill during most of the journey and some did not survive. Numerous factors contributed: the different climate, the blazing heat, the lack of adequate cleanliness during the voyage, and the unfamiliar food. Digestive problems were most common. It is estimated that between thirty and forty children died during and shortly after the journey. Eleven had died in the first group before reaching Gimli. Jon from Mæri wrote that "quite a few people remained behind in Gimli during the winter as they did not have the strength to continue. Some have estimated that close to sixty people passed away in New Iceland."[10]

Another pioneer, Benedikt Arason, wrote 15 September to a friend in Iceland, who later had the letter published in *Norðanfari.* Arason, who homesteaded ten kilometres south of Gimli, stated that close to 1200 people had arrived in the colony from Iceland during the summer. In his opinion, that was too many. He recommended that migration from Iceland be put on hold for a year or two, or until those already in the colony had settled. Haymaking was adequate on some farms but not on others, and some areas were completely useless, as the land was much too wet. He found three major disadvantages with the site: the long and cold winter, the marshy lands, and the vicious bugs. Of the newcomers, he wrote, "Most of the people are exhausted and sick following the journey and at this stage about sixty people have died, most of whom were infants around one year of age." He warned fathers of such young children against emigration, insisting that children under eight years of age should not go on such a demanding journey. He also suggested that elderly people who led a reasonable life in Iceland should carefully consider all their options before deciding to emigrate.[11]

Although many settlers were exhausted or ill upon arrival in the colony, most recovered gradually and had gained full strength by the fall. But illness was not the only reason for unexpected deaths. The accidental drowning of two men, one in the Red River, the other in the lake, left no one in doubt that the waters of the new land could be dangerous.

The settlers in New Iceland had not been aware of Aboriginal people in the area during their first winter in the colony. Aboriginal hunting grounds were further north, perhaps as a result of the Icelandic reserve or because hunting was poor in the area around Gimli. In the summer of 1876, three Icelandic settlers moved north to the mouth of the Icelandic River. One was Olafur Olafsson, who had explored a possible settlement in Alaska, and who brought with him a twelve-year-old stepson, Fridrik Sveinsson. There were ten people in this group, who initially lived in an old Hudson's Bay Company log cabin. The cabin was later given the name Pox because the smallpox epidemic, which later swept through the colony, supposedly started there. Olafsson was the first to begin to build a house on land he had claimed by the mouth of the river. And here they noticed Aboriginal people for the first time.

The only permanent resident in the area was a man called Ramsay. He lived with his wife and five children in his teepee on the north side of the river, not far from where Olafsson was building his home. The Icelanders noticed him and his wife tending to a vegetable garden and were under the impression that Ramsay grew mostly potatoes. At first, there was no contact between the two groups. But one morning, when the three men crossed the river on their boat to continue the work on the house, Ramsay was standing right where they normally landed. The men attempted to land but Ramsay pushed the boat out each time it struck ground, and, at the same time, tried to make it clear through hand signals that he was forbidding them to land. After a second attempt had failed, Olafsson made a threatening gesture with his axe. This time Ramsay stepped aside, they landed and went to work, but, a little later, saw Ramsay canoe upriver. That evening, after the Icelanders had returned to their log cabin, they heard shots and, looking upriver, they saw several canoes, from which it seemed Aboriginal men were firing at birds, though they may have been shooting in the air to startle the Icelanders. Two or three of the children had been playing outside, some distance away from the cabin, but hurried home once they heard the noise. The men landed their canoes in front of the log cabin and walked inside. They sat at one end of the building in a semicircle, holding their firearms, facing the Icelanders on the other side of the building. Time went by in total silence, each group staring across the cabin.

As it grew dark, another canoe approached and, shortly afterwards, Ramsay appeared with another man who spoke English. He informed the Icelanders that the Aboriginal people considered the Icelandic claim of land by the river illegal and that the area was rightfully Aboriginal. They insisted that no part of the Icelandic reserve was on the north side of the river. The Icelanders had to admit that they did not know if that was the case and it was agreed that before further construction continued, the exact boundary line would be established.

The Icelanders resolved that Olafsson, his stepson Sveinsson, and another adult would row south to the mouth of the Red River and meet with Sigtryggur Jonasson, who was expected soon with the first group from Iceland. They arrived at Gimli during the night. Winds were strong from the north the following day, causing high waves on the lake. Still, they made it to where the river enters the lake. They had travelled through here only once before, the previous year on their way to New Iceland. The closer they got, the more turbulent became the water about their vessel and, as they went through the surf, the boat nearly capsized and was almost full of water once they entered calm water again.

Much to their delight, they spotted the steamer. The Icelandic immigrants and Sigtryggur Jonasson were aboard, and, as luck would have it, also aboard was a government representative who was on his way to meet with the Aboriginal people to explain to them the arrangement made for the Icelanders. He stated that the Icelandic reserve stretched north, across Icelandic River. Once this news reached Ramsay's camp, he and his people never bothered the Icelanders in the area again. Olafsson and Ramsay made an agreement that permitted Ramsay further use of Olafsson's land. He maintained his vegetable garden and teepee on the land for the rest of his life. Ramsay became a good neighbour and on many occasions assisted the Icelanders. He was an excellent shot and hunter.[12]

By the fall of 1876, the entire coastline, from Boundary Creek in the south to Sandvik in the north, had been settled. Only a few of those who arrived later could get a lakefront lot north of Arnes. From there up to Sandvik and the Icelandic River, all the land was soon claimed and settled. Many people rowed with their belongings across to Hecla Island and homesteaded there. A small community developed there in the fall, consisting of numerous families, many of whom initially shared housing. The survey team from Winnipeg never arrived at Hecla Island that fall and, in fact, the island was not surveyed for several months. This was a great inconvenience for the settlers, as they did not know the exact limit of their homesteads.

Some activity already existed on the island. There was evidence of lumber work and a sawmill. At first, the Icelanders were pleased to see the mill, as they expected that here they could have their timber cut for their houses. But the owners were anything but cooperative. A few men got jobs working at the mill, but never received their salary. Trees the settlers intended to leave standing on their property were unexpectedly chopped down, and about 200 logs, which the settlers had neatly piled up and intended later for a church building, were confiscated without any explanation.

Those settlers who planned to farm had much to do during September and until the first frost and snow. They had to get supplies for the entire winter, build a cabin, prepare a shed for the cow, make hay for the animal, and carry the hay to the cowshed. Two, even three families shared one cow and lived close to one another. But the first task of every farmer was to have his land surveyed. The survey north of Icelandic River was carried out most often by Stefan Eyjolfsson, who did such an excellent job that when the government land survey specialists did finally arrive, few changes needed to be made to Eyjolfsson's work.[13]

The federal government appointed Sigtryggur Jonasson in November as its agent in New Iceland. His major business was to assist John Taylor with the government loan to the settlers. Taylor was in charge of ordering necessities, while Jonasson tended to the distribution of supplies among the settlers and looked after the bookkeeping. From the day Sigtryggur Jonasson was appointed until the Colony Council was established at the end of February 1877, the population was divided into groups of forty to eighty people. A group leader was appointed who received monthly food supplies, which were to be distributed evenly to group members in accordance with the size of each family. Other supplies were handed out according to needs or requests.

In 1876, there was an unexpected visit to the colony. Pall Thorlaksson had served his compatriots in the small Icelandic colony in Shawano County, Wisconsin, and also in a few, small Norwegian congregations in the area. In the summer of 1876, he learned that "well over one thousand of his countrymen were expected to arrive in Canada and head west to New Iceland."[14] Thorlaksson was convinced that the colony was not ready yet to receive a large number of additional people.

For many years the Norwegian Synod had a committee to assist Norwegian immigrants who were without the services of a pastor. The committee urged Thorlaksson to travel immediately to New Iceland to offer his assistance. He agreed and after an uneventful journey by train to Fisher's Landing, he caught a steamer to Winnipeg. He later recalled of the journey that "a straight line was perhaps 150 miles but the trip along the Red River made it more like 400-500 miles due to the constant curves and bends, almost full circles of the river as it flows down to Winnipeg."[15] He reached Winnipeg 18 August and accompanied the large group from Seydisfjordur (the second group) downriver to Gimli.

On Sunday, 23 August, Thorlaksson performed the first religious service in Icelandic in New Iceland. In a clearing in the woods, just north of Gimli, 500 settlers gathered for the service. However, many of them sensed a new approach when he so enthusiastically advocated the literal interpretation of the Bible. Said one pioneer: "He strongly emphasized the reading of the Bible; I had never heard the pastors in Iceland do that."[16]

Thorlaksson performed the usual clerical duties such as burials and christenings, and, despite his different preaching, which some people found hard to accept, he earned the respect of all who heard him. When the need for a pastor was so strongly felt, it is not surprising that many settlers accepted him as their future pastor when he offered his services without remuneration. His offer must have been made in consultation with leaders of the Norwegian Synod, who probably paid part of his salary. Although circumstances in the colony had not given the Icelanders much time to discuss such issues as churches and schools, most of the settlers realized that they needed a pastor for their congregations, and would have to financially support him and the church. The immigrants could scarcely afford to turn down his generous offer, but yet they hesitated, so Thorlaksson left the colony before any decision was made.

Until Thorlaksson's visit to the colony, only John Taylor had performed religious services. When Taylor suggested that the Icelanders become part of his church, all agreed that while there was no one else to perform a religious service, his was accepted, with Fridriksson translating. The settlers acknowledged Thorlaksson's dedication to Icelandic immigrants in North America. They recognized his sincere efforts in finding work or accommodation for newcomers and his financial support through the Norwegian Synod for needy immigrants in Ontario. But the news had also spread that he and Rev. Jon Bjarnason were not in agreement as to the doctrines of the synod, which may be the reason the settlers hesitated to accept Thorlaksson's offer.

Thorlaksson had just left the colony when news reached Gimli that a few people had died in the Icelandic River region from an unknown disease. Some time in September, a disease had surfaced suddenly. No one in the area recognized it. For about six weeks, the disease did not seem to spread and, consequently, not enough attention was paid to it. Then it did begin to spread and, by November, had reached every home in the river region. One woman suffering a severe attack of the disease went to Gimli and died shortly afterwards, and still the nature of the plague remained a mystery. On 9 November, Sigtryggur Jonasson wrote from his home in Modruvellir to Taylor in Gimli, reporting that three Icelanders and seven Aboriginal people had passed away during the previous four days. John Taylor reacted immediately and, on 13 November, wrote to Winnipeg for medical assistance. Four days later, two doctors, David Young and James S. Lynch, arrived in Gimli. Dr. Young remained in Gimli while Dr. Lynch travelled to Icelandic River. A few days later, another doctor, Dr. A. Baldwin, reached Icelandic River. Before the doctors arrived, a new warehouse, which the federal government had built in Gimli, had been converted to an infirmary.[17]

These doctors determined that the disease was smallpox and took immediate steps to prevent it from spreading and to help the sick. Although a smallpox epidemic had not plagued the Icelandic nation for many years, all settlers in New Iceland recalled descriptions from previous times of the disease sweeping the island and leaving thousands dead. In panic, families chose to be isolated in their homes, but those dwellings were anything but the ideal infirmary. The isolation slowed the disease down, but official reaction to the raging plague still came surprisingly late. It was not until 27 November that the whole area was placed in quarantine. A watch post was established at Netley Creek, about twenty-four kilometres south of the south boundary of the colony. The three medical doctors stayed three to four months in the colony, though not without relief. Once the plague began to retreat, a single doctor was sent as a replacement for the original three. He did not leave until June, by which time there had not been any new signs of the plague.

Magnus Stefansson and Kristjan Jonsson interpreted for the doctors. Stefansson claimed he had entered every home in the colony during the epidemic, witnessing suffering and pain wherever he went. Not only were the people physically spent, but also mentally broken. In addition to the suffering of the afflicted and the loss of loved ones, there was much hardship caused directly by the quarantine. No one was allowed to leave the colony and the people had to depend on supplies reaching them from the outside. As there was no supervision of deliveries, food such as beef was often stolen on the way from Winnipeg. Dogs and other animals also managed to get to the food supplies, as no one was there to watch them. People were either too sick or busy at other duties.

Those who could help in any manner kept busy all the time, and there were cases of almost unbelievable courage and endurance. Aldis Laxdal served as midwife in the district. After she had been vaccinated, she got permission to cross the quarantine post at Netley Creek in order to obtain some medication in Winnipeg. There was a desperate need for medical supplies in the settlement the entire winter, and she walked all the way to Winnipeg and back, not once, but three times. It took her several days and she had to spend at least the first night of each trip outside in the heavy bush. The distance between Winnipeg and Gimli is close to 100 kilometres.

In March 1877, it was evident that the plague was retreating; it caused only one more death. In total, nearly a third of the New Iceland settlers caught the disease and 102 died, mostly children and teenagers. No one ever knew how the disease was brought to the region. Many Icelanders blamed it on a piece of clothing bought in Quebec City by a young Icelander who, due to illness, had remained behind for a while in order to recover. He arrived in New Iceland in early September. Another theory is that the plague was brought to the colony by Aboriginal people. Historian W.L. Morton has noted that the disease had "flared and smouldered periodically along the Indian frontier during these years of rapid immigration by whites."[18]

On 7 April, Colonel Osborne Smith, Head of the Keewatin Board of Health, announced that not one case of smallpox existed in the settlement, but the quarantine was not immediately lifted. Traffic to and from the colony, which had been prohibited, was now allowed to cross the boundary line after certain procedures had been carried out. If a person had not been infected, he was required to wait for two weeks, then bathed thoroughly and was provided with new clothing before he was allowed to proceed into Manitoba. Those who had caught the disease and were recovered waited a shorter period, but had to take the bath and accept the new outfit. Letters could not pass, either, unless they had been soaked in carbolic acid.[19] April and May passed and still the guard stood his ground at Netley Creek, and no steps had been taken by the authorities to have the quarantine lifted. This situation crippled all attempts by settlers to improve conditions in the colony. Their products, mainly fish, could not be transported out of the settlement so there was no income. The settlers survived by using the government loan and eating the fish they caught.

Authorities were still not at ease by early June and not ready to lift the quarantine. The settlers were becoming increasingly restless; many intended to leave the colony to find work somewhere in Manitoba for the summer. Moreover, the two governments, Manitoba and the Dominion, could not agree which one was to cover the expenses resulting from keeping the guard at Netley Creek. At a meeting attended by Jonasson, Taylor, and Manitoba authorities, it was resolved that every house in the settlement be thoroughly cleaned and disinfected. This was done during the period from 8 June to 30 June. Houses were whitewashed, and bed linen and all clothing washed in soap. Down, and anything else that could not be washed, was burnt. Once this was done, people expected the immediate lifting of the quarantine, but still nothing happened. The Manitoba government received some strong letters from the settlement, but to no avail. Government employees in the colony showed neither support nor sympathy, and were accused of using insulting and threatening language. The situation had become intolerable.

On 20 July, several hundred settlers gathered at a public meeting in Gimli, where they decided to break through the quarantine. The meeting had begun with a religious service, and then plans were made for the march to Netley Creek. Weapons of any sort were not to be carried. In fact, no particular method of breaking through the hated barricade at Netley Creek was mentioned. But before people began the walk, news reached the meeting that the quarantine had finally been lifted and the guard had abandoned his post. Ten months had passed since the discovery of the disease and four had gone by since the last case was reported in March. Most young men and women immediately left the colony in search for work on Manitoba farms or in Winnipeg.[20]

More than two years had passed since the Icelandic delegation had explored the region on the western bank of Lake Winnipeg and chosen an area large enough to establish the exclusive Icelandic colony. Approximately 1500 people had arrived in the colony in those two years, but between 150 and 160 had died. These two years had been a period of suffering and pain. During the first winter, many suffered from scurvy and hunger, and then from the smallpox during the second winter.

Work on the land was limited to haymaking and growing crops on a very small scale. The settlers had made good progress in fishing, which kept them alive. But the settlement still lacked the characteristics of a community. Although a school had been started and three issues of a handwritten newspaper had been read to people in their homes or at public gatherings, much more was needed. Some kind of community council was required to establish order with laws and regulations. The provisional council, which had been formed in January of 1876, served the purpose of supervising the distribution of necessities the first winter. With the arrival of the large group in the summer, the need for a permanent form of a local government became clear. The epidemic had delayed all discussions on the issue, but in January of 1877, two meetings were held, one in Gimli on the 22nd and the other at Icelandic River on the 26th. Each meeting elected a committee of five to draft a provisional form of constitution for the settlement.

On 5 February, at a public meeting for the entire settlement in Gimli, the provisional drafts were combined and then presented to the meeting. The proposal, which was approved, divided the settled New Iceland into four districts, each with an Icelandic name. From south to north, the districts were Vidirnes district, Arnes district, Fljots district, and Mikley district (Hecla Island), in townships 18 to 23. Township 24 was actually part of the Icelandic reserve, but since no one had homesteaded there at that time, it was excluded. The agreement was not to assume jurisdiction over an area from which there was no representation.[21]

Nine days later, on 14 February, elections were held for the first time. In each district the approval of all residents had to be obtained and a council of five elected. The council was then to elect its chair or reeve. A week later, on 21 February, the four district councils met at Sandvik, where a provisional chair, Sigtryggur Jonasson, and a vice-chair, Fridjon Fridriksson, were elected for a regional council, which governed the entire region. This council also included the four reeves. The chair was given the title "Governor of the Region."

The Regional Council began to consider issues regarding the organization of the settlement. These issues, which required the approval of settlers as being appropriate, were passed on to the district councils, who then discussed them, each in its own region. Several significant agreements were reached. First, each male, twenty-one years of age or older, contributed two days' work or paid a fee of $2.00 to the building of roads in the colony. The district council was to decide each time where, within its boundaries, such work was planned. Second, widows and orphans were to receive enough support. Widows who, according to the district council, had the ability to homestead would be assisted in every manner. Third, five individuals were to be appointed in every district to look after the general well-being of the residents. They were expected to examine the general cleanliness of homes, the state of wells, and the protection against fire. Proposals for a temporary constitution for the region were accepted. These consisted of eighteen sections and were to be in force for the remainder of 1877. These sections were much shorter and more suitable for the common people, and more Icelandic in spirit, than the eighteen articles that made up the final constitution. As an example, the agreed proposals concluded with a clause that indicated that the name of every individual was to be registered in the records of the region. Unfortunately, this was ignored, for the most part, and such records, if they were ever kept, have since been lost. But the clause reads: "Until a pastor has arrived, settlers shall provide the reeve of every district with population count at the end of each year; in addition, dates of birth in every home, within a week from the event."[22]

Framfari, the first Icelandic weekly published in America, printed the final articles of the constitution on 22 December 1877, and with them an exhortation that reveals the optimism of the leaders in the community and explains the duty, not only of every board member, but also of every individual in the settlement:

> We must not regard ourselves as immature children, or people on relief, but rather as fully developed free men who are quite competent to manage their own affairs. We must not regard ourselves as foreigners, but rather as a part of

the national structure in which we find ourselves. We must remember that we hold in our hands the honor and the reputation of the Icelandic national group in this hemisphere. Our aim must be to be the equals of our fellow citizens and we must seek to reach the same levels of culture, practical training and learning as others in the nation of which we are part.

The story of this land is full of examples which show that others, large groups as well as individuals, equally poor and lacking opportunities, have through hard work and unabating determination achieved success and good repute. Why cannot Icelanders do the same? If we only have the same courage, the same enthusiasm, support one another as brothers, there is no reason why we cannot reach the same goals. In closing we ask you to urge every man to study the Agreed Proposals and make suggestions, if deemed necessary, in accordance with Section 17.[23]

The settlers were then encouraged to complete the constitution so that it would be ready for the approval of the Parliament in Ottawa, which was expected to meet as usual on 10 February. The constitution must also have been written in English because it was to be sent to Ottawa. How it was received in the capital city was never discussed in the paper.

The settlers reacted positively and studied the proposals carefully. One interesting change was made: the word for "agreed proposals" in Icelandic is *samþykktir*, which was struck out, and *Stjórnarlög*, "Laws and Regulations," inserted. Also, the name of the colony was hyphenated from Nýja Ísland (New Iceland) to Nýja-Ísland (New-Iceland). This was probably done to prevent the misconception that men desired to establish a colony of Iceland or a new Iceland. Sigtryggur Jonasson undoubtedly made this change, as he was the editor of the first eight issues of *Framfari*. From the beginning of publication to the last issue, the spelling in the masthead of the weekly was always a hyphenated Nýja-Ísland. Elections were held on 2 January 1878, and, on the 11th, all elected representatives met at Sandvik where the laws and regulations were finally approved.

The preparations and planning of those responsible for drafting the laws and regulations clearly demonstrate their consciousness of the rights of every individual in a democratic state, and of the collective duties imposed on all. Some of the men who so diligently put the draft of the constitution together must have had knowledge of Icelandic laws and practices, but several items clearly are based on Canadian municipal regulations. Another remarkable feature was the democratic process by which the constitution had to pass before it was accepted. Before the final meeting at Sandvik, delegates from each district had attended meetings at which the general public gave instructions to the delegates through their voting. This process was then followed at the last meeting at Sandvik. Significantly, the delegates and planners repeatedly emphasized that the settlers were a part of the Canadian nation, and their laws and regulations were subject to the powers of the Parliament in Ottawa.[24]

7

New Iceland: A Religious Controversy

The early history of Icelanders in North America shows a considerable lack of practical knowledge about their new homeland. The difference between farming in America and in Iceland was much greater than they had anticipated. This caused more hardships than many other ethnic immigrants had to endure. Yet, just when the smallpox epidemic was taking its toll, and bitterly cold winters and lack of wholesome food added to the suffering, one of the most discussed issues was the founding of a newspaper for the colony. The desire for a printed newspaper reflected the general spirit in Iceland during the second half of the nineteenth century. The national awakening in the early part of that century had had its roots in printed matter. In all kind of publications, newspapers and periodicals, the nation had been encouraged to endure, despite the elements of nature and Danish suppression. A newspaper not only spread news, but served as a medium for the exchange of opinions and ideas, like a present-day forum. The settlers in North America found it unthinkable to live without a newspaper.

Following the arrival of the large number of people during the summer of 1876, it became clear that Gimli's handwritten newspaper was inadequate. As the construction of new homes went on, numerous issues such as schools, churches, and communication were considered. Discussions on such matters were most often confined to talks between neighbours in every part of the settlement, but the settlers wanted to hear the views of others and to express their own. Newspapers in Iceland had been open to the exchange of opinions on any issue and the general public was used to taking sides in disputes when they occurred. The settlers in Iceland also felt that the founding of an Icelandic newspaper in their colony was essential if they were to transplant their heritage on this foreign soil.[1]

The smallpox epidemic in the fall delayed any serious plans for an Icelandic newspaper. However, in January of 1877, the plague began to retreat, talks were resumed again, and at a public meeting held at Gimli on the 22nd, it was agreed to found a publishing company. A stock company would be formed to meet the expenses of the business, including the purchasing of a printing press. Settlers were to be offered shares in the business. It was agreed that the principal sum would be $1000.00 and each share issued at $10.00, to be payable in cash forthwith. Settlers could purchase any number of shares.

On 5 February, at another meeting at Gimli, it was reported that enough individuals in the settlement had promised to purchase shares. The news warranted the launching of the project and the New Iceland Printing Company was established. The three individuals mostly responsible for the project were Sigtryggur Jonasson and Johann Briem at Icelandic River, and Fridjon Fridriksson at Gimli. These three made the largest financial contributions and were the first directors of the company. Sigtryggur Jonasson was to be the first editor of the new newspaper.[2]

The matter of a printing press was obviously of utmost importance. The settlers contacted the Rev. Jon Bjarnason, residing in Minneapolis at the time, and his connections in the publishing world enabled him to find and purchase a printing press. Before it could be transported to the colony, special dies for the extra letters in the Icelandic alphabet had to be made. This was apparently not easily done and caused such delay that the press did not reach the settlement until June. Even then, a few of the letters needed to complete the Icelandic alphabet were missing, as is evident from the first few issues of the paper, but these were acquired later. The first issue of *Framfari* appeared on 10 September 1877. It was a paper of four pages and was to be published three times monthly. At first it was published in Lundi (Icelandic River), but then it was published in Gimli, where there were better communications and transportation.

The "Laws and Regulations" of the publishing company appeared on the front page of the first issue in a single column on the right. But in two columns on the left, in an address to subscribers and readers, the following appeared:

> Shortly after the Icelanders began emigration in large numbers to this continent, the fear of losing their language and heritage became evident unless necessary steps were taken to preserve both. They have agreed all the while that in order to succeed in this venture, two things were essential: First, the Icelanders establish their own colony and second, a newspaper be published in Icelandic in America. The two are so closely linked that one surviving without the other was unthinkable. A lot has been said regarding the founding of Icelandic settlements and

some attempts to that effect even made in different parts of this country but nothing permanent has developed until the establishing of this colony. On the other hand, no attempts have been made to publish a newspaper but that was among other things the aim of the Icelandic Organization of America, which was founded at the Icelandic celebration (1874) in Milwaukee.[3]

Sigtryggur Jonasson was editor of the first eight issues, but on 24 January 1878, he was replaced by Halldor Briem. Briem was editor until publication of *Framfari* ceased 30 January 1880. One additional issue, which was edited by Sigtryggur Jonasson, was published 10 April of the same year. Jonas Jonasson, brother of Sigtryggur Jonasson, was the printer of *Framfari* for the first thirty-six issues, having learned printing in Akureyri. A young apprentice of his, Bergvin Jonson from Mikley (Hecla Island), joined the printing staff at the beginning and officially became the assistant printer in September of 1878. Together, these two men printed the newspaper until publication ceased. The annual subscription fee was $1.75.[4]

With the establishing of *Framfari,* the Icelandic immigrants in Canada had achieved the exclusive Icelandic settlement and a publication in their native tongue. It had been their conviction that this would be the foundation on which Icelandic heritage in North America would be built. This might have been the case under different circumstances, but instead of *Framfari'*s concentrating on promoting Icelandic sentiment and urging the settlers onwards to greater accomplishments, the newspaper was used mostly to promote very one-sided views in a heated religious controversy. Instead of encouraging the two sides to settle their grievances and improve conditions in the colony, *Framfari,* edited by Halldor Briem, added fuel to the dispute. This controversy resulted in complete division and the departure of more than half the settlers from the dream colony of New Iceland.

Ever since Jon Bjarnason had arrived in North America and became acquainted with the teachings of the Norwegian Synod, he fell into disagreement with his friend, Pall Thorlaksson. Bjarnason could not accept the doctrines of the synod, believing they contradicted those of the Icelandic State Church to such a degree that any reconciliation was impossible. He also opposed Thorlaksson's opinions on the immigration of Icelanders, especially the view that the Icelanders needed to learn new ways of farming, preferably on a Norwegian farm. In Bjarnason's opinion, such an arrangement would not only result in the direct influence of the synod on the Icelandic settlers, but also hinder any attempts to found the exclusive Icelandic colony.

The fact that Thorlaksson urged his compatriots to learn about agricultural methods before beginning their own farming was interpreted by many as the synod's effort to attract the Icelanders, and this had led those opposed to such ideas to hasten the search for a colony site. Jon Olafsson went to Alaska, Olafur Olafsson arranged for an exploration in Nebraska, and Sigtryggur Jonasson made attempts in Ontario. The toasts delivered at the Milwaukee Festival of 1874 had made it clear that the two men, Bjarnason and Thorlaksson, held different opinions about the Icelandic settlement in America. Although people attending the Milwaukee Festival had sensed this difference of opinion, also expressed in Bjarnason's warnings not to follow the example set by Norwegian settlers, no one appeared interested in the religious side of the disagreement. Bjarnason wrote to friends in Iceland and explained to them why he felt he could not accept the doctrines of the Norwegian Synod, but in North America people had other things on their minds during the years from 1875 to 1877.

The question of a pastor for the Icelandic settlement, wherever it might be founded, was seldom addressed. No effort was made to secure a pastor directly from Iceland. But once Bjarnason expressed his willingness to consider serving his countrymen in an Icelandic colony, those in favour of such a settlement made him their first choice. This is understandable, as he would perform his religious services in accordance with the doctrines of the Icelandic State Church and such an arrangement would be in harmony with their intentions of establishing an exclusive Icelandic settlement.

On the other hand, those who followed Thorlaksson's advice and later founded the small colony in Shawano County saw nothing wrong with his becoming their pastor. Thorlaksson repeated his former offer to the settlers of New Iceland in a letter in the late fall of 1876, requesting at the time a list of the names of his supporters. The positive reaction to his offer prompted Fridjon Fridriksson to write to Bjarnason on 27 November to inform him of Thorlaksson's second offer. He added that 200 settlers already had entered their names on the list and that more might follow if no alternatives were offered. Increasing pressure was put on Bjarnason and the frightening prospect of the synod's control over church life and schools was frequently pointed out. In addition, Bjarnason was made aware of the fact that he was the only one in North America who could provide the appropriate defense against such impositions. In spite of all this effort, Bjarnason was not easily persuaded.

During the winter, discussions about a pastor for the colony gave further evidence that the two candidates were Thorlaksson and Bjarnason. In the early spring of 1877, at meetings held throughout New Iceland, it was generally agreed that a pastor was needed immediately.[5] This had been strongly felt during the entire winter when smallpox affected every home. Fridriksson wrote to Bjarnason on 30 April 1877, and described a meeting held two days earlier on the question of obtaining a pastor. It had been agreed that a Lutheran Synod would be established, whose doctrines should be in precise harmony with those of the Icelandic State Church and be completely independent of other synods in North America. During this meeting, a committee was organized for the purpose of obtaining a pastor and collecting funds to build a church. The same committee was to inform Thorlaksson that his offer had been turned down.[6]

Clearly, these meetings were called and chaired by those favouring Bjarnason. In an effort to meet the cost of pastoral services, each family agreed to pay $4.00 a year or as much as they could afford. In his letter, Fridriksson pointed out that those who could afford to, should pay more, whereas others might have to be completely exempted from payment. This was the first time payment was ever mentioned to Bjarnason and that may have been encouraging enough for him to finally make up his mind and visit the colony. In July of 1877, Bjarnason saw New Iceland for the first time. During his short visit of three weeks, he examined the conditions of the colony and the spirit of the people. The immigrants were impressed with his services and other clerical performances, and he was equally pleased with their response.

Following Bjarnason's visit, a meeting was held at Gimli on 31 August, where yet another formal call to Bjarnason was signed. This call from four congregations, consisting of 130 families or about 650 persons, stated that this was a renewal of an earlier request. Those who signed pledged to guarantee Bjarnason's maintenance as long as he would serve the congregations. Among those who signed were Sigtryggur Jonasson and Fridjon Fridriksson. Eventually, Bjarnason agreed. He resigned his position as the editor of *Budstikken* and, on 18 October 1877, left Minneapolis for an uncertain future in New Iceland. Meanwhile, Thorlaksson received his list of supporters and arrived in Gimli on the 19th, just ahead of Bjarnason.[7]

The presence of two pastors so opposed in their religious conviction inevitably left a division in the community, but it is interesting to speculate on what grounds it occurred. Immigrants in New Iceland ranged from relatively well-to-do farmers to poor farmhands; the economic condition of these people varied widely. This fact must have played a very important part in their choice of pastor. Thorlaksson's offer did not involve the burden of maintaining a pastor, just as had been the case back home in Iceland. There is little doubt that there were many who accepted his offer for this very reason, especially those who struggled at the level of mere subsistence. These people were not extremely concerned whether each word of the Bible was inspired by God, as Thorlaksson maintained, or only a part of the Holy Writ, as had been taught in the Theological Seminary in Iceland. The well-to-do who favoured Thorlaksson did so primarily because they felt that as citizens in a new country, they should be ready to accept new ways in North America, such as different religious teachings. Their knowledge of religion did not matter as much as their firm wish to become new citizens. They also wanted to enjoy the protection and the overall assistance the Norwegian Synod could offer. Finally, Thorlaksson's personality strongly impressed anyone who met him; his ability as a leader was never questioned and, as a result, many people gathered around him. It is tempting to say that the question of which pastor to choose was less a matter of doctrine than one of qualities of leadership.

Many of the immigrants favoured Bjarnason, because they saw in him a representative from the church in Iceland. These people were opposed to any interference from a foreign organization, fearing that it might severely limit their jurisdiction over their church and their schools. They argued, for example, that if they became involved with a large synod, like the Norwegian Synod, their votes would count for little at the synod's conferences. These settlers also pointed out that if a foreign body ran their schools, subjects such as Icelandic and Icelandic history might not be taught. In brief, this group wanted complete control over their church and schools. They were convinced that Bjarnason would make much greater efforts to preserve the Icelandic language in the colony and generally promote Icelandic culture.

There was a concomitant upheaval in ecclesiastical affairs in Iceland. The introduction of the new theology appeared first in 1542 in the translation of the New Testament. In 1584 Bishop Gudbrandur Thorlaksson included this translation in the first full edition of the Bible in Iceland. These were by no means his only publications; he worked tirelessly on religious studies, many of which became extremely popular in the country. One example of such work was the *Gradule*, a service book and hymn collection. This book was not replaced until 1801. Gudbrandur Thorlaksson's efforts consolidated the position of Lutheran doctrine and rite in the country. These publications also helped greatly in preserving the Icelandic tongue, preventing it from becoming tainted with foreign linguistic influences.

Soon, other works appeared, which contributed to the fervent personal and communal piety that marked the whole nation in the early post-Reformation period. One example was the work of Hallgrimur Petursson, who was born in 1614 and moved to Holar with his family, where his uncle, Gudbrandur Thorlaksson, still reigned. Whether Thorlaksson had much influence on the young man is unknown, but his works certainly did. Petursson was a great poet; his hymns are still regarded as the most beautiful works ever written in Icelandic. *The Passion Hymns*, which deal with the last days of Jesus Christ, are undoubtedly his masterpiece.

Lutheran orthodoxy gradually was strengthened during the seventeenth century and soon this religious tradition became important to every Icelandic family. In these times the religious tradition achieved a unity and strength that have not since been matched. On each farm religion was practised and, in addition to normal church attendance, prayers were said daily together with reading, usually the sermons of Bishop Jon Vidalin, and singing, under the supervision of the master of the house. The sermons of Jon Vidalin, first published in 1721, became very important to most Icelanders; they were still widely read in the early nineteenth century. The unity of tradition and practice was significant during the peak of Lutheran orthodoxy in the seventeenth and eighteenth centuries.

During the period from the Reformation in 1550 to 1800, the influence of Bishop Thorlaksson, Petursson, and Bishop Vidalin was very strong, and the unadulterated Lutheran orthodoxy in their works dominated religious exercises in Iceland.[8] This religious expression gradually gave way to new tendencies in the nineteenth century. The Theological Seminary in Reykjavík based its teachings on these new currents. Some of Rev. Bjarnason's contemporaries had few positive things to say about the age of Lutheran orthodoxy in Iceland. Matthias

Jochumsson, for example, a poet and editor, attacked Lutheran orthodoxy and blamed Bishop Gudbrandur Thorlaksson and Danish authorities for reducing the nation to extreme misery and poverty—Thorlaksson through his preaching, and the Danes by their trade monopoly. Bishop Petur Petursson was more moderate and said only Bishop Vidalin's sermons better fitted Vidalin's age than the nineteenth century. In other words, the late nineteenth-century Icelandic State Church renounced Lutheran orthodoxy as it had been practised from the Reformation. This was the orthodoxy that, in Rev. Thorlaksson's view, came closest to the doctrines of both the Norwegian and the Missouri synods.

The faith the Icelandic immigrants brought with them was one of tolerance and trust in merciful divine powers. This faith was quite different from the seventeenth- and eighteenth-century Lutheranism. Therein lay the difference between the modernistic views of Bjarnason and the traditionally entrenched dogma espoused by Thorlaksson, Hallgrimur Petursson, and Jon Vidalin. Seventeenth-century Icelandic orthodoxy adequately suited Thorlaksson's education and training at Concordia University, St. Louis, Missouri. Although Bjarnason was not completely at ease with the new Lutheran orthodoxy, if one can thus designate it, it remained the basis for his own conviction.

In New Iceland, the two pastors commenced immediately upon arrival to organize their congregations. Thorlaksson named his three congregations after the three most influential religious men in the age of Lutheran orthodoxy: Gudbrandur Thorlaksson, Hallgrimur Petursson, and Jon Vidalin. Naming his congregations in this manner probably served to strengthen his case when he insisted that his congregational laws were in accordance with Lutheranism as practised in Iceland. His laws were in twenty-one articles, which clearly indicate the relations with the two frequently mentioned synods. The third article of Thorlaksson's laws is identical to Article 1, Chapter 2, of the constitution of the Missouri Synod. Thorlaksson's article reads: "The congregations accept the Holy Scripture i.e. canonistic books of the Old and New Testaments as the Word of God and the only true fountain, rule and norm of faith and life." The Missouri article reads: "Acceptance of Holy Scripture of the Old and New Testaments as the written Word of God and the only rule and norm of faith and life."[9]

In the spring of 1877, when those Icelandic immigrants who did not ask for Thorlaksson's services discussed the need for an Icelandic pastor, they agreed to establish an Icelandic synod, based on laws the Icelanders understood were in accordance with the faith in Iceland. Rev. Bjarnason and Halldor Briem in the United States, who were both known for their opposition to the Norwegian Synod, wrote the laws in eleven articles and in New Iceland they were passed unchanged.

When Bjarnason arrived in the colony in November of 1877, some changes were made then to the laws. For example, one dealt with the creeds. Originally the article read: "The Synod considers the creeds of the Lutheran Church valuable evidence of how the Church has at various times interpreted the teachings of the Bible and defended itself against heresy." After the change it read: "The creeds of the Lutheran Church are especially honored as evidence of how the founders of that Church, which our nation has accepted for three hundred years, have understood and taught the learning of the Holy Scripture and defended itself against heresy. But neither these Lutheran creeds nor any other confessions do we match with the Holy Writ, which any doctrine must be judged by."[10]

No explanation exists for these changes, but they may have been made to conform more closely to the Icelandic State Church. Since both pastors maintained that their laws were in accordance with what had been practised in Iceland, these changes may also have been made as an attempt to prove Thorlaksson wrong. The fourth article of his laws reads: "The congregations accept the learning of the Holy Bible in the same manner as the Lutheran Church in Iceland does in its creeds because they do not only accept evidence of what the church has taught at various times, but also as a pure and correct interpretation of the Word of God which never changes. These creeds are: 1) the Apostolic, 2) the Athanasian, 3) the unaltered Augsburg Confession, 4) the Nicene, 5) Luther's Small Catechism."[11]

When Thorlaksson's laws were finally published in *Framfari,* 19 March 1878, the editor, Halldor Briem, found reason to comment on some of the articles. His main interest was in the creeds, some of which—particularly the Nicene and Athanasian—he insisted had never been translated into Icelandic. He maintained that these were unknown to Icelanders and he doubted if Thorlaksson ever explained them to his congregations. In a brief answer to Briem's comments in *Framfari,* on 12 April 1878, Thorlaksson referred to a meeting held at Gimli in March of the same year, where he claimed he answered all such accusations.

In comparison, Bjarnason's laws were much more tolerant. For example, Thorlaksson did not consider women as full members and they were not given the right to vote. This was in accord with the dictates of the Norwegian Synod. Bjarnason, on the other hand, equated women with men in every respect. Thorlaksson insisted that only a pastor with proper education should perform religious services, whereas Bjarnason maintained that in congregations without a pastor, religious practice should be performed as was done in Iceland. Thorlaksson served three congregations, while Bjarnason organized five, located in Mikley (Hecla Island), by Icelandic River, on the border of Arnes and Icelandic River districts, at Gimli, and in southern Vidirnes district.

Thorlaksson faced stiff opposition. Each pastor had supporters, Bjarnason with 142 families, Thorlaksson with 132, but the most influential men in the settlement, Sigtryggur Jonasson, Fridjon Fridriksson, and Halldor Briem, were on Bjarnason's side. Jonasson and Briem were editors of *Framfari* during the debate, a tremendous advantage to Bjarnason.

Thorlaksson did not become fully aware of the seriousness of this dispute and the accusations made towards the Norwegian Synod until late in 1877. He felt it his duty to rectify what he called "a misunderstanding of the nature and tendency of the Norwegian Synod,"[12] which he found dominant in the arguments of the opposition. In an article in *Framfari,* 24 January 1878, he began by briefly recounting the history of the synod. He described the new Norwegian Theological Seminary in Decorah, Iowa, and compared it to the one in Reykjavík, Iceland. He maintained that the subjects taught were basically the same in both schools but that greater emphasis was placed on theology at Decorah than in Reykjavík. He concluded this first article of three by comparing students at the two educational centres, claiming that the students in Reykjavík were so liberal that they doubted the superiority of the Lutheran church over other Christian churches. They even doubted the superiority of Christianity over other faiths. The students of Decorah, on the other hand, were grateful for the truth that God had granted the Lutheran church. His comparison of the students clearly reflected the difference in religious education and doctrine at the two institutions: the liberalism or tolerance of the Icelandic students compared to the fundamentalism of the Decorah students.

Bjarnason shared Thorlaksson's views on students at the seminary in Reykjavík in the sense that he found them lacking all enthusiasm in their studies. In his "Apologia pro vita sua," he gives the following description:

> When I entered the school I became very disappointed. The students were fewer than ever before, just over thirty. One tends to think it needed not be disadvantage, much rather the opposite, but such was not the case. I found the spirit among the students cold and repellent. Later I found out, however, that there were exceptions. This dreadful spirit appeared, for example, in the attitude of the students to the study. It was not considered honorable to be diligent; in fact they even detested those who made any effort in that direction.... This attitude was at times beyond my strength; it hurt me tremendously.[13]

Halldor Briem immediately commented on Thorlaksson's article, stating that Thorlaksson's intention should be appreciated because nothing was as important as a true, clear picture of the synod. He claimed that Thorlaksson had failed to give any explanation of the misunderstanding. In fact, it had not even been mentioned. The comparison between the students at Decorah and in Reykjavík was not justified, Briem maintained. He felt that the accusations against the faith of Icelandic students were of such a serious nature that they could not be left unanswered. The majority of these students were ordained upon graduation, and served as pastors throughout Iceland. In conclusion, he pointed out that if Thorlaksson seriously intended to clarify any "misunderstanding," he had to be a lot more accurate.

Briem did not discuss Bjarnason's case. The latter had been an outstanding student at the seminary, receiving top grades, but upon ordination no benefice was offered to him, even though he applied on several occasions. Bjarnason had expressed his views on the Icelandic State Church while he was at the seminary and more strongly upon graduation. His disappointment with the seminary and the Church of Iceland may well have been the reason church authorities in Iceland ignored his applications for a benefice. He had emigrated to America partly as a result of his disappointments with the church in Iceland. In New Iceland, however, where he was considered its representative, Bjarnason never expressed any criticism of the Church of Iceland.

At this stage in the debate, only Thorlaksson and Briem were exchanging opinions. Bjarnason had yet to become involved. It was apparent, however, that more was to follow. Briem's comments were of such a nature that Thorlaksson was forced to react. Yet, he avoided entering discussions on the doctrines or tendencies of the Norwegian Synod, which was exactly what Briem had asked for in his conclusion. Briem wanted him to admit, for example, that the Norwegian Synod had never considered slavery sinful, which had been one of the accusations against the synod from the beginning.

The second part of Thorlaksson's article was published in *Framfari* on 12 February 1878. This time he gave a detailed account of the educational system of the synod and described the schools to which it had access.

He explained why he was offered a scholarship by the synod, maintaining that the prospect of his assistance to Icelandic immigrants to North America was the only reason for this award. Their need for a pastor had been known to the synod, who had asked him to become the Icelanders' pastor.

Briem's comments appeared in the same issue. He discussed, among other things, his own experience of the Norwegian Synod. After attending classes at their seminary for some time, he realized that he could not accept the "bigotry and narrow-mindedness" of the synod. He admitted that one day, in front of some students, he spoke his mind to some of the teachers and then left the seminary for good. He also discussed the synod's assistance to poor immigrants: how it offered to meet the expenses of a pastor, church, and school buildings. It was his firm belief that if immigrants accepted such help, they had either to join the synod or to repay the sum of money provided for their assistance.

His last remark reflected one of the most frequent accusations against the Norwegian Synod. It was blamed for forcing its power upon poor, trusting immigrants by offering money and the services of a pastor. Many immigrants accepted such help, the critics believed, but then found themselves deprived of any influence on their church life. Such accusations were by no means new. As early as 1873, Jon Olafsson had expressed these views in a letter to Bjarnason. To prove the point, Briem quoted Norwegian immigrants who opposed the synod. *Framfari* also referred to an article by Professor R.B. Anderson in Madison, Wisconsin, which had been published in the *Skandinaven*. In the article, Thorlaksson was accused of purposefully describing conditions in New Iceland so incorrectly that the Norwegian Synod had immediately offered a large sum of money for his congregations. Thorlaksson had, indeed, requested assistance from the synod for his congregations.

The conclusion of Thorlaksson's article appeared in *Framfari* on 20 February. Again he raised the question of the misunderstanding about the synod; now, however, he blamed Rev. Bjarnason and Halldor Briem. He maintained that their constant accusations against the synod and himself during the winter of 1876-

1877 resulted in suspicion and even distrust among many of the settlers in New Iceland. He insisted that at meetings or whenever he had the opportunity, he had tried repeatedly to explain his concept of the role of a pastor, the organization of the Norwegian Synod, and its doctrines. His congregations had, therefore, been thoroughly informed. He said that he had found some of his greatest friends among the Norwegians, and he expressed his appreciation of the synod and his admiration for its leaders.

In his reply, Halldor Briem maintained that Thorlaksson undoubtedly had tried to explain the nature of the synod and its doctrines. Whether he succeeded was a different story. Nothing in Thorlaksson's article had clarified anything regarding the so-called "misunderstanding," which he originally intended to rectify. Consequently, there were reasons to doubt that Thorlaksson's attempts elsewhere had been any more successful. Briem concluded his comments by comparing the financial situation of the two pastors.

Rev. Bjarnason had given up an advantageous post in Minneapolis and had to rely on his countrymen in New Iceland. Thorlaksson, on the other hand, was maintained by the Norwegian Synod and had no financial worries. Thus, Briem said, "when he brings presents to members of his congregations we will not say that the intention is directly to allure them, but I have witnessed that such gifts from the Synod are not always due to charity."[14]

For the first time, Thorlaksson then publicly accused Bjarnason of being involved in an attack on himself and the Norwegian Synod. No evidence of such an attack exists. However, by not coming forth in *Framfari* to defend Thorlaksson, Bjarnason can be said to have approved of Briem's charges.

The dispute, as it appeared in *Framfari*, had become bitter and frustrating. Discussion of doctrine had yet to appear and yet both men tried their utmost to cause distrust in the other's church. Thorlaksson insisted that Icelandic pastors had limited faith; Briem claimed that the Norwegian Synod forced its authority upon immigrants, including Icelanders. Although these were the opinions of only two men, they probably reflected the arguments of others in the colony. Laymen probably never discussed the difference in doctrines, for they lacked knowledge of them, but they certainly had their own opinions on the synod as a powerful religious body.

The harvest in New Iceland during the summer of 1877 was disappointing and so was the fishing. Scarcity of food became evident as Christmas drew closer. The Regional Council, therefore, asked that reports from every district be forwarded to a meeting at Gimli on 28 December. It appeared that no fewer than one-fifth of the population was in desperate need. The council calculated that 116 families were well off, another 116 could manage, but twenty-three families were in a desperate situation. The council decided that those who were comparatively well-off could help those in need and that assistance from outside the settlement was not required. However, Thorlaksson and his people were of a different opinion. At a meeting held at Gimli on 5 January 1878, an appeal to the Norwegian

Synod was signed by representatives from Thorlaksson's congregations, and accompanied by a request that he submit it along with his own assessment. Apparently Thorlaksson was not in attendance at the meeting, nor did he know of its intention beforehand. On 11 January, he wrote a long letter describing what he considered to be the hopeless situation in the colony. These two letters and a note from H.A. Preus, the president of the Norwegian Synod, were then published in one of the synod's papers and all Norwegians in North America were urged to help their friends in New Iceland.[15]

The reaction to this appeal among Bjarnason's people was very critical. Bjarnason wrote to *Budstikken* in Minneapolis in March of 1878, expressing the view that Thorlaksson's statement was greatly exaggerated. *Framfari* published the views of both Bjarnason and Thorlaksson. The matter revolved around the question of survival without outside help. Bjarnason maintained, as the council had done, that although many settlers were impoverished, others could come to their rescue and that the synod's assistance would give it a hold over the community. Thorlaksson, on the other hand, insisted that the situation among his people was serious; many a household had been forced to slaughter its only cow and others were eating the seed potatoes intended for next year's crop.

This dispute reached every Icelander in North America and brought divergent reactions. For example, Icelandic settlers in Lyon County, Minnesota, called a meeting and agreed to send a letter to future emigrants in Iceland to warn them against settling in New Iceland. They gave Thorlaksson's letter to the synod as a reason for their warning. People of non-Icelandic extraction also contributed opinions. Professor R.B. Anderson of Madison maintained in his article that if the Norwegians intended to help the Icelanders, they should not exclude Bjarnason's followers.

This is an interesting suggestion and may have affected the synod's leaders because on 13 March, Preus stated in the paper *Norden* that he had written to Thorlaksson and asked for more detailed information. He may have been inquiring whether all the immigrants in New Iceland needed help, or he may have wanted more information on the economic circumstances of those belonging to Thorlaksson's congregations. One suspects the latter; after all, Bjarnason had declared that the situation in New Iceland was not as serious as Thorlaksson's submission had indicated.

There were others who took honourable stands. For example, J.A. Heiberg, a Danish pastor in Chicago and the president of a Danish Lutheran organization, asked Bjarnason for information on New Iceland because the Danes in his community had collected a sum of money intended for starving Icelanders. In *Framfari*, 22 May 1878, Bjarnason explained that on behalf of his congregations, he had turned this generous offer down.[16]

In early 1878, the dispute widened to include many other topics. The Regional Council called a public meeting at Gimli on 25 and 26 of March, where the pastors were asked to account for their theological doctrines. The intention was to reach some kind of an agreement between the two groups. It is estimated that at least 300 immigrants attended this meeting.

The meeting was to start with the singing of a hymn and a prayer, but Thorlaksson refused to participate on the grounds that he could not accept Bjarnason as a brother in Christ. His refusal is interesting because it was in harmony with the standard practice of both the Missouri and the Norwegian synods and their complete disapproval of other religious bodies. That it was by no means a step towards a reconciliation between the two groups shows how determined Thorlaksson was to follow the rules of the Norwegian Synod.

At the meeting, almost two days were devoted to interpretive aspects of the Bible. Since this question has remained fundamental to every religious debate among Icelanders in North America, it requires close examination. Pall Thorlaksson accepted the Plenary Inspiration, whereas Bjarnason followed the theory of the Partial Inspiration. In the latter, theological components of the Bible are said to reflect the inspiration of God, whereas its historical constituents and formal presentation can be ascribed to human endeavour.

In his attempts to dispute this theory, Thorlaksson invoked the words of one of the most prominent theologians of the Missouri Synod, D. Gaussen, who had stated: "No arrogance can match that of him who believes that the Bible is God's apocalypse but dares to read it and distinguish what is inspired and what is not."[17] Thorlaksson added that this theory would demolish the very foundation of religion and would allow people to believe what they wanted to believe, not what God had said.

In their effort to prove each other in error, the pastors repeatedly quoted theologians and books of dogma in various languages. Initially, the lay participation in these discussions was limited, but during the second day of the meeting, participation began to widen the scope of the controversy. Halldor Briem repeated his accusations against the Norwegian Synod, probably using arguments similar to those he had printed in *Framfari*. As before, Thorlaksson spoke in its defence. It is unfortunate that no detailed account of the meeting exists because, according to a report in *Framfari*, Thorlaksson answered Briem's accusations more directly than he had done in the paper. *Framfari* stated that it intended to publish an article on everything that was said but this was never done. However, the conclusion of the minutes is quoted:

> Everybody is convinced that the pastors hold extremely different opinions. Despite this it appeared that the members of the two factions departed with a friendly feeling and with much better understanding of the differences between the two pastors and between Christian sects. It was especially apparent that the people were of one accord that while each person held to his own point of view in religious matters, this should not mar public concord and brotherly co-operation.[18]

In spite of this optimism, these words, unfortunately, turned out to be no more than wishful thinking. The dispute grew increasingly serious, demoralizing both civil relations and brotherly cooperation. The constant disagreement led to hostility; good neighbours became bad; even families were split as a result. Jon Jonsson from Mæri wrote later that what really had made life miserable in New Iceland was the religious controversy. Wherever people met they would argue. Another settler said that the extremes of the weather, the bloodthirsty bugs in the summer, the hunger and scurvy, floods, smallpox epidemic, the isolation and lack of transportation had been bad but worst of all was the dispute between the two pastors.[19]

As Thorlaksson still had obligations in Shawano County in Wisconsin, he left New Iceland in April 1878 and did not return until October. His people began preparing for spring work but at the same time began to discuss a possible settlement elsewhere. Thorlaksson had frequently pointed out that there were still some attractive, unsettled areas down south. A group of five Icelanders left the colony in May and explored both north and south of the border. They returned in June, some determined to leave the colony of New Iceland for good. Their decision led to the beginning of a new phase of the dispute: the future of New Iceland.

The Canadian government had agreed to assist the immigrants from Iceland in their effort to get settled in New Iceland. This was done through loans amounting to $80,000.00, which meant that each homestead was mortgaged. The first loan of $15,000.00 was granted to the people moving west from Ontario in the fall of 1875. This money was intended for the purchase of supplies and livestock in Winnipeg. Because there was no hay available in the colony, the livestock plan was dropped and, instead, the money was used only for supplies.

The second loan, $5000.00, was to cover the cost of transportation from Quebec to New Iceland for those who only had enough money to cover the fare to Canada. The third loan, $8000.00, was granted to the same group in Toronto for the purpose of purchasing equipment, nets, and food for the journey to Winnipeg, where another $9000.00 awaited the same group, which was used to buy food supplies for three months and to cover the cost of transportation to the colony.

In October of 1876, the fifth loan, in the amount of $18,000.00, was granted to the inhabitants of New Iceland for the purpose of buying food supplies for the winter months, stoves, equipment, and forty cows. The last loan, $25,000.00 in April of 1877, was for the purchase of sufficient seed, tools of various kinds, yarn for net-making, stoves, food supplies, and livestock. By end of April about 250 cows had been bought.

The first payment of the total amount was due 1 January 1879, but by 31 December 1878, interest would be charged. In ten years' time, or at the end of 1888, the loan was to be repaid in full. Those who intended to remain in New Iceland would not be expected to pay either interest or capital until after five years; then, one-sixth of the capital sum plus interest was due. Similar payments were expected annually until the entire amount plus interest had been paid in full before 1 January 1884.[20] The government did not actually pursue collecting the debt from those residing in New Iceland, nor from those who later chose to settle elsewhere in Canada. In fact, the loan was never repaid. But when the news spread through the settlement that some of Thorlaksson's people were determined to leave the colony and possibly Canada, the payment of the loan became an issue of utmost importance. It was emphasized that the loan was for the inhabitants of New Iceland only and that the first instalment was due to be repaid in 1879. Those supporting Bjarnason argued that if many people left the colony, the payments would become unbearable for those remaining behind. They demanded that no one be permitted to leave without paying his share, either in cash or by leaving behind livestock and tools.[21]

Thorlaksson was again blamed for having urged his followers to leave; people said he had never liked the idea of a settlement in Canada and had always greatly exaggerated the shortcomings of New Iceland. *Framfari* maintained that everyone knew that the first years in an unsettled area were always difficult; such had been the case throughout North America for years. People would simply need to unite in their effort to conquer the pioneer problems. Divided, as they gradually were becoming, progress would be slow.

This was an interesting change of tone and an appeal to both factions to settle their grievances. Up to this point, *Framfari* had shown little, if any, effort to support reconciliation. On the contrary, under the editorship of Halldor Briem, the paper had been instrumental in keeping the controversy going through constant accusations of Thorlaksson and his flock. Not once had Halldor Briem suggested previously that joint effort by all inhabitants would make the settlement a success.

Since Thorlaksson was not in the colony at the time, his people made no effort to defend their plans of leaving. However, in July, unexpected support came from Bjarnason. In a long article in *Framfari*,[22] he expressed his views on an all-Icelandic settlement and admitted that since his arrival in North America he had thought that maintaining a separate colony would suit the Icelanders best. It had been his dream to see the Icelandic language and culture flourish under such circumstances. Now, having witnessed the struggle in New Iceland and its limited progress over the last two years, he saw only two alternatives for the Icelanders. One was to open up the reserve to people of other nationalities with necessary experience and economic ability to start an organized agriculture. The other was to leave the colony and scatter among others, either in Canada or the United States; he personally had always favoured the United States. The Icelanders had to face the fact that they had come to North America to become either Canadians or Americans. Being isolated in New Iceland would only prevent progress and normal adaptation. He maintained that had it not been for the fish in the lake, no one could have survived the first two years. He concluded that future immigrants from Iceland should not settle in groups in North America; they should scatter among others familiar with North American soil.

This sudden change of heart is perhaps not surprising. The settlers still had not made any progress in their agricultural effort and it had become increasingly evident, as attempts were made to break and cultivate the land, that this district had poor soil in many places. The settlement was not, by any means, self-sufficient and a large number of families barely survived. Bjarnason, like Thorlaksson, had witnessed in the United States how progress had been made and how new settlers, scattered among others, could benefit from the experience of those already settled. He now went as far as to suggest a complete depopulation of New Iceland when he recommended they scatter among other settlers. In other words, he now approved of what Thorlaksson had recommended from the very beginning. He no longer appeared to be as concerned with maintaining the language or culture or religion, because survival itself was now an issue.

His article came as a shock to those of his followers who had dreamt of a separate Icelandic settlement. They expressed their disappointment in a long sequence of articles in *Framfari* during the remainder of the year. Of greatest concern was the possible opening up of the reserve. The major question was how to keep undesirables from the colony. Both Sigtryggur Jonasson and Halldor Briem addressed this issue in the paper, arriving at similar conclusion: that the matter of opening up the reserve would need careful thought and consideration. The Regional Council made no decision in the matter.

The controversy between the two religious factions remained very much alive throughout 1878. It was apparent that most settlers were not ready to depart from New Iceland and scatter all over Canada and the United States. Quite a few were determined to remain and discussions on opening up the reserve were much more frequent. In February of 1879, men from both groups agreed to call yet another public meeting. The purpose was to have the pastors continue their discussion of matters raised at the Gimli meeting of the previous year, as well as other topics of public concern, one of which was the future of New Iceland. It had occurred to many people, after Bjarnason's famous article in *Framfari,* that he might even have changed his opinion regarding the Norwegian Synod.

Those who had doubts regarding Bjarnason's views on the Norwegian Synod must have been relieved on 13 March 1879, when *Framfari* began to publish a long article entitled "Necessary Exhortation" by Bjarnason. Here he attempted at length to explain the vast difference between the two synods and the Icelandic State Church. In his book *The Icelandic People in Manitoba*, Wilhelm Kristjanson gives the following summary:

> Reverend Bjarnason said, in substance, that it was evident from the disputation of 1878 that the religious beliefs of Thorlaksson differed on many fundamentals not only from his own views but also from those generally held in Iceland. From the first, Thorlaksson had objected to a common cemetery for church groups in New Iceland; he had refused to join Bjarnason in a prayer at the public disputation of 1878 because he considered him a heretic, and he had stated that his conscience forbade him to call Bjarnason his brother in Christ. The Missouri Synod where Thorlaksson and most of the Norwegian ministers had received their religious education, was by far the most conservative Lutheran organization of all time. A burning question among the students at their seminary had been whether it was sinful to accept interest on money; the Synod had officially forbidden the marriage of a man to his deceased wife's sister; one of

its chief publications claimed that the sun moved around the earth; it demanded acceptance of beliefs not concerned with Christian religion and it claimed that Luther's teachings after 1523 were infallible and was elevating Luther to papal stature. Reverend Thorlaksson's preaching of predestination was contradictory to God's wish that all would be saved in truth.[23]

It should be added that in his discussion of the Plenary Inspiration, Bjarnason maintained that one person among many who had strongly opposed it was Bishop Martensen of Denmark. In his comments on Bishop Martensen, Prof. Walther at Concordia had stated: "The so-called religious work of Martensen is a collection of the most revolting heresies."[24] Almost every Icelandic pastor would therefore be considered a heretic, since Martensen's dogma was not only taught at the University of Copenhagen but also at the seminary in Reykjavík, Iceland.

Since only the first of three parts of Bjarnason's article had appeared in *Framfari* before the second public meeting at Gimli, Thorlaksson did not have an opportunity to comment. However, after the meeting and once Bjarnason's whole article had appeared, he stated in a short note in *Framfari* on 22 April that this whole matter was too complicated and extensive for any brief explanation. He added that he planned to publish a pamphlet in which he hoped to explain his point of view once and for all.

The second disputation took place at Gimli on 17 and 18 March. Many people have referred to this meeting as the most remarkable gathering ever to take place among Icelanders in Canada. Never before had the Icelanders been so enthusiastic on matters of religion, but the constant disagreement over the past three years had left its mark. Again, the two different theories of the inspiration of the Bible were discussed. Bjarnason claimed that the Bible was partly inspired but it was written by men who made errors. Contradictions could, then, be found in it. None of these, however, upset the text of the Holy Writ. In his answer, Thorlaksson insisted that the Bible must reflect an instance in which men of limited education must have been divinely inspired, since they wrote complicated sentences that were beyond even their own understanding.[25]

Again both pastors referred to various sources. Thorlaksson normally gave passages in the Bible as proofs. Bjarnason, in his rebuttals, repeatedly insisted that no passages could be found to vindicate Thorlaksson's point of view. This meeting made it clear that reconciliation between the two factions was impossible. It was also obvious to all, although no one brought it up, that the two factions no longer could live in harmony, side by side, in New Iceland. This was less of a problem than might have been expected because most of Thorlaksson's people were seriously considering a new settlement in North Dakota.

Thorlaksson may have been on the losing end in the dispute with Bjarnason, in the sense that he failed to convince his opponent and his followers, but he was right about the exclusive Icelandic settlement. In order to avoid any misunderstanding regarding Thorlaksson's view on settlements, it must be emphasized that he wanted his mother tongue to be preserved in North America. He always maintained that, having obtained the necessary training and education in the States or Canada, the Icelanders would be in a position to establish their own colony. He sincerely believed that nothing was of greater importance for the Icelanders during their first years in America than to learn proper agricultural methods. This, he was convinced, could only be achieved through work on farms already engaged in the production of wheat, corn, and other cereals, not by settling totally without experience in a remote area.

He was quite right, as far as the first years in New Iceland were concerned. Even his opponent, Bjarnason, admitted as much. It is possible that both Sigtryggur Jonasson and Halldor Briem, especially the latter, who tried everything they could to make Thorlaksson's presence in the colony look suspicious, may have come to the same conclusion. Unable to admit as much, they blamed all the problems in New Iceland on Thorlaksson. A majority of the immigrants, both in Canada and the United States, saw in Thorlaksson's proposal a threat to their dream. This, however, did not emerge until Bjarnason expressed his opinions on the Norwegian Synod. Before his arrival, no one had objected to assistance from the Norwegians because the doctrines of the Norwegian Synod did not bother them. Thorlaksson had found the kind of Lutheranism that suited his faith and, bearing in mind the declining influence of the church in Iceland, he never doubted that the synod could be of considerable help to the Icelanders, spiritually and economically.

Had Bjarnason never immigrated to North America, and had employment for Icelanders been available in Wisconsin, they might have settled in accordance with Thorlaksson's suggestions. Neither Jon Olafsson nor Sigtryggur Jonasson expressed any opposition to the synod until Bjarnason spoke his mind. Bjarnason, therefore, may have started the controversy through his objections to the synod's doctrines, and carried it further by encouraging the Icelanders in Wisconsin to search for a site where they could settle as a united ethnic group.

Public debate on the religious disagreement between the pastors was limited. Many people expressed their dislike of the synod and usually based their arguments on the synod's attitudes towards matters such as slavery, dancing, and interest on money, but they seldom spoke out with theological or religious conviction. The reason for this was probably a lack of sophisticated understanding of such matters and this, in turn, explains why people hardly ever expressed themselves in print about the entire dispute and why their voices were somewhat unclear at the meetings at Gimli.

This lack of training in religious dogma and in the administration of ecclesiastical affairs can be attributed to the traditions of the Church of Iceland, which had made no allowance for public participation in the governing of its affairs. When the Icelandic settlers suddenly had to choose between the kind of Lutheranism represented by the synod and the one practised in Iceland, their own views of their roles as citizens of a new country took precedence over religious consideration. Both factions would remain Lutheran, and although the synod's approach differed from the one in Iceland, the prospect of assistance amply compensated for this difference.

Those who felt they needed to adjust to a new, North American way of life considered the synod a means by which such an adjustment could be achieved. On the other hand, those who were determined to remain loyal to their Icelandic culture and religious tradition were firmly opposed to any interference from a foreign religious organization. Although Thorlaksson had been an active leader of his countrymen in Wisconsin before 1875, he did not perform a religious service for the majority of them until August of 1876 in New Iceland. This marked the first point at which people in New Iceland sensed what, to them, must have been a deviant scriptural exposition. But this did not concern them as much as the thought of losing control over their church and schools. Thus, they did not argue about Thorlaksson's literal interpretation of the Bible. Their main concern was freedom of language and culture.

The insinuation from both Bjarnason and Briem, that the synod threatened the participation of the Icelanders in church and school matters, was perhaps overly cynical. There is no evidence from the period of Thorlaksson's tenure in New Iceland of unsolicited interference by the synod. Thorlaksson undoubtedly followed the procedures of the synod during his service in Canada. Therefore, his congregations may be said to have been part of it unofficially, although the general membership never saw it that way. Being in the synod's employ, Thorlaksson naturally maintained close relations with it and may even have attended some of its conferences and meetings as a concerned individual, since his congregations never elected him their official delegate. The only time they ever sought his assistance in their relations with the synod was in January 1878.

The synod, therefore, never gained the control in New Iceland that Briem and others had feared. Whether any such possibilities ever existed is doubtful. After Thorlaksson's death in 1882, for example, the synod's influence among the Icelanders gradually vanished. Briem's continued accusations against the synod in *Framfari* were, therefore, probably unjustified and although he frequently maintained that he knew of immigrants in the United States who had accepted assistance from the synod and later found themselves helpless under its power, he never provided any evidence or substantiated his allegations.

Briem's writings on the synod were often lacking in logical coherence and seemed primarily designed to malign Thorlaksson and the synod. It certainly seems doubtful whether Briem, in his opposition to Thorlaksson, ever received any encouragement from Bjarnason; their strategies were quite different. Briem, a quick-tempered man, often reacted spontaneously to views opposing his own and was reluctant to accept advice from others. He had the opportunity to study the synod and claimed that he had learned enough to criticize it, so any consultation on his part with Bjarnason seems improbable.

Bjarnason, on the other hand, made his statements cleverly and argued them logically. His "Necessary Exhortation" is proof of such work. The name of his article indicates that what Briem had written, in Bjarnason's opinion, had in no manner clarified the difference of opinions between the pastors. Although Bjarnason never expressed any dislike of Briem, at least not in writing, it may perhaps be suggested that through his article he silently disapproved of his methods. Others, however, did not hesitate to express their views on Briem. Fridjon Fridriksson at Gimli was one. Before Bjarnason had left New Iceland, he had ordained Halldor Briem in order not to leave his congregations without the services of a pastor. Briem, incidentally, had graduated from the Theolgical Seminary in Reykjavík in 1875 and emigrated from Iceland the same year without ordination. In a letter to Bjarnason from Gimli, 19 December 1880, Fridriksson expressed his dislike of Briem, and criticized his immature conduct and his inability to stir the hearts of the members of his congregations.

Even though Halldor Briem advocated unity among the settlers in New Iceland, his contributions had a contrary effect. He appears to have wanted Thorlaksson and his strongest supporters out of the colony. Prospects of unity were perhaps never good, and Thorlaksson may also have stood in the way as his attempts to win support in New Iceland was never very successful. However, hopes of reconciliation were high among the general public at the first meeting. On the other hand, Briem's articles in *Framfari* aggravated an already sensitive situation, since they were excessively critical of the synod and its interference in the affairs of the Icelanders.

During the course of the debate, most of the settlers realized that before they came to North America, their participation in religious affairs had been very limited. It was clear that in the absence of meaningful individual contributions, their church in the New World could not provide the foundation for an active religious life. As a result, religion became more important to them than ever before. The disagreement between the pastors undoubtedly contributed to the crystallization of a new religious awareness, which marked the beginning of a process that led to renewed religious controversies for years to come. However, the encounter between Bjarnason and Thorlaksson came to an end with the departure of Thorlaksson from the colony in 1879 and Bjarnason's return to Iceland in 1880. The dream of one, exclusive, Icelandic settlement in North America, where all Icelandic immigrants could live together, had come to an end.

8
New Iceland: On the Crossroads

Despite their ongoing controversy, the two pastors worked hard to support members of their congregations. The life of the pastor in New Iceland during these pioneer days was anything but easy. Bjarnason's congregations were scattered throughout the entire colony, from Boundary Creek in the south to Hecla in the north, a distance of many kilometres. Halldor Briem occasionally took his place by leading religious services at Icelandic River and in Hecla.

The Bjarnasons made many trips during their tenure in New Iceland. Their schedule was always tight. Every month they made one trip north and another south in the colony. The summer journeys were tougher as the road was difficult and the bugs a constant pest. In addition, they often were obliged to spend nights under difficult circumstances. Poverty in many places was such that the food offered consisted only of fish, milk, and potatoes. Many of the homes in the colony were in poor condition. In addition to the general hardship endured during his travels, Bjarnason never received the promised pay. His congregations had agreed that his annual fee would be $600.00 but he never received full payment. *Framfari* stated that he had been paid $284.00 the first year, and $374.00 in the second.[1]

In many ways, Thorlaksson had a much easier time in New Iceland. His congregations were close to one another so his travels were never as difficult as

Bjarnason's. He only resided in the colony during the winter months, as he still served congregations in Wisconsin. But during his time in the colony, Thorlaksson never stopped working. He was constantly out among his people, assisting in every way he could and always ready to help, including those of Bjarnason's congregations in times of desperation. The following excerpt from a settler's diary gives some indication of Thorlaksson's activities:

1977
Friday, 19 October: Rev. Pall Thorlaksson arrived.
Sunday, 21 October: Rev. Thorlaksson held a meeting in this house and explained why he became a pastor and explained in detail his faith and religious conviction.
Monday, 22 October: Rev. Thorlaksson returned from Arnes district.
Tuesday, 23 October: Rev. Thorlaksson examined the population of his congregation in the southern part of the Vidirnes district.
Wednesday, 24 October: Rev. Thorlaksson was here to take a member's count.
Sunday, 28 October: Seven of us in this household traveled to Dadastadir in order to attend a religious service performed by Rev. Thorlaksson.
Sunday, 18 November: All seven of us attended Rev. Thorlaksson's service.
Monday, 19 November: Rev. Thorlaksson along with two others walked west to explore lands.
Wednesday, 21 Nov.: The group returns.
Wednesday, 28 Nov.: Meeting at Hofn in Arnes district to discuss congregational Laws. Some nine people attended along with Rev. Thorlaksson.
Monday, 3 December: Service at Jon Hjalmarson's.
Wednesday, 5 Dec.: Choir practice at Rev. Thorlaksson's. [2]

Thorlaksson also frequently travelled south to Winnipeg to see how his countrymen lived in the town. He helped young men find work and placed women in jobs as housemaids. However, his assistance was not always appreciated. Many of the influential men in the settlement considered him a threat to the progress in the colony. There is, perhaps, little wonder that he began to pay attention to those of his supporters in New Iceland who contemplated a settlement elsewhere.

During the winter of 1876-1877, the Canadian government arranged for the survey of all of New Iceland. Only the southernmost part had been surveyed in 1875. The district was about fifty-seven kilometres by fourteen, 1296 homesteads. Straight lines were chopped around each section, one and a half kilometres by one and a half, and marks were left clearly visible to show how each section could be divided into four homesteads.

Areas for three towns in the colony were surveyed at the same time; Gimli, one and a half kilometres along the lake and about a kilometre in width; Sandvik, located in the northeast corner of the settlement, one kilometre along the lake and 650 metres in width; and Lundur, located about five kilometres up Icelandic River on the southeastern side and the same size as Sandvik. Each town lot was about twenty-two metres wide and forty-four metres long.[3]

Shortly after the arrival of the large group in 1876, the government also had surveyed to build a fifty-eight-kilometre road along Lake Winnipeg from the south to the north. Work was started immediately. The building of this road was quite simple: trees and other vegetation were cleared, roots pulled, and the road path evened. The northernmost road in Manitoba only reached Netley Creek in the south, about twenty-two kilometres from the border of New Iceland. The road through New Iceland was, therefore, continued until it was connected with the one in Manitoba. The new road was eighty kilometres long. The task was completed in the winter, and the total cost, covered by the Canadian government, was $10,500.00. This road remained the highway of the settlement for a long time and was normally difficult to travel in the fall and spring, and even in rainy summers. Winter use was better as the ground froze solid under a layer of snow. Though settlers often cursed the road, it was an important means of transportation.[4]

Pay for the road-workers was low, about sixty to seventy cents per day, but it was supplemented with good meals for all workers, much better meals than most settlers were used to. Icelandic women found work in the kitchen and were paid the same as the men. Here they gained valuable experience in handling and cooking local foods. The men also gained experience in the use of the axe and other tools. These were mostly young men who worked in two groups, one working from Gimli north towards Icelandic River, while the other chopped and dug on the path south to Netley Creek.

Lord Dufferin was Governor General in Canada from 1872 to 1878. He had assisted the Icelanders in Ottawa and thus had had a hand in the settlement of New Iceland. He had already travelled west to British Columbia and had visited the eastern regions of Canada, so only the Territory of Keewatin, North-West Territories, and Manitoba had yet to be visited. He was well received wherever he went and there was considerable excitement among the Icelanders once news reached the colony that he intended to pay a visit. As a young man of thirty in 1856, he had sailed his yacht, *Foam*, from England all the way north to the small island of Svalbard. During this journey he had stopped over in Iceland and spent considerable time on the island, travelling and exploring.

The original plan was that the Governor General would visit Gimli on 6 September and on that day a large crowd had gathered, waiting with great anticipation. But a problem with the steamer *Colville*, which was supposed to pick up Lord Dufferin at Fort Alexander, changed all plans. The steamer became grounded in the mouth of the Red River and was not freed until the 9th. It immediately headed for Fort Alexander, but the Governor General had become tired of waiting and had just left the harbour on a sailing boat, heading for Mikley. However, when the *Colville* caught up with him, Lord Dufferin decided that since he was already days behind the scheduled visit to Gimli, he would go on to Grand Rapids, about 288 kilometres northwest of Gimli, where the Hudson's Bay Company had a trading post.[5]

On his return from the north, the Governor General wanted to visit Gimli on the 13th, a week late. The settlers of New Iceland made hasty preparations at Lundi near Icelandic River. The captain of the steamer complained about a shortage of coal aboard his vessel and refused to approach Icelandic River. Neither would he stop in Gimli, but continued south, up the Red River to Stone Fort. All women aboard went ashore but early the next morning, on 14 September, Lord Dufferin managed to persuade the captain to make the return trip to Gimli.

No one was expecting the Governor General, but suddenly *Colville* appeared on the horizon, sailing straight for Gimli. John Taylor went out to meet Lord Dufferin, and took him to visit every home in Gimli. Afterwards, he wanted to inspect local farming and, with Taylor and Fridriksson, walked five kilometres west, where he examined three farms. It was noted that he took his time and studied the buildings and fields without comments. He later asked for reports on the economic situation in New Iceland and if the farmers were content and what their plans were.

By 4:00 p.m., more than 100 Icelanders had gathered in a semicircle in front of a platform on which were seated the Governor General and his entourage. Fridjon Fridriksson addressed him in Icelandic but handed Lord Dufferin a translation in English. He recalled the hardships endured by the settlers in New Iceland during the last two years, including the shortage of food, scurvy, floods, and the smallpox epidemic. He thanked the government of Canada for the financial support, describing how that assistance had kept the settlers alive. He then moved on to more positive issues. He claimed the soil in numerous parts of the colony was good for agriculture, and he noted the abundance of fish in the lake and trees for the construction of future homes. The program concluded with toasts to the Governor General, Queen Victoria, and the British Empire, of which the settlers in New Iceland had become part.

Lord Dufferin then rose and addressed the gathering. He discussed his visit to Iceland, the kindness bestowed upon him, and his general fondness of the Icelandic people. He stated he was well aware of the hardships endured during the last two years by the Icelandic settlers in New Iceland and the suffering during the smallpox epidemic. However, he claimed he had yet to speak to one settler in the colony who expressed discontent with New Iceland. Good knowledge of three things was essential for the Canadian settler—wood-chopping, tilling of soil, and construction of roads—he said, "but as you, in your native land, never gazed upon tall trees, vast green fields or proper roads, it cannot be expected that you will immediately show much skill in such areas."[6] He encouraged everyone to work hard, stating that in due course they would gain valuable experience and that progress in the colony was inevitable. It was his conviction that the Icelanders in Canada would adjust to their new environment in a short while, due to the high standard of education in Iceland and the general thirst for printed matter.

The Governor General repeatedly complimented the Icelanders on the accomplishments of their forefathers, who also faced calamities. The ability not only to survive but to overcome hardships was in the blood of every Icelander, he said, and the settlers in Canada would put this ability to use in adjusting to Canadian ways. He praised the many young women who had spent some time in a Canadian household, learning not only the English language, which every immigrant needed to learn, but also the economy of the home. Several of these women had returned to the colony and their homes reflected what they had learned. Diplomatically, he made suggestions for improvements or changes including, for example, the general use of open fireplaces.

He concluded by pointing out that the settlers from Iceland should remember that once they were in Canada, they became a part of a nation that was supportive and generous. Becoming subjects of the British Empire and adjusting to different ways of life did not signify the severance of ties with their Icelandic heritage and culture. On the contrary, Lord Dufferin encouraged the settlers to preserve their love of Icelandic literature and hoped that one generation after the next would inherit the same interest in ancient Icelandic culture. Finally, he wished them every success in their settlement, claiming that in his conversations with his Canadian friends, he always maintained his faith in the Icelandic settlers.

Only three days after his departure, on 17 September, two government ministers, David Mills and C.A.P. Pelletier, appeared in the colony aboard the steamer *Lady Ellen*. During their voyage downriver, they picked up a few Icelandic women also travelling to New Iceland. These were newly arrived settlers just in from Iceland. Their husbands remained on the scows, which floated downriver and were eventually pulled to Gimli. The ministers visited homes in Gimli, asking every settler questions relating to their general well-being and the prospects of the settlement. They also visited nearby farms, south, west, and north of Gimli. Not only did they examine every home, but also walked around each farmland to see what improvements had been made. The ministers pointed out that nearly all the hastily constructed huts from the fall of 1875 had been demolished, and new buildings erected. Although signs of poverty were evident, all the houses were clean and tidy. Approximately 600 cows had been brought to the settlement, many of which had been purchased with money earned by young people in Winnipeg or on Manitoba farms. The gardening was improving, especially the growing of potatoes, but also turnips and cabbage. While grain had not grown well, hopes were high for the following year. The settlers had built boats and their fishing nets had improved.

The inspectors thought there were plenty of supplies available for the winter. They were impressed with the youth, the increasing knowledge of English, the Regional Council, and the publishing of *Framfari*. They departed convinced that New Iceland had all the necessary ingredients to succeed. The report by Mills and Pelletier pointed out that the settlement contained many qualities of a successful pioneer settlement.[7]

Caroline Taylor, or Carrie, who was John Taylor's niece, organized the first elementary school in New Iceland during the winter of 1875-1876, and instruction began in early January of 1876. The following winter, Caroline's sister, Janet Taylor, took over instruction at the school. The school was in operation for two years and was well attended, but the actual number of students each year is unknown. There are no records of any other schools in the colony at this time, nor is there any clear evidence of elementary or Sunday schools in Thorlaksson's congregations. However, as *Framfari* is the chief source of information, the absence of such information from the pages is perhaps to be expected. *Framfari* was critical of everything Thorlaksson did, and may have chosen to remain silent regarding the education of children in Thorlaksson's congregations. Had he neglected the children, there is little doubt that Halldor Briem would have made it known to all his readers. However, in Thorlaksson's congregational laws, an elementary school teacher is mentioned twice: Section 12 refers to "legal reasons for the dismissal of a pastor or elementary school teacher"; and Section 19 reads: "The majority of votes of all eligible voters in the congregation is required for a pastor or an elementary school teacher to be elected."[8] Thorlaksson, true to the rules and regulations of the Norwegian Synod, must have seen to it that a teacher was elected in each of his congregations. Schools may not have been established but teachers who travelled between the districts provided instruction. It is most likely that the children visited the home of the teacher or gathered in somebody's house, just as people did to hear Thorlaksson's service. In the new settlement in Dakota, Thorlaksson had organized a school during the first winter of 1879-1880. A Dakota settler, Jon Jonasson, wrote on 7 January 1880 to a friend in Iceland that "three schools have been established this winter and the instruction goes well."[9] In a newsletter written in Gimli, 9 October 1878, and published in the synod's *Evangelisk Luthersk Kirketidende* in Decorah, Iowa, Thorlaksson stated that "Fr. Bergmann from Decorah has kept school here in my congregations during my absence much to the delight and support of all during times of suffering and mockery on behalf of our rivals in religious matters."[10] A short note in *Framfari* mentioned the same Bergmann: "Fridrik Bergmann, son of Jon Bergmann in Gimli, a student at Decorah, arrived here in the colony late in June. He keeps school in Thorlaksson's congregations this summer."[11]

Rev. Jon Bjarnason established a Sunday school in New Iceland in November of 1877, during his first journey through the settlement. After his religious service at Icelandic River, 18 November, a regular Sunday school was established for children and teenagers. Four individuals were responsible for instruction at four different locations in the northern part of the settlement. The first lessons took place the following Sunday. Illiterate children were taught how to read, and both children and teenagers were examined in general knowledge, and given religious texts to read and interpret. The principal purpose of Sunday school was to teach reading and prepare children and youth for their Christian instruction. Older children and teenagers were also taught the basics in math. Bjarnason established such schools in all his congregations.

Following a tiring journey in the fall of 1877, he suggested the establishment of a school in Gimli, which was started before Christmas of 1877. The principal teacher at the school was his wife, Lara Bjarnason, but others contributed to the instruction. Children attended the school, which was held in the old supply building at Gimli, for five days a week but on weekends it was used for religious services. Everyone was welcome to attend, regardless of the faction to which they belonged. During the first winter, forty-two students attended and were taught reading, writing, math, geography, English, and music (singing). In addition, Rev. Bjarnason gave instruction in religious matters when time permitted. Children were only required to be partly literate in order to be accepted, and all the instruction was free of charge. School was out on 22 April.[12]

This elementary school should have been the precedent for every Icelandic community in North America. Lara Bjarnason continued with the school the following year with the support of her husband and Fridjon Fridriksson. School was adjourned on Maundy Thursday, in the spring of 1879, following a religious service. The principal teacher tested the students that day in reading, singing, geography, and in the English language. Kristjan Jonsson kept a similar school that same winter, 1878-1879, in Vidirnes district, where the children met on Wednesdays and Sundays. At Icelandic River, another school was organized, with teachers Sigtryggur Jonasson, his wife Rannveig, Torfhildur Thorsteinsdottir Briem, and Halldor Briem. Twenty-two children were in attendance that school year. On 14 October 1879, *Framfari* stated that school would be operated in Gimli in the same fashion as before but would commence considerably earlier. For that purpose, the old assembly hall (originally the supply house in 1875) was being prepared.

That school may have been in operation at Icelandic River the following year and possibly during the next few years. But once the pastors had gone and more than half the population had left, regular schools were not common. Only by Icelandic River was there any sign of community; elsewhere, people were scattered. There is little doubt, however, that children received instruction in reading, writing, math, and religious works in most homes, but other important subjects such as English were neglected. Icelandic remained the spoken language in the colony.

Written sources frequently mention the construction or use of churches or chapels in New Iceland.[13] The dream of the exclusive Icelandic settlement included having control of their churches without ties to any foreign religious body. But religious harmony was never achieved. Never before had a group of Icelanders become part of such heated religious controversy. *Framfari* devoted more space to this dispute than any other issue. It is, therefore, surprising that none of the congregations on either side ever managed to build a church, especially as there was ample wood. As soon as it was clear that Thorlaksson and Bjarnason would serve congregations in the colony, both sides did plan to build churches and schools. One of Thorlaksson's letters from Dakota stated that his people had to walk away from partly built churches in New Iceland when they moved south. Skafti Arason, who settled in Kjalvik in the Vidirnes district and later became a successful farmer in Argyle, wrote in his diary around 1880 that a few chapels had also been constructed.[14] Judging from reports in *Framfari,* the buildings in question originally were intended to be used as churches but were also used as assembly halls and schools. New Iceland was not to be the site for the first Icelandic church in America.

A report translated from the *Free Press* in Winnipeg was published in *Framfari* in July 1878, discussing progress made by Mennonites in Manitoba since arriving in 1875.

> As is well known to everyone, Mennonites secured themselves a reserve in the south of Manitoba. This year they expect to harvest some 18,000 acres and crops look promising. Aside from wheat they also seeded 350 bushels of flax. They already have sixteen threshing machines and recently they purchased a steam threshing machine. A wheat windmill has been built in their settlement.... The Mennonites have accomplished some great things. Recently they built a road through the St. Norbert Swamp, some eight miles long towards their colony. In all it is sixteen miles long. Through the swamp it is some four feet high and wide enough that two carts, each pulled by two horses, can be driven along it side by side. The road is impressive but 500 people with some 380 oxen completed the task in six days....[15]

Framfari occasionally reported on issues pertaining to agriculture, fishing, or commerce in the colony. On 24 July 1878, a report from the Vidirnes district, the only area in which raising sheep was attempted, stated that wolves and bears had appeared in the district and sheep were missing from the area. Health in the district generally was good and haymaking had begun on 1 July.[16] Wheat and potatoes appeared to be doing fine and free of all insects. The last remark refers to a common concern throughout the settlement. A letter from Mikley stated that farmers in some places had had to seed three times, as everything that came up was destroyed by some type of larva or worms. Farmers were hopeful that their last seeding might make it.

Initial attempts to break the land and raise crops in different parts of the settlement often failed, because the land chosen was too soggy, sandy, or rocky. Nevertheless, in 1878 a few farmers were successful. One of the largest wheat fields was by the Icelandic River, on a farm called Unaland, belonging to Eyolfur Magnusson and his sons. Its size was estimated at about one hectare. Another "big" field was on Mikley, where Magnus Hallgrimson supposedly had cultivated a little more than a hectare.[17] A year later, *Framfari* reported that the biggest farm was that of Eggert Gunnlaugsson, who lived just west of Gimli. His field covered one and a half hectares. Skuli Arnason, who had lived in the south of New Iceland, purchased Dvergasteinn, west of Gimli, and had crops growing in a field of one hectare. Neither Magnusson at Unaland nor Hallgrimson in Mikley were mentioned in this report, which indicates that neither farmer had expanded.

Despite the fact that most reports on agriculture were negative, progress was made in a few years. For example, Sigtryggur Jonasson purchased a mowing machine in the summer of 1878. One person could work the machine, which was pulled by a team of oxen. A young man from Unaland, Stefan Eyolfsson, son of Eyjolfur Magnusson, operated the machine. He managed to cover, on even land, about two hectares in one day, which was four times more than an individual could do by hand.

News from Mikley in the fall of 1878 stated that Sigurdur Jonsson had harvested just over thirty kilograms of beans from the eight kilograms he used for seeding. Asmundur Gudlaugsson, in the district of Vidirnes, had eighteen kilograms of the same type of beans. In that district, potatoes grew well, most of the farmers getting about forty to forty-eight bushels, but exceeding them all in Vidirnes was Jon Jonsson, who harvested 330 bushels.[18]

Pall Thorlaksson wrote from Gimli, 9 October 1878, to *Evangelisk Luthersk Kirketidende,* in Decorah, Iowa, that:

> Considering all circumstances here the future looks as can be expected. Most families, I hear, have harvested from 50-200 bushels of potatoes but potatoes appear to be the only item families grow with some success. It is time for fall fishing but to this point catches have been small. If the fishing becomes a success and people will have both plenty of fish and potatoes, then everyone should last the winter. But if the fishing fails I cannot foresee how men shall survive....[19]

Although such reports brought hope and optimism, the settlement was still vulnerable and ill-prepared for any additional hardship. *Framfari* published a report by Fridjon Fridriksson at Gimli in late November 1878, describing conditions in Arnes and Vidirnes districts.

> The fall was windy and wet; fishing was minimal here in these parts and also in Arnes district. Potatoes were damaged in numerous homes, as basements of houses were flooded and could therefore not be used. Attempts were made to store them outside, under layers of soil and hay but frost got to them. Consequently, what remains of quite a decent crop is insufficient in many homes. Food supply in many homes, especially in the Arnes district, is low but many families have nothing but potatoes. Many are extremely worried as food obviously will not become available at this time of year. It appears that yet another winter will be one of famine and suffering. Quite a few in these parts have become very tired of the struggle on their farms and long to get away. However, that is not by any means easy if people want to go free of all debts and other obligations. Dakota appears to be the main attraction. Talk of moving south has become just as common as discussion of moving to America from Iceland. This movement is quite normal and can be beneficial to many but at the same time it is discouraging to all who want to go but cannot.
>
> Winds have subsided and the last three weeks have been calm and quite

nice. However, ice on the lake has prevented men from fishing. Roads are in an awful state making impossible all transportation of goods from Winnipeg. This hurts my business as I am running out of so many important items.[20]

Clearly, the general outlook had worsened considerably from the time Thorlaksson wrote his newsletter in October until *Framfari* published Fridriksson's letter at the end of November.

The settlers in New Iceland were aware from the beginning that fishing in the big lake would be different from fishing in Iceland. From 1875 until late in 1877, they experimented with differently sized nets, in different places on the lake. Fishing was a necessity rather than a commercial activity. However, whenever their catch was good, fish could be traded for other important articles such as flour, wheat, or tools. After two years of settlement in New Iceland, settlers began to spend part of the winter out on the lake, many kilometres north.

On 8 December 1877, because food had become so scarce in the colony and fishing through the ice near Gimli was poor, Magnus Stefansson, Josef Schram, and Jon Gudmundsson travelled north to investigate fishing opportunities. John Taylor had learned from the Aboriginal people that fishing was good in the northern parts of the lake during the winter, and he had urged Magnus Stefansson to lead the small exploration party. *Framfari* stated that "if they are successful we hope others will join. Fridjon Fridriksson at Gimli is willing to pay eight cents for each whitefish caught."[21]

Stefansson had three excellent dogs but needed a sledge; his partners had two dogs and a sledge. Jon Bergman, with whom Stefansson was residing just west of Gimli, built a sledge three metres long. They started their journey on those two sledges with five dogs, a tent, some tea, grain, and pemmican. They travelled for two days and on the evening of the second day they placed their nets in the lake and prepared themselves for the night. At dawn, they examined the nets and discovered twelve whitefish. Magnus Stefansson later said they became so excited with their first catch that they stayed there for three weeks. The food supplies lasted a week; after that they ate only fish for another two weeks before they returned. In Gimli, John Taylor was in the midst of arranging a search party. *Framfari* brought the good news of their return and good fishing:

> It has been pointed out in Framfari that three young men went from Gimli north to Grindstone Pont searching for whitefish. After trying their luck in different places, without catching much and their food supplies running out, they persisted and just southwest of Grindstone Point their luck changed. In just ten days Magnus Stefansson, Josef Schram and Jon Gudmundsson caught more than 500 whitefish. Each brought back 200 fish, so the total catch was 600. The first two mentioned arrived in Gimli just before New Year, bringing 300 fish and were quite pleased with their trip. They stated that there had been just as much fish when they left so they were determined to return. They pointed out

that very little had been caught in some nets as they were too small but other types brought more success. These fishing grounds are some twenty miles north of the mouth of Icelandic River and the depth is some 40 feet. When they started there was heavy current but it was much less by the time they left. Jon Gudmundsson decided to stay but was joined by Petur Palsson from the Icelandic River area. He had caught some 100 fish just as Stefansson and Schram were leaving.

The discovery of these excellent fishing grounds is the work of intelligent, energetic young men to whom we all are grateful. This gives hope of survival to many families not only just this winter but is evidence of excellent, future winter fishing.

The news of this success was most encouraging as some 20 men left from Vidirnes district, 12 from the district of Arnes and some 10 from the Icelandic River area. These men brought with them nets from others who opted to stay home. In return for fish these performed all necessary chores on the farms. This exchange of duties is a positive sign of communal enterprise, which we hope will continue.[22]

The winter of 1877-1878 turned out to be the mildest in New Iceland and was uncharacteristically mild throughout all of central North America. Had the winter been of average temperature, when frost and snow make dwelling outside quite dangerous, there would not have been much fishing and the food shortage would have been most serious. The Rev. Bjarnason pointed this out in one of his sermons in the spring:

One thing is certain, and that is, God has been more generous to these people this winter than anyone dared to hope for last fall as He has removed the extreme cold and thus minimized people's lack of proper outfits. He maintained almost a steady calm throughout the winter, thus enabling everyone who needed, to find food ... the little food available last fall has been multiplied in quantity.[23]

Men were also experimenting elsewhere. A report in early January of 1878 stated that men had had good luck fishing at the mouth of the Icelandic River. Two brothers, Halldor and Thorgrimur Jonsson, had been most successful. Halldor Jonsson had caught on a single hook 150 pike in shallow water a little distance upriver. The ice was sixty centimetres thick and 120 centimetres deep. The average weight of the fish was one and a half kilograms but one pike weighed seven kilograms. Later in the winter, on 12 March, a few Aboriginal people arrived in Gimli from Doghead Point and brought the news that some Icelanders had fished well north of Little Grindstone Point. At the same time, men were also catching fish in nets in the river and, in various places off the coast, pike, pickerel, and goldeye. At Easter, numerous nets were lost in the lake, both in Arnes district and Breidavik, when ice drifted up to the shore. In March, eighteen men in the southern region of the district of Arnes caught 2538 fish and at the end of April, one man by Icelandic River caught fifty fish overnight, mostly goldeye. Good-sized pike were caught in Breidavik in the following summer.

During the first half of May, fishing near Gimli was good; sometimes, a few hundred fish were caught daily. Fishing near Mikley was also good in May, especially in the second half. All types of fish were caught, mostly whitefish in the northern waters, and catfish just south of the island.

A report in *Framfari*, 16 July 1878, stated that Eyjolfur Benediktsson in Breidavik had caught 2500 fish since he started fishing in the spring. In October of the same year, Johannes Sigurdson at Icelandic River caught 250 whitefish and a few of other kinds. But fishing in the fall began to decrease and catches of whitefish became smaller. Overall, the catch of whitefish this fall was much less than in previous years. This was probably due to unexpectedly cold weather.

As the whitefish more or less vanished from the waters next to the settlement, settlers again decided to go north. In October, twenty-five people from the Arnes and Vidirnes districts and Icelandic River tried their luck around Mikley and Deer Island. A few tried areas near Little Grindstone Point, where 400 fish were caught, but only seventy whitefish. Some people went as far north as Moose and Reindeer islands, and fished for three weeks, bringing back 500 whitefish and 100 of other types. Tomas A. Jonasson and his companion, Thorstein Antoniusson, built their camp on the south shore of Mikley and had by far the best catch that fall. Each landed close to 400 whitefish during a period of just under three weeks. Jon Bjarnason (not the pastor) in Mikley had netted 450 whitefish in a little over three weeks.

In the Vidirnes district, fishing was reasonable throughout the summer—mostly pike, pickerel, and goldeye—but in early November only a few whitefish were caught. Miserable conditions throughout the fall made fishing strenuous. On 15 November, a bad storm caused the loss of nets. In Sandvik, for example, twenty-nine nets were lost. A week later, *Framfari* finally printed a good fishing report: "The good news reached the paper from Mikley earlier this month, that in the middle of the worst fishing season experienced here, Magnus Hallgrimsson and another man had in two weeks caught more than 1000 whitefish by Bad Throat River on the east side of the lake."[24]

It seems clear that the settlers became more dependent on fishing during 1878. They not only improved their fishing technique but also discovered some very important fishing grounds. However, the poor catches in the fall made it clear that more than just fishing was needed in the colony. The spring seeding was somewhat neglected due to the excellent fishing and few attempts were made to improve the state of agriculture.

On 7 January 1879, *Framfari* reported that whitefish were abundant by Little Grindstone Point and that many men were on their way to the area. The next issue, 4 February, reported that the fishing in the Grindstone Point area was essentially over and that the catch was a tremendous benefit to all. Petur Palsson from Icelandic River had the best catch, more than 1000 whitefish, having begun fishing in mid-December. Sixty people fished in the area, and the total catch was estimated at 60,000.

Fishing was attempted in different parts of the lake. For example, in the second half of February, six men from the Vidirnes district went up to the mouth of the Red River and, during five days of fishing, caught 2150 pike. On Easter Sunday the ice broke near Icelandic River and right away there was some good fishing just north of Lund. It was poorer closer to the lake. Throughout the summer, fishing in general was good but the number of men fishing was decreasing as so many were leaving. Just as vital experience had been gained, other factors meant only a few people benefitted.

The commercial transactions of 1878 show how important it was for the settlers to be within close range of a large market. Whatever their original dream had been, life in New Iceland during the previous three years left no one in any doubt that communication of every kind with the surrounding settlements and communities was necessary. It had been their dream to grow grain and all the vegetables needed, catch all the fish required, and make all necessary tools and equipment themselves. However, one year of settlement convinced them that such would not be the case.

The settlement needed a store, where the settlers could exchange their wares for necessities. The function of such an establishment depended on two crucial factors: first, access to a bigger market, where the merchant could trade the settlers' products and where he could purchase necessities; and second, in order to succeed in his transactions at a bigger market, the merchant had to offer quality goods in demand. New Iceland was isolated; transportation to and from the settlement was always difficult and, at certain times of year, dangerous. The settlers could not compete with more skilful settlers in agriculture so fish became their most valuable commodity, especially whitefish.

The first Icelander to establish a store in North America was Sigtryggur Jonasson, who hired Fridjon Fridriksson to operate the primitive store in Kinmount, Ontario. Young Fridriksson gained valuable experience and John Taylor chose him to operate the original government supply store in New Iceland. Fridriksson dominated the commercial scene in New Iceland during the first two years.

In early January in 1878, Jon Julius and Arni Sigvaldason arrived in the settlement from Winnipeg. They brought 115 sacks of flour, all of which they sold quickly in the colony. Another settler, Sigurdur Kristofersson, sold seventy sacks. The price of a sack at the time was $3.00 to $3.30. About the same time, in early 1878, a Canadian toured the settlement, offering a sack of flour for forty whitefish.[25]

Samson Bjarnason operated a small store in the Icelandic River community, trading flour and other necessities for fish. Bjarnason, who also travelled to Mikley and the Arnes district to do business, was aware of the needs of his countrymen and travelled long distances to meet their demands. In April of 1878, he went on his boat all the way to Minnesota to obtain supplies. Fridjon Fridriksson also went south for supplies at the same time and both he and Bjarnason returned to New Iceland after a week. Bjarnason proceeded north along the coastline to Sandvik, making numerous stops on the way to trade. He returned south in the middle of May, having sold nearly all his goods.

Two weeks after his return from Winnipeg, Fridriksson advertised the following goods:

Linen— 5-16 cents per yard
Tobacco—45-60 cents per lb.
Coffee—35 cents per lb. (3 lbs. for $1.00)
Sugar—16 cents per lb.
Bacon—12.5 cents per lb.
Quality flour—$3.00 per sack [26]

Fridrikson also advertised that he bought whitefish at nine cents per fish, which was the going rate in the settlement, but it was neither the highest nor the lowest rate. Others bought whitefish at eight to eleven cents each, but the highest price per fish was paid in Winnipeg, which at one point went as high as sixteen to twenty cents per fish. Normally, though, prices in the city were lower.

Samson Bjarnason returned to the colony in June and, along with his companion, Sigurdur Myrdal, took his boat full of supplies to Hecla to do business. On their way back, they stopped at Icelandic River and Sandvik. Bjarnason returned to Icelandic River on 9 October. Among the items he offered and sold were:

Flour—$3.35 per sack (he sold 45)
Coffee—35 cents per lb. (3 lbs. for $1.00) (sold 35 lbs.)
Sugar—6 cents per lb. (sold 80 lbs.)
Tobacco—40-75 cents per lb. (sold 30 lbs.)
Salt—2.5 cents per lb. (a barrel for $5.00) (sold 5 barrels)
Kerosene— 15 cents a quart, 12.5 cents for 10 quarts or more (sold 20 gallons)[27]

In addition, he sold different items such as linen and soap pipes (for stoves) for $50.00 to $60.00. On this trip to the Icelandic River community, he sold goods for around $280.00.

Sigurdur Myrdal was now operating his own small store in Sandvik. On 21 November, he intended to go to Winnipeg in order to buy supplies but, due to heavy storms, he only made it to Gimli. He sold some whitefish at eight cents per fish in Fridriksson's store and purchased supplies for his own store for $200.00.

Samson Bjarnason made it to Os, near Icelandic River, just before Christmas on a sledge pulled by two oxen. He sold his wares and purchased whitefish at ten cents each.

Shortly after Christmas, Stefan Eyjolfsson from Unaland brought whitefish from Little Grindstone Point on his sledge to Manitoba. He had bought each fish for eleven cents and at Sandvik he was joined by Sigurdur Myrdal, who also had some business interests in Manitoba at the time. This convoy, two sledges pulled by teams of oxen, each filled with whitefish, must have been quite a sight. The fact that such a trip was made at this time of year indicates that the settlers were becoming accustomed to the Manitoba winter.

In early 1879, a Canadian merchant travelled to the Little Grindstone Point, offering eleven cents' worth of flour for each whitefish. He left with 230 but returned six weeks later, this time paying eight cents per fish. He returned to Winnipeg that time with 550 fish.

Johannes Kristjansson, who later emigrated to Utah (in 1885), ran a small shop in the Icelandic River community and later in the Arnes district. He travelled to Winnipeg late in August and sold potatoes at thirty cents per bushel. He returned to Arnes, offering a sack of flour for $2.80 and a kilogram of sugar for seven cents.

Fridjon Fridriksson in Gimli had been the first person to operate a store in New Iceland, and by 1880, he was the only one. He travelled to Winnipeg late in the fall of 1879 to obtain supplies for the winter. Most of his customers in the Vidirnes district had left for either Dakota or Winnipeg. By 1881, he sold out in Gimli and bought Sigtryggur Jonasson's estate by Icelandic River, where there still remained a small community. Jonasson had left for Winnipeg.[28]

Conditions in the woods of New Iceland remained difficult. Cultivated land was limited; trees were piled up but went unused. The settlers did not invest in a vessel and a sawmill to process the lumber for sale, although there must have been a market for timber in Manitoba. However, the two most important ingredients for such an enterprise were lacking: familiarity with communal work, and knowledge of the lumber industry. The latter could have been overcome easily by hiring skilled workers to train the Icelandic settlers, but the general lack of interest in any type of communal effort was the major obstacle. A portion of the government loan devoted to such purposes would have proven more beneficial in the long run than the purchase of sacks of grain for seeding in non-existent fields.

The original dwellings were of poor quality and unwholesome. Lord Dufferin pointed out the mistake of using the cooking stoves as heaters because little or no fresh air was allowed inside. Children and older people suffered illnesses in these conditions and many died. The smallpox epidemic was one of many diseases that harassed the population in New Iceland.

Only a few months had passed from the day the quarantine from smallpox was lifted to when scarlet fever spread around the settlement. It was brought to the colony from Manitoba and was foreign to the settlers, just as the smallpox had been. *Framfari* reported: "Some inflammatory disease has been detected in children in the Arnes and Vidirnes districts. To our knowledge, three children have died."[29] On 4 January 1878, *Framfari* reported that the disease had been diagnosed as scarlet fever. Three children in the district of Arnes and one in the Vidirnes area had passed away. The report states that of those, three had had an uvulotomy just prior to catching the disease and died very quickly. The paper recommended that people refrain from such foolish practices. It also discussed a new medicine, which was believed to cure both diphtheria and scarlet fever but was "actually just nothing but sulpho-carbonate of soda."

According to *Framfari*, the settlers' health improved as they adjusted to the different climate, food, and water. On 20 February, *Framfari* reported that general health in the colony was better and that the scarlet fever was retreating, although the odd case was still reported. Deaths were few but on 5 April, the death of a young man just over twenty years of age was announced. The paper reported in the same issue that three young children had caught the disease in the home of Sigurdur Myrdal in the Arnes district.

Measles appeared in the summer and spread to every corner of the settlement in the next few months. The disease, like scarlet fever, was brought to New Iceland from Manitoba and first appeared in the southern regions of the Vidirnes district. Pall Johannsson, also known as Colonel Paul Johnson, reported from the area on 31 July that seven people were sick but no one was seriously ill. On 2 November, measles had reached every home in the district and apparently one child had died. On 11 December, it was stated in *Framfari* that the editor himself had caught the disease on 1 December 1878 but was slowly recovering. This means the measles had reached the Icelandic River area.

9
Migration from New Iceland

The growing discontent in New Iceland reached new heights in 1878. That year marked a turning point in the settlement. Rev. Thorlaksson had never approved of the colony site and Rev. Bjarnason, in his article in *Framfari* in July, had come to the conclusion that its future was bleak. Both men realized that the settlers needed a drastic change. While Rev. Bjarnason believed that non-Icelandic immigrants might be tempted to settle in New Iceland, Rev. Thorlaksson felt the only solution was a move out of the colony site onto the open, fertile prairie.

On 2 February 1878, a letter by Rev. Thorlaksson, addressed to a periodical in Iceland, was published in the pages of *Framfari*. In it, the clergyman compared New Iceland to the settlements of Icelanders in Minnesota and Wisconsin, where conditions were much better. There was unlimited pasture and hayland, and roads were good in the United States, while most of New Iceland was too low and wet for settlement. He was convinced that the colony would never prosper.

The editor of *Framfari* commented in reply that, once the woods had been cleared, conditions would improve. He believed that the market for fish had already been established, and that the river and lake provided adequate transportation to and from the colony, both in summer and winter. He concluded by saying there was very little room available in the Minnesota and Shawano settlements for additional Icelanders.

Neither *Framfari* nor community leaders managed to persuade the discontented to reconsider their plans for departure. The mud, the roads, the distance from markets, and the swarms of flies that gave the livestock little peace during the summer and greatly affected the yield of milk were only a few of the reasons for their decision. The appeal for help to the Norwegian Synod, which had been ridiculed by *Framfari,* resulted in hard feelings between neighbours. The animosity brought about by the religious controversy, which led to a lack of unity and cooperation in the settlement, had much more to do with the decision to depart than did the poor conditions.

Members of Thorlaksson's congregations met frequently. Jon from Mæri reported: "Meetings were held late that winter in Arnes district to discuss ways and means of improving conditions, for they had neither fish nor cattle to sell and there was no market for wood. So the conclusion was, although many did not like it that they must move away."[1] Thorlaksson left the colony for Minnesota in early April, and agreed to look for suitable land for those of his people in New Iceland who wished to leave.

The advance party that had originally secured the land for New Iceland had reserved the entire region for Icelanders only. At the Regional Council meeting held at Sandy Bar, 11 January 1878, Bjorn Jonsson, reeve of Vidirnes district, moved that settlers of all nationalities be allowed into the colony.[2] His motion was defeated in the council but the matter was referred to the district committees for further discussion. This was a democratic way of dealing with the issue because it permitted a general discussion throughout the colony.

Rev. Jon Bjarnason then raised the matter again in *Framfari,* 18 July 1878. Halldor Briem, editor of *Framfari,* responded that by opening up the reserve, they would have lost the battle to preserve Icelandic heritage and would soon Americanize their nationality, language, and thought. Briem did not want to give up the dream of an exclusive settlement so quickly. He thought the settlers had done as well as could have been expected, considering the circumstances in the colony during the first two years. He was convinced that practical knowledge would come soon and that progress would then be good. He asked how colonists could guarantee that only desirable settlers of other ethnic groups would find their way to New Iceland, arguing that there were many criminal organizations in North America and nothing could prevent them from reaching the colony. Moreover, he concluded, the reserve had not only been secured for the settlers already there, but also for future Icelandic immigrants whose rights should be safeguarded.[3]

Bjarnason responded that the Icelanders should accept the fact that they were becoming members of a new nation. To preserve the Icelandic heritage in North America should not be their chief concern. He asked if the English had come to America to establish a new England, the Germans a new Germany, or the Irish an Ireland. Every settler in Canada should accept new Canadian citizenship. Although he did not bring up the religious controversy, he mentioned the fact that there were some, in most respects honourable, people who refused to pay their subscriptions to *Framfari* on the grounds the paper had been and was too biased in church matters. The same people renounced their allegiance to the colony because they felt the government agents had not aided them fully in dealing with the government loan. It was the duty of all to pay their dues and to be obedient to the district reeve. Bjarnason repeated his previous statement that a closed reserve would never prosper and maintained that the more flourishing the colony, the better for the Icelandic settlers. He concluded by mentioning all the vacant land in the west of the colony, where there would be plenty for future settlers if the present site would be filled.[4] The debate continued. Briem responded that exclusive settlements existed in North America, even in Manitoba. The English had one and the Mennonites another.

The discussion on the issue was widespread. The major concern appeared to be the selection of appropriate people. It appeared that Briem's warning about criminals flocking to New Iceland troubled many of the settlers. The Regional Council presented no official statement regarding the issue. However, *Framfari* published an article by Sigtryggur Jonasson, who had resigned from the position of the governor of the Regional Council in March.[5] He had remained silent, perhaps understandably, since the shock of Bjarnason's change of heart still lingered in the colony. He warned people that migration was not a permanent solution to their present problems. In leaving, they escaped existing difficulties but should expect to find fresh reasons for discontent in another environment. Nonetheless, those settlers who so strongly desired to leave should go, as their discontent was harmful to all. Still, he insisted, it was the duty of everyone in the colony to unite in an effort to find a solution to the problems and to create a community life. He maintained that it was more true to the Icelandic spirit to face and overcome difficulties than to run away from them into uncertainty. He then began to discuss conditions in the colony and mentioned the wet land, pointing out that ditches needed to be dug and bridges built. He hoped that the Dominion government could be persuaded to contribute more towards the construction of the highway and that the provincial government would improve the road to the south and bridge Netley Creek. However, the settlers themselves would have to build all lateral roads. And, to those complaining of shortage of hay, he said they only needed to clear more land for grass.

In regard to possible future industries, he mentioned the selling of cordwood, pointing out that the treeless Red River valley was being settled, railroads were under construction, and steamers were increasing in number, and, consequently, Manitoba offered a fast-growing market for cordwood. He offered several solutions to getting the product to the market. One was to arrange with dealers to buy cordwood located in designated areas along the shore. Another was to establish a cooperative association in the settlement and build scows on which to transport the wood to market at Crossing and in Winnipeg. The cost of transporting the product might be as high as $3.00 to $4.00 per cord but the price at the market was between $4.50 to $5.00. He concluded that the present transportation cost was only half of what it had been at the beginning of settlement.

Elections for the councils had been held 2 January 1878. Sigtryggur Jonasson was elected governor of the Regional Council, and Olafur Olafsson, vice-governor. Elected reeves were Bjorn Jonsson from the Vidirnes district, Johann Stefansson of Arnes, Johann Briem from the River district, and Halldor Reykjalin from Big Island.[6] A committee appointed to study and make changes in the provisional constitution met at Sandvik on the 11th, and the New Iceland constitution became law with its publication in *Framfari* on 14 January. Some minor amendments were made, the most noteworthy of which clarified the duty and function of the Regional Council. It was to consider and advise on all matters pertaining to the progress in the colony, such as admission of non-Icelanders, supervision of the colony highway, lateral roads and bridges, and extension of the colony boundaries. The limited progress in the colony the previous year, the lack of initiative, and the increasing tension between the two factions undoubtedly were the main reasons for the clarification. People must have blamed the district committees and, above all, the Regional Council, which was considered the governing body of the colony.

As the committee at Sandvik finalized the constitution, Honourable David Mills, Minister of the Interior, was preparing Bill No. 23 to be introduced at the ensuing session of the Dominion government in Ottawa. It was referred to as the Keewatin Municipalities Bill. It was, in essence, based on the New Iceland constitution but more comprehensive because it provided for public schools. When he introduced the bill, Mills said that it conferred upon the future township municipalities powers like those exercised by the municipal councils in the provinces of Ontario and Manitoba. It provided for the appointment of assessors, uniform property rights, election of councillors, and division of the district into school sections. It granted powers to appoint trustees, employ teachers, and impose taxes for the purposes of building schools.

Mills defended his support for the bill by saying that all 1500 immigrants in the colony were well informed and intelligent. They were in Canada because of Danish oppression in Iceland. They were able to converse in the English language and, as an example of their literary activity, Mills pointed out that the Icelanders mailed four or five times as many letters, in proportion to their number, than other Manitoba settlers. He concluded by describing the literary society in the colony and the public library it had founded, which consisted of donations of books by members.

In his comments on the bill, Prime Minister Alexander Mackenzie stated that it was of such a nature that there could be hardly any objection. But members of the House rose one after another to express doubts and strong opposition. As an example, a Mr. Boswell questioned extending the franchise so widely, pointing out that Ontario had restricted the power given to the voters very materially by limiting the franchise to those directly affected by the creation of debt. Mr. Pope insisted that the councillors should be people with considerable stake in the country. A property qualification should be essential, perhaps possession of property valued at $300.00 to $500.00. Mr. Mills accused Mr. Pope of lack of faith in people, adding that a certain property qualification would be adopted immediately following the first election. Mr. Boswell was not finished and asked if aliens would have the vote. Mr. Mills said that all settlers except one were aliens, and added:

> The principle is perfectly sound. We have adopted an entirely different principle in this country from what prevails in England. We want the country settled, and aliens can hold property. In municipal institutions you represent property and the rights of property. Whether sound or not, there is no other principle applicable in a country like the North-West where we are seeking to secure the settlements of large communities of people who are not, but are going to be, British subjects.[7]

However, the Opposition was not finished, either. The ballot system came under fire. It was pointed out that the secret ballot was not in use in Quebec, yet the system there worked well. Recently, secret ballot had been introduced in Ontario but, in Manitoba, it had been abandoned after a brief trial. Mr. Mills pointed out that the reason it had been abandoned in Manitoba was the inability of people to write. Mr. Mitchell was appalled that the government was wasting time and effort on 1500 ignorant Icelanders, of whom only approximately eighty were voters. None of them, he believed, had ever had any opportunity of understanding the proper administration of municipal affairs. He concluded that it was a mistake to give to people who had no understanding of Canadian institutions the responsibility for working out such a measure.

Bill No. 23 was withdrawn at the close of the session and the government of New Iceland was obliged to carry on without the benefit of legal sanction from Ottawa.[8] The conclusion of this affair in Ottawa changed nothing in the colony. The New Iceland constitution was in full effect for almost twelve years.

People in the old country continued to contemplate immigration to North America. In 1877, only fifty-nine people emigrated from Iceland, all going to the Canadian colony, but in 1878, the steamer *Waldensian* arrived in Quebec in late summer, bringing 422 immigrants from Iceland. Fifty-one others found their way to different parts of North America that year, for a total of 473 immigrants from Iceland in 1878. Of the Quebec group, 186 decided to go to Winnipeg, 106 were destined for Toronto, and nine intended to travel to Nova Scotia. The remaining 121 intended to travel south to the United States but, having discussed prospects in Canada with Sigtryggur Jonasson, who was on hand to meet the group, thirty-five of the US group changed their minds and headed west, raising the total for Manitoba to 221. Of those, only forty remained in Winnipeg while the rest went to New Iceland.[9]

As an agent for the Dominion government, it was Jonasson's duty to persuade his compatriots to remain in Canada, but how he managed to convince them to travel to New Iceland remains a mystery. At the time, he knew that many people were seriously considering a move out of the settlement. He also knew that conditions were unfavourable and, although fishing had improved, farming, especially the growing of crops, had not met expectations. All financial assistance from the government had been terminated. However, as his article in *Framfari* indicated later that year, he still hoped to unite people in the colony. It just may have been his own firm conviction that eventually progress would be made and the colony would prosper.

The financial situation of this group was not much better than of those who arrived in 1876. It has been estimated that after paying the travel cost from Quebec to Winnipeg, the entire group had a little over $5000.00 between them. Those who had stopped in Ontario did not do so in order to find land, but out of necessity—they could not afford the fare all the way to Winnipeg. Many of them resolved to work until they had saved enough money to buy a ticket to Manitoba. Others remained uncertain about their future.

Travelling with the group destined to New Iceland was Jon Olafsson, who represented a group in Iceland and whose assignment was to examine conditions in New Iceland and then return to Iceland with a report. Olafsson's journey was sponsored by the Allan Line, which granted his return passage. He spent several weeks in the colony and returned to Iceland in October, reasonably impressed with the Icelandic River area.[10]

This was the first time someone had been sent from Iceland to explore areas and prepare potential emigrants for migration to North America. Reports from New Iceland had given a confusing picture of conditions. On one hand, Sigtryggur Jonasson and Halldor Briem described the situation as difficult but emphasized that a brighter future was just around the corner. Thorlaksson and his followers painted an entirely different picture, often describing the situation in the settlement as being hopeless. In Iceland, people were left confused and had no choice but to arrange for an independent exploration and an unbiased report.

Discouraging news from Icelandic settlements in North America was often magnified in the Icelandic media, especially by those who opposed emigration from Iceland. The criticism concentrated on two main aspects of the entire emigration movement; first, it attempted to describe all emigrants as useless parish-recipients; and, second, it gave a bleak description of Icelandic settlements in North America. The purpose was to discourage people from emigrating to North America. The ridicule in the media must have been disheartening.[11] People awaiting passage were described as sleeping in the streets and crowding restaurants and cafés. If a ship did not appear, they would return to their former district, most of them in quest of parish-relief.

Immigration reports from these years (1878-1879) also show that, in every group destined for New Iceland, a certain number always remained behind in Winnipeg. These people were often teenagers who were left in the city by their families for the purpose of finding work and earning some money while the rest of the family became settled. The plan was, of course, that they would join their parents in New

Iceland and many did. But there were always a few who did not find their way to the new home in the colony as planned. Young women or men found love and got married; employment turned out to be both satisfactory and rewarding; or, as the struggle in New Iceland certainly was not over, parents encouraged their offspring to hold onto secure prospects. There were also those who never intended to go any further, who realized they were a short distance away from the Icelandic settlement and could take up residence in the colony at any time they desired. Many of these immigrants were single and, to them, New Iceland had nothing to offer. As the years went by, a strong Icelandic community developed in Winnipeg.

Records show that 322 Icelanders emigrated to America in 1879. Only seventy made New Iceland their final destination. Two hundred and fifty-two arrived in Quebec and scattered over North America. There were 150 who went south to the United States, thirty-seven remained in Ontario, and sixty-five continued westward to Manitoba. Of them, thirty-four went to New Iceland.[12]

A new Canadian government had withdrawn its subsidy to immigrant fares, raising the fare from Quebec to Winnipeg from $12.50 to $20.00. The Icelandic immigrants had no knowledge of this increase and many were not prepared to meet this additional cost. Consequently, many people did not go on to Manitoba. A similar situation arose in New York, where many families intending to travel to New Iceland could not afford the fare. As the New York group wandered through the streets and contemplated the future at Castle Gardens, they became the sensation of the day. The *New York Star* gave the following account:

> The men were all of medium size and build, but they all had a hardy look. The women were small of stature, but showed evidence of qualities of great endurance. All the adventurers appeared to be happy, and they chatted together right merrily. The men were dressed plainly but not outlandishly, except that several of them wore shoes similar to the moccasin of the North American Indian.... The women were attired in dresses that reached down below the top of their shoes, the material being mainly alpaca. Their peculiar headdress consisted of a flat black pad about the size of a regular saucer. This was worn directly on the caput, while from it was suspended a tassel nearly a foot long, which swept the left shoulder at every step the wearer took.[13]

The immigration of 1879 reveals a change in the pattern of the previous three years. The majority of immigrants no longer went directly to New Iceland. Conditions in the colony deterred many. Moreover, Bjarnason's suggestion that future settlers scatter throughout North America rather than attempt to establish an all-Icelandic settlement made a considerable difference. No longer did immigrants dream of a large, exclusive, Icelandic settlement.

The people in New Iceland who contemplated a move out of the colony faced the problem of paying their share of the government loan. The land of each settler was the surety for the payment of the loan. Everyone felt obliged to pay their debts but most couldn't afford the payments. Discussions led to arguments over the terms of payment and some people were unjustly accused of evading their responsibilities. In the end, Sigtryggur Jonasson, the Assistant Icelandic Agent, was asked to clarify the issue. He responded to the request in *Framfari*. The loan was to date from 1 January 1879, with six percent interest, and paid in full by 1 January 1889.

Bjorn Petursson responded to Jonasson's article in *Framfari* on 28 March. He said that initially both settlers and the government had believed that the chosen colony site was a good one and that the small Icelandic community would prosper. However, the experiences of the last few years showed that the land site had certain serious drawbacks, which, in the views of many people, outweighed its good qualities. He believed that the government had intended the loan for the development of the settlement site but had been as disappointed with the outcome as the settlers had been. In short, the speculation simply had failed. Therefore, he thought that both parties should share the loss; it was unfortunate that the government should lose any portion of the loan, but it was worse that the settlers, who had worked hard for three years, should see no return. He said the government hitherto had shown the Icelandic settlers considerable nobility in all its dealings, which should encourage every settler intending to leave to pay as much as he could. His suggestion was that the government retrieve implements that had been bought with the loan but forgive money spent on food.

The Dominion government agreed with Petursson's suggestion: those moving out should be held responsible for stock and implements that had been bought with government money. In an effort to assist the settlers in earning money towards payment of their debt, the government made a $1000.00 appropriation in July of 1879 for the completion of the highway south of Gimli. This marked the end of the Dominion government's financial assistance to New Iceland.[14]

Sigtryggur Jonasson had commented on the possible move from New Iceland in an article in *Framfari* in December of 1878. He spoke his mind again in January 1879 when he clarified a misunderstanding regarding the government loan. These two articles make his position clear: he believed that improvements could be made in the colony; and, in order to succeed, all settlers must approach the monumental task with positive minds. In a three-page article in *Framfari,* he expressed his arguments for a closed colony and also his thoughts on what was needed to ensure progress in the settlement. He began by asking why the Icelanders should not be able to learn new, progressive methods in the isolation of New Iceland. In his opinion, adjusting to the North American way could just as easily be done in the colony as somewhere else on the continent. He then asked if there was no one in the settlement willing to build rather than tear down. " What is the role of the pastors in this matter?" he asked, and then answered, "To foster Christianity and if Christian faith is fostered in the hearts of people, other things would follow."[15]

He described how, from the time of his arrival in Canada, it had been his dream to establish an all-Icelandic colony where the Icelandic language would be spoken, and where books and papers in Icelandic would be published. Such an endeavour would not only preserve the written language but also enrich the literature of the Icelandic people. A colony of this nature would maintain the religion as practised in Iceland and ensure the promotion of Icelandic sentiment in North America. He recalled how it had been the intention of all the original settlers in New Iceland to be a credit to their motherland and that segregation was essential to fostering the Icelandic heritage. Despite all the setbacks, he was convinced such a colony could prosper. However, in order to succeed, those who supposedly were leaders should guide the people to work in harmony. The promotion of discontent and factions prevented progress. If the Icelanders scattered throughout America, all hope of publishing papers and books and maintaining the Icelandic religion would vanish. To expect Icelandic sentiment to survive under such circumstances was the same as to expect blood to flow through the veins when the heart had been removed, he said. An Icelandic colony would keep much stronger ties with the motherland and receive from it an important inspiration in years to come: the inspiration to maintain the language and heritage. Such an all-Icelandic settlement could then offer this gift to the mixed Icelandic settlements in the United States and Canada. Jonasson opposed Thorlaksson's view that the settlers would gain valuable experience working elsewhere before establishing their own colony. Experience could be gained in New Iceland. The all-Icelandic settlement had been established and seeking sites elsewhere for the same purpose made no sense. He claimed that only Aboriginal peoples were given reserves in the United States.

Jonasson continued by pointing out that at this stage there was no reason to open up the colony to people of other ethnic backgrounds. This did not mean that the colony could not prosper; although segregated, the settlers would be open to outside ideas and different ways of life. He was convinced that the continuing migration from eastern Canada to the prairie regions would gradually benefit the Icelandic colony, suggesting that the Canadian authorities could be approached to move the boundaries of the settlement further west. This would open up a vast area for those Icelanders who preferred the prairie.

He then changed his tone somewhat and appealed to his compatriots, reminding them of past accomplishments in Iceland despite endless hardship. He recalled Lord Dufferin's words when, at Gimli, he had encouraged the settlers of New Iceland to cherish the achievements of their ancestors. Jonasson stated that the Governor General had actually put his reputation at stake when he had claimed that he was in no doubt that the Icelanders would make their colony a success.

At the conclusion of his article, his bitterness, even anger, became evident. He attacked Thorlaksson, stating that the clergyman had encouraged migration from the colony at congregational meetings where religious matters alone were supposed to be discussed. Jonasson questioned Thorlaksson's legal right to encourage people who had received financial support from the Dominion government to move south to the States. He pointed out that Thorlaksson truly could be considered a US agent. Icelandic settlers should keep in mind the fact that it would be bad for their reputation in this country if they ran away from their obligations in New Iceland and failed to make their colony prosperous. He added that, even if they left, there was no need to leave Canada, as there was plenty of good land available in the northwest.

Who wrote the article? Sigtryggur Jonasson, the government agent who felt he was responsible to the Dominion government in the event the colony was abandoned? Or was it Sigtryggur Jonasson, the "Father of New Iceland," who only thought of how he could persuade his compatriots to continue their struggle in the colony? In view of his arguments, the obligations to both government and settlers guided his pen. His own reputation was at stake. He had been instrumental in selecting the site for the settlement; he had met with the Canadian prime minister in Ottawa and secured financial assistance; and he had continuously met with and encouraged Icelandic immigrants to choose the colony as their future home. He firmly believed that conditions would improve and the colony would prosper. His contributions to New Iceland bear witness to his strong conviction.[16]

Those settlers who wanted to remain in the colony continued to try to improve their living conditions. During 1878 to 1879, there were signs of increased competition in trade and economic growth. The price of flour dropped in 1879, for example, due to the growing competition. Stefan Eyolfsson was the first man in the colony to take his grain to a flour mill. In early 1879, he hauled 665 kilograms of wheat to Pritchard's mill on the Red River.[17] Soon he became engaged in other ventures, including an attempt in the fall of 1879 to export railway ties to Manitoba. Johann Briem and Eyolfsson had struck a deal with a Winnipeg businessman who was ready to pay twenty-five cents a tie. They decided to try to buy 25,000 ties from the settlers in the colony for eight cents each at the place of cutting. Eleven settlers attended a meeting at Sandy Bar to discuss the project and were willing to produce 7100 ties. But just as the plans had been made, news reached the colony that the required ties were already being shipped to Winnipeg by trains. The project was never launched.

However, at Hecla, the sawmill, which had been in operation off and on ever since the Icelanders came to the island, was put to permanent use in 1878. The company proposed to buy wood from the settlers at fifty cents per 1000 feet at the place of cutting, or $1.00 at a certain point on the shore. In 1879 another sawmill on the east side of the lake by Bad Throat River was to commence operation, providing employment for a few men.

Upon the purchase of *Victoria*, the owners, Sigtryggur Jonasson and the brothers Arni and Fridjon Fridriksson, along with Jon Bergvinsson and Jon Pjetursson, offered to purchase 300 to 400 cords of wood at Icelandic River and more farther down the lake at sixty-five cents per cord.

Sigurdur Jonsson, who had offered room and board in his home, announced in *Framfari* that, due to increasing traffic on the island, he was forced to raise his fees.[18] Meals would be sold at ten to fifteen cents, a single bed for ten cents; a straw mattress on the floor was to cost five cents. Hay and stable for horses or oxen would cost fifteen cents. Thus, the hotel industry in New Iceland was born.

Home industry of various kinds had existed in the settlement from the beginning, as it had in Iceland. For example, Vigfus Sigurdsson placed a notice in *Framfari* in February of 1878 that he would bind books. Payment could be in the form of cash, well-made butter, or whitefish. The settlers' love of books obviously prompted this rather interesting announcement. Other items that were homemade and sold include fishing nets and small boats. All wooden parts of tools and implements, such as axes, hammer-handles, mallets, barrows and sledges, skis and snowshoes, were most often manufactured at home, and, as the number of sheep increased and wool became more available, women knitted socks, sweaters, and mitts.

When the New Iceland Printing Company had announced on 5 February 1877 that a newspaper, *Framfari,* would soon be published in the colony, everyone welcomed the effort. Not only was the publication welcome as a newspaper, but even more as a sign of progress in the colony. Printed matter gave the settlers a sense of society, a new feeling of being part of a community rather than a group of individuals fighting for survival in a setting isolated from the rest of the world. However, by mid-1878, people in the settlement held considerably different views on the publication. The editor, Halldor Briem, had never withheld his opinions in such important matters as the religious controversy, and this led to growing dissatisfaction in Thorlaksson's followers. In their opinion, *Framfari* had become a tool in the hands of their opponents, which understandably left them contemplating the cancellation of their subscriptions.[19]

The New Iceland Printing Company called a meeting of shareholders on 2 September, almost a year after printing the first issue. The reeve of the Arnes district, Johann Stefansson, called the meeting to order and immediately brought up the main item on the agenda: the increasing discontent with the management of the paper and the hesitation of shareholders to pay their shares as a result. He presented a document, signed by twenty-four people in his district, in which they expressed their dissatisfaction with the management of both the company and the paper. All had agreed to withdraw their financial support (shares) and cancel their subscriptions if seven demands were not met:

1. All shareholders to have equal voting power; intellect, not wealth, should rule.
2. The printing press to be removed to Gimli in order to reduce expences.
3. Change of management, at least to a certain extent.
4. All expenses to be greatly reduced.
5. Editor change and the adoption of a new policy. All signed articles accepted for publication.
6. An unbiased board of three to decide whether to publish article if previously declined by editor.
7. Annual meetings and annual elections of officers.[20]

The demands reflected discontent with the existing situation and showed that Bjarnason's people ruled both company and paper. Clearly, there had been occasions when Halldor Briem had turned down an article without justifying his decision. It is apparent that all the "wealthy" settlers belonged to Bjarnason's group.[21]

Sigtryggur Jonasson replied that it was unreasonable for an individual holding several shares not to have more voting power than a person holding only a single one. He opposed the proposed move to Gimli on the grounds that the paper would have to be sent to subscribers in the north. If this was not done by mail, then delivery would be uncertain. He also mentioned the possible cost of a new building for the press at Gimli, and commented that the reduction of price obviously meant reduction of size. Halldor Briem responded that he had carried on his work according to the best interest of the colony and that he would continue to do so. He was not opposed to the suggestion of an editorial board. No direct action was taken at the meeting regarding these demands, Sigtryggur Jonasson suggesting that the annual meeting should address them rather than a meeting of some of the shareholders.

It should be added here that Gimli was the first postal centre in the colony and the only such office in the settlement. *Framfari* was carried south to Gimli from Lundi by Pall Johannsson. Mail service in the colony was greatly improved in December of 1878, when a direct link between Gimli and Peguis, near Lower Fort Garry, was established and, in July, another post office in the southern part of the colony at Husavik was opened.[22]

The financial picture was bleak. In June, the editor and the printer had received $166.12 from shares, of the expected $228.84. The sum of $166.97 was owed at that time on thirty-seven shares and outstanding subscriptions totalled $650.00. With everything accounted for, the assets of the six-months-old publication were exceeded by $353.49 in liabilities.[23] *Framfari* published a statement and appealed to the shareholders and subscribers to clear their debts. Despite the financial difficulties, publication continued until 1880, when the last issue of *Framfari* was printed.

The settlers in New Iceland had endured hardship of various kinds. Leaders such as Sigtryggur Jonasson were convinced that the times of significant struggle were past. However, there was still more to come. In 1875, when the site had been selected, everyone agreed that the land was somewhat low and that, if the level of the lake rose, flooding would be inevitable. During the early years in New Iceland, land had occasionally been wet, but flooding had never threatened the homes and farms of the settlers. But the summer of 1879 was unusually wet. Almost constant rain resulted in minimal haymaking and few potatoes, although brief, dry spells in August and September permitted a small harvest.

In the fall, Willow Creek was flooded, greatly damaging low marshlands in the region. The lake had risen about sixty centimetres over the average level. The cattle suffered from lack of pasture and there was a shortage of hay during the winter. In some cases, livestock perished, while in other instances, animals had to be killed due to the lack of fodder. A herd of 100 cattle and sheep was driven out of the colony to a farm in Manitoba for winter feeding.

All agricultural attempts failed dismally as a result of the wet summer. Operations that had begun in April, as was the norm, came to an abrupt stop in May and were never re-started. There was no opportunity to sow more grain and the little seed already in the ground was destroyed. Some potatoes and beans were planted during a short break in the rain in June but were ruined by an unexpected 5 July frost. The settlers attempted to cut hay in the marshes, as was the normal practice, and to carry it to higher ground for drying and stacking. However, the hay was either washed away in the heavy storms in the fall or spoiled as the water rose.

On 5 November, a great flood occurred in the northern region of the settlement. In the Icelandic River area, on the farm of Jon Guttormsson, which stood on a one-metre-high foundation close to the river, the waters reached almost to the floor of the house. In the barn, the farmer found his cattle standing in water up to their bellies, leaving him with no other alternative but to bring his livestock to his house. For two days, the Guttormssons shared their home with cattle. Other houses in the vicinity were surrounded by water but because they stood on higher land, they escaped the flooding. Haystacks became waterlogged and many collapsed.

However, John Taylor's annual report to the government was positive, despite the awful summer and bleak outlook for the winter:

> I have the honor to report that during the year 1879, the Icelandic Colony has successfully passed through a crisis such as all similar colonization efforts are liable to, namely: the disaffection of some of the settlers. . . . The prairie lands in Dakota were represented to be far more desirable than those in Canada. During the season 20 to 30 families have gone away to North Dakota, having been assisted by co-religionists in the States. . . . The departure of these persons has left the colony in peace. There never was a better or more hopeful spirit among the people than at the present moment. . . . The general health of the people has been good, although much wet weather prevailed in June, making bad roads and seriously injuring the crops. The land improves every year it is ploughed and cultivated. . . . Notwithstanding the wet state of the hay marshes a large amount of hay was provided, sufficient for all demands. . . . Cattle are much increased and beef is now added to the diet of the settlers.[24]

Taylor reported that the departure to Dakota of close to thirty families was to the advantage of the remaining settlers. He stressed the fact that those who left had been unhappy, and hinted that they had been the main source of discontent in the colony. With their absence, peace had finally arrived. He minimized the effect of the wet summer, stating that there would be "sufficient hay for all demands." This may be wishful thinking; he would have been aware of the result of the flood in the Icelandic River in November and that a herd had been driven out of the colony to a Manitoba farm for winter feeding.

The Regional Council requested from each district a thorough economic survey for the year 1879. The result was published in *Framfari*.[25]

	Vidirnes	Arnes	River	Hecla	Total
Population	405	112	320	192	1029
Householders	80	31	82	41	234
Place of residence	80	31	67	36	214
Wells	52	22	32	9	157
Cleared land (acres)	313	138	304	129	883
Cultivated land (acres)	154	57	122	100	432
Potatoes (seeded) bushels	529	214	518	285	1546
Potatoes (harvested)	4150	1893	4603	2522	13,168
Wheat (seeded) bushels	46	4	32	14	96
Wheat (harvested)	272	48	219	122	661
Cows	191	47	179	59	476
Oxen and bulls	65	9	42	14	130
Young cattle	266	62	217	66	611
Pigs	30	8	30	5	73
Sheep	25				25
Poultry	300	7	83	65	455
Horses	6		3		9
Boats (bigger)	37	17	47	29	130
Boats (smaller)	527	124	1950	230	2831
Gill-nets	171	100	239	148	658
Fish lines and hooks	1115	1077	1684	1229	5105
Whitefish	3799	3188	16,050	13,752	36,789
Other fish	50,626	46,525	63,050	41,401	201,602

The most striking figure is the total population of 1029. Since the migration out of the colony to Dakota in 1878 and the constant stream of people south to Winnipeg, many of whom found permanent work and a new place of residence, the total had dropped dramatically.

The following table shows migration to New Iceland in the period from 1875 to 1879:

Migration to New Iceland, 1875-1879

Year	Migration
1875	approx. 270
1876	approx. 1150
1877	8
1878	180
1879	80
Total	1688

Source: Kristjanson, *Icelandic People in Manitoba*, 102;
Thorsteinsson, *Saga Islendinga,* vol. III, pp. 160-366.

The total population of New Iceland during this period probably never reached 1688. The number of births and deaths is not taken into consideration, nor the number of people away working. However, the population figures in 1879 leave no doubt that migration out of the colony had started and the number of people leaving exceeded those arriving.

Another significant figure in the above report is that of cultivated land. Only 175 hectares had been cultivated at the end of 1879, while, according to a report in *Framfari,* more than 7000 were seeded in the Mennonite reserve in southern Manitoba. One of the reasons the site of New Iceland had been originally selected was the possibility of raising livestock, because that sort of farming was more suited to the Icelandic immigrants. The explorers in 1875 thought there was good opportunity to make enough hay. Fishing in the lake could complement farming, and growing grain would gradually be developed. These expectations had not been met. There were just 476 cows for 234 households, and two and a half young cattle (611) per household. The low number of sheep (twenty-five) shows that the typical Icelandic farmer was having problems in his new environment because, in Iceland, sheep had been the main livestock. Farmers were getting closer to self-sufficiency, but a long way from prosperity: more than 400 people left the colony for employment in Manitoba during the summers of 1879 and 1880.

Although Rev. Thorlaksson had accepted the call for a pastor from New Iceland, he had maintained his ties in Wisconsin and Minnesota. Normally he spent the winter with his flock in New Iceland and moved south of the border in the summer. He was in Canada in 1879 long enough to take part in the second public meeting on the religious controversy, held at Gimli in March, but left shortly afterwards. With a few others, he had explored regions west of Pembina in North

Dakota and, on his own, had travelled farther south in Minnesota. As soon as the first Icelandic families settled in Dakota, he became involved in their community.

Rev. Bjarnason had stirred up the people in his article in *Framfari* in which he declared that the dream of an exclusive Icelandic colony would never come about and that such a goal should be abandoned. In the fall of 1879, he announced to his congregations his intention of leaving the colony for Iceland. The reasons he gave were of a personal nature but there were undoubtedly other contributing factors, including the generally difficult economic circumstances in New Iceland.

In an article published in the periodical *Áramót*, he mentioned his controversy with Thorlaksson:

> There are many who consider this religious dispute a misfortune, but the bless-
> ing was greater than the misfortune or rather the misfortune turned out to be a
> blessing for the immigrants. The importance of Christendom has probably never
> in the history of the Icelandic people been pondered as much. We all had to go
> through that experience.[26]

From that time on, he insisted, this small portion of the Icelandic nation began to examine its role in a new world, which to him was a sign of survival in America.

The year 1880, a significant time for so many settlers, began with the colony elections. A new Regional Council had agreed to make plans for the construction of roads and bridges, and the reeve from Vidirnes proposed that steps be taken to encourage Canadians to settle in the colony. However, after its first meeting, the council lapsed into inactivity as its members struggled on their farms and many prepared to move. The winter was hard, and spring was wet and cold. Once it became clear that farmers could not expect a good crop, many decided to leave.

In July, John Taylor approached Skafti Arason, who had been a member of the advance party in 1875, and asked him to explore regions at Shoal Lake, west of the Lake Winnipeg basin.[27] Taylor suggested that perhaps the summer could be used for making hay there and then families could move into the region in the fall. However, Arason was not impressed with the prospect and the project was abandoned upon his return to the colony.

Sigurdur Kristofersson and Kristjan Jonsson, who both had also been in the 1875 advance party, left the colony in August and explored areas in the Tiger Hills district, several hundred kilometres southwest of Winnipeg. They returned with a favourable report on the region. During what remained of summer and through the following winter, many people prepared for the move to Tiger Hills, later to be named the Argyle settlement. Most of the early settlers in the new district came from the Vidirnes district, and were original members of the Ontario group that arrived in New Iceland in the fall of 1875. They had all chosen Canada over the United States and had been strong followers of Bjarnason. It is ironic that these very men, who had been instrumental in the decision to claim the present site for New Iceland, should become the first settlers to explore new areas.

As the new settlement was born in the summer of 1881, John Taylor moved to the Carberry district. Halldor Briem and his wife, Susie Taylor, left New Iceland about the same time. They spent some time in Winnipeg and in the United States before travelling to Iceland, where Briem was hired as principal of a newly established school. Sigtryggur Jonasson did not wait this long to leave; he had moved in 1880 to Crossing, which by now had been renamed Selkirk. This did not mean that he had completely abandoned New Iceland. He continued to work for the welfare of the people there and provided employment through his business enterprises, the steamer *Victoria* and a sawmill.

Those who packed their things and prepared to move did not do so filled with joy. It had been a difficult decision and, although life in New Iceland at times had been almost unbearable, part of their life would always be linked to the colony. Quite a few settlers made a stop in a small cemetery in Gimli or in a clearing in the wood, to bid farewell to a grave where a loved one rested, perhaps a victim of the smallpox or the scurvy or scarlet fever. By the end of 1881, only around 250 people remained in the colony: there were twelve homes in Vidirnes where there had been eighty at the end of 1879; five remained in Arnes of thirty-one in 1879; twenty-five of eighty-two in the Icelandic River district; and nine on Hecla.[28]

Those who chose to remain in the settlement did so out of pride and loyalty more than because they had a decent financial standing. They believed that moving away might mean starting similar struggles elsewhere and that, by remaining in New Iceland, at least most of the initial problems were behind them. They had experienced mild winters in the colony during their tenure and also productive summers, even though the last two had been discouraging. They had come to terms with the lake, knew which type of nets or hooks to use at any given time, and where to go in each season. It would only be a matter of time until their farming would become productive. Communications and transportation had improved so the isolation was much less. Also adding to their decision to stay was the fact that on 21 March 1881, the north boundary of Manitoba was moved to the twelfth base line, which meant that it was extended to the north boundary line of Township 44 across the province. Consequently, the entire settlement site of New Iceland became a part of Manitoba. Unpatented lands remained the property of the Dominion of Canada.

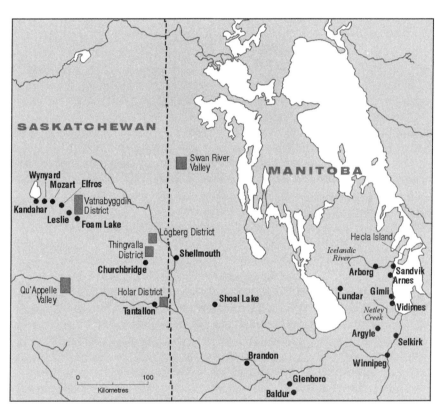

Early Icelandic Settlements in Saskatchewan and Manitoba, Canada.

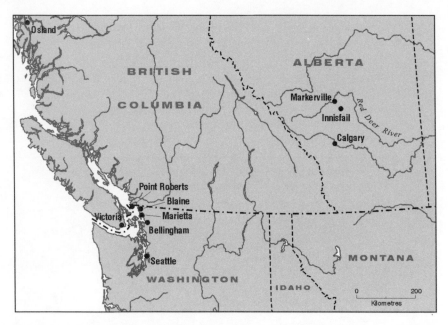

Early Icelandic Settlements in Alberta, Canada, and on the Pacific Coast.

Woodcarving with Runic inscription by Icelandic craftspeople, showing a fishing scene from Norse mythology. (Wisconsin Historical Society, Whi-4041)

Stephansson family and home in Markerville, Alberta, August 1907. (Glenbow Archives, NA-270-2)

Petur Asmundsson ploughing with oxen in 1905 in the Wynyard, Saskatchewan, district. He emigrated from Iceland in 1889 and earned his living working on Icelandic farms in Saskatchewan. (Saskatchewan Archives Board, R-A18382)

Ólafur Guðjón Arngrimsson (who changed his name to Anderson) was born in Iceland 23 April 1859, and emigrated in 1879. He moved to Minneota, Minnesota, in 1889, and in 1896 established what became O.G. Anderson and Company. Before he died 10 September 1903, he was considered one of the most noteworthy merchants in Minnesota. (Society for the Preservation of Minnesota's Heritage)

O.G. Anderson's Big Store was the biggest Icelandic store in North America in 1901 when it was completed. The wing was added in 1915. (Society for the Preservation of Minnesota's Heritage)

The steamboat *Manitoba*, on Red Lake River at Fisher's Landing, Minnesota, 1875. All the Icelandic settlers moving to Winnipeg or New Iceland travelled this route. (Polk County Historical Society)

Vidir School, c. 1915. (Provincial Archives of Manitoba, N11341)

The Sigurdsson General Store, c. 1915, Arborg, Manitoba. (Provincial Archives of Manitoba, N11305)

First post office at Icelandic River, 1907. (Provincial Archives of Manitoba, N11468)

Winnipeg, c. 1890s (Provincial Archives of Manitoba)

Icelanders at Steep Rock, Manitoba, packing frozen fish in crates, c. 1916-1917. (Glenbow Archives, NA-2483-3)

Brailing salmon (using a special net to scoop up the fish) into a scow from a fish trap at Point Roberts, Washington, c. 1898. (Point Roberts Historical Society)

West Point Roberts, Washington, c. 1900 (Point Roberts Historical Society)

Early school class, Point Roberts, Washington, c. 1914. (Point Roberts Historical Society)

10

Explorations in Dakota

During the early months of 1878, a few people met at Thorlaksson's to consider where those intending to leave New Iceland should go. They concluded that Magnus Stefansson and Sigurdur J. Bjornsson would accompany Thorlaksson on his travels south to Minnesota. However, the following is a part of Stefansson's own description of an event that led to his decision to explore regions in Dakota:

> It was Saturday, first day of summer, 27 April, when we boarded the steamer, *Ellen*, and headed for Winnipeg. Quite a few young women had joined us but they intended to find work, which I agreed to assist them with. The trip to Winnipeg went smoothly; we arrived early Sunday morning. I placed a notice in the window, which read: Housemaids looking for work. This went quite well and I was kept busy for three or four days, by which time all the girls had been hired except one. A man arrived at the house where I lived, and asked: "Do you have a maid for me?"
>
> "There is one left unemployed."
>
> "Can I hire her?"
>
> "It is quite possible." Once at his place, she and I liked what we saw and the matter was settled.
>
> I returned downtown with the man, who shortly afterwards stopped by a tall building and said: "My office is upstairs. Please, I want you come in with me;

my name is Hunter and I am the editor of the *Winnipeg Standard*. I need news from New Iceland."

I provided him with enough material for a long article, after which he asked, "But where are you heading?"

"To Minnesota to claim land for everyone presently staying in New Iceland."

"You should not bring them to Minnesota, there is no available land that I know of large enough for all the people except in the northernmost regions, east of the Red River and not much better than that of New Iceland. Go to Pembina; there is plenty of good land available." I determined to follow his advice.

"Wait while I write two letters of recommendation for you. Can you wait or would you rather come back tomorrow?" Hunter ... completed two letters. One was addressed to N.E. Nelson, the other to Billy Goodfellow, both quite well known to all Icelanders who ever travelled through Pembina. "Now, it is settled. You shall go to Pembina. I shall send you the *Standard* and I shall find out from the girl whether you kept your promise. You will write her, of that I am certain. Good-bye."[1]

This conversation throws light not only on the decision to go to Pembina, but also on the circumstances surrounding employment of the young Icelandic women in Winnipeg. Evidently it was common practice that an adult male monitored the hiring of the Icelandic women and went to great lengths in securing them a decent workplace. In this instance, Stefansson went with the woman and her future employer to examine his home before the woman gave her consent. In 1876, when there was a great demand for female domestic servants, Fridjon Fridriksson had opened his own employment agency in Winnipeg for the purpose of assisting people—mainly women—to find work.

The conversation does not indicate that other settlement prospects in Canada were even discussed. Either Stefansson had somehow made it clear that the United States was where the people intended to go, no matter what, or Hunter knew of no better land in Manitoba large enough for all the Icelandic people in New Iceland. Stefansson exaggerated somewhat in saying that he intended to bring *all* Icelandic settlers from New Iceland. He had neither the authority nor the approval of the people in the colony to make any plans for the departure of them all. However, he may have believed that others would soon follow once a new and better site had been selected.

Stefansson managed to convince Thorlaksson and Bjornsson to explore regions in northern Dakota. In Pembina, Stefansson and Bjornsson met with Nelson and Goodfellow and decided to explore regions west of the town of Cavalier in Pembina County. Stefansson and Bjornsson started their journey westward on foot and often had to wade through half-melted snow for hours. In Cavalier they met a man named John Betchel, who had arrived in the area in 1875 and who thereafter was most helpful to the Icelandic settlers in the area. The following day, he conveyed them further west to meet a Norwegian man, Butler Olson, who had fought in the Civil War of 1861 to 1865. He moved to Canada in 1887 and settled near Morden in Manitoba.

Stefansson and Bjornsson stayed with Olson for a week, during which he drove them west and south to examine possible settlement sites. They approved of the land, and then returned to Pembina, where they met Thorlaksson and three other Icelanders, all of whom planned to explore lands in Dakota. Thorlaksson's party wanted to see the region they had selected. Thorlaksson's travel companions were Johann Hallsson, his son Gunnar, and Arni Thorlaksson. Olson provided them with a guide, a Métis man named Amab Loose, who brought five ponies and two Red River carts, and they travelled for four days. Olson had provided bread and butter while Loose shot some ducks and collected eggs for food. They went south to Gardar Creek and examined the land where the towns of Mountain and Hallson are now located. Stefansson wanted the eastern boundaries of the new settlement to be where the town of Crystal now stands and then to proceed westward along the creek, but the others rejected his proposal.

Finally they chose the Mountain/Hallson region and all the explorers claimed land before returning to Pembina.[2] The Pembina County region that was so appealing was mostly flat prairie, protected by trees, with large, grassy meadows. In the distance, the Pembina Hills rose, much to the pleasure of the Icelandic explorers, who expected the area to be considerably more dry than that of New Iceland.

It was to be a much longer journey for Stefansson and Bjornsson than they had anticipated. For the second time in Pembina, they changed their minds and, instead of proceeding with the others to New Iceland, they accepted summer jobs on the farms of Olson and Betchel. The others returned to New Iceland, arriving 19 May 1878.[3]

Only five days later, the first group of Icelanders destined for Dakota left New Iceland. Samson Bjarnason conveyed the people to Crossing on his sailboat, from where they caught the steamer *Lady Ellen* to Winnipeg. They sailed aboard the *Manitoba,* reaching Pembina on 4 June. They rested for two days and prepared for the journey to the new settlement site. They bought two teams of oxen for the transportation of their belongings and the women and children, but the men walked. In the early morning of 6 June, this small group of settlers left Pembina and, after an uneventful journey, reached the farm of Butler Olson. The men in this pioneer group were Johann Hallsson and his son Gunnar, Benedikt Jonsson, Jon Jonsson, Gisli Egilsson, and Jonas Jonsson.[4]

The first log cabin, the home of Johann Hallson, was completed on 23 June. At one time that first summer, nine people resided in Hallson's cabin and on 6 July 1878, the first Icelandic child was born in the settlement when Ragnheidur Johanssdottir gave birth to a boy.[5] During the next two years, a new Icelandic settlement was gradually established. Many of the newcomers had lost everything in New Iceland. The little they had was invested in tools, nets, and livestock. The question of the Canadian government loan troubled many people. Some decided simply to leave whatever they had acquired in New Iceland as payment towards their debt.

News that people were moving out of New Iceland and settling in northern Dakota reached Icelandic settlers in both Wisconsin and Minnesota. The Icelanders in Shawano had followed events in Canada and learned of the migration to Dakota from Rev. Thorlaksson, whose father, Thorlakur Jonsson, and three brothers, Haraldur, Jon, and Bjorn, all worked and lived in the Wisconsin colony. They had reached the conclusion that the prospects in Shawano were not promising enough and that their progress in the woods had been too slow. Once they heard Thorlaksson's positive description of the land west of Pembina, they sold their properties in Shawano and headed west. Joining them were three others in the colony, Sigurjon Sveinsson, Benedikt Johannesson, and Kristinn Kristinsson.[6]

They went north on wagons, driving their livestock ahead of them. In Minnesota, they sold their six horses and replaced them with cows and oxen. After a slow and uneventful journey, they came to a halt in Dakota on a large, grassy area sheltered by two hills, and decided to claim this land. This was mid-summer, 1879. When the post office was opened in the colony in 1881, it was called Mountain. These people were followed by others in 1880, among them Stephan G. Stephansson and his wife, Helga Jonsdottir.

A few farmers from the Shawano County settlement lived in Minnesota for some time. Six families moved to Dakota in 1880 and claimed land in the region known today as Gardar. The people arriving from Wisconsin and Minnesota were considerably better off than their compatriots coming from New Iceland and had obtained farming experience from their Norwegian neighbours during their tenure in Wisconsin and Minnesota. With the increasing migration to Dakota from Manitoba in 1881, more land was claimed and the so-called Sandhills in the northern part were soon settled.

The new Icelandic settlement was located in the centre of Pembina County, which stretched from the west bank of the Red River in the east to the western side of the Pembina Mountains.[7] When the Icelanders first began to pour into this region, three laws regarding the claiming of land were in effect: Preemption, Tree Claim, and Homestead. The same settler could choose any one or all three. A settler selecting to claim land by the first and the last regulations was obliged to live on his land for at least three years. Anyone claiming land by the Tree Claim Act was required to plant 6000 trees during three years and, if the trees survived, the land became the settler's.[8]

The hardship and disappointment in New Iceland had left their mark on the new settlers. Many of them were mentally and physically exhausted when they reached Dakota. Of the early settlers in the summer and fall of 1878, few had supplies for the coming winter. Everyone looked to Thorlaksson for help and, through his connections with the Norwegians in Wisconsin and Minnesota, he was able to find support, or he managed to obtain assistance from local farmers, leaving promissory notes for the provisions.[9]

During the winter of 1879-1880, it became clear that Thorlaksson was in poor health, but, despite that, in the spring, he went to Northfield, Minnesota, where he had an appointment with Harald Thorson, a wealthy Norwegian trader. He managed to persuade Thorson to lend the Icelandic settlers in Dakota 100 barrels of flour and forty cattle, to be paid in full in two years' time. By travelling alone from one Norwegian farm to another in Minnesota, he managed to get thirty-five additional cows. This was all transported free of charge for the Icelanders from Northfield to St.Vincent near Pembina.[10] Thorlaksson was back in Minnesota during the summer of 1880 and, from other Norwegian farmers, he obtained an additional eighty-five cattle and sixty-five sheep, as well as some money. Most of this was a loan but some farmers made a donation to the Icelandic colony.

Gradually, land was cleared and tilled and a few acres put to use. At first men seeded their fields by hand, but that proved inadequate. They required mowing machines and oxen and horses. Unfortunately, many people ran into debt to purchase animals and machines. The trader, Harald Thorson, moved into the region and began to trade in the Icelandic settlement. He operated a store for ten years—unfortunately, with disastrous consequences for several farmers. Thorson sold a team of horses for $400.00 and a team of mules for $500.00, which was considerably higher than the going rate, and he obtained liens on the properties of buyers. Before he left the region, some settlers had lost their lands. In such cases, the farmers had to find work elsewhere, which resulted in the relocation of families.[11]

When the Icelanders took up land in the United States, they were required to renounce their obligations to the King of Denmark as Icelandic subjects, which they probably did not fully understand and may have done gladly in most cases, but they also had to agree that in due course they would become citizens of the United States of America. In 1882, Pembina County obtained municipal status and elections took place. The county commissioners handled all general welfare issues in the county and each township elected a three-person committee, supervisors, a secretary, an assessor, two Justices of the Peace, two constables, and a school board. Soon, Icelanders filled some of these positions, all of which were poorly remunerated.[12] The position of the assessor was perhaps the most appealing as it was better paid than the others and more prestigious. The assessor was required to be a good-tempered and patient man, as his duty was to record everything of value on the farms, both outside and inside the homes. The settlers were taxed according to his report.

Although a new Icelandic settlement was developing, the approach to establishing the new colony was entirely different from that in New Iceland. The most significant difference was the attitude of the settlers themselves; none of them had any illusions about founding an exclusive Icelandic colony. They all arrived in Dakota aware that there were settlers of other nationalities in Pembina County, Norwegians like Butler Olson, Germans like John Betchel, and Americans like

Nelson and Goodfellow. For those arriving from Wisconsin and Minnesota or other parts of the United States, the adjustment was not as difficult as for the people from New Iceland. In Dakota there was no doubt that they were part of America. The district followed the same laws and regulations as other counties in Dakota; elected officers carried the same titles and authority in the new settlement as they did elsewhere. By accepting their position within American society in this fashion, Icelanders had taken a first step towards assimilation. Never again did they contemplate an all-Icelandic colony.

Agricultural efforts began the summer of 1880. Many settlers had selected land in partly wooded areas and their initial task was, of course, to clear the land and prepare the soil. Horses or oxen were few, perhaps one animal for every five to ten settlers. This meant that many people could not get started right away and needed to earn some money. They worked wherever employment was available, some as far as 300 kilometres to the south, where there were established settlements. Here they worked during harvest and threshing in the fall for a month and a half at a wage of $1.00 to $1.50 per day plus meals. Those remaining in the settlement worked for themselves or for others who could pay a few dollars. Most settlers had to make do with $100.00 or even less for provisions for an entire winter.[13] Many attempted to increase their income by working in the woods on their land, often hauling cords of wood to a market many kilometres away, only to return with some syrup or half a sack of wheat. But after two or three years, everyone began to benefit from their land. More animals, horses and oxen, were purchased and tools and equipment became readily available. Non-Icelanders noted that the new settlers were exceptionally reliable when it came to payments on loans or the prompt return of borrowed machines or animals. A growing faith in the Icelanders resulted in the offer of loans of money or provisions, often with alarming consequences at a later date. During the decade from 1880 to 1890, there was progress in breaking land, and improved homes and barns, but the settlers still struggled financially, most often due to these loans.

The livestock increased in number every year. Settlers built fences around pasture land and made certain that enough fodder filled the barn in the fall. Gradually, raising domestic animals became a noted profession in the settlement as the Icelanders appeared to be more skilled in the art of raising cattle, pigs, or sheep than the average farmer elsewhere in Pembina County. Although the economy of the new Icelandic settlement in Dakota remained in poor condition throughout the 1880s, general optimism existed from the beginning, especially among those arriving from New Iceland. In a letter to a friend in Iceland, Jon Jonasson described the positive feelings.

> Cavalier 7 Jan. 1880
> My dear compatriot!
>
> I thank you most heartily for your letter dated 2 December of last year, which I received on the 23. I welcomed it specially since I have not had time to write any letters since arriving here in this new settlement, which you ask me to tell

you about. It really was established by a few Icelanders the summer before last but last year more than a hundred people moved in and I can safely assume that the population is above two hundred. (I do not have the exact number.) Sixty have already claimed land and many are expected to arrive here in the spring from places like Minnesota, Wisconsin, Fargo (a town south of here by the Red River) and New Iceland. Consequently it seems likely that a large section of land will be settled by our fellow countrymen. Presently, most have settled near the Pembina Mountains, south by the Tongue River, which flows east into the Red River. The land is wooded in parts but in between one finds grassy meadows and flatland for cultivation. Some homesteads offer woods, rich pastureland as well as excellent soil for grain. The overall scenery is beautiful, moderately wooded but mostly flat, an ideal agricultural site. South, east and west of here are large sections of land which have yet to be claimed. The air is clear but winters apparently can be cold and summers quite warm. The general health in the colony is good.

The harvest of last fall consisted of 25-35 bushels of wheat per acre, 50-60 bushels of oats; maize turned out well but I do not have any figures and potatoes were 14-28 times seeds.

The closest market is still some 28 miles away but we are hopeful that the railway will come this way in the nearest future. Regarding my own future here, I cannot but state that it is much brighter than in New Iceland despite all our hardships in getting here, exhausted and financially ruined by the New Iceland council. The land here is much drier, roads among the best there are (some need work) and your land is truly yours from the start. There are three ways of claiming land: first is the preemption, 160 acres free but you pay $17.00 for the paperwork, the second is homestead at $200 and the third tree claim (one is supposed to grow trees on 8 acres) at $17.00 like the first.

The Government here is quite good and there are no obligations or duties required from the settlers except roadwork. As far as I know, the Icelanders in the settlement have some 18 oxen teams between them, which is quite good after such a short stay but I do not know the number of other livestock. Some 160 acres have been cleared and are ready for seeding in the spring. Rev. Thorlaksson, who is our pastor, has received assistance for us from Norwegians, which we are all very grateful for. Without it this winter would be hard for many as last summer was mostly used for the construction of homes and shelters for livestock and the clearing of land. Very little seeding took place.

If this group manages until next harvest and can continue to improve their lands then I am convinced that we shall accomplish more here than we ever could in our previous settlement. As a token of that I point out that here more land has been cleared and broken in one year than was done in New Iceland in four!

My family and I, especially myself, are quite content and at ease with our present situation. I am especially happy for my children who I feel will have greater opportunities here. I have claimed land and have ploughed some six acres, which I shall seed with wheat in the spring. I expect to have two cows, two oxen calves and an oxen team, which I share with my son, Jonas, so that we can plough our fields. I still have not moved in but am presently staying with my son-in-law, Samson, but expect to be in my own house at the beginning of summer.

Church matters are still in the preliminary stages yet three elementary schools are in operation this winter and are well appreciated. Men in these parts are expecting higher salaries in the upcoming summer as the wheat is growing in price, up to 90 cents to a dollar per bushel....[14]

The letter reveals Jonasson's bitterness regarding New Iceland and the leaders, Sigtryggur Jonasson and Halldor Briem and members of the Regional Council, all of whom made the departure from the Manitoba colony exceedingly difficult, in the opinion of those who left. Jonasson is not concerned in his letter with Icelandic sentiment; having suffered in New Iceland for some time, he had other, more urgent needs on his mind. This was probably the general attitude of all those who left New Iceland. But the letter mentioned elementary schools, indicating that the settlers strove to educate their youth despite the primitive conditions in the settlement during the winter of 1879-1880.

Jonasson mentioned religious issues and stated that little had been accomplished in church matters. However, he had not long to wait before Thorlaksson organized his congregations in the colony.

The first Icelandic sermon in Pembina County was delivered by Thorlaksson in the house of Butler Olson on 5 December 1878. No attempt was made on that occasion to organize a congregation; the number of Icelanders in the colony was low and future settlements had yet to be selected. But in the fall of 1880, Thorlaksson brought up the issue. At that time, he had given religious services in three districts of the colony, at Vikur, Gardar, and Tongue River, and had continued to work in Minnesota. In order to establish a church in Dakota, he called a meeting at Gardar on 24 November 1880. Thorlaksson was appointed chair and Stephan G. Stephansson was secretary. Thirteen settlers were in attendance, representing more than fifty immigrants. Thorlaksson's congregational laws of New Iceland were essentially approved and everyone present signed a promissory note for his salary of $50.00.

Six days later, a similar meeting was called at Mountain, where Thorlaksson was again appointed chair and his father secretary. Thirty-one settlers attended, representing close to 140 people. It was agreed that a congregation be formed, that Thorlaksson be called on as pastor, and that his annual salary be $95.00. Thorlaksson's church laws were accepted and it was agreed that three religious services would be held each month.

The third meeting was held 2 January 1881 in the home of Johann Hallsson near Tongue River. Thorlaksson was chair and Palmi Hjalmarsson was secretary. Church laws were decided on, and fourteen settlers present agreed to pay a salary of $55.00.[15]

But Thorlaksson did not serve his congregations in Pembina County for long. He passed away on 1 March 1882. Although everyone had been aware of his failing health, no one was prepared for this loss; he had been the leader in the colony, the individual everyone called on in need. His funeral did not take place until 12 April, due to miserable weather. A Norwegian pastor, Kristjan Flaten, spoke in Norwegian, while Niels Steingrimur, brother of the deceased, addressed the gathering in Icelandic. Despite heavy snow and bitter cold, a large number of people travelled to Mountain in order to pay their respects.

Although Rev. Thorlaksson's sojourn in North America was just under ten years, his contribution to the history of Icelandic people in North America was most important. He was one of the few Icelandic pioneers who was prepared to accept his role in the very complex American society of the 1870s. Knowing that Icelanders would be part of a young, fast-growing nation, he made every effort to convince his compatriots to adjust to American ways. Blamed for his lack of patriotism, his involvement with the Norwegian Synod, and for his enthusiasm for everything American, Thorlaksson nevertheless had shouldered his responsibilities with dignity and conviction. Although he had originally wanted to lead his flock from New Iceland to Minnesota or southern regions of Dakota, he conceded to the desire of his people to settle in Pembina County. If Sigtryggur Jonasson was the "Father of New Iceland," then Rev. Thorlaksson surely deserves the same title for the Icelandic community in Dakota. He was instrumental in obtaining livestock and grain for the settlers and, although he did not see his settlement flourish, he knew that considerable progress had been made. Thorlaksson organized congregations in his community that accepted the same laws he established in New Iceland. This is interesting for two reasons. First, his followers, many of whom had been members of his congregations for some time, were content with his services, even though he had been educated and trained by a foreign religious organization. They agreed that his sermons differed from that of pastors in Iceland, yet the difference did not matter to them, nor were his strong ties with the Norwegian Synod objectionable. Stephan G. Stephansson, for example, said that it was not a religious conviction that led to his participation in Thorlaksson's church; rather, he agreed with Thorlaksson's approach to the settlement of Icelanders in North America.

Second, the Norwegian Synod was absent in the Dakota settlement. Rev. Bjarnason, Jon Olafsson, and Halldor Briem were among the many opponents of Thorlaksson who were concerned that the synod eventually would control not only the church but also the schools. They had gone as far as stating that Icelandic sentiment would be eliminated in a colony controlled by the synod. However, the synod was not present, and both the Dakota and Minnesota Icelandic communities have, to this day, preserved and promoted Icelandic sentiment just as strongly as any other Icelandic community in North America, including the Interlake region in Manitoba. As evidence of this, one only needs to point to the fact that the Icelandic language is spoken in both American communities.

Knowing that the end was near, Thorlaksson prepared for his successor and strongly recommended that Rev. Hans Thorgrimsen be called. He was the son of Gudmundur Thorgrimsen of Eyrarbakki in Iceland, who had been instrumental in planning the 1872 immigration of Thorlaksson, Hans, and others. Hans had graduated from the Theological Seminary in St. Louis in the spring of 1882 and had planned a journey back home to Iceland, so he did not arrive in Dakota until August of 1883.

The first church belonging to the Icelandic community was built at Mountain in 1884. In order to meet the cost of the construction, members of the Mountain congregation obtained a loan of $1000.00 from Harald Thorson. A few farmers offered liens on their properties, which were accepted, but soon it appeared they might lose their lands as Thorson wanted their properties more than his cash. In the end, two farmers, Bjorn Einarsson and Jon Jonsson from Mæri, took over the loan and paid it in full. They were duly rewarded later when the congregation paid back the full amount with interest.

As more land was claimed and settled by Icelanders, Rev. Thorgrimsen organized new congregations. In 1884, a congregation was established in Cavalier County and in 1885 one was organized at Gardar and another in Pembina.[16]

In the early part of 1884, Rev. Thorgrimsen introduced the idea that all Icelandic Lutheran congregations in North America should be joined in one Icelandic synod, and on 2 December a committee was elected to write up the laws for such an organization. All the Icelandic congregations in Dakota were invited to send delegates to Mountain for a joint meeting. Called to order on 23 January 1885, the meeting lasted three days. The proposed laws were discussed, modified, and prepared for a further discussion at yet another meeting on 31 January, where all sections of the laws, except one, were approved.

The first conference of The Icelandic Evangelical Lutheran Synod in America was held in Winnipeg, 24 June 1885. Half the delegates, twelve, came from Dakota, among them Rev. Thorgrimsen, Stephan G. Stephansson, and Thorlakur Jonsson (Rev. Thorlaksson's father). Other delegates represented Icelandic settlements in Manitoba—New Iceland, Argyle, and Winnipeg. Rev. Jon Bjarnason attended, having just returned from Iceland. The strong representation from Dakota reflected the size of the congregations, which at that time equalled the number in Manitoba.[17] This was an extraordinary event in the history of the Icelandic people in North America, as it was the first effort to develop an Icelandic religious body for all Icelandic settlers in both the United States and Canada.

Both Thorlaksson and Thorgrimsen wanted to establish active church organizations. The Mountain congregation was one of the first to set up a women's society, but soon others followed. Sunday schools also were organized in the early days and played a significant role in the education of youth. The dedication of the pastors and the general involvement of all parishioners, young and old, in the various functions of their church brought about greater awareness of the difference between the Icelandic State Church and the independent American church. Few of these settlers had had a similar opportunity in Iceland, where direct involvement of the general public in church matters was minimal. One event in particular caused increasing interest in religious affairs. This was the annual meeting of the pastors of the Icelandic Synod, normally in the fall, when discussions of religion attracted a large attendance.

The settlers organized their own social events. Each community within the settlement, often just a few farms, held its own gathering at which people sang, recited poetry, or participated in debates. Dances were common and featured the music of an accordion, fiddle, or harmonica; the attendance varied from place to place, as young people often had to travel a great distance.

The desire to publish Icelandic material was not only confined to the shores of New Iceland in Manitoba. During the winter of 1879-1880, an Icelandic periodical was established by a few pioneers in the Gardar district. Stephan G. Stephansson was the editor and the paper was to appear twice a month. He gave the publication the name *Fjalla-Eyvindur*. It was a handwritten newspaper, which was read on every farm in the district as well as in Winnipeg and even Iceland. Numerous Icelandic pioneers contributed articles to the newspaper, but, like the handwritten weekly in New Iceland, this publication in Dakota was too time-consuming and didn't last.

An Icelandic festival, the first in Dakota, was held at the farm of Jon Jonsson, on 5 July 1880. Many settlers travelled from Gardar in the south and Tongue River in the north. Rev. Thorlaksson gave a speech and discussed the prospects of the new settlement. This was followed by entertainment of various kinds, such as sporting events and games in which young and old participated. The women provided pancakes and coffee. A year later, a 4 July celebration was staged at Gardar. A committee had been chosen to prepare the events of the day and Stephan G. Stephansson had been asked to write a play:

> Men were on my back, insisting I write a play. I declined but to no avail, I was forced. I toiled every day but the night was bright. In the evening I'd lie down in the slope by my hut and write. What I wrote each night was then studied, memorized and rehearsed the following day. I was up the entire night, prior to the celebration, during the events of the day as well as the next night. Fell asleep working with horses and a mowing machine in the field the day after. Neither animals nor myself suffered.[18]

The play was a success and became known in the Icelandic community as *The Immigrants, Teitur, and the Magistrate*. At Gardar the leading actors were Baldvin Helgason as the magistrate; Jakob Lindal as Teitur, the young student; his sister, Ingunn, as Teitur's girlfriend; and Caroline Dalmann as the older woman who misunderstood everything, especially the English language. Another event that always attracted widespread attention was the June festival of the Sunday schools. It was a full-day event involving both children and adults in sports, games, and singing.

The Culture Society was established 4 February 1888 in the home of Stephan G. Stephansson near Gardar. In addition to the poet, the founding members were Skafti and Magnus Brynjolfsson (brothers), Bjorn Petursson, Olafur Olafsson,

Einar Jonsson, Jonas Hall, Bjorn Halldorsson, Sveinn Bjornsson, and Brynjolfur Brynjolfsson. The society was expected to promote Icelandic culture and freedom of thought, and support independent examination of modern, scientific literature. Study groups were organized and public addresses and debates planned. Each study group was given a specific subject to study and share with others, who then took part in a general discussion. Topics ranged from natural science and psychology to comparative religion and poetry. Discussion on religion, which was a most sensitive issue in a community struggling to establish its church, was common. The society allowed for complete freedom of speech and thought, which resulted in leaders of the Icelandic Synod having to take a stand against the society in the matter of religion. Rev. Jon Bjarnason, having fought Thorlaksson's extreme orthodoxy in the early days of Icelandic immigration to North America, now was confronted with its opposite. In the synod's publication *Sameiningin*, he blasted the society and its stand on religion:

> A society which proposes to promote culture and morality with the aid of books such as those of Robert Ingersoll will break the old bonds…. An association made up of farmers who have never attended school now challenges the might of the Christian church, the greatest power in the world, and seem confident that they will topple it. Such excess of boldness in America! An association of Antichrist has raised its standard.[19]

Although this remarkable organization was short-lived, it left a lasting impact. The society was instrumental in establishing a reading organization and arranging numerous talks as well as planning several cultural events. The first reading club had been established in the Sandhills district in 1887 and another one at Mountain a few months later. By 1889, six reading societies had been founded in the Icelandic settlement in Dakota. These organizations strove to provide members with material in Icelandic as well as English.

The Icelandic settlers soon began to take part in local politics. Most of their neighbours were Scandinavian Republicans and, initially, Icelanders joined the same party. But as Democrats increased in number, many Icelandic settlers were attracted to that party, too. Eirikur Hjalmarson Bergmann was one of the young Dakota settlers who became involved in political and social matters. He emigrated from Iceland in 1873 and went first to Milwaukee, where he lived during the next four years. In 1876 he homesteaded in Lyon County, Minnesota, but was never content with his land and decided to explore southern Dakota in 1878. The following year, he claimed land in Pembina County, further north, by Park River. He was the first family man to settle in the Gardar district. He married Ingibjorg Petursdottir Thorlacius in 1876 and together they spent forty years at Gardar. They were known for their devotion to the Icelandic settlement in Dakota and contributed in various ways to the developing community. Bergmann was the first post officer in his district and operated a store. He was one of the founders of the Gardar congregation and its president for many years. His significant role in the Icelandic church in Pembina County led to his participation in the founding of the Icelandic Evangelical Lutheran Synod in

America. He attended the first conference in Winnipeg in 1885. He was a member of the local school board, the County Commissioner, and a member of the first legislature in Bismarck after Dakota was divided into two states, north and south, in 1889. That year marked the admission of North Dakota as the thirty-nineth state in the Union.[20]

Thorlaksson had always maintained that the Icelanders could contemplate a settlement in either the United States or Canada after they had prepared themselves for the task. To him, assimilation was inevitable, but nothing should prevent the establishment of an open Icelandic colony. The settlement in Dakota became exactly this, a part of a larger community in which the language was preserved and Icelandic sentiment promoted, but, at the same time, settlers were actively involved in all other aspects of American life.

Minnesota has always been known as being the most Scandinavian state in the US. Early Swedish immigration, mostly to east-central Minnesota, paved the way for Norwegians, who had first intended to work in the lumber industry but took up farming in the Red River valley and the southeastern regions. Later, regions of the west and southwest were settled by Scandinavians and Germans.

Gunnlaugur Petursson, the first Icelandic settler in Minnesota, had arrived in Lyon County in July of 1875. He claimed land on the banks of the Yellow Medicine River, ten kilometres northeast of Minneota. By 1880 several Icelanders had arrived in Minnesota in the towns of Marshall and Minneota. The first Minneota settler from Iceland was Johannes Halldorsson, who later adopted the surname Frost. The towns offered employment to labourers and store clerks, but other people started their own commercial ventures or became civil servants. In 1883 Johannes Frost and Jonatan Jonatansson, later Peterson, opened the first Icelandic store, which bore their names and was called Frost & Peterson.[21] A year later Peterson sold his share and Frost ran the store alone for another year and a half. In 1886 he moved to New Ark in South Dakota, where he opened another store.

The Icelandic Trading Company was established in 1886. Its purpose was twofold: to invest the shareholders' funds, and to improve commerce in their region. Several Icelanders bought shares, each worth $25.00. The leading men of the trading company in the beginning were Stefan Sigurdson, Josef Josefson, Björn Gislason, Einar Jonsson, Sigurbjorn Hofteig, Gudmundur Grimsson (later G.A. Dalmann), and Sigfus Runolfson (later F.R. Johnson). In 1896, the company ceased operation and sold all its stocks and properties, except one building worth $3000.00. During its heyday, it had been valued at more than $10,000.00.[22]

Icelandic businessmen in Minneota caught the attention of their rural compatriots who frequented the Icelandic shops, not only to do their shopping but also to hear the latest news from other Icelandic communities in North America. On occasion, farmers landed a job for a daughter or a son in such shops or the shop owners were helpful in finding work. As time passed, Minneota became the centre for Icelandic settlers in southwestern Minnesota.

The settlers in Minnesota were keen on organizing religious work in their Icelandic community. As early as 1878, the communities in Lincoln and Lyon counties joined forces and put together a committee to write congregational laws. Snorri Hognason, Eirikur H. Bergman, and Gudmundur Henry Gudmundsson represented settlers in Lyon and Yellow Medicine counties, the so-called "Eastern settlement." Arni Sigvaldason and Stefan Sigurdsson sat on the committee on behalf of the settlers in the Lincoln County settlement, or "western settlement."[23]

This committee met just before Christmas in 1878; a problem arose immediately. The religious controversy in New Iceland had reached the Minnesota colony and men held opposing views. Bergman and G.H. Gudmundsson supported Thorlaksson, while the others favoured Bjarnason. However, it was agreed that the committee should avoid any controversial statements. Proposals for congregational laws and regulations were approved and presented to the general public the following spring. These were accepted and two congregations immediately organized. The congregation in the western settlement was called Lincoln County Congregation, and the one in Lyon was named the American Congregation. The third Icelandic congregation was established later in Minneota and called St. Paul's Congregation, and the fourth, which followed in Marshall, was called the Marshall Congregation. All these were later accepted by the Icelandic Evangelical Lutheran Synod in America.[24]

Unfortunately, the minutes of the meeting are lost, as are the congregational laws and regulations as accepted in 1879. The members of the committee were laymen who had no education or training in theology, but had a reputation for being both intelligent and tolerant. As they were not only aware of the religious controversy in New Iceland, but felt they knew enough to take sides, they must have seen and studied the laws of both Thorlaksson's and Bjarnason's congregations. Both sets of laws had appeared in *Framfari* and had been discussed a great deal, as had the controversy itself. The committee members, like most Icelandic immigrants elsewhere in North America, were more concerned with the effect the controversy had on the relationships of families and friends than with its religious content. The division in the North American Icelandic community troubled them and they wanted to seek a solution acceptable to both sides. But whether they chose to base their proposals on those of either or both Thorlaksson and Bjarnason, or ignored them and wrote their own, is not known.

Both Thorlaksson and Bjarnason had visited the colony before the meeting of December 1878. Thorlaksson was in the settlement in the fall of 1877, when he gave religious services and carried out other clerical duties. At that time, his differences with Bjarnason, in the eyes of the public, were more concentrated on settlement issues than on matters of religion. Neither pastor had publicly denounced the faith of the other. Thorlaksson returned to Minnesota in the spring of

1878, on his way to his congregations in Shawano County. Again he was asked to perform clerical duties, among them the confirmation of two boys. This time, however, he must have been asked about the religious controversy in New Iceland, as articles and reports on the issue had filled the pages of *Framfari* since January.

Bjarnason was in Minnesota in the fall of 1878 and, like his colleague, performed religious duties when asked. On his way to Iceland in 1880, he travelled through Minnesota again and visited his compatriots in the settlements. At this time, people in the colony were considering how to obtain the permanent services of a pastor. A general meeting concluded that since Rev. Bjarnason was on his way to Iceland, he would be asked to make recommendations about four pastors in Iceland: Jon Halldorsson, Thorvaldur Bjarnason, Valdimar Briem, and Jens Palsson.

How enthusiastically Bjarnason complied with this request is hard to guess; he may have written or met each one of them, or contacted the Icelandic church authorities, asking for assistance in the matter. He may have known that none of the four would be interested in leaving the security of the Church of Iceland for the uncertainty he himself had endured among Icelandic settlers in America. In view of his debate with Thorlaksson, he surely must have preferred an Icelandic pastor to someone trained and educated in America. Be that as it may, he was unable to find anyone, but he recommended the Minnesota settlers call Rev. Halldor Briem in New Iceland, and congregations in both districts agreed. Briem received his call late in 1880 or early 1881, and arrived in Minnesota in the spring of 1881. He served in the colony for a year before returning to Iceland, where he stayed.[25]

Records do not indicate whether Thorlaksson was ever asked to assist in securing a pastor for the Minnesota congregations. This is understandable, as his connections with a foreign religious body, the Norwegian Synod, were stronger than those with the Church of Iceland. The Icelandic congregations felt their pastor should be Icelandic because part of his duties included teaching the language and promoting Icelandic sentiment. The settlers stood firm on this issue, and this left the congregations without a pastor for several years.

In 1886, Rev. Fridrik J. Bergmann, who had just graduated from the Lutheran Theological College in Philadelphia, visited the settlement and happily complied with the request that he perform religious services for a while. He was on his way to Dakota, however, and was never considered the permanent solution for the colony. It was not until 1887 that the services of a pastor were obtained. Niels Steingrimur Thorlaksson, brother of Rev. Thorlaksson, was completing his theology studies in Norway, and accepted the call and served in the community for the next seven years. After he graduated, he was ordained pastor in America in the summer of 1887 by Rev. Jon Bjarnason, who was in the States after spending four years in Seydisfjord in Iceland.[26]

The Minnesota colony must be considered the most successful of the Icelandic communities in North America in the 1880s. Founded in the same year as New Iceland, it never received the same attention for the simple fact that the Minnesota settlement was never supposed to be an all-Icelandic colony; people settled in small groups among settlers of other ethnic backgrounds. The American settlers were nonetheless equally determined to preserve their Icelandic heritage, which is borne out by the fact they insisted on an Icelandic pastor for their congregations. They also successfully established organizations for the purpose of promoting Icelandic culture.

The settlers in Minnesota had several advantages. They were close to markets in the towns of Minneota and Marshall, and all transportation and communication were more advanced in Minnesota than in Manitoba or northern Dakota. The almost daily contact with Americans and Norwegians contributed to their assimilation and stimulated their progress in farming. The following report appeared in *Leifur,* the first Icelandic weekly published in Winnipeg, when the Minnesota colony was only nine years old. It was provided by G.S. Sigurdsson and described the eighty property holders, and the twenty-four labourers and store clerks, in the total population of 575. Sigurdsson discussed the Icelandic Association in Lincoln, adding that thirty-five settlers had become members and the annual fee was fifty cents per person.[27]

Production in Minnesota in 1884

Wheat—23,060 bushels
Oats—11,325
Barley—330
Flax—120
Maize—900
Potatoes—5430
Roots—1000
Hay—2835 tons
Cultivated land—2240 acres
Properties—10,690
Total value of all properties in the colony—$133,725.80

The two large Icelandic settlements in the United States, the ones in Minnesota and Dakota, experienced considerable progress in the 1880s. The population figures grew considerably in Dakota, and steadily in Minnesota. The first Icelandic settlement in North America in the 1870s on Washington Island also experienced growth in population, although on a much smaller scale than the other two. The last person to arrive on the island in the 1870s was Oddur Magnusson, who immigrated to Milwaukee in 1873 and spent a year in Wisconsin. He then went to Washington Island. Seven years passed before the next Icelandic immigrant arrived. In the summer of 1881, Jon Gunnlaugson crossed the border into the United States from New Iceland. He had arrived in 1873 in America and went to New Iceland in 1876, where he suffered from smallpox and was bedridden for five weeks. From New Iceland he went to Pembina County in Dakota. From 1881 to 1895, twelve householders—single men and families—settled on the island. Most of these settlers came directly from Iceland but some had been elsewhere in America. For example, Thorgeir Einarsson had immigrated to Milwaukee in 1873, found work on Norwegian farms, and lived in Racine and Walworth counties for fifteen years before moving to the island.

Gradually, more land was cleared and broken, and, by 1896, fourteen Icelandic settlers were farmers, two concentrated on fishing, one operated a store, another had a small merchant vessel in operation on the Great Lakes, and two were blacksmiths. Several of them soon became active in the small Washington Island society, which consisted mostly of Danes, Norwegians, Germans, Americans, and, of course, Icelanders.

11
The Winnipeg Icelanders

Icelandic records show that 2857 people left the country for America between 1870 and 1879. The same sources reveal no steady increase in emigration from one year to the next. For example, the largest group of 1190 people migrated in 1876, but the following year only fifty-nine people migrated. In 1878 and 1879 the number of migrants was 473 and 322, respectively.[1] In 1879 most of the Icelandic immigrants in North America resided in Canada but with the establishment of the Dakota colony and the large migration from New Iceland, the number of Icelanders in each country became more equal. During the next ten years, from 1880 to 1889, there is a direct link between emigration totals and unusually cold weather in Iceland

Immigration from Iceland, 1880-1889

1880 — 94	1885 — 141
1881 — 144	1886 — 504
1882 — 347	1887 — 1947
1883 — 1215	1888 — 1109
1884 — 121	1889 — 702

Source: Krisinsson, *Vesturfararskrá 1870-1914*, Table 3.

This decade was the busiest of the entire migration period: 6324 people emigrated from Iceland to North America. In 1883 alone, 1215 people emigrated to North America. In Iceland, *Ísafold* stated:

> Emigration to North America has been tremendous this year. Most emigrants came from Borgarfjord, Skagafjord, Eyjafjord and western Hunavatns-district. Many left from other parts as well. We have been unable to obtain any concrete figures but the total number of emigrants exceeds twelve hundred. Quite a few who were willing to go were forced to remain behind as they were unable to dispose of their properties. Around a half went to Winnipeg while others went south to Pembina and a few to Minnesota. Beside these, some thirty headed for Utah.[2]

The fact that these Icelandic immigrants were destined for at least four different locations in America shows that the dream of an exclusive Icelandic settlement in North America was no longer alive. Those people heading for Winnipeg often chose to remain there for a period of time while making a decision on their future home in North America.

Living conditions in Iceland in 1882 were so bad that a fundraising campaign was started abroad, in countries such as Denmark, Norway, Sweden, Germany, England, and North America. The circumstances forced many people to emigrate. The misconception always arose during times of hardship that the people leaving were somehow unable to cope because of their own lack of effort. No farmer in Iceland in those times had the opportunity to make enough hay one summer to last a few years. When severely cold weather prevented spring and summer grazing and haymaking, farmers could do nothing to save their livestock. It is true that young men often attempted to farm on land they knew had little to offer. Ruins of such farms speak for themselves. However, these men were ready to make another attempt to improve their lives even if it meant emigration to America. It is quite likely that a few, perhaps many, people left Iceland filled with bitterness.

The following years, 1883 and 1884, were easier in Iceland. Again, emigration figures bear witness. Only 121 people left Iceland in 1884, and 141 in 1885. The snowfall of early 1885 was tremendous, preventing all transportation on land in many regions. The spring and early summer were marked by freezing cold, northerly winds, and overnight frost well into July. The number of emigrants in 1886 rose to 504 as a result.

The year 1886 greeted the Icelandic nation with continuous snowstorms and below-average temperatures, which lasted until the end of February. In many places in the north, snowmelt did not occur until June, and hail and frost were frequent that summer. Grass grew poorly in all parts of the country, severely damaging the farming industry. More and more people contemplated emigration, and when the following winter of 1886-1887 turned out to be extremely hard, their decision was made. In 1886, the largest number of people ever to leave Iceland in one year that century, a total of 1947, emigrated to North America. Conditions in the northwestern regions were described in the *Fjallkona*: "Awful prospects, most farmers without any hay, feed cows 4-5 weeks but nothing available for the sheep, which are dying. Lack of supplies is such that many are suffering from scurvy. At Strandir there are people dying of hunger and the same is happening here at Skagi. Most people want to go to America but no one is able to."[3]

Sigurdur Ingjaldsson of Gimli, Manitoba, described the situation in his district in Iceland and his departure:

> Yes, this winter was extremely hard and the quality of hay very poor, so poor that the animals were underfed. I began to despair and began to contemplate a move to America. I had actually never been fond of the idea, in fact had been rather opposed to any migration there. But it was not easy to get there. Selling livestock or household goods was next to impossible due to the poor economic conditions and I was hard up but wanted at all cost to try. It has always been my custom never to give up anything I have already started, no matter how difficult it may be. I began to try to sell my animals. All were in good condition and I managed to sell them all but at a very low price. Tools and household goods were much harder to dispose of but I needed to in order for both of us to make it. But then arctic ice moved into bays and fjords preventing any traveling on sea until mid summer.
>
> Blizzards in May dumped so much snow that traveling on land now became impossible. Many farmers had already put the sheep outside, as weather conditions were not so bad. A lot of sheep were lost in those storms. I had already sold my sheep and did not suffer any losses. But the ice delayed our departure and I needed to spend money in order to live. At the same time, those who had intended to purchase my tools and household goods would not as they fell on hard times and could not pay. I realized then that the two of us were unable to go and I was about to give in and abandon my plans. Many neighbors and others encouraged me to stay suggesting that I still could lead a decent life even if I stayed but my Margret insisted I should go, pointing out that I could always send her money for the fare later, provided God gave me good health and I agreed. I left her some money but she was also to attempt to collect from our debtors. I had just enough for the transportation but expected to find work and was not worried, believing that God would lead me as he had always done.
>
> The arctic ice closed all harbors in the north until July when our ship eventually reached Saudarkrokur. It was the steamer *Miaka*, captained by her owner, Otto Wathne. A large number of people intended to emigrate and it took quite some time for them all to reach the harbor from the various places in the district. Many had hesitated following the storms in May thinking that there would not be a ship.
>
> We left Saudarkrokur 11 July 1887, a large number of people, I do not know how many though, and at each place we stopped there were additions. Our last port was Seydisfjordur from where we sailed to England.[4]

Ingjaldsson's preparations for emigration from Iceland were probably typical for the vast majority of the Icelandic migrants. The only way to finance the venture was to sell livestock and household goods but evidently the market for such goods was unstable. One can just picture the despair of those who lost their sheep, either in the storms in May or due to lack of feed during the winter. Ingjaldsson had enough money to cross the Atlantic to Canada and was assisted to reach Ottawa. He worked in mining miles away from the city and eventually earned enough to travel to Winnipeg, where he was later joined by his wife.

Three men aboard the *Miaka*, Sveinn Solvason, Magnus Josefsson, and Solvi Thorlaksson, discussed the situation in Iceland and the general famine that faced a large number of people in northern regions. They resolved to write an appeal to all Icelanders already in America, asking for their support. Their article, entitled "What can be done to avert starvation and human death in Iceland?," was published in *Heimskringla,* the newly established Icelandic weekly in Winnipeg. It described the dismal conditions in the northwest areas:

> It seems that nothing can prevent famine and death in the North of Iceland if no significant assistance is offered. The common people desperately want freedom and the chance to immigrate to America. However, most have no means of meeting the cost as livestock, the only valuable commodity, has been lost. A large number of able and willing people is unemployed and in many cases unable to find temporary or permanent accommodation.
>
> It is the general opinion in North-Iceland that the only solution to this life threatening problem is if the people of North America can lend a helping hand. We, people from Skagafjordur, who sign this appeal, request from every man of Icelandic background in America to arrange for this appeal to appear in American newspapers. Also, to organize fund raising committees in every district in the same fashion as was done in Scandinavia and elsewhere in Europe in 1882 and that the money thus raised be used to transport poor people from Iceland or assist them in any other way.[5]

This appeal did not go unnoticed. It had been translated into English and appeared in newspapers in America, including *The Tribune* in Minneapolis, where a committee had already been arranged with Cyrus Northrop, the president of the state university, to chair. In Winnipeg, a well-attended meeting was called on 12 September 1887 by the Icelandic Society, chaired by its president, Sigtryggur Jonasson.

At the meeting, the editor of *Heimskringla,* Eggert Johannsson, reported that he had learned from Iceland that improvements were in sight: a better fishing catch around the island was expected and the gathering of hay had been better than previously expected. But Johannsson was not ready to say that the crisis was over. Sigtryggur Jonasson read an article from the Icelandic paper *Ísafold* in which the Icelandic Althing (the Parliament) insisted the situation was not as bad as many people claimed. Rev. Jon Bjarnason, who had returned to America in 1884, spoke for a long time. He believed that people in Iceland needed help, and that Icelanders in America should protest against the stand taken by the elected members of Althing. This was an opportunity for Icelandic immigrants in America to be accepted as cousins of the Icelandic people and matters concerning them would then be more likely to be fairly considered in the Icelandic newspapers. He recommended that the committee in Minneapolis continue its collection of funds, but also cautioned that the funds be dispensed wisely. He opposed the idea of handing monies over to the Icelandic authorities, and suggested that people recently arrived from the hardest-hit districts in Iceland should be consulted. They could provide names of reliable individuals in every region to manage funds and guarantee that those in desperate need would benefit.[6] A committee was appointed, which was to call another meeting within ten days. It was not called until 5 November 1887, but was so poorly attended that it was rescheduled for the 14th of the same month; this time many people were in attendance. In the absence of the chair of the society, Sigtryggur Jonasson, Rev. Bjarnason read from letters and articles intended to prove how bad the situation in Iceland was. The committee had gathered the material and sent copies, translated into English, to Minneapolis.

Another meeting was to be held 21 November but was never called. No further attempts were made to organize any collection of funds in Canada. It appears that general interest in the matter was minimal and conflicting reports from Iceland prevented many people from taking a stand. Most Icelandic immigrants in North America were in no financial position to donate much money. But the discussion on emigration from Iceland to North America had never before been so heated. Newspapers on both sides of the Atlantic Ocean became involved and in the next year or two, publications in Winnipeg encouraged people in Iceland to emigrate to North America, especially Canada, while the Icelandic media used more degrading terms for Icelandic emigrants than on any previous occasion.[7]

The vicious verbal battle, which took place in newspapers as well as at public meetings in Iceland during the 1880s and well into the 1890s, left lasting scars. Icelandic patriotism in North America had been damaged, and people in Iceland tended to accept the much-publicized image of the "good for nothing" Icelandic immigrant in America. This unfortunate picture, drawn in the 1880s, was still regarded as accurate in Iceland well into the twentieth century. Authorities in Iceland believed this type of propaganda was their only efficient tool in the effort to discourage mass emigration from Iceland. It must have worked to a degree, as numerous sources indicate that people changed their mind and struggled on in Iceland. Another significant constraint on emigration was the system of labour engagement. The poor and homeless were placed on farms at the discretion of authorities and had little or no chance of emigration to America.

Meanwhile, despite such strong and somewhat cruel opposition in Iceland, some emigration to North America continued, and significant numbers of people emigrated from the country in 1888 and 1889. In 1890 the population of Iceland was 70,240, about 2200 less than in 1880. Emigration to America was mostly blamed for this decrease but diseases also played a part, including German measles in 1882 and an influenza epidemic in early 1890. The Icelandic publication *Fjallkona* gave slightly higher numbers, listing the population of 1890 as 70,927.[8]

Since 1875, when the first Icelanders came west, Winnipeg had been the destination of a large number of Icelandic immigrants. A decision whether to proceed elsewhere or remain in the city was often not made until after the immigrants had spent some time in Winnipeg. Gradually, the number of Icelanders finding permanent homes in the city grew and Winnipeg became the centre of Icelandic immigrants in North America. By the end of 1882, between 500 and 600 Icelanders were residents of the fast-growing city.[9] Usually, the Icelandic immigrants found temporary work, normally somewhere in Ontario, and then continued to a chosen destination. In some instances, the temporary work became permanent and a home was established in the province. Occasionally, such families would later surface in an Icelandic community elsewhere in Canada or the United States. Both *Heimskringla* and *Lögberg,* the two Icelandic weeklies established in Winnipeg in the late 1880s, published reports from communities that mentioned the arrival of new settlers from Ontario. Although some remained in the eastern provinces of Canada and a few moved east from Manitoba or came up from the States, Manitoba was the main attraction.

Icelandic immigrants were certainly not the only ones heading west: 40,000 immigrants arrived in Manitoba between 1876 and 1881. This period has often been referred to as the "Manitoba (land) fever," when farming on the vast prairie was firmly developed. Winnipeg grew in accordance with this great influx of settlers—its population rose from 5000 in 1875 to 8000 in 1881, and 15,000 or more in 1884. This population was diverse in race, origin, and religion, but gradually became amalgamated into a united whole, of which the Icelanders became a part. The first Icelandic settler in Winnipeg was Bjorn G. Skagfjord, who, due to his wife's illness, had to stay behind in Winnipeg in the fall of 1875. It is not known if Skagfjord built a home in the fall of 1875 but Fridrik Sigurbjornsson did, either late in 1875 or early 1876, at No. 6 Hudson's Bay Flats. He is generally considered the first Icelandic homeowner in Winnipeg. Sigurbjornsson married Sigridur Jonsdottir on 6 September 1876, with Rev. Thorlaksson performing the ceremony. The couple had two children, the first born 26 September 1877 and christened at Grace Church by Rev. Frank Walter. The boy was named Frank after the pastor.[10] This was a significant example of a step taken towards integration into Canada because the custom in Iceland for centuries had been to give the newborn boy the first name of either one of his grandfathers, which would have been Sveinbjorn or Jon.

A year later, when the large group from Iceland went to New Iceland via Winnipeg, about 200 Icelanders remained in the city. In the early spring, many people arrived from New Iceland in search of employment, including young women bound for domestic service, and several young men who found work unloading steamers and barges on the Red River, or in the construction of the Main Street sewer, or even sawing wood. There was also work outside Winnipeg; for example, on the transcontinental railway east of Selkirk and on the road from Selkirk to Winnipeg.

Although manual labour was nothing new to most of them, these Icelandic settlers were not used to the pick and shovel. The different type of food and the warm weather in the summer also required adjustments. But for many immigrants, especially the middle-aged who had been their own masters back in Iceland, suddenly having to accept orders was perhaps hardest to accommodate. The first Icelandic community in Winnipeg was in the so-called Shanty Town,[11] located on the Flats, south of Broadway, where the Canadian National Railway yards later stood, extending along the banks of the Red River north to Water Street. The Icelanders built their own shanties, which were, in most instances, little more than poorly constructed huts.

Winnipeg was not a large city in the late 1870s, but it was different from anything the Icelanders had experienced. Nearly all had come from rural Iceland, where the largest communities were small seaside ports, Reykjavík being the largest. Regular working hours also were not followed on an Icelandic farm. During the bright summers, men were accustomed to working late into the night, using every minute of daylight to make hay, and the dark winter months offered little outdoor labour. In Winnipeg, most employment called for a certain number of hours per day, leaving evenings and nights free. Most of the young people planned to work temporarily in the city while their parents established themselves in New Iceland and, later, other Icelandic rural communities in Manitoba. They dutifully contributed some of their earnings to the family farm, believing that one day they would move out there. And quite a few did. But as the problems in New Iceland increased, and it became evident that establishing a farm in the colony was much harder than any Icelandic settler anticipated, many young people remained in Winnipeg. There were also quite a few single men and women who chose to stay in the city.

These people, perhaps more than the others, seemed determined to adjust quickly. They abandoned some significant Icelandic customs for North American ways, of which the anglicizing of their names or adoption of English names were most noteworthy.[12] This also meant abandoning the Icelandic custom of husband and wife each carrying their father's first name, and their children also carrying the husband's first name. The adjustment to city life also required intensive study of the English language, which many Icelanders undertook. This reduced the purity of spoken Icelandic in Winnipeg, as the Icelandic language lacked words for many of the new ideas. In order to overcome the problem, the English word was simply used, though given Icelandic inflections, and a new hybrid language, Western-Icelandic, was born. Some people incorporated English words in every sentence, thus greatly changing the spoken Icelandic. This trend caused great concern in the North American Icelandic community, many people mocking what they called the "preposterous language" spoken by Winnipeg Icelanders. Winnipeg Icelanders were more heavily criticized for the use of this type of language than settlers in any other Icelandic community in North America. At the same time, they also integrated with more ease into Canadian ways. Settlers in rural communities accused the Winnipeg settlers of abandoning Icelandic heritage. A certain division, therefore, can be detected in the Icelandic community in Manitoba in the late 1870s. A comparison between communities in rural Manitoba and Winnipeg is unfair in this case as settlers in small but predominantly Icelandic communities were in much less direct contact with people of other races.

Although many Winnipeg Icelanders could be accused of mixing foreign slang with their mother tongue, they certainly did not ignore or forget their ethnic background. However, there are examples of young people immigrating on their own, both men and women, who, as they adjusted to the city life, drifted away from the Icelandic community, and never became involved. As well, employment or change in marital status often led to a loss of contact with fellow countrymen or loss of interest in maintaining such ties.

From the beginning, the Icelanders in Winnipeg formed a distinct Icelandic community and attempted to establish their place in the multicultural city. The diversity of population probably was beneficial to all the ethnic groups. As these groups were mixed together in one prairie community, all had the opportunity to establish themselves. There was room for numerous religions, different social groups, and ethnic celebrations.

The small group of Icelanders in Winnipeg wanted a leader or an organization to assist them in their adjustment to Canadian life. Jon Thordarson had immigrated to Wisconsin in 1873 and attended the 1874 Milwaukee Celebration when the first Icelandic organization of North America was established. He arrived in Winnipeg in 1877 and was instrumental in establishing the Icelandic Society on 6 September of that year. Although the original membership was small, the purpose was lofty; *Framfari* of 19 October 1877 stated: "It is to promote the honor of the Icelandic people on this Continent and to preserve and cultivate among the Icelanders that liberal and progressive spirit of culture, which has throughout the ages characterized the Icelandic nation."

Thordarson was elected chair. Others on the committee were Arngrimur Jonsson and Magnus Jonsson. The annual fee was to be fifty cents and meetings were to be held every other week. New officers would be elected quarterly, probably in order to provide as many members as possible with experience in office. Women were just as active as the men and, after the first quarter, Helga S. Thorsteinsdottir was elected treasurer.

Despite good intentions, the Icelandic Society seems to have struggled from the very start. The officers changed frequently and left Winnipeg permanently without notice. The membership was always low. On 6 May 1878, for example, only fifty members were recorded. The lack of interest is difficult to explain but the purpose of the organization was perhaps too vague. To state that an organization is to preserve and cultivate among the Icelandic people a liberal and progressive spirit is honourable, but to make it work is another matter. For example, there was no Icelandic publication in Winnipeg during the period from 1875 to 1883 to promote Icelandic culture, and *Framfari*, during its short life in New Iceland (1877 to 1880), was focussed on the hardship in the colony and paid little attention to events in the city. However, before it ceased publication, *Framfari* found room to accuse Icelanders in Shanty Town of drunkenness and other disorderly conduct. The editor (Halldor Briem) pointed out the increasing number of Icelanders in the city, and he stated that although there was work available, rumours had reached New Iceland of idleness and disorder. Drinking in excess was becoming a problem among the Icelanders because many only worked a few days at a time and then spent days in the taverns. He encouraged his compatriots to mend their ways, insisting that jobs in stores were available for young men and that Icelanders should capitalize on what he considered the bright prospects in Winnipeg.[13] A response to the accusations was printed in the paper on 23 May 1879. Ten Icelandic residents of Shanty Town signed a statement in which they maintained that the Icelanders in Winnipeg attended to their employment and were in no manner engaged in any disorderly conduct. Briem responded that his intentions had been good and he still maintained there was some truth to his story.

The consumption of alcoholic beverages among Icelandic immigrants in Winnipeg in the late 1870s is not the real subject of this debate. It must be remembered that Halldor Briem and Sigtryggur Jonasson were fighting for the survival of New Iceland. The Winnipeg Icelandic community was a dangerous alternative, a multicultural city in which the consumption of beer and other spirits was a daily occurrence. The participation of the Icelanders in such "foreign" customs was considered proof of their willing acceptance of assimilation.

The reaction outside Winnipeg to "Western-Icelandic" and the "drinking habits" of the residents of Shanty Town is significant. It illustrated a certain dislike of the urban way of life. As the community in Winnipeg grew in strength and became more influential in the North American Icelandic society, debates between Winnipeg and other Icelandic communities became more frequent.[14] The lack of interest in Winnipeg in the Icelandic Society has also been attributed to the determination of people to adjust to, and become actively involved in, their new environment. For many people, this meant learning and accepting the Canadian way of life. Both men and women keenly observed the way Canadians dressed for different occasions, how they carried themselves in public places, and what were considered proper manners. Making such efforts in adjusting and learning new ways resulted in the neglect or even abandonment of traditional Icelandic ways. It is understandable that anyone so busy learning "foreign" customs and traditions would not at the same time be actively involved in an organization whose sole purpose was to preserve the old ways. Members of the society even attempted to introduce foreign customs into their own Icelandic organization, including foreign rules at meetings.[15] The most active members of the society were dismayed by the lack of general participation by their countrymen, and in 1878 they decided to try a new, more appealing name for the organization. The Icelandic National Society of America replaced the Icelandic Society and its purpose was somewhat clarified by placing importance on assisting the needy, educating the young, and promoting Christian culture. Despite the new name, interest actually dwindled during the next few years.

On 6 May 1881 the society was reorganized again and given a new name, Icelandic Progressive Society. The aim of the revised constitution was to promote the progress of the Icelandic people on the continent. Equal rights to men and women were accorded and the age limit for membership was set at sixteen. Meetings were to be held weekly if circumstances demanded, but otherwise, every other week.[16]

The immediate task was to build a community hall. The founder of the organization in 1877, Jon Thordarson, whose house had previously been used, had left Winnipeg. An Icelander named Helgi Jonsson had been in Winnipeg for some time and, through profitable real-estate transactions, had acquired considerable money and lots. He proposed to donate a lot, provided the entire Icelandic community in Winnipeg would collect funds and guarantee that a hall would be built. This was approved and, with several members involved, the construction was completed on time. The first meeting, held at 137 Jemima Street, took place 10 July 1881 with over 100 people in attendance. The new hall became the community centre, where various Icelandic organizations in Winnipeg held meetings, religious services, concerts, debates, and dances. During the next two years the society was active, but then, as *Leifur,* the first Icelandic periodical published in Winnipeg, edited by Helgi Jonsson, stated, "Committee members are so much on the move that some did not have time to attend more than one or two meetings before departing . . . our Progressive Society is as dead and inactive as can be, possible more so now than when I first became involved. Unemployment and lack of money is mostly to blame."[17] This was only partly the reason. Other Icelandic organizations had taken over some of the original functions of the society.

Since 1877, Icelandic women in Winnipeg had concentrated on two significant aspects of community life. One was assistance to the needy, especially new immigrants; the other was to educate the youth. As people moved out of New Iceland, they often stayed in Winnipeg and required shelter and work. Immigrants from Iceland arrived without money and uncertain about their next move. In 1881 a group of women resolved to organize their own society, independent from the existing one, in order to concentrate on aiding the poor, the unemployed, and the new immigrants.

Eight women, Rebekka Gudmundsdottir, Gudrun Jonsdottir, Kristrun Sveinungadottir, Svava Björnsdottir, Thorbjörg Björnsdottir, Signy Palsdottir, Helga Jonsdottir, and Hildur Halldorsdottir, met at the end of September 1881, and the Women's Society was established. In order to raise money, the new organization staged the play *Sigridur the Sun of Eyjafjord* at the hall, using the proceeds to establish a fund for their society. The ladies worked hard at raising money and soon made donations to various causes. In less than two years, the Women's Society expended almost $400, and about $150 remained in the treasury. The constant support to the needy in Winnipeg was valuable but probably more outstanding was the help provided over the years to new Icelandic immigrants.

More than 900 new immigrants arrived in Winnipeg in 1883 and, although the Icelanders in the city opened their doors and attempted to accommodate as many as possible, there was not enough room in private Icelandic homes. Many people had no alternative but to remain at the Immigration Shed. Members of the Women's Society worked tirelessly for two weeks at preparing meals and tending to other needs of the immigrants. A banquet arranged by the ladies netted $50.00, all of which was donated to these needy immigrants. The ladies of the society also arranged for assistance for the immigrants to obtain work and to become acquainted with the city. The Women's Society continued its praiseworthy work for years. This was the first Icelandic organization in America almost entirely committed to the task of assisting their compatriots upon arrival in Manitoba.[18]

Other Icelandic organizations were established in Winnipeg in the early 1880s. One was the Choral Society: The Harp. The members' vocal and instrumental contributions greatly enriched every program and were always appreciated. Other organizations included the Oriental Society, which encouraged the reading of good literature, including English literature. It was founded in the fall of 1882 and was very much a typical North American organization patterned after college and university societies in America. Its founder, Bjorn Stefan Brynjolfsson, had studied at Thiel Lutheran College in Pennsylvania, originally intending to join the ministry but never did. This organization was short-lived, however, because Brynjolfsson moved to Dakota in 1883 and several other members moved from Winnipeg. The Temperance Society was established in 1884, with fifty-three members. A year later it listed eighty-six members. It worked with other temperance societies in the city to fight against the admission of juveniles to saloons and to prevent the sale of alcoholic beverages to young people.[19]

An IOGT lodge (International Order of Good Templars) had been formed in Iceland in 1884 and, during 1886 and 1887, several eager Good Templars immigrated to Winnipeg from Iceland. On 23 December 1887, the lodge Hekla was formed, with a membership of twenty-four, of which seventeen were men and seven were women. This organization held weekly meetings in the Progressive Society Hall, which included entertainment of various kinds. By March 1888 the number of members had risen to seventy. However, as was becoming the norm in the Winnipeg community, people holding such different views on politics and church matters could not work together in this new organization. About fifty members of Hekla withdrew and established a new lodge, Skuld, on 27 September 1888. A keen rivalry in finding new members commenced with the establishing of Skuld and both lodges offered a variety of entertainment in order to attract members. This competition moved both lodges somewhat off-track; for a while, greater effort was placed on obtaining new members than on the actual temperance work. The activity benefitted the community in the sense that greater cultural awareness was inspired by such programs. Skuld, for example, offered readings of prose and poetry in Icelandic as well as the singing of Icelandic songs. Soon, most Icelanders belonged to one of the lodges. The membership of Hekla in 1900 was 281 and rose to 430 in 1906, the largest such lodge in western Canada.[20]

The Icelandic Labour Association was established on 3 April 1890 as a result of an uncertain labour market. Unemployment in Winnipeg was high and the prospect of improvement was slim because the supply of workers exceeded demand. Approximately sixty Icelandic labourers joined the new organization, which held meetings biweekly and demanded dues of ten cents. It was an independent organization but one delegate was appointed to the Trades and Labor Council. Increased building activity in 1891 led to more demand for workers in the summer and forty Icelanders were employed by Thomas Kelly & Sons, a building contractor. The rate of pay for sewer work was $1.25 a day and construction paid $1.50, but the association demanded a raise to $1.75 and $2.00. The company offered only the best workers a raise, which was rejected, and on 21 July, Icelandic labourers in construction and street maintenance went on strike. It lasted three days, each worker receiving $5.00 from the association, but the eventual settlement was an increase to $1.75 per day. Another strike in 1892 resulted in a twenty-cent increase in pay on sewer construction, but after this the association began to lose ground, mostly due to the lack of unity, and after 1896 it ceased operation.[21]

These organizations were patterned after other, similar, North American societies. But instead of joining "foreign" organizations, the Icelanders established their own, an indication that they wanted control of their own affairs.

Like other Icelandic immigrants in the 1870s, with the exception of New Iceland, Winnipeg Icelanders led a religious life without a resident pastor. However, both Bjarnason and Thorlaksson visited them and performed religious services. Many of the settlers from Iceland in Winnipeg held to their religious heritage, and organized prayer meetings and read scripture. Others, keenly exploring foreign ways in everything, also turned their attention to local churches.

Of the two pastors in New Iceland, Bjarnason had a larger following in Winnipeg. During his tenure in the colony, he visited the city twelve times to hold services. Most of these meetings took place at the home of Jon Thordarson, but at least three are known to have taken place in the Zion Methodist church. His adherents organized and established the Trinity congregation there on 11 August 1878.[22]

Following the departure of Bjarnason and Thorlaksson, and, eventually, also of Halldor Briem in 1882, the Icelandic congregation in Winnipeg was on its own. In the absence of Icelandic pastors, people continued to arrange prayer meetings but also began to attend services of Anglo-Canadian churches.

The Trinity congregation held a meeting in Winnipeg on 30 July 1882, when Halldor Briem departed without resolving the problem of finding another pastor. The next meeting was not called until 8 April 1883. On 22 April, the congregation decided to hold weekly Sunday prayer meetings at 3 p.m. Despite the dedication of several laymen, attendance dwindled and a congregational meeting was not called again until 21 October. The main item on the agenda was a letter from Rev. Bjarnason from Iceland, in which he asked if a call he had received from the Winnipeg congregation in 1881 still stood. In the spring of 1884 he no longer would have any commitments in Iceland and therefore he could return to Manitoba if there still was interest. Apparently, someone from Winnipeg had visited Iceland in 1881 and was asked by members of the Trinity congregation to discuss with Rev. Bjarnason the possibility of his returning to Canada.[23]

The Bjarnasons arrived in Winnipeg in early August of 1884. His arrival brought much-needed life to the congregation, which recorded 140 members at that time. Of those, just 100 were considered active members. By the end of August, after Bjarnason had held two services, an additional 176 members had joined.

Bjarnason's arrival brought religious life back to the Icelandic community in Winnipeg. On 7 September 1884, a Sunday school was established. The enrolment grew from twenty-one in 1884 to 124 in 1885 and 399 in 1891. Students attended classes twice during the week from 9 a.m. to noon and on Sunday afternoons for an hour and a half.

While the arrival of Bjarnason in Winnipeg was appreciated by all his people from New Iceland and also those newcomers who wanted their pastor to be Icelandic, the community he met in Winnipeg was unlike any other he had encountered in North America. The most obvious differences were the absence of so many Icelanders from the only Icelandic congregation in the city and the lack of community spirit. Although the membership rose considerably after his arrival, he never attracted all Icelandic settlers in Winnipeg. Many of the Icelanders believed that their involvement with other religious bodies was an important part of their assimilation, and that in order to become Canadian, they had to accept a new way of life, including a different religion. Even members of the Icelandic congregation who had experienced religious services in other churches, such as the Congregational and Methodist, suggested changes to the Icelandic services. Foreign influences were affecting the Icelandic church in the city. The name of the congregation had been changed in August of 1884 to the First Lutheran Congregation of Winnipeg. Many people insisted on a more simple form of worship service, and the intoning and the use of cassock, traditional Icelandic elements, were abandoned. To make such concessions was uncharacteristic of Bjarnason, but since they were not central to the service, he yielded.[24]

The increase in general participation in church activities led to frequent discussions about the construction of a church for the congregation. Religious services had been held at the community hall but, because the hall was also used for concerts and dances, many people considered it unsuitable for divine services.

Eventually, a lot was purchased on the corner of McWilliam and Nena streets for $500.00. The cost of building the church was $4000.00. It was dedicated on 18 December 1887 and was known as the First Lutheran Church of Winnipeg. The *Free Press* in Winnipeg stated:

> The Icelanders constitute by far the most numerous portion of the foreign ele-
> ment in the city, as well as the oldest, and their church work is proportionally
> ahead. From the beginning of their settlement in this country in 1875, they have
> kept up their religious services, though they have not during the whole of the
> time had a resident clergyman among them. Rev. Jon Bjarnason, their present
> pastor, has been settled in Winnipeg for several years, and is the pioneer resi-
> dent minister among the foreign population. Though his congregation has not
> been first in church building in the order of time, having until now occupied a
> hall belonging to an Icelandic society, it has just entered into a church which is
> by far the largest one devoted to services in a foreign language, being capable of
> comfortably seating eight hundred people on ordinary occasions and a thousand
> at times of special gatherings, although built no larger than was deemed abso-
> lutely necessary.[25]

Although the number of members in the Winnipeg Icelandic congregation had risen considerably since the arrival of Bjarnason, the absence of many others did not go unnoticed in the city. In 1888, Dr. George Bryce, professor at Mani toba College, who had been involved with many of the charitable institutions in Winnipeg and was interested in the Icelanders, met Jonas Johansson, who was eager to work as a missionary for the Presbyterian church in the Winnipeg Ice landic community. (He was later joined by his brother, Larus, who attempted street-corner preaching.) According to the *Free Press,*

> Dr. Bryce announced the formation of a new mission in the western part of the
> city. A suitable site had been examined, a subscription list opened and over
> $400 promised to the building. It was agreed that it should be regarded as a
> mission under the care of the Presbyterian and that the church and the manse
> building fund be asked to grant a loan of $500 for the purchase of the site. [26]

This announcement stunned the leaders of the Icelandic Church in Winnipeg and Bjarnason reacted in *Sameiningin* in June of 1888. He pointed out that the Icelanders had recently built their own church and their congregation had grown in strength during the last few years. He stated that he failed to understand this interest in the Icelanders, as no efforts had been made by the Presbyterian church to influence the Catholics, French and Irish and Italians, in the city. Neither had any attempt been made to reach the thousands of Canadians of various ethnic backgrounds, such as American, Scottish, and English, who stood outside the church. The thought of this mission succeeding and eventually bringing about the destruction of the Icelandic congregation worried him. He stressed that Ice landers would not benefit at all from religious services performed in a language other than Icelandic.

The Icelandic Lutheran Synod also strongly opposed the new mission, but to no avail. In 1889, the Kate Street Chapel was enlarged and its name changed from the Manitoba College Mission to Martin Luther Icelandic Church. The worries of Bjarnason and others within the Icelandic church were unnecessary, however, as the mission never became a threat to the First Lutheran Church. The Icelanders in Winnipeg never crowded the chapel on Kate Street; upon the death of Jonas Johannsson in 1891, the mission lost the little following it had in the Icelandic community.[27]

The First Lutheran Church probably did not expect its next opponent to rise from within. Bjarnason had visited Iceland in 1889 in an effort to find Icelandic pastors for the Icelandic Synod in America. He was unsuccessful; only Rev. Hafsteinn Pjetursson travelled with him to Canada. A lengthy illness from 1892 to 1893 forced Bjarnason to minimize his duties at the First Lutheran Church and he was replaced by Pjetursson. As Bjarnason regained his strength, he returned to his duties but he soon noticed a change.

The Icelanders in Winnipeg in the late 1880s and especially in the 1890s gradually had become divided into two groups, one north of Notre Dame Avenue, the other on the south side. People in the south began to ignore the services at the First Lutheran Church and eventually asked Pjetursson to become their pastor. He accepted and held his first service at the Mulvey School on 3 May 1894. A new congregation was established, called the Winnipeg Tabernacle Congregation. These dissidents from the First Lutheran Church warned Pjetursson against any attempt to establish the new congregation within the synod. They believed that Bjarnason and others in the synod would attempt to gain control.[28] The building of a church on the corner of Sargent Avenue and Furby Street was begun on 15 October of 1894 and the dedication took place 16 December that year.

The pastor and his flock worked well together in introducing innovations to the otherwise Lutheran service, such as delivering the sermon without notes, emphasizing choir music, and bringing in soloists, which was new to the traditional Icelandic service. Sunday school was immediately established and the activities of young people were supported. There had been only nineteen original members of this new congregation in 1894, but their number was up to 450 in the summer of 1899. Two groups within the church were established, the Ladies Aid Society and the Young People's Society. Rev. Pjetursson resigned from his congregation in Winnipeg in 1899 and moved to Copenhagen. He was replaced by Rev. Bjarni Thorarinsson.

The Tabernacle Congregation never did apply to become a member of the synod, much to the annoyance of some Icelanders. *Lögberg* published a threat: "In the present circumstances we must seriously advise all those belonging to the First Lutheran Congregation not to become members of the Tabernacle Congregation. If the Tabernacle continues on its present course it will cause a division in our church and will at the same time harm all work of Christianity among our people in America."[29]

The ever-present difference in religious views in the Icelandic community reflects the liberalism in such matters among Icelandic immigrants to North America. Religious controversies in various forms and of different consequences were common throughout the years from 1870 to 1914. North America had such a variety of religious bodies, synods, and churches that it was inevitable some would influence Icelandic immigrants. Bjorn Petursson was one who had a very open mind. He was born in Iceland in 1826 and immigrated to America in 1876. He had attended the Latin School in Reykjavík, taking courses in theology. He founded the Unitarian movement, which was active in Icelandic communities both in Manitoba and Dakota.[30] He lectured on both sides of the border and gradually built up a large following. In 1890 he worked in Winnipeg as a missionary of the American Unitarian Association, establishing a Unitarian congregation on 1 February 1891. The original membership was small, but building a church was an important, immediate goal. A fundraising gathering on 10 February 1892, attended by more than 200 people, raised $60.00. After the Winnipeg congregation received a donation of $1000.00 from Unitarians in the United States, the construction began. The building site was on the corner of McWilliam and Nena streets, just across from the First Lutheran Church, and the construction was completed in December 1892. Not subscribing to any creed, the Unitarians believed in the unity of God, insisting that Jesus Christ was his son in the same way all people were his children. They emphasized the humanitarian and ethical teachings of Christ. The Lutherans, led by Bjarnason, opposed the Unitarians, considering them, as he had the Norwegian Synod, a threat to the unity of the North American Icelandic community.[31]

However, the ecclesiastical history of the early Icelanders in Winnipeg not only reflects their liberal views on religious matters, but also reveals their keen desire to assimilate. A large number abandoned the First Lutheran Church, which, through Bjarnason, represented the faith of the Icelandic nation. However, even Bjarnason made certain adjustments to North American Anglican ways. Later, after his mission in Iceland to recruit pastors for the synod had failed, he admitted that "the theology training in Iceland does not adequately meet the demands which church life in this country makes."[32]

This remark indicated that even his own church in Winnipeg and his role within it were different from the Icelandic State Church and the function of the pastor. In his sermon in the Milwaukee church in 1874, he had stated that when the faith of the homeland is abandoned, the ethnic background is also abandoned. In 1874 he believed that the Icelanders could find a site in North America where they would continue to live as Icelanders. In 1890, he knew differently. Icelandic customs were giving way to foreign influences, perhaps nowhere as obviously as in Winnipeg.

The decision to settle in Winnipeg required that the settlers have daily contact with the English-speaking majority. This meant that Icelanders immediately emphasized the study of English. During the winter of 1876-1877, several adults met regularly to learn the language. Children and young people received some home schooling during the first few years. The children began to enter public schools in 1879, when six Icelandic children are recorded at the Carlton school.

Sunday schools were established early. The Icelandic Society, founded in the fall of 1877, for example, immediately established Sunday school, at which three ladies gave instruction in reading and catechism. Stories in English were read to the students. By 1880 an evening school was established with eighteen students the first winter. Due to the sharp rise in the Icelandic population in Winnipeg in the next few years, the school had to expand. A day school was established at the beginning of 1881.

If fifteen students were registered, one permanent teacher was to be hired, and if the enrolment exceeded twenty-five, a second teacher would be added. The fee per child was $2.00 a month; orphans and the very poor were exempt from payment. These were the times of increasing immigration to Winnipeg from Iceland and also a steady flow of settlers from New Iceland. The majority of these newcomers were poor and the Progressive Society forwarded $232.00 to the school in its first winter of operation. Subjects taught included English, geography, math, and Icelandic.

An Icelander named Frimann B. Anderson arrived in Winnipeg in 1884 after completing a three-year arts course in Hamilton. He noted that the Icelanders would need ministers, doctors, and lawyers in their communities, and introduced the idea of an Icelandic high school. The proposed educational centre would unite the scattered Icelandic communities in North America and foster the Icelandic spirit. His plans were met with scepticism. Opponents argued that their children would manage well through the existing public school system, and that such an exclusive Icelandic institution might be too burdensome for the community. The plan failed to materialize but was not forgotten.[33]

Helgi Jonsson arrived in Winnipeg in 1878 and immediately became active in the Icelandic community. He joined the Icelandic Society and enthusiastically advocated for the construction of a hall for the organization, and the establishment of an Icelandic newspaper. *Framfari* had ceased publication. Jonsson had a difficult time finding financial support, but he bought the *Framfari* press and the first issue of the new weekly, *Leifur,* was published on 5 May 1883. It was four pages and the subscription per year was $2.00. Jonsson appealed to all Icelanders in North America for support, because "it is the Icelandic people I have in mind. They will lose more than I without a good newspaper in their own language."[34]

Leifur was met with mixed feelings in the Winnipeg community. Many people appreciated a newspaper in their own language, bringing news, poetry, and other cultural material. The critics pointed to the lack of experience of the editor and his inability to write in proper Icelandic. Also, the typesetting was of poor quality—an inexperienced printer had been employed in haste. The first few issues contained little of quality or literary value. The editorials concentrated more on the problems of publishing an ethnic newspaper in North America than on discussing matters of concern to the Winnipeg community. The editor, heavily criticized for the poor content, responded angrily: "Changes in the editorial policy of Leifur should not be expected while I am the owner and publisher."[35] Jonsson maintained that people were expecting too much too soon; he had already paid $600.00 and expected his risk to be close to $2000.00. He pointed out that many subscribers did not even bother paying the annual subscription fee of $2.00.

The struggle to publish the paper continued throughout 1883, but early in 1884, an improvement was noticeable. Jonsson hired a young man, Eggert Johannsson, who had immigrated to America in 1876 at the age of twelve. Although he lacked experience in writing, he was taking his first steps as a newspaperman and later blossomed as a writer. Jonsson and Johannsson agreed that the paper should be relevant to every Icelandic community in North America, and they succeeded in obtaining reports on conditions in many communities, on immigration, and on farming developments.

With a break in publication from 18 November 1884 to 3 January 1885, *Leifur* continued to appear until 4 June 1886, six months after Jonsson had moved from Winnipeg and had handed over the editorship to Eggert Johannsson. Even though the quality of *Leifur* can be questioned, the fact it ceased publication due to lack of support is significant. Jonsson had obtained financial backing from Ottawa and contributed regularly out of his own pocket to meet the cost, but his subscribers were always heavily in arrears. The issue of ownership and influence, especially in the Winnipeg community, was growing to such a degree that unity in almost any matter seemed impossible.

However, only three months passed until a new weekly publication appeared in Winnipeg. Frimann B. Anderson's *Heimskringla* was introduced to readers on 9 September 1886. Eggert Johannsson became associated with Anderson from the beginning, as did Einar Hjorleifson, who had just arrived in Winnipeg. The policy of the paper appeared on the last page of the first issue: "The paper is first and foremost for Icelanders in Canada. We will take a keen interest in all questions which are of much concern to them whether they are matters of public affairs, employment or education." All questions concerning the people of Iceland, including government and cultural affairs, would be addressed. It declared that "the paper is to be politically independent and is free to deal with questions which in the opinion of the editor appear appropriate." *Heimskringla* was not to be an agent for emigration from Iceland, but immigration and any other subject might be discussed. The first issue was of much higher literary quality than *Leifur* had ever been. It included poems by Anderson and Hjorleifson, a book review, and a report on Gladstone's government. The editorial asked if Icelanders in North America should become involved in politics; the editor maintained that as citizens of this country, and in no manner inferior, Icelanders should take part.

Heimskringla, like *Leifur,* soon ran into difficulties and publication stopped for several months. This was mostly due to financial problems but also because Anderson and Hjorleifson could not work together. From 9 December 1886 to 7 April 1887, no issue was published. Anderson then took charge until November of 1888, when he moved from Winnipeg, leaving the paper in the hands of Johannsson and a new stock company.

As the Icelanders in Winnipeg adjusted to their new environment, they began to pay attention to politics. By the mid-1880s, most of them had chosen one of the traditional political parties in Canada, Conservatives or Liberals. When *Heimskringla* declared her support for the Conservatives in Canada and Democrats in the United States, opponents of these parties demanded another weekly, and on 14 January 1888, *Lögberg*, a second Icelandic weekly, was launched. In the next few years, both papers strove to employ highly literate and experienced editors, even bringing in some from Iceland.

Both papers addressed issues of interest in the community. *Lögberg*, for example, in the first year, discussed Icelandic immigration, public school education, Icelanders in North America, relations between Iceland and Icelanders in America, conditions in Iceland, literature, and Canadian politics. Debates were frequent between the two papers on many issues. In fact, it was rare that the papers agreed on important matters. However, both papers fully promoted the well-being of Icelandic immigrants in America. For example, both eagerly encouraged all Icelanders to preserve their heritage and language, but held different views on how that could be best accomplished. At least initially, contributions to the papers from every Icelandic community, as well as regular news and articles from Iceland, added to the variety in their columns. Geographically divided in America, the Icelanders were united through the two papers. Both papers allotted room for North American Icelandic literature, both prose and poetry, much of which undoubtedly would otherwise have been lost. Reaching nearly every home in the early days, both papers also contributed greatly to the preservation of the Icelandic language.

Other publications concentrated chiefly on religious matters. *Sameiningin* was launched in December 1885, but did not become a regular monthly publication until March of the following year. It was the religious periodical of the Icelandic Synod and was established to unite the scattered congregations in America. Edited by Bjarnason for almost thirty years, it upheld his religious views and those of the synod, and was often engaged in bitter disputes with opponents of the Icelandic North American Lutheran church. *Aldamót,* written by the pastors of the synod from 1891 to 1903, was published annually. It featured lectures given at conferences as well as articles on religion and ethics.[36]

Two brothers became the first Icelanders to establish businesses in the city. In 1876, Fridjon Fridriksson opened an employment agency for Icelanders looking for work in Winnipeg. His brother Arni arrived in Toronto in 1873 and, recovering from a permanent injury—frozen feet—he found a job in a shoe factory, where he worked for two years. He moved to Winnipeg in the fall of 1875 and in 1879 he opened a store and a shoe-repair shop on Main Street, the first Icelandic shop in Winnipeg.[37]

As immigration to Canada increased in the second half of the 1870s, Winnipeg grew rapidly. The Canadian government strongly supported settlement on the prairie, with the eventual goal of settling the entire region between the Red River and the Rocky Mountains. To this end, the construction of the transcontinental railway pressed forward and Winnipeg prospered. In 1880 the first boom in Manitoba began. Prices of lots in Winnipeg and some towns, and farmlands in settled communities, rose quickly.

Although they were unfamiliar with the real-estate world, several Icelanders in Winnipeg paid close attention. Helgi Jonsson, the founder of *Leifur,* bought a lot in Winnipeg in 1880 and resold it at six times the original price. His house stood originally on McWilliam, now called Pacific Avenue. His sudden wealth enabled him to travel back to Iceland for pleasure in October 1881, where he was labelled the richest Icelander in America.

During the late summer of 1881, a plan for an Icelandic investment company began to circulate, which would enable all Icelanders to take advantage of the sudden boom. It was registered in November under the name John Julius & Co, probably under the Partnership Act. Forty-five members invested sums ranging from $100.00 to $2000.00. However, in January of 1882, speculators in eastern Canada showed signs of hesitation and by the summer the boom was over. The value of property suddenly plummeted, rents dropped from $40.00 to $8.00, and opportunities for employment ceased. The Icelanders suffered, as did so many others. Many members had all their money invested but suddenly there was little or no sale for their properties. Finally, in early 1883, the Icelandic Company was liquidated, forcing many people to sell their lots at whatever price was offered. A lesson in booms and busts had been learned.[38]

However, in 1883, Icelanders in Winnipeg established their businesses. Arni Fridriksson expanded and opened a second store. W. Johnson & Co, owned by Thorvaldur Johanneson and Baldvin L. Baldvinsson, operated a new shoe store on Main Street, and Thomas Paulson, a joiner by trade, advertised a new business on Jemima Street (now Elgin). In addition, Helgi Jonsson ran a dry-goods shop, and Walter Gudnason repaired and cleaned watches and clocks in his shop on Notre Dame Avenue.

The boom had not only increased property values but had also increased employment and opportunities in various industries. By mid-1883, twelve Icelandic merchants operated their own stores. There were also twelve dressmakers, as well as carpenters, printers, painters, and one blacksmith.

12

Manitoba Rural Settlements

When the New Iceland settlement failed to materialize in the late 1870s and people moved to Winnipeg or Dakota, settlers began to consider rural regions elsewhere in Manitoba. Although the Icelanders had struggled in New Iceland, immigration to Manitoba had continued and, once the railroad from Ontario to Winnipeg was completed, the flow of immigrants increased. Many settlers looked at regions southwest of Winnipeg. In August of 1880, Sigurdur Kristofersson, who was in the original advance party of 1875 that selected the site for New Iceland, and Kristjan Jonsson decided to explore southwest Manitoba.

A vast region of the prairie, the fertile area between Emerson and the Assiniboine River, had been settled by only a few people. Everett Parsonage, who had worked for John Taylor in New Iceland, was one of these pioneer settlers, and had recommended the district to friends in New Iceland. Kristofersson (later Christopherson) and Jonsson sailed to Winnipeg and then south to Emerson. From there they proceeded to the Land Claim Office in Nelsonville, where they gathered information regarding available land and how to find Mr. Parsonage's home near Pilot Mound. They reached his home after walking for three days.[1]

About fifty kilometres northwest from Pilot Mound, they found Oak Creek, a stream they followed westward until they found a site. South of the site they chose were the rolling Tiger Hills, and north and west was the prairie, possibly the most fertile part of Manitoba.

At the Land Claim Office in Nelsonville, Christopherson filed entry on a homestead and, true to the Icelandic custom, he named it Grund. Jonsson also filed an entry on a homestead nearby and then returned to New Iceland while Christopherson invested in a scythe and went back to his land. Two Englishmen, living in a tent at the time, had claimed land nearby and all three worked at making hay for Christopherson's expected livestock while he, in turn, built a log cabin for them. Sigurdur Christopherson spent two months on his new homestead before returning to New Iceland for the winter.

On 25 September 1880, two others from New Iceland, Skafti Arason and William Taylor, claimed land in the same district for themselves and others. By the end of 1880, eight settlers from New Iceland had claimed land in this part of Manitoba, referred to as Argyle.[2] On 15 March 1881, the first group, consisting of five men, three women, and ten children, left New Iceland for Winnipeg. They used sleighs pulled by oxen to transport their belongings and drove the livestock they owned ahead of them. They reached Winnipeg on 17 March. After resting for a day, they continued westward and, after covering close to 320 kilometres, often across rough terrain in sleet or hail, they arrived on 31 March. Before leaving New Iceland, Skafti Arason had placed on his sleigh a caboose three metres long and about two metres wide, in which his wife and children found shelter. A small stove was inside, which kept everyone in the group warm at night. Sigurdur Christopherson had arranged for the use of the log cabin he had helped build the previous fall because the two Englishmen, the owners, were away. Others in this first group hastily constructed huts near their land. The first two or three weeks remained cold, as snow still covered the ground. However, as soon as it warmed up, each settler moved onto his land and built more adequate temporary dwellings.[3]

In the spring and summer, several others claimed land. These immigrants were all poor, some arriving with nothing but the clothes they wore. Despite their poverty, no one suffered. There was an abundance of hay and large meadows for the livestock. Soon chicken and pigs were added to these farms and everyone helped to raise the log cabins for each settler. The homes had sod roofs and dirt floors, but provided good shelter. The most important task was to clear and plough the land. The crop the following year was good. Most farmers used reapers, and some had access to haymowers. No one had horses; the oxen were busy animals on every farm. Homemade wagons transported the sheaves from the fields.

The considerable distance from the nearest market was a problem. The closest town was slowly developing at Carberry by the CPR main tracks, about sixty kilometres away. It was a rough journey and, because the settlers had to take their crop to market, most chose to travel to Brandon or Manitou, even though both places were further away.[4] These journeys to market often lasted up to four days, so many people travelled together. The trips took place in the fall and, because the weather could get bad, men often travelled day and night, stopping in bushes only for short rests or to cook meals. In 1886 a railway was built just north of present-day Glenboro. Another town, Cypress River, developed later about fifteen kilometres further east. In both towns, shops provided a range of conveniences for the settlers in the district. This brought about positive changes in everyday life as the Icelandic farmers could invest in adequate tools and equipment. Many settlers became heavily indebted, but their farm products not only increased in quantity but also in quality. All farmland in this district soon became valuable.

The main occupations in Argyle district were growing grain and raising cattle. As farms developed, employment became available to single young people. Many farmers had only young children and depended on outside labour, especially at harvest time.

The number of settlers grew steadily:

New Settlers in Argyle, 1881-1890

Year	New Settlers
1881	7
1882	17
1883	15
1884	18
1885	10
1886	10
1887	11
1888	15
1889	0
1890	2

Source: Kristjanson, *The Icelandic People in Manitoba*, 139.

At the end of the first decade, the total number of settlers and their families was 527 and the entire population of Icelanders in the Argyle district was just under 700. The council for the Argyle district consisted of seven elected members, six councillors, each in a constituency, and one reeve, elected at large. Icelanders took active part in politics and, from 1883 on, they had at least one representative on council, the first one being Sigurdur Christopherson.

Obtaining supplies was a priority. Sigurdur Christopherson operated a small store in his home, but, as the railway reached the area and new towns developed, he closed his shop. In 1886, when the railway reached Glenboro, Fridjon Fridriksson, formerly of New Iceland and Winnipeg, arrived in the town and established a new store, which he operated until 1906.

In 1889, another railway was built south of the community, nineteen kilometres south of Glenboro. Kristjan Jonsson, one of the pioneer settlers in the community, opened a hardware store in Baldur, a new small town on the rail line, and his father opened a bookstore not long afterwards. Although the demand for young people on the farms was great at seeding time and especially during harvest, young Icelanders began to seek more permanent work in the towns, such as

Glenboro, Baldur, and Cypress River. Many young men learned a trade and, later, some opened up stores next to their workshops.[5]

By this time, the Icelandic settlers understood the importance of assimilation. They had to adopt new ways of farming; their construction of houses on the prairie was unfamiliar; and, in the homes, much of the food was as foreign as the means of cooking and preserving it. Even the clothes were different. However, the Icelanders made progress. On 25 January 1884, Skafti Arason wrote to *Leifur* that "we have in all some 650 acres plowed, 250 cattle including 62 oxen, around 70 pigs, 60 sheep, 9 horses and 2 ponies, 6 mowing machines, 6 horse-rakes, 3 single reapers, 2 combines, 1 threshing machine, 13 wagons, 23 ploughs and 12 harrows." There were forty settlers in the community in early 1884 and Arason's report illustrates their success in just over three years. They had cleared and ploughed 294 hectares in this short period of time, a clear evidence of progress in new agricultural ways. In Winnipeg *Leifur* reported on 26 February 1886 that 14,147 bushels of wheat were harvested in the Argyle community in 1885. In comparison, in 1879 the total production in all the communities of New Iceland was a little over 660 bushels.

Young men from Iceland who arrived in Winnipeg during the 1880s often went to the Argyle settlement, at first as summer hands, and then remained in the district as the towns developed. As they did in Dakota, Icelandic settlers in Argyle took an active part in the community. For example, Christopherson was elected to join a delegation to Winnipeg to discuss the development of railroads in the district. The Icelanders may have settled close to one another and established their farms, but they were a part of a multicultural community, benefitting from the experience of others as well as contributing from their own.

A letter by Jon Olafson published in *Leifur,* 26 February 1886, stated that the Women's Society, established 24 October 1885, had arranged for the staging of the play *Sigridur, The Sun of Eyjafjord*. This society was active for a long time and contributed in numerous ways to cultural as well as religious activity in the community. During the construction of the first Icelandic church in the area, for example, the society arranged for the collection of funds on numerous occasions.

Perhaps the most unique association founded by Icelanders in the early days of immigration to America was established on 23 March 1884 at the home of Kristjan Jonsson. Skafti Arason was instrumental in introducing and establishing the Reform Society. The purpose of this organization was to improve social behaviour and strengthen Christianity. Drinking alcoholic beverages was prohibited and those people who were not already smoking tobacco regularly were not to start. Members were urged to refrain from the use of uncouth expressions and profane language.[6] Although the society flourished for only a few years, its aims and the stringent rules for social and personal conduct demonstrate at least one prevailing line of thought among the Icelandic Argyle settlers.

Most of the pioneer settlers from New Iceland had been strong supporters of Rev. Bjarnason. Some said they had never considered Dakota as a future home because it had been settled largely by followers of Thorlaksson. Many of the leaders in Argyle, including Skafti Arason and Sigurdur Christopherson, had been very involved in the Lutheran church established in New Iceland by Bjarnason. Therefore, once they were comfortably settled in a new colony, the settlers looked to organizing a Lutheran congregation.

On 1 January 1884, the Free Church Congregation was founded. As the name indicated, it was not to belong to any religious body in North America. The congregational laws were similar to those of Bjarnason's congregations in New Iceland in the 1870s. The first congregational board included both Skafti Arason and Sigurdur Christopherson, who extended, on behalf of their new church, a call to Bjarnason to serve a certain part of the year in Argyle. He arrived in the colony in October 1884 and agreed to devote six weeks to the new Icelandic community. He commuted from Winnipeg and never resided for any length of time in Argyle, but he visited on numerous occasions during the first two decades.[7]

A second Lutheran congregation in the community was established 26 July 1885. According to an article in *Leifur*, "A congregational meeting held in the Free Church July 13th revealed a deep difference in opinions on numerous congregational matters. This controversy resulted in the resignation of many settlers from the Free Church and presently the same are engaged in organizing a new congregation, which they propose to call Liberty Congregation."[8] Fifty-seven members registered in the Liberty Congregation, all of whom had belonged to the Free Church. Skafti Arason and Sigurdur Christoperson now belonged to different congregations.

Even though Christopherson and his people had organized a new congregation, they were willing to work with the older church to obtain a pastor who would serve both congregations. Christopherson led a delegation to a congregation meeting at the Free Church on 2 August, and asked to be allowed to address the meeting on the issue. Skafti Arason rose and opposed their involvement in the proceedings of the meeting. Nevertheless, Bjorn Jonsson, chair of the meeting, overruled Arason, asking Christopherson if the Liberty Church was a member of the Icelandic Lutheran Synod of North America. The following reply is quoted from the minutes of a meeting held 9 August in the Liberty congregation, at which Christopherson was asked to give a report on the joint meeting of the two congregations. He stated:

> I addressed his question in the following manner saying that as all members of the Liberty congregation had been members of the Free Church when the laws of the Synod were accepted and approved, we all consider ourselves members of the Synod. If, however, this situation was unacceptable to the Synod it would immediately be corrected as a written request to join the Synod would immediately be forwarded. The Chairman found my answer unacceptable and opposed

any participation on our behalf in their search for a pastor. He then ordered us to remain silent, calling us fools before the meeting was adjourned.[9]

This short quotation illustrates the bitterness between the two Lutheran congregations, who were both people of the synod and both comprised of members who formerly supported Bjarnason.

The Liberty Church held a meeting 6 March 1886, chaired by Rev. Bjarnason. He agreed to serve the Liberty congregation in Argyle unconditionally, in the same way he was serving the Free Church. He urged the meeting to support *Sameiningin*, the official publication of the synod, and Sunday schools, and concluded by warning against indulgence in alcohol.

The controversy between the two congregations dissipated and in a few years people in the community appeared to have forgotten it. Joint efforts became possible and in 1888 the Argyle congregations announced they would be holding the annual conference of the synod in the summer of 1889. The matter of a church building became of utmost importance.

The Liberty congregation held a meeting 25 November 1888 to address the church construction. The meeting concluded with the election of four members to a committee of seven who was to represent the Liberty Church congregation in a joint meeting with a committee of the same size from the Free Church. The sum of $731.75 was collected, and the church was erected at Grund, about eight kilometres north of Baldur and eleven from Glenboro.[10]

On 31 March, it was announced that the services of Rev. Hafsteinn Petursson of Iceland had been obtained and the sum of $90.00 been sent to Iceland as an advance payment. He served the community until 20 March 1893, when he joined the Tabernacle Church in Winnipeg. The Icelanders in Argyle then formally called Thorkell O. Sigurdsson, a theology student from Philadelphia, in 1894. He accepted and was ordained at the conference of the synod in Pembina, North Dakota, in 1895, but his health failed. While he was recovering at Park River in North Dakota, the congregations in Argyle advanced him some money and their best wishes for a speedy recovery. However, in a letter dated 17 December 1895, addressed to Jon Olafson in Argyle, Sigurdsson expressed his gratitude and concluded, "The wonderful, glorious Christmas celebration is approaching. But all I am able to do is to send you and the congregations my best Christmas greetings in the name of the Lord."[11] He passed away 27 December 1895 in Park River. The congregations then employed Rev. Jon J. Clemens, who had immigrated from Iceland to Chicago, where he studied and was ordained. He served the Argyle community from 1896 to 1901.

The reconciliation of two congregations was good for the entire community. A Reading Society was organized at Baldur on 28 January 1893 with the aim to increase the reading of Icelandic literature in the Argyle community and to make the literature readily available to all. The founding members worked diligently in obtaining books and magazines, and membership rose steadily. New reading organizations were formed, some of which were in existence well into the twentieth century. A good collection of books and magazines in Icelandic and also in English on Icelandic matters has always been invaluable to the Icelandic community. In the early years it helped maintain the Icelandic language, but it also greatly contributed to the promotion of Icelandic sentiment in the district.

By 1890 three Icelandic settlements in North America—Minnesota, North Dakota, and Argyle—clearly stood out as prosperous communities. However, during the 1880s and 1890s, the colony at New Iceland also prospered and other Icelandic settlements in Manitoba were developed. New Iceland became a part of the Province of Manitoba in 1881 as the provincial boundaries were extended. This did little to improve conditions in the colony, as the settlers were reluctant to establish a municipal government, which the founding of the County of Gimli permitted. In their opinion, new taxes, which would automatically be introduced, outweighed possible benefits of a municipal government. Some settlers believed a municipal government would make obtaining grants for roadwork, drainage, bridges, and school construction easier. But most people wanted to find a way to solve New Iceland's problems without outside assistance.

The settlers in New Iceland who refused to leave were convinced that life in the district could and would improve. With more than 750 people gone by 1881, the remaining 250 felt that the out-migration might, after all, benefit the rest. However, it was obvious that the soil was not well suited for grain and so the settlers made no attempts to clear more land for grain; the same fields were seeded year after year. This did little to improve the economy of the settlement.

The people in New Iceland were scattered, the majority residing at Icelandic River and in Vidirnes district. Gimli village was nearly depopulated; in 1883 ten homes were occupied, and five in 1885 when the population was only twenty. However, by 1891, there were forty residences in the village, and although most of the newcomers were poor, the community showed signs of revival.

The local government was no longer functioning, although a council of five still existed in Vidirnes. The sudden exodus from New Iceland had aggravated the issue of the Canadian government loan. A certain amount had been paid back, but although the government made little effort to collect the money, it was an impossible situation for those who remained, since homestead patents were withheld as long as the debt was outstanding. There had been a drop in land values immediately following the migration, and new, destitute immigrants needed help if they were to settle successfully. Eventually, after tireless efforts by Fridjon Fridriksson, who was soon to move to the Argyle community, the rest of the amount due was cancelled.[12]

Sigtryggur Jonasson and Fridriksson had built a sawmill in 1881 at Icelandic River. Neither of them had sufficient funds to raise the estimated cost of $12,000.00, but an outsider named Osenbrugge provided the balance and the mill began operation. In addition, the steamer *Victoria* and two barges were purchased by Jonasson and two brothers, Fridjon and Arni Fridriksson, for $7,500.00. Only Fridjon Fridriksson and Sigtryggur Jonasson directly managed the company—Fridriksson was in charge of the sawmill and Jonasson managed the transportation on the lake.[13] This venture kept the small community in New Iceland alive, especially the one at Icelandic River, during the critical period from 1881 to 1885. Employment at the mill was steady, as it was in operation year-round. The winter salary was $13.00 to $15.00 a month, and often reached $20.00 in the summer. At the busiest times, more than eighty people earned a living from the company, either at the sawmill or aboard the steamer. By 1886 the two brothers, Fridjon and Arni, sold out, and Jonasson moved his business to Big Throat River on the east side of the lake.[14]

The years from 1881 to 1885 are often referred to as a critical period in the history of the New Iceland settlement. These were the years when the future of the settlement would be decided. Another flood, unseasonably cold winters and springs, or another plague would have driven out the remaining settlers and terminated the Icelandic community on the western bank of Lake Winnipeg. However, despite the trying times, a small trickle of immigration into the settlement occurred in the first half of the 1880s. A few previous inhabitants returned after spending some time in Winnipeg, but most of the new settlers came directly from Iceland. Gradually, the population began to climb. In 1883, for example, Vidirnes district had only around fourteen families or between sixty and seventy inhabitants. By early 1885, the number of families had risen to fifty-four and the population was around 250. The number of families in Arnes district had risen from just six families in 1880 to twenty by 1885. The total population continued to grow, reaching almost 1600 by 1894. This was higher than it ever had been during the period from 1875 to 1880.[15] If 1886 marked the beginning of better times, 1887 certainly witnessed more progress than had been made since the Icelanders' arrival. The newcomers brought with them the renewal of a much-desired community spirit. Larger homes were constructed, more land claimed and fenced, and trade and travel increased. *Heimskringla* reported that "many of the immigrants have constructed new houses, brought in new mowers, wagons, sleighs and plows. They have extended their land and fenced it."[16]

Fish had been the main staple for most of the decade and certainly the most important trading commodity. Once the lake had reached lower levels, old fishing grounds were revisited with excellent results. In 1884, for example, it was common for fishermen with first-rate equipment to return ashore with up to 2000 fish, after spending around ten days on the lake. Still, the fishing boats were not yet decked, and the best fishing grounds had yet to be discovered.

Farming was not neglected but most settlers concentrated on fishing or on work at the sawmill at Icelandic River. Grain growing didn't increase for the next ten years or so until more settlers claimed land further west. Thus, the Icelandic River settlement began to expand westward, up along the river away from the lake.

Sigtryggur Jonasson and other influential men in the Icelandic community began to urge the benefits of a municipal government. They pointed at the poor roads and lack of bridges and schools. Finally, in 1886 the Municipality of Gimli was created and legally constituted in the fall of 1887 after an election. Johann Briem, one of the pioneers of 1876, was elected the first reeve for the new municipality, and councillors were Johannes Helgason, Thorgrimur Jonsson, Gudlaugur Magnusson, and Kristjan Kjernested. The new council elected Gudni Thorsteinsson as secretary-treasurer.[17]

After the departure of the majority of settlers in 1880, the schools at Icelandic River and Gimli were closed. The settlers remaining in the colony and later arrivals had to rely on home education conducted by parents or grandparents until the fall of 1885. Without a permanent pastor, settlers could not depend on the spiritual guidance offered through Sunday schools, but Gudni Thorsteinsson offered private instruction at three different locations in the colony from 1885 to 1887. He spent three months during the winter in each place. He requested a fee of fifty cents per student, but many were unable to pay. His lessons were attended by fifteen to twenty students in each community. A private school was also in operation for one month of 1886 at Icelandic River. A report from Hecla Island in *Leifur*, 11 May 1886, stated that that district had had a school for three months. One teacher, receiving $9.00 per month, had taught twenty children.

In these years, education in the settlement did not follow any regular pattern in terms of school buildings, subjects, or language of instruction. This situation changed when the Province of Manitoba in 1887 became financially responsible for public school education in the settlement. However, this was something many settlers were unwilling to accept and a debate arose over whether the Icelandic immigrants should continue the private, locally financed system of elementary education or accept the provincial public school system. One settler, Stefan B. Johnson, addressed this problem in a letter published in *Heimskringla* on 14 February 1887:

> The question is this and must be considered in all earnest: which is preferable, provincial schools under Manitoba laws or free schools—independent private schools. The merits of both need careful examination. One's immediate concern is of an ethnical nature. This is one merit the private schools have and is in my opinion on its own greater than all merits one can imagine of schools bound by provincial laws. The public schools, within the provincial laws, have one legally constituted language of instruction (English), they have revenues determined by provincial laws.... The free schools could have a self-declared language of instruction (Icelandic) and legally decided revenues.... They could have subjects of study selected as would appear appropriate, including English.

Eggert Johannsson, editor of *Heimskringla,* opposed Johnson and those of similar opinion. His message reflected the views of those who encouraged assimilation. He said that all Icelanders in North America should learn the national language, learn the history of their adopted countries, and become North American citizens. Separate schools, he believed, would do the Icelanders immeasurable injustice.

By 1889, the issue of private Icelandic schools had disappeared, and that year, five public schools were built in Gimli municipality and an additional two a year later. This was a major step towards assimilation; from then on, Icelandic children received the official educational program of Manitoba, the same as children of any other race. The policy that all subjects should be taught in English was adopted generally in Icelandic communities both in Canada and the United States. Oddly, Icelanders were indifferent to the enactment in 1897 by the Manitoba legislature of a compromise school law, which provided that if ten or more students in any school spoke French, or another native language, "the teaching of such pupils shall be conducted in French, or such other language, and English, upon the bi-lingual system."[18] It is remarkable that a community so predominantly Icelandic in nature, with schools in which nearly all children were of the same ethnic background, should ignore this opportunity to establish instruction in the Icelandic language and to encourage its use. Instead, they sought another compromise.

The first Icelandic high school in Gimli municipality was built and in use by the turn of the century. A proposal accepted and supported by School Inspector A. McIntyre, and welcomed by the Gimli School Board, declared that the Icelandic teachers hired must be fluent in English but stress the importance of Icelandic culture. This would improve the English of the high school students while ensuring that they could keep in close touch with older people, parents, relatives, or friends, and maintain an appreciation of the Icelandic heritage. The language itself could be taught at night or on weekends.

By the 1890s, New Iceland had become the largest Icelandic settlement in North America, excluding that in Winnipeg, and even though settlers from other ethnic groups lived among them, the community was predominantly Icelandic. However, the original idea of an exclusive Icelandic colony where the language would be spoken and heritage promoted had faded and, in 1897, when the Icelanders were presented with an opportunity by their own province to educate their children in Icelandic, an opportunity they would have jumped at twenty years earlier, the Icelanders said no. Perhaps their experience in North America taught them the importance of being able to converse in English. There is no doubt that many of the Icelanders in Manitoba were not satisfied with only understanding and being able to express themselves. They wanted to speak English flawlessly, without an accent. The criteria for hiring high school teachers at Gimli is clear evidence.

To become Canadian citizens and establish themselves in the Manitoba community, the Icelanders chose not to be a secondary minority but to be accepted as equals by the British majority. The pioneers knew they might never attain that goal but in order for their children to have the opportunity, they needed a good command of English and education of the highest standard, and this meant that instruction in Icelandic throughout primary school would be of little, if any, advantage. On the other hand, understanding and speaking the language of the parents was certainly valued and emphasized. Thus, interest in Icelandic culture was fostered and encouraged after school hours and in the home.

Once the critical period from 1880 to 1885 was over and the settlers realized that the worst was behind them, slow but steady improvements occurred in every aspect of community life. Immigration to the settlement continued, but since most of the newcomers arrived empty-handed, considerable time and effort were required for them to get settled. New areas were claimed and a log cabin or hut built on the property. Land was cleared and prepared for seeding. The typical pioneer life, therefore, was present in some parts of the growing colony almost to the end of the century. Settlers sometimes attempted to form small-scale stock companies in order to invest in expensive machinery. One such effort was made in 1887 when Stefan B. Jonsson and Isak Jonsson organized the Progressive Society. A year later some members joined forces and bought a steam engine that was to be used to saw and plane wood, to plough, and to thresh. Transportation in the settlement was still difficult, as roads were few and, other than the main highway and the road west from Gimli, their conditions were poor despite more maintenance work after the organization of the municipality in 1887. In 1896, for example, when a creamery was established at Gimli and a year later another one at Icelandic River, farmers from inland regions were obliged to carry their cream cans on their backs through the thick woods to the lake where a boat would pick them up.

The lake was the main transportation route during the summer; by 1894 more than twelve steamers were regularly in use on the lake, most of them skipped by Icelanders, and there were also some sailboats. Ever since they had first landed at Willow Point in the fall of 1875, the settlers had built vessels to be used for various purposes on the lake. The wood of the barges on which the belongings of the first group had been transported from Winnipeg to New Iceland was used for the first boats. As time passed and settlers gradually learned what type of wood to choose and how to work it, they built improved vessels. The steamer *Aurora* was built in 1884 when seven settlers had financed the $22,000.00 project. During the 1890s, decked ships were built regularly, including, for example, the *Lady of the Lake* in 1897.

Lumber and fish were the important trade commodities in the 1880s. Jonasson's mill at Big Throat River produced 370,000 feet of lumber in 1886, and another one at Icelandic River in 1900 shipped out 400,000 feet.[19] In 1886 a store was opened again at Gimli in the old house of Rev. Bjarnason and a more elaborate building was constructed in the following year.

Despite the exodus from the settlement, in the two most densely populated regions, Icelandic River and Vidirnes, there existed strong community bonds. The 1883 immigrant group from Iceland had consisted mostly of people from the Eyjafjord district, all of whom were community-minded. Fishing and the Icelandic River sawmill provided work, and food was never short. Social gatherings always existed. In 1886 a large community hall was constructed at Icelandic River and another one in Gimli in 1893, where Icelanders attended plays, choir singing, and prayer meetings. Two IOGT lodges were established in the colony with regular meetings, weekly in the winter months but less frequently during the summer.

Just before the turn of the century, two women's organizations were established at Gimli: the ladies of the Lutheran faith formed the Framsókn ("Progress"), and the Unitarian women established Tilraun ("Experiment"). The latter was mostly responsible for raising funds for the construction of the community hall.

The community was without the regular services of a pastor but after Rev. Bjarnason returned to Manitoba in 1884, he always visited New Iceland, travelling on foot from one community to the next. Churches were built at Hecla in 1890 and in Gimli in 1891. In 1887 Rev. Magnus J. Skaptason arrived at the settlement directly from Iceland and after that the community enjoyed regular religious services. He assumed all pastoral duties for the congregations in the settlement.

The Icelandic Synod was responsible for Skaptason's presence and, in spite of adjustments to the spirit of the Free Churches of North America, the synod still maintained strong bonds with the Icelandic State Church. Some of the adjustments made by the synod were unacceptable to Skaptason and, although this became apparent almost immediately upon his arrival, both he and the congregations kept peace until Easter of 1891. In his sermon that day he "renounced the doctrine of total depravity and eternal punishment," and this caused a split in the community. The Fraternal Congregation at Lundi, for example, voted thirty-five to six to ask Skaptason to resign, but other congregations, like the one at Hecla Island, in Arnes, Gimli, and Vidirnes, withdrew from the synod and stood by their pastor. Skaptason sent a letter of resignation to Bjarnason, the president of the synod. Skaptason's position took everyone by surprise, and disappointed Bjarnason and those who had supported his appointment. Upon his resignation, Skaptason still claimed to be a Lutheran but only a few years later he accepted a call from the Icelandic Unitarian church in Winnipeg.[20]

It is noteworthy that both the two pastors recruited in Iceland in the late 1880s, Petursson and Skaptason, caused a split in their parishes. The Tabernacle congregation in Winnipeg chose not to join the synod, and congregations in New Iceland followed Skaptason out of the synod.

Despite the establishment of the Municipality of Gimli in 1887, with all the changes in the status of the Icelandic colony this step involved, the settlement still remained an exclusive Icelandic reserve until 1897. The question of opening up the colony to foreigners had been debated in *Framfari* in the late 1870s. The exodus that followed undoubtedly encouraged other immigrants to look elsewhere. But steady immigration from Iceland and from other parts of Manitoba and the United States had gradually filled up all vacant land and new sites further west were considered as the century was coming to the end. A large Ukrainian settlement was established west of Arnes and the Icelandic River settlement grew westward along the river.

The 1890s were a period of considerable unrest in most Icelandic settlements, both in the United States and Canada. Settlers in North Dakota and Minnesota as well as in Manitoba began to explore new possibilities, especially in western Manitoba and the territory further west, which later became Saskatchewan. The vast territory between the Manitoba border and the Rocky Mountains tempted young men from the farming communities of the midwestern States. Some Icelanders came north to explore regions in the Interlake. For example, in late November of 1900, four young men arrived in New Iceland from Hallson in North Dakota. They claimed land by the Icelandic River, about thirty-two kilometres northwest of Lundi. Here, the communities of Riverdale (Ardal) and Framnes were developed a year later by about seventy people from the Icelandic communities in North Dakota. Later centred on Arborg district, this community grew steadily after 1900 and stretched north to Vidir and Sylvan.[21] A large portion of these new settlers in the Interlake area were actually second-generation New Icelanders whose parents had moved south in the late 1870s.

The new influx of settlers further strengthened the Icelandic Interlake community and by 1910 it was the largest Icelandic community outside Winnipeg. It was not, however, the exclusive Icelandic settlement originally planned. Rather, Icelanders welcomed the arrival of immigrants of other ethnic groups and strove to become respected members of the diverse Manitoba population. In their effort to establish their identity in the community, emphasis was placed on the adoption of Canadian ways. This was noted by visitors from Iceland, who had become more frequent around the turn of the century. Many of them returned to Iceland disturbed by what they had seen, especially the emphasis on the adoption of the English language. Some people commented on the issue in newspapers published in Iceland, accusing their cousins in Canada and the United States of having abandoned their heritage. This, in turn, was equally upsetting for the Icelanders in America who had worked hard through cultural societies, reading clubs, and many publications to promote Icelandic sentiment in their communities. The accusations in Iceland were true in one sense: learning English was emphasized, and sometimes it meant the loss of spoken Icelandic. Rev. Bjarnason, for example, was saddened in 1906 to witness, at a confirmation of youth in the First Lutheran Church in Winnipeg, their inability to express themselves in Icelandic.[22] This trend was more obvious in the urban communities where daily use of English was necessary.

The Canadian Sessional Papers (A 1890 No. 6) estimated that in 1889 approximately 8600 Icelanders resided in Canada. Approximately 5000 were inhabitants of rural communities, and the rest lived in urban centres. Apart from the steady stream of settlers into New Iceland and the Arborg district, the Icelanders had also settled in other parts of Manitoba. By 1885 the Argyle region had only limited land available and sites further west were being explored. Helgi

Jonsson of Winnipeg, the former owner and editor of *Leifur,* wanted to leave Winnipeg and he examined regions on the western boundary of Manitoba. A clever businessman, Jonsson chose a site in 1885 at Shellmouth, reserving land for future Icelandic settlers. Like so many others, he was convinced that the North-Western Railway would pass nearby and increase the value of adjacent land. However, the railway route was changed and the Shellmouth settlement never became very large. Ten settlers had made homestead entries in December of 1885, an additional twelve in the following year, and sixty persons arrived in the area in 1886 directly from Iceland. At the end of 1887, thirty-five Icelandic families were in the district. This was not to become a permanent home for many of them: sites across the border in what is now Saskatchewan at Langenburg and Churchbridge drew their attention.

The Interlake region, the area of land between Lake Winnipeg and Lake Manitoba, included the Icelandic reserve in the east half. In the west were a few small settlements, notably a Roman Catholic and Métis colony at St. Laurent, an English settlement at Seamo, a French community, and the Hudson's Bay Company trading post at Oak Point. It was the custom to refer to two Icelandic communities in the region; in the west was the Swan Lake colony, and in the east, Shoal Lake. The small town of Lundar became the centre of the two communities and the area was called the Lundar District.

Two Icelanders from Winnipeg, Frimann B. Anderson and Bjorn S. Lindal, concentrated their exploration on sites in the western half of the Interlake region, the area between Shoal Lake and Lake Manitoba, in 1886. They had previously explored regions near the Moose Mountain and the Qu'Appelle Valley, along with a third Icelander, Stefan Gunnarsson, and a Canadian guide, but nothing in that vicinity impressed them as much as certain areas in the Interlake. They went as far north as Mulvihill village and eventually selected a stretch of land further south. It was dry and covered with tall grass, and an abundance of trees provided building material and firewood. Apparently, as the wagon carried them through the land, Anderson often ordered it to stop, then jumped off with a small shovel he had brought along to test the soil. The Canadian guide and an English farmer also involved in the exploration often disagreed with Anderson about whether the land was fertile, and he would then dig into the ground to prove his point. The explorers did agree that the site in the present Lundar district had many advantages. Not only was the land ideal for mixed farming, with its abundance of pasture and hay land, but the prospect of having the railway from Winnipeg running through the region would bring future settlements within reach of the big market in Winnipeg.[23] The rail project was launched in October 1886 but once it had reached Harperville, about sixty-four kilometres north of Winnipeg, work discontinued. The railway eventually reached Oak Point in 1904. Fishing was also good, both in Shoal Lake and Lake Manitoba, and the pioneers knew that this valuable commodity was not only a supplement to their diet but an item of trade.

Immigration to the region commenced immediately and in 1887 ten settlers reached the site, with an additional nine in 1888, eight in 1889, and, of the arrivals in 1890, forty-six came from North Dakota. The total number of people in the settlement in 1892, according to the Sessional Papers of 1893, was 238.[24] That number rose steadily during the next ten years.

The Icelandic settlement in Lundar was a pioneer community but, although a large number of settlers had little experience and often arrived empty-handed, the necessary help was usually available. Newcomers were taught how to built their cabins, and how to mix clay and straw for the roof, and often were provided with a cow or two, the necessary farming equipment, and household supplies. There was ample pasture land and meadows for haymaking. Soon farmers started selling dairy products such as butter. Meat was readily available as part of the diet. The land was best suited for raising livestock, although a few settlers grew grain. In fact, this district was perfect for animals and soon farmers had increased their herds. The French Métis sold their land and although Canadian farmers remained, the settlement increasingly became an Icelandic colony.

In ten years a number of the settlers had raised good-sized herds and had begun to sell cattle on a large scale. Herdsmen would round up the animals and drive them westward to the new settlements near the Saskatchewan border. A yearling often sold for $14.00. For six years, from 1897 to 1903, this was a lucrative business but as the regions in the west were settled, the visits of the herdsmen decreased, and finally this venture came to an end. Animals were still sold to the butchers in Winnipeg, although this was never a guaranteed transaction as the animals had to reach a certain weight. For animals who were fed on hay and grazed during the summer, reaching the required weight could be accomplished by the fall only if the summer had been favourable. The price for cattle dropped, consequently, and remained low.

Despite the support they received in their early years in the community, young men had to seek employment elsewhere, most often outside the colony. The settlers worked at harvest jobs in the grain-growing regions in the United States or around Portage la Prairie and Argyle. This had positive aspects as young men earned extra money and gained valuable experience in threshing wheat. However, their annual absence prevented progress not only on their own farms but also in the joint undertakings in the colony. Because clearing land and attempts to grow grain were secondary obligations, the settlers imported nearly all the grain consumed in the colony. The women and children were left on the farm to tend to the animals and the men sometimes returned to a certain amount of disorder, with all the fall work still to be done before the first frost. In addition, the long, tedious journey to Winnipeg, approximately 128 kilometres away, would have to be made to get all the winter supplies. This trip often lasted ten to fourteen days, depending on the condition of the roads.

Some settlers returned home to find everything on their homestead burnt to ashes. Prairie fires were common, especially in the early years of the settlement. Helgi Einarsson was only seventeen when he experienced his first prairie fire:

> When the grass began to wither in the latter part of September, people began talking about the danger of fire. We made preparations for our own safety by burning a firebreak around the house site, but before we had it completed, the sudden arrival of a whirlwind spread it out of our control. During the night, with the assistance of all the men in the neighborhood, we succeeded in beating it out, but not before it had burned out an area half a mile wide and a mile and a half long to the south and east. That fire eventually proved a blessing, for had it not occurred, we would in all probability have lost all our possessions in the prairie fire which swept across two weeks later.
>
> About eleven o'clock the morning of 30 September I noticed a little smoke about fifteen or twenty miles to the south. Impelled by a brisk south wind, it billowed rapidly until it hid all the sky in that direction. We realized that this was the fire people had been apprehensive of. Until this summer there had been no brush fire here for many years. The dried vegetation of previous summers lay thick on the ground and was highly inflammable. We began to protect ourselves as best we could. Although the house and haystacks were close to the spot where we had lost control of our first firebreak, we nevertheless made another one, about twelve to fifteen feet across.
>
> South of us there stretched about two miles of prairie with grass three to five feet high. Around three in the afternoon we saw the fire sweep out of the woods across the prairie, all of which was ablaze within five minutes. I have never witnessed so awesome a spectacle. Impelled by a strong wind, the flames, twenty to thirty feet high, swept away everything in their path. The noise and smoke were overwhelming.
>
> As soon as we saw the fire break out of the woods, we set a counterfire on the windward side of the firebreak we had just finished making. It had time to burn about fifteen to twenty feet against the wind before the big fire met it and that was our salvation. With pails of water and wet bags we extinguished the sparks blown by the wind onto the hay and area around the house. We managed to save everything, but came close to losing the hay, for on two occasions the grass caught fire a few feet from the stacks. It took only five or ten minutes for the fire to burn out around our place, but it rapidly swept north until the middle of the night, when its progress was impeded by the dew and dampness.[25]

The settlers fished in Lake Manitoba both for commercial sale and for domestic consumption. When fishing was good, it took considerable time and effort, which often resulted in farming receiving less attention. In the fall of 1887 some of the pioneers who had brought nets with them began to fish. They did not have boats of their own but occasionally borrowed vessels from Métis people who lived on the coastline. In spring 1888, soon after the ice broke up, the Icelanders noticed that creeks and streams flowing into the lake were teeming with fish of various types, pickerel being the most common. From then on, spring fishing in the creeks became an annual event. The fish was either dried or salted for preservation during the warm summer months.

Commercial fishing increased when in 1891 an Englishman operated a steamer on the lake, accompanied by smaller sailboats, which made it possible to take the fish to market during the summer. The first Icelander to fish commercially during the summer was Helgi Jonsson. However, summer fishing was prohibited by law in 1900 as an attempt to prevent decreasing stock. This did not severely affect the Icelanders, as winter was always the main fishing season for them, from mid-November, once the lake froze, to 15 March. The winter freeze prevented any spoiling of the fish. As time passed and fishing techniques improved, many settlers stopped farming. Lake Manitoba gradually became just as important to the Lundar district as Lake Winnipeg was to New Iceland.

Most settlers in the pioneer days had to travel to Winnipeg for necessities, where they normally bought supplies from Arni Fridriksson. There were times when settlers arrived in Winnipeg with little or no money and in desperate need for winter supplies, and, often, Fridriksson provided them with what they requested. His trust in people may have resulted in an occasional loss but most settlers settled their account with him at their earliest opportunity. As time passed, however, many people began to shop at Stonewall, a town about ninety-six kilometres southeast of Lundar, which was connected to Winnipeg via a rail line of about thirty kilometres. This shortened the distance to market considerably.

As the population grew, so did the need for local stores. In 1896, Halldor Halldorsson established a small store, which he managed for four years. His son Johann succeeded him and was to became one of the main businessmen in the community in the next ten years. At first he operated from Lundar, then Oak Point. His commercial enterprise touched just about everything in the business world of those settlement years; he supplied the locals with all necessities, such as food and household supplies, and farming and fishing equipment. He was active on the livestock market, trading in cattle, horses, pigs, and sheep, and his company competed with Winnipeg-based private corporations in the fishing trade. Jon Sigfusson, one of the pioneer settlers, also became involved in the cattle trade as early as 1890. In 1897 he opened a store, which he operated for a few years. Other store owners were Helgi Oddson at Cold Springs, whose store came into operation in 1907; and Thorsteinn Johannsson and Thorarinn Breckman, who ran a shop at Mary Hill from 1905 to 1908. Pall Reykdal's operation in Oak Point lasted from 1904 to 1908, but he concentrated on fodder and wheat as well as conventional food supplies for the community. He and Johann Halldorsson, both second-generation settlers, were raised in the same community but later became competitors in commerce as well as in politics. Jon H. Johnson of Shoal Lake operated a successful fish-trading post at Oak Point for many years.[26]

The first Icelandic settlers in the Shoal Lake district did not arrive in a completely uninhabited region, as had their compatriots across the Interlake in New Iceland in the mid-1870s. The settlement was actually the Municipality of Posen since 1886 but, due to the small population in the area, the slow influx of settlers in the first few years, and their inability to pay taxes, the region lost its status as a municipality in 1893. One Icelandic pioneer had the honour of sitting on the Posen Council: Jon Sigfusson at Clarkleigh was elected and sat for one year. Most of the Icelanders arriving in the area in the late 1880s either came straight from Iceland or from the Icelandic settlements in North Dakota. Many of them lacked knowledge of the English language and were ill-prepared to take on any responsibilities in running their community. Others, however, fared better.

Pall Reykdal immigrated with his family to Canada in 1887 when he was nine years of age. In the two years his family spent in Manitoba prior to their arrival at Shoal Lake, he learned how to speak very good English; in fact, it was better than that of most settlers and many of them called for young Reykdal's assistance in any written communication with Canadian authorities.

The eventual demise of the municipal council at Shoal Lake indicated to the Icelanders that they could manage without a council, which they did until 1910. However, this meant that funds for any major communal venture, such as construction of roads and schools, were not available. As in so many out-of-the-way settlements in those times, roads were scarce and poorly maintained. The railway from Winnipeg had been started in 1887 but its construction was stopped before reaching the settlement. This drove many Canadian settlers away, and some of the Icelanders bought cheap land. For example, 160 acres were purchased by one settler for the total of $35.00 and this was not by any means land of poor quality. An acre nearby sold for $8.00 in 1908. The railway finally reached Oak Point in 1904. There was just one main road at the time, from St. Laurent along the shore of the lake to the Narrows.

The settlers began to organize various community associations. The Farmers Institute, founded in 1900, was intended to pave the way for agricultural progress in the settlement. The institute received a small provincial grant for the purposes of improving farming and its greatest achievement was the lowering of prices for stock medicine.[27] A second community effort was the establishment of a creamery. Hitherto, the settlers had made their butter at home, and either sold it locally or preserved it until the fall journey to Winnipeg. The quality varied under such circumstances and sometimes was so poor that it did not sell. A well-attended meeting resolved to establish a stock company, each share worth $5.00. Subscriptions were collected and soon 400 shares were sold. The company was called the Maple Leaf Creamery Company.

The construction of the creamery was completed late in April of 1902. There were two buildings, one eighteen metres by seven, and the other five metres by four. Machines were purchased from a dissolved creamery in western Canada and additional equipment from Winnipeg. The total cost of starting this enterprise reached $2600.00 and the shareholders realized they required a loan. The first board of directors was elected in March 1902. Jon Sigfusson was elected chair, Thorsteinn Johannsson was secretary, Gudmundur Breckman was treasurer, and Skuli Sigfusson was elected manager. The creamery was in operation for four to six months every summer. In the spring of 1908, new and more efficient machinery was purchased. The Maple Leaf Creamery soon earned a reputation for first-rate production and received recognition at annual Winnipeg expositions between 1906 and1910.[28]

A reading society was established on 4 February 1904. Its founder and first president was Gunnar Holm. In a community that numbered a little less than 500 Icelanders in 1900, membership was always low. The record high of forty-seven was reached in 1907, but in 1910 it was forty-five. That year it had 252 volumes in its possession.

The settlers in the Lundar district made no effort in the first ten years to hire a pastor. They met at the Mary Hill schoolhouse on Sundays for prayer meetings and organized a Sunday school. Instructors were local farmers. As the synod began to sponsor visits of pastors or deacons to the Icelandic communities in Canada and the United States, religious services began in the colony. In late September 1900, Rev. Jon Jonsson arrived in the district from Iceland, and a year later the first Icelandic Lutheran congregation in the Lundar region was founded. Religious services were offered at the Mary Hill School once every month. Thirty-seven settlers became members of this congregation in 1901. This Icelandic community, like so many others, could not live in religious peace. In 1904, the majority of the congregational board of directors had resigned and left the congregation, which was dissolved. Rev. Jonsson continued to serve in the community, at first for $60.00 a year but later for whatever was contributed at each service.

In 1908 the synod organized a congregation in the community. At first it appeared interest was minimal. But when Rev. Jonsson and his wife became members, sixty additional people joined. Other settlers organized a Unitarian congregation, which was led by Rev. Rognvaldur Petursson. That membership reached thirty in the first year, 1906. The schoolhouse at Mary Hill was bought for religious services and meetings, and the Unitarian movement in America provided financial support.

The Icelanders in Lundar may not have been in any hurry to establish their religious organizations, but they wasted no time in arranging for the education of their youth. The first school, the Franklin School, was established in 1889 where Lundar Post Office later stood. Additional schools were established at Mary Hill, Cold Springs, Stone Lake, Rabbit Point, and Deer Horn. Icelandic teachers were in high demand and the first four sites had at least one Icelandic teacher during the first decade of the twentieth century. These were often young people who had graduated from Wesley College in Winnipeg.[29]

Between 1880 and 1900, many Icelanders in North America moved from one place to another in search of the ideal permanent home. For example, a large portion of the settlers of New Iceland had moved south to the States, most to the new colony in North Dakota. But after the mid-1890s, a wave of Icelanders from the States moved north to Manitoba. On 18 January 1900, *Heimskringla* reported that the total number of Icelanders in Winnipeg was one-tenth of the city's entire population of 54,778; in its March edition, it estimated the population of Icelanders in Manitoba at slightly more than 10,000. According to the paper, more than 5000 resided in Manitoba cities such as Winnipeg, Selkirk, and Brandon, and another 5000 lived in the seven largest rural communities.

Sigtryggur Jonasson estimated in 1901 that the Icelandic population of Manitoba was 9800 and divided in the following manner:

Icelandic Population of Manitoba, 1901

District	Population
Winnipeg	4000
New Iceland	2500
Argyle	1000
Selkirk	700
Lundar District	500
Big Point	250
Dauphin	200
The Narrows	150
Morden	50
Pipestone	100
Piney	100
Elsewhere	250

Source: Jonasson, "Early Icelandic Settlements."

The town of Selkirk (Crossing) is significant in the history of Icelanders in Manitoba. It was established in 1875 when the Canadian Pacific Railway had its western offices at the site but at that time the transcontinental railway was expected to cross through the town. This influenced the Icelandic explorers of 1875 when they chose the site for their colony just north of the town, because the settlement in New Iceland would have been much closer to main transportation lines and big markets. However, this plan was changed and the railway went through Winnipeg.

Since the beginning of settlement of New Iceland, travellers often stopped in Selkirk. When the exodus from New Iceland began, a few settlers went only as far as Selkirk—Sigtryggur Jonasson being one, although he continued his business transactions in the colony. As Selkirk grew, it became a fishing centre where steamers from northern parts of Lake Winnipeg unloaded their cargo of fish. The

Icelandic community began to develop there in 1885, and in 1889 an Icelandic Lutheran congregation was established and a church erected. The IOGT lodge Einingin ("Unity") was established in 1891 and then a community library. The Icelanders became active in every aspect of community life. They found work at common labour, fishing, and in sawmills, but before the turn of the century the town had an Icelandic blacksmith, a shoemaker, a butcher, a jeweller, and a baker.

Brandon was incorporated as a town in 1882 and within five years, a small community of Icelanders, mostly farm workers, had developed there. By 1892, the number of Icelanders had reached 150, although the number fluctuated over the following years. A Lutheran congregation was established in 1889 but prior to that, regular prayer meetings were held on Sundays and in 1891 a church had been built. Pastors from Argyle and Winnipeg visited regularly and held religious services. Sunday school had been established through the church by 1900 and an Icelandic Society was founded to promote Icelandic culture. Shortly after the turn of the century, when settlements in Saskatchewan and Alberta were being established, some members of the Brandon Icelandic community moved west.

The Pipestone colony, which the Icelanders called Laufás, was settled in 1892, approximately thirty-two kilometres from Melita. It was primarily a grain-growing community, a treeless region with rocky soil in places, but by 1896, 255 hectares had been cleared and cultivated. The agricultural settlement was scattered, but a small congregation of thirteen homes was founded in 1896, with a community hall and a small library.

The Icelandic immigrants to America usually chose either farming (grain growing) or fishing. In Manitoba this became apparent in the 1890s as small settlements either were established on the middle of the prairie or by one of the large lakes. Pipestone is a good example of the former, and Big Point on the west shore of Lake Manitoba serves well as an example of the latter. Big Point is approximately fifty kilometres east of the town of Gladstone and the first Icelanders arrived there in 1894. The settlement grew steadily and by the early twentieth century, forty settlers were established there. A log schoolhouse was built in 1898 and a community library established. Visiting Lutheran pastors performed religious services but a congregation was established only in 1906 when a permanent pastor, Rev. Bjarni Thorarinsson, accepted a call.[30]

There was plenty of good hayland and the settlers raised livestock but they also fished. The closest markets were at Gladstone and Westbourne, but when the railway reached the town of Langruth, it gradually became the centre of trade. In his *Sketch of Early Langruth*, the founder of the town, George W. Langdon, described his first encounters with Icelandic settlers:

> The late Mr. Olafur Thorleifson accompanied me about Big Point and I met a number of very agreeable people indeed. They were enthused as one might suppose over the prospect of perhaps a little town so near their settlement and I was pleased to find that they had already sent a petition to the railway company making the request for a station where we also desired it or at least convenient

to the Big Point road. So it was unnecessary for me to go further on that quest. That was my introduction to the Icelanders and I cannot speak too highly of the part they have continued to take in all matters affecting the advancement of the community and general welfare. They took a special interest in the development of the little town from the onset and many of their young men were among our pioneer merchants. The Icelanders adopted Canada upon their arrival in the country as perhaps no other nationality from a non-British country and there are no better Canadians.[31]

The first resident of Langruth moved onto the townsite in 1910 and later that year three partners from the Big Point settlement, Bjorn Bjarnarson and the Helgason brothers, Soffanias and G. Freeman, built a store, the Langruth Trading Company. The second store of Langruth, also built by Icelanders, opened in the following year.

The settlement of Big Point led to further exploration of the land in the vicinity and at least one site was settled, that of Big Grass, which in 1905 was given the name Marshland. The name explains the type of land. It literally was a sea of grass, ideal for livestock. A small Icelandic community developed in 1900, with settlers coming from Big Point as well as North Dakota. A Lutheran congregation was established and two schools organized. The farming in this untouched region went well until drainage was introduced. As the land dried, its yield of hay was seriously affected and several settlers left.

Further north, along the west shore of Lake Manitoba, four, small, island communities developed in the early twentieth century: Reykjavík, Bay End, Wapah, and Lonely Lake. Initially, fourteen Icelandic settlers established the Reykjavík colony, where they fished and raised livestock. Another small settlement was at Lake Winnipegosis. In 1896 Dauphin was founded and a year later, the railway reached Sifton. The abundance of fish in Lake Winnipegosis appealed to the Icelanders, who first arrived in the fall of 1897 and spent the winter fishing on the lake. Settlers came from North Dakota as well as from the Interlake region in Manitoba and more than 100 Icelanders moved to the town of Winnipegosis, finding work at common labour or fishing. The Icelanders also established themselves on Red Deer Point and in 1903 thirty-seven families were reported living there. In 1907, however, many moved to the town of Winnipegosis and others west to Saskatchewan.[32]

Regions in western Manitoba gradually opened up for settlement just before and immediately following the turn of the century. One such area was the Swan River Valley in the northwest, approximately 480 kilometres from Winnipeg. Those Icelanders either just arriving from Iceland or those discontented in their present place in America keenly followed these developments. Sigurdur Christopherson of Argyle had arrived in the valley in 1897 and filed entry for his compatriot in Argyle, August Vopni. He and a friend, Gunnar Helgason, left their Argyle settlement on 15 June 1898, and became the first Icelandic settlers in the Swan River Valley region. Others soon followed, mostly from Argyle and the

Mouse River colony in North Dakota. The Icelanders were dispersed among settlers of other nationalities, so a strong Icelandic community did not develop there. However, they became actively involved in the overall development of the region, and organized an Icelandic community life. Those who came to the Swan River Valley prospered and few ever left the region.[33]

Two more prairie communities in Manitoba require mention. One, south of the town of Morden, just north of the US border, was called the Brown settlement and was originally a part of the Mennonite reserve. But, as the land was heavily treed and wet, it was only partly settled and when, in 1898, the Icelandic communities in North Dakota were becoming too large for that district, the search for land nearby commenced. The first Icelandic settlers arrived in 1899 but the next two years were the busiest, when forty-five settlers arrived in the fall of 1900. Most of them came from North Dakota, some of whom had originally settled in New Iceland in the late 1870s. A community library was established in the fall of 1899, a Lutheran congregation in 1900, and a choir in 1902. Community life flourished; most of the settlers had had previous experience in establishing a new settlement.

The other community of Icelanders in the southern region of Manitoba was at Piney, about 110 kilometres southeast of Winnipeg, near the border with Minnesota. It was originally settled by Norwegians in 1897 but the Icelanders soon followed as everyone expected the southwestern railway to cross through the region. Fifty-four Icelanders settled there, but the land is poor and the settlement never flourished. Still, the settlers organized their Lutheran congregation in 1901 and built a school in 1903.[34]

The movements of Icelandic immigrants in Manitoba at the close of the nineteenth and the beginning of the twentieth centuries indicate that many people were not settled permanently. There were numerous reasons for this: people arrived from Iceland every year; new regions were opened up by governments; and overpopulation in some colonies, North Dakota for instance, drove the people into new areas.

13
Settlements in the Western Provinces

Helgi Jonsson of Winnipeg, former publisher and editor of *Leifur*, moved west in 1885 to Shellmouth, where he expected the arrival of the Canadian Pacific Railway to spur the development of a prosperous settlement. This did not materialize—the railroad was diverted southwest to Birtle and then to Yorkton. Jonsson sold his small retail store in Shellmouth and moved to Langenburg, where he and Bjarni W. Westmann entered a partnership in the retail business. Bjarni Westmann later moved to Churchbridge. This farm district extends from the town of Churchbridge northeasterly toward Calder, a distance of approximately thirty-two kilometres. The original Icelandic settlement was east and northeast of Churchbridge and was named Thingvalla, after the historic site in Iceland, Thingvellir. In 1885, three Icelanders filed on homesteads: Jon Magnusson, who was the first Icelander to build a cabin on his land; Einar S. Sudfjord; and Bjorn Olafson. All three had their families at Solsgirth ready to proceed to Shellmouth and the new district.[1] On 30 April 1886, fourteen people departed. It was a cold day and they made frequent stops at farms in order to give the women and children, shivering on the wagon, a chance to warm themselves. They travelled to Shellmouth, where Bjorn Olson, who was employed at a sawmill, chose to stay while the others continued the journey.

Fourteen families joined these pioneers later in the summer of 1886 and homesteaded in the Thingvalla settlement. A special type of home was built by several of the settlers. These were partly dugouts cut into the south of a hill. The walls on the south end were made of sod, often higher than two metres, and tapered out at the north end almost to the level of the ground. Roofs were made of poplar trees and sod. These homes were quite warm and many families lived in them for several years.

The immediate task for these farmers was to gather hay for the few cattle they brought. Some machines had been brought into the settlement but were in constant use by their owners and therefore of little help to the others. Companies that provided the settlers with necessities, and took security in their homesteads for the advances they gave, recommended oxen for these pioneers, as they were cheaper than horses. For many Icelanders this recommendation was advantageous as they lacked experience in handling animals with machines. In the winter of 1886-1887, six teams of oxen were available to twenty-three families in the settlement.[2]

Early in January of 1888, a Lutheran congregation was formed and thirty-six people in the district became members. Thomas Paulson was elected president, Arni Johnson became secretary, and Jon Ogmundsson was appointed treasurer. Others on the executive committee were Sigurdur Johnson and Christjan Helgason. Sunday schools were organized at the same meeting and teachers elected for the two parts of the settlement, the east and west. The executive committee in Thingvalla invited Rev. Jon Bjarnason to the settlement, who arrived in October 1888. He gave a sermon at a schoolhouse, where he also baptized twenty-two children and married eight couples.[3] A permanent pastor was not available for the community but visits from pastors from Winnipeg or other Icelandic communities in Manitoba were common, and some pastors stayed much of the summer.

In 1890 another Icelandic community, called Lögberg, was established nearby in the northeast part of the Churchbridge-Calder region only a few kilometres from Thingvalla. A German community separated the two Icelandic settlements but the Lögberg settlers had to travel through the Thingvalla community to reach the markets at Churchbridge, and consequently became frequent visitors in the district. The first two settlers in Lögberg were Johannes Einarsson and Gisli Egilsson.

In Thingvalla district, social events were deemed just as essential as religious services. At a meeting on 14 March 1891, the community endorsed the building of a community hall. Einar Sudfjord donated land, and Thomas Paulson took charge of the construction, supported by everyone in both the Thingvalla and Lögberg settlements. A forest of poplar trees was in the Lögberg district, where skilled men chopped and hauled the logs to the site. The hall stood about seven metres wide and twelve metres long, with an additional building of five by six metres for a chancel. Families and individuals donated money and funds were received from events organized by the already established ladies' societies, for lumber, windows, and doors. In two years, the hall was completed and the first religious service was given. Other gatherings at the hall included concerts and plays, as well as dances.

However, it became clear that the location of the hall was suitable only for a part of the growing communities in Thingvalla and Lögberg. The distance of twenty to twenty-five kilometres between the hall and the Lögberg settlement was too great for many of the Lögberg settlers, who now wanted their own church. Settlers in the south were not only in agreement with this proposal, but offered some financial assistance as well, and in 1904, a new church was opened in the Lögberg district.[4]

A division occurred in the congregation in Thingvalla, and in the fall of 1901, settlers in the west left the original congregation and, supported by Rev. Jon J. Clemens, organized a separate congregation in October. It was called Concordia Lutheran Congregation and a church was built by 1904, eight kilometres straight north from Churchbridge. The first pastor to serve on a yearly basis was Rev. Hjortur J. Leo, who was ordained in 1909. He served all three congregations from 1909 to 1912. He objected to conducting his services at the Thingvalla Hall and, at a meeting on 12 January 1910, he encouraged the congregation to build a church, which was eventually done. Thus, there were two congregations and two churches in the Thingvalla settlement.[5]

The Lögberg community was always small, both in population and area. The settlers had made the mistake of expecting one quarter-section to suffice for a mixed farm. The railroad had already reached beyond Churchbridge, where the settlers unloaded and then travelled by oxen the twenty-four kilometres to the new site. Even though there were quality building materials nearby, most settlers initially were content with small huts. However, as the years went by, improved housing replaced the small, often worn-out dwellings. Here, as in the Thingvalla settlement, a few settlers brought livestock and had to make hay. Some brought farm implements such as mowers and rakes but there were not enough of these to serve all the farmers, and the use of scythes and hand-rakes was the only alternative.

Community life in Lögberg resembled that of Thingvalla in many ways. The education of youth was important, at first through Sunday school but later, in 1891, a school was built to serve the entire northern community, which consisted of the Icelanders in the east and a mixed German-Scottish community in the northwest. The Rothbury School came into existence in March of 1891, but was too far away from the centre of the Icelanders' community, as some of the children had to walk nearly six kilometres. A new school district was organized in 1895 and a second school in the settlement was built approximately ten kilometres east of the Rothbury School.

The Canadian prairie, a vast region, has recurring wet and dry cycles, and none of the settlers in the Churchbridge region had been warned about the prairie's dry spells. The rush of settlers to the new community reached its height in 1891, and by then, many settlers were becoming increasingly aware of the shortage of water, especially underground water for their wells. By mid-summer of 1892, most wells were dry. Despite constant effort and digging of numerous new wells, there was no water. Even the largest sloughs had dried completely by early summer. Appeals to the government of Canada resulted in well-drilling outfits being sent out, but to little avail, as most of them failed. Many farmers were thus driven off their land, and a few searched for water in other parts of the settlement. Farmers from Lögberg, for instance, moved south to Thingvalla where prospects were supposedly better. But, following a record-breaking cold winter of 1892-1893, which began with a snowstorm in October of 1892 and finished with a three-day blizzard at the end of April 1893, many settlers moved back to Manitoba, most to Big Point or other regions on the western shores of Lake Manitoba. The Icelandic communities at Lögberg and Thingvalla lost more than half their population.[6] Eventually new settlers arrived, some of different ethnic backgrounds. Still, the characteristics of this first Icelandic community, in what was to become the province of Saskatchewan, were retained.

The Churchbridge region at the time was part of the North-West Territories. In 1887 the legislature for the territories passed a Statute Labor Ordinance, which provided for the organizing of Statute Labor Districts for work on roads and bridges. The Icelanders in the Lögberg community took advantage of this legislation and Johannes Einarsson led a group of people who formed a district in their own township.

A Local Improvement Ordinance, which was passed in 1901 by the legislature, provided for the election of councillors from each township in every Local Improvement District. On 5 April 1904 Local Improvement District No 12-A-1 was established in the Thingvalla-Lögberg area. Three Icelanders served on the first council: Sveinbjorn Loptsson, Fridrik Fridriksson, and Gisli Egilsson, who was named secretary-treasurer. His salary was $40.00 a year and ten cents mileage for all travel necessary for district business.[7]

Johannes Einarsson (one of the two pioneer settlers of the Lögberg region; Egilsson was the other) became a councillor in the fall of 1904 and sat on the council until 1913, when the Local Improvement District became the Rural Municipality of Churchbridge. He then became reeve, the leader of the rural municipality council. Einarsson was involved in other organizations in his settlement. In partnership with several other settlers, he organized a cooperative store through which the pioneers bought supplies. In 1891 he took an active part in organizing a creamery at Saltcoats and was president for several years. These two cooperative enterprises may have been the first of their kind in the area. The Churchbridge Creamery was formed in 1898 and quickly became the largest in the North-West Territories.

The town of Churchbridge, although somewhat on the outskirts of the Thingvalla settlement, soon attracted Icelandic shopkeepers. Bjarni Westmann opened his store on the south side of the railway tracks in 1888, and in 1889 Johann G. Thorgeirson arrived from Winnipeg and opened a store on the north side of the tracks. Apparently he was too lenient with his customers and granted too much credit, and in 1894 he was driven out of business. Another Winnipegger, Olafur J. Olafsson, reached Churchbridge in 1889 and opened a harness shop. Palmi Sigtrygsson and his wife operated a guest-house just before the turn of the century, and in 1903 Magnus S. Thorlaksson built the first hotel. Sveinbjorn Loptsson purchased a retail store in the town in 1904, where he operated for several years.[8]

Icelanders also began businesses in other villages or towns developing in the region at the time. In Bredenbury, for example, Chris Thorvaldson opened a butcher and livestock business, and Hjalmar Loptson started his general store just before the turn of the century. Icelandic settlers also opened up businesses in Saltcoats, Calder, and MacNutt.[9]

The beginning of the Holar settlement occurred from a chance encounter. Frimann B. Anderson wrote numerous articles in *Leifur*, the Winnipeg-based weekly published by Helgi Jonsson. Together, the two became interested in prospects in the North-West Territories. Jonsson had settled at Shellmouth, and Anderson guided settlers around sites in western Manitoba and the eastern territories. During one exploration, he met a former employer from Ontario, Thomas Douglas. The pair met as Anderson was escorting a small group of young Icelanders to a Swedish colony called Stockholm in the Tantallon district, which is on the rim of the Qu'Appelle Valley, east of Tantallon village. The Stockholm colony was further west but Douglas, a government agent, suggested to Anderson that he consider the area on which they stood. It had been intended for settlers from Scotland who apparently were not coming, and Douglas offered it to the Icelanders. He mentioned the fertile regions all around, the large poplar trees growing on the slopes of the valley, and the scattered willow bushes, all of which favourably impressed the Icelanders. Their journey westward ended there.[10]

By 11 October 1887 three settlers had brought their families to the new site. All had arrived from Iceland in mid-summer and had limited knowledge of English. The immediate task was to make hay for their animals. The North-West Loan Company, a colonization company, had advanced the Icelanders $250.00 each to buy a team of oxen, a cow, and a wagon. Instead of buying three teams, the settlers decided to join together and save some money. Hay was cut by a Canadian settler already in the district but the Icelanders raked and stacked themselves.[11] Instead of every family attempting to complete a hut, all worked together to construct a sod house, which was about seven metres long and four and a half metres wide. The roof was made of poplar rafters and sod. The house had only one window and a door facing south. Here, the entire group, three families, spent the winter together.

The Icelanders referred to this small Icelandic community as Holar District but to the Canadians it became known as Tantallon District. The area is rolling and cut with ravines and flat depressions. Due to poplar bluffs and willow bushes, breaking land was difficult in places but the soil was good for grain farming. The Qu'Appelle Valley is deep and wide, and the slopes are steep, offering a beautiful view from the top. More experienced settlers from other Icelandic communities soon moved into the region. As was often the case under similar circumstances, this combination worked to the benefit of the young community. The new arrivals brought with them renewed Icelandic spirit and contributed greatly to the promotion of Icelandic culture, and their presence guaranteed that the Icelandic language continued to be spoken. The experienced settlers assisted the new settlers in adjusting to this different way of life. Small but steady increments of new settlers in the 1890s helped strengthen the community life. Only two years after the arrival of the first settlers, an Icelandic celebration was held, which became an annual event for several years. Speeches in Icelandic were delivered, Icelandic songs sung by all present, and sports events arranged.

There was a strong emphasis on teaching the Icelandic language in the homes, so most of the children spoke little or no English when they started school. Formal education began early in the life of the community and the first school, Holar School, was built from 1892 to 1894. The settlers built a community hall on a site donated by one of the settlers, on top of a hill providing a beautiful view over the district in all directions. It was completed in 1898 and in 1900 the school was moved to this site.

The two buildings became the centre of all activities in the community, including a small theater group. Popular Icelandic plays were selected, among them *The Outlaws*. Another play, *The Immigrants,* perhaps closer to the new home, was equally popular; both were written by the Icelandic poet Matthias Jochumsson. Three men were mostly responsible for the community entertainment and gatherings — John Anderson Hjaltalin, Jon Julius, and Sigurdur Johnson. Along with another settler, Gudmundur Olafsson, who had donated the land for the hall, they provided music for the community dances and concerts. Hjaltalin, who was a qualified teacher and music instructor, put together a choir around the turn of the century, which was in demand far beyond the limits of the Holar district. A reading society was organized in 1895 and a growing collection of good books became the foundation for a library. Most settlers brought books with them from Iceland, some of which were old publications. There were even cases of valuable manuscripts from the Middle Ages, which had been family treasures, that were brought to North America by settlers. The reading society at Holar was just as popular as in other Icelandic communities. Most books and magazines were in Icelandic and helped preserve the reading of the language for many years. A handwritten newspaper called *The Pioneer*, edited by Hjaltalin, came into existence in 1897. He took his paper to gatherings at the hall, to plays, concerts, or prayer meetings, and read it out loud to the audience. When there were no public events, he travelled from one home to the next and read it to every family.

The women in the community established an organization that was active in all church and social matters, as well as attended to other community needs in time of accidents or misfortune. One of the women, Helga Sigridur, an educated and trained midwife, contributed tremendously to the general well-being of the settlers, as she also performed the work of a doctor and a nurse. Like so many others, the small community did not enjoy the permanent presence of a physician, the closest ones being in Yorkton, Moosomin, or Russell.

Without the regular services of a pastor, these settlers organized prayer meetings on Sundays, especially during the winter months. The first pastor to visit the colony was Rev. Gislason, just before the turn of the century. Visits by pastors became more regular in the early 1900s, however, and steps were taken to establish a Lutheran congregation.

The Holar community, small in number compared to other rural Icelandic communities, became prosperous from the beginning. In contrast, the dry seasons in the Churchbridge district left many settlers convinced that their chosen site had been poor. Unaware of the dry and wet cycles, they believed that a move out of the area was their only option. The lack of moisture affected every aspect of farming and those people who concentrated on raising stock foresaw problems in making enough hay.

In 1891 work on the railway to present-day Yorkton was underway and explorers of regions further west and north reported that there were lakes in the vicinity, surrounded by fields of tall grass. The news reached the Thingvalla community and two settlers, Ingimundur Eiriksson and Christjan J. Helgason, decided to examine these regions. Both had come to the Thingvalla settlement in 1886. They had a team of horses and a wagon and travelled about 184 kilometres until they had reached Fishing Lake, which was, even in those dry days, a lake of good size. On the lower south side, there was plenty of hay, but on the higher ground, poplar buffs surrounded taller trees ideal for the construction of houses. Eiriksson and Helgason moved their families to Fishing Lake on 27 June 1892. Three settlers, Eiriksson, Helgason, and Gisli Bildfell, had brought their families and were joined by two more settlers in the fall, Sveinn Halldorsson and Stefan Olafsson, both of whom brought their spouses.[12]

There was little time to build their own homes so they decided to construct one large dwelling and a stable. Walls were made of logs and the roofs were covered with rafters and sod. A section of the stable was partitioned off for Stefan Olafsson and his wife, while the remaining families, nine adults and six children, shared the other house.

These settlers brought animals with them and had made enough hay for the coming winter, when a prairie fire swept through the region, burning their stacks to the ground. Fortunately, they found a meadow full of hay about six kilometres away. This was what today is known as Foam Lake, but in the fall of 1892 it was completely dry. The settlers made enough hay, but decided to leave it on the meadow where it was stacked, and they made numerous trips during the winter to haul it to the stable. During the summer of 1893 they realized that the large meadow they had used the previous fall and the surrounding area was in all likelihood the most desirable settlement site. The settlers, therefore, moved to Foam Lake in the following spring, and settled on the shore of what, in a few years' time, became a lake. In the next few years, more settlers arrived from the Thingvalla district, adding to the number of this tiny Icelandic community. In 1902 nineteen farmers had settled in the colony and the adult population of the community reached thirty-five. Most of the shore and the land up from the lake all around had been settled by the end of the century.[13]

Life in this isolated community was difficult in the first few years. The lake was far from the nearest market at Yorkton, and transportation was both time-consuming and strenuous. Twice a year, spring and fall, the settlers undertook a shopping trip to Yorkton. The trips became part of community life, as many people travelled together—husbands, wives, and older children. If market cattle were included, the journey usually lasted three days. The community spirit was good—people met on special occasions such as Christmas or Easter and, as was customary in Iceland, always celebrated the arrival of the first day of summer. In the first few years, people took turns holding gatherings in their homes. From 1902 to 1904, or until the railroad reached Sheho, more settlers arrived, most of whom continued westward beyond the shore of the lake. Foam Lake was gradually filling up as a result of a wet cycle and in 1904 had reached its normal level of a metre and a half. The arrival of the railway increased the traffic into the region and it had reached Leslie in the winter of 1908. All the early settlers at the Foam Lake settlement, with one exception, had come from the Thingvalla district, and by 1902 the first Icelandic settlement era in Saskatchewan history came to an end.

The second settlement period began at once as the Canadian Northern Railway main line reached just north of Tantallon (Holar District), as well as a new Canadian Pacific line. The Icelanders arriving in Canada in the late 1890s and during the early twentieth century were caught in a sudden upheaval in every aspect of life in western Canada. Gradually, as settlement expanded west, Icelandic settlements of different shapes and sizes became a part of the western Canadian cultural mosaic. In the 1910s the Icelanders were on the leading edge of the frontier, exploring and establishing new colonies as occupation of the west progressed. Icelanders from overcrowded regions in North Dakota and Minnesota moved to regions in Saskatchewan, Alberta, or British Columbia. Also, numerous settlers from Icelandic communities in Manitoba joined those searching for permanent homes in the west.

During the 1880s, more people emigrated from Iceland to North America than at any time in the past, an exodus which was not repeated. Most of the 6324 people who left in this decade first attempted to settle in different parts of Manitoba. Records show that immigration peaked immediately following unusually cold years, when farmers were forced off their lands as frost remained in the ground, preventing summer grazing and hay-making. Overcrowded rural regions prevented young people from starting their own farms, and the small fishing villages and towns were ill-prepared to sustain a sudden increase in population. Increasingly, people moved to the urban areas. At the same time, the population in Iceland had risen to almost 79,000 in 1901, from the 47,000 of 1801, in spite of the heavy immigration to America during the last two decades of the century.

In politics the main issue since 1874 was what type of government system should be granted to the Icelanders, who wanted more executive power. The demand for home rule grew stronger, but a very conservative Danish government rejected the demands. In fact, it was not ready to accept any progressive ideas about political reforms in Iceland.

Valtyr Gudmundsson was elected Member of Parliament in 1894 in Iceland, and immediately put his mark on politics there. He introduced a compromise in which an Icelander should take over the office of Minister for Iceland. He would be responsible to the Parliament in Iceland but sit in Denmark. This bill was rejected in 1897 and again in 1899, but was at last accepted, somewhat modified, in 1901. The passing of the bill could not have come at a worse time, as the Conservative government of Denmark had been defeated by Liberals. However, led by Hannes Hafstein, the so-called Home Rule Party won in the next general election of 1902 and again in 1903. In 1904, Hannes Hafstein assumed the office of Icelandic Minister with an office in Reykjavík.[14] Although the legal status of Iceland changed little, as the Danish constitutional laws of 1871 were still in force, the foundation of executive power had been brought to Iceland. A cabinet comprised of three departments was established, one for ecclesiastical affairs and justice, another for industries and communication, and a third for public finance.

Despite progress in the struggle for independence, and improvements in communication and important social issues such as education, opportunities to improve the lives of Icelanders remained limited. America offered two attractions: one was the many success stories of families and friends; the second was the effort by agents of both Canadian and American governments to encourage people to emigrate. Opposition to emigration had continued to grow in Iceland since the late 1870s and, in the 1890s, agents were met with open hostility. One Icelandic newspaper on 10 March 1893 reported:

> The American-Icelanders, Baldvin L. Baldvinsson and Sigurdur Kristofersson recently arrived in Reykjavík after touring most of the country preparing intended immigrants. They have given lectures in numerous places on the glory of America but the reactions have varied. The opposition to immigration to America has clearly grown tremendously in this country. The agents are accused of misleading the crowds by glorifying conditions in America and at the same time blasting the situation in this country. Baldvinsson published this winter a report on progress in Icelandic communities in America, which has been considered inaccurate and unreliable. Recently, the pair conducted a meeting at Akranes at which the place caught fire when an oil lamp in the building

accidentally fell. The crowd on hand escaped unharmed and the fire was extinguished before major damage was done to the building.

This accident may have been a premonition as the next meeting planned in Reykjavík was a total disaster. The meeting was scheduled at the Good Templars Hall where Baldvinsson intended to deliver a major speech. Long before the meeting was called to order the house was packed and a crowd gathered outside as well. As soon as Kristofersson attempted to call the meeting to order he was silenced by whistling noise and horns from the two hundred people in the house. This naturally was a message to them to keep quiet and that the meeting should be cancelled but at least ten times they attempted to call the meeting to order but to no avail. In the end they left but the crowd remained in the building long afterwards just in case the agents would return again.[15]

No available sources throw light on how effective the opposition to the immigration movement actually was. One suspects that, when newspapers continuously criticized and demeaned those people intending to leave, and magnified the hardships endured in the United States and Canada, and when groups of people disrupted meetings, and even threatened to use violence, emigration was discouraged significantly. As is often the case in the absence of proof, those people strongly opposing emigration from Iceland seldom argued their case with facts and logic, but used humiliation and questionable reports from America. However, there were no simple solutions to the problems in Iceland, and, despite opposition, emigration continued.

Emigration 1890-1899

1890—217	1895—.9
1891—216	1896—10
1892—290	1897—.55
1893—725	1898—87
1894—113	1899—157

Total—1879

Source: Kristinsson, *Vesturfaraskrá 1870-1914*, Table 4.

Compared to figures for the previous decade, emigration from Iceland had dropped considerably. The climate was milder, economic conditions were slightly better, and perhaps the fierce opposition was having some effect. Even in the wake of a severely destructive earthquake in the late summer of 1896, an immediate increase in emigration from the country did not occur. However, emigration rose sharply during the first five years of the twentieth century.

Emigration 1900-1914

1900—725	1908—4
1901—258	1909—.41
1902—313	1910—87
1903—677	1911—90
1904—313	1912—84
1905—282	1913—156
1906—57	1914—85
1907—36	

Source: Kristinsson, *Vesturfaraskrá 1870-1914,* tables 5 and 6.

The sudden drop in 1906 and after was undoubtedly due to the establishment of Home Rule. The few people emigrating from 1906 to 1914 were mostly relatives or friends of people already in North America. Migration to the United States had slowed considerably after most of the land in the North Dakota and Minnesota colonies had been settled, but those who had relatives in these colonies or elsewhere in America continued to emigrate to the United States, if only for a while.

In Canada, Manitoba continued to attract attention and the population of communities in the Interlake region grew steadily, as did the Icelandic population in Winnipeg and major towns. As these settlers moved into Manitoba, many established settlers in the province, as well as in North Dakota and elsewhere in the United States, went west to Saskatchewan and Alberta.

The first Icelandic settlements in Saskatchewan had been comprised of combinations of immigrants from Iceland and settlers from Icelandic communities in Manitoba or North Dakota. During the first decade of the twentieth century, established Icelandic settlers from overcrowded parts of North Dakota and Manitoba, such as Argyle, formed a large Icelandic community in Saskatchewan, extending from the west side of Foam Lake as far west as the present Dafoe and to the north and east, almost to Fishing Lake.[16] This new settlement was an extension of the existing Foam Lake settlement westward; at seventy-two kilometres long and thirty kilometres wide, this was to become the biggest Icelandic settlement in Saskatchewan.

Thomas Paulson, who previously had settled in the Thingvalla district, had moved to the west margin of Foam Lake in 1898 and shortly afterwards was appointed agent for the Canadian government. His duties were to direct new Icelandic immigrants to the area and assist them in the selection of land. Although many of the Icelandic newcomers to the developing colony had been in North America for some time, most of them still preferred land best suited for mixed farming. Some already had gained experience in grain growing but continued to raise stock as well. In the thirty years of Icelandic settlements in North America, only once had the settlers from Iceland chosen land without a guarantee they could establish mixed farming—when they selected land on the west bank of Lake Winnipeg where they expected to fish and raise livestock.

Thomas Paulson advised his compatriots to settle as closely together as possible in order to facilitate the creation of Icelandic colonies, perhaps unnecessary advice as that was their custom, but there were Canadian colonization leaders who advocated complete assimilation of immigrants. Rather than directing the Icelanders onto the open prairie near the present Kandahar, Paulson recommended areas in the eastern part of the district, which was broken by sloughs, poplar bluffs, and willow bushes.[17] Most settlers followed his advice, but a number of people from the Argyle district in Manitoba chose the open prairie, as they were accustomed to it.

These settlers certainly were much better prepared for the pioneer task ahead than those who had arrived directly from Iceland a few years earlier. Not only had they gained valuable experience in North American farming, but they also had acquired a sufficient command of the English language. In addition, most of them arrived with important material resources, whereas those from Iceland lacked just about everything. But the most significant difference was the new way of looking at their role in the Canadian cultural mosaic. Many of these newcomers had emigrated from Iceland as children or teenagers with their parents in the 1870s. Some of them were, in fact, born on North American soil. Their upbringing had been Icelandic in nature and the use of the Icelandic language was still very much a part of their daily life. To them, Iceland and her heritage were significant, but their future was going to be Canadian and, therefore, they tended to look ahead rather than back. Their outlook differed from that of their parents in the sense that they lacked the spirit of dedication and sacrifice to the past. Rather, they were brimming with a growing sense of new values and appreciation of new opportunities. This clearly marked a very decisive step towards integration, a step from the childhood years in the dominant Icelandic environment to adulthood in the multicultural society settling the Canadian west.

Most of the settlers arriving in Saskatchewan after the turn of the century came from either North Dakota or the Argyle district in Manitoba. Some came from Winnipeg, others from the regions on the western shore of Lake Manitoba, Winnipegosis, or New Iceland. A few came directly from Iceland, and one individual, Magnus G. Isfeld, arrived with his family all the way from Brazil. A few had been born in North America, including Jakob F. Bjarnason, who was born in Kinmount, Ontario, in 1874. These settlers established the largest Icelandic colony in Saskatchewan, a settlement always referred to by the Icelanders in America as Vatnabyggðin (the "Lakes Settlement"). Although many of these settlers had a different outlook from that of their parents, they maintained Icelandic values and traditions, such as teaching Icelandic in the home. Prayer meetings were held in the homes or a hall in the absence of pastors.

The basic chores of a pioneer farm remained the same. Land had to be cleared and broken, stables and barns and a family home constructed. For the preparation of soil, oxen were still very useful because horses were expensive, but farm implements had made cultivation a little easier. The pattern of settlement, though, had changed. Pioneers in New Iceland, North Dakota, or Argyle had wandered into mostly uninhabited regions and developed communities that remained isolated for years. The Saskatchewan settlers had better communication opportunities because the railway was being built through their regions as they worked their land, which meant the quick development of villages around each new railway station.

The Lakes Settlement was predominantly Icelandic and most of the halls built in the villages were constructed by the Icelanders and used as Icelandic cultural and community halls. Reminiscing in the *Almanak*, Fridrik Gudmundsson of Mozart wrote, "Some years ago community halls were erected in almost all the villages along the railroad. Half of them were exclusively owned by the Icelanders but some of the others, owned and mostly used by other ethnic groups, were still built by Icelandic settlers."[18]

Nine congregations in the Lakes Settlement were established, from Foam Lake in the east to Kandahar furthest west. Pastors serving in the community in the first decade included Rev. H.J. Leo, Rev. Pjetur Hjalmarsson, Rev. Guttormur Guttormsson, Rev. Einar Vigfusson, and Rev. Runolfur Fjelsted.

Although the entire region of the Lakes Settlement can be considered one Icelandic colony, smaller communities within the settlement retained their own characteristics.

The immediate area surrounding Foam Lake had been settled by the turn of the century. A steady influx began in 1903 and reached its peak in 1905 and 1906. Most of the newcomers settled west of the already established community but also claimed land in the north and south. The railway reached the region in 1907 and immediately a village appeared. Several Icelanders moved to the village and started their businesses. A hardware store, partly owned by Olafur Petursson, and a lumberyard owned by Ingvar Olafsson were started in 1908. Soon, retail stores were opened as well as an implement business. A school was built shortly after the Westside School District was formed in 1905 and the Rural Municipality of Foam Lake was incorporated in 1910. In 1912 Gudbrandur Narfason was the first Icelander elected as reeve.

In 1903 settlers began to move to Kristnes, north of Foam Lake. Jon Thorlacius settled there that year and established a post office the following year. To serve this predominantly farming community, Jonas Samson opened a small store on his farm in 1903, Fred Vatnsdal operated a small trading post on his farm in the northern part of the community, and Thomas Hordal had a blacksmith shop on his farm. Although they were essentially a rural community, settlers in Kristnes became involved in all community and municipal affairs and organizations. John Arnason, for example, was one of the first councillors of the Rural Municipality of Foam Lake. During the first decade of the twentieth century, the Icelandic population of Kristnes was just above seventy.

The community of Leslie was centred around one of the small railway villages in the region. Work on expanding the railway onwards from Leslie was suspended for the year in the winter of 1907-1908, which meant that the small village was the end of the line. That situation resulted in an excellent start for anyone involved in business, as settlers arriving on the train would buy the necessary supplies before going to their homesteads. Thomas Paulson started an implement store and his brother, W.H. Paulson, who moved to Leslie from Winnipeg, opened a hardware store. W.H. Paulson was later a successful Liberal candidate in provincial elections and served as MLA for several years. Thorvaldur Thorvaldson also moved to Leslie and opened a general retail store.

Leslie grew fast as a result of the delay in rail construction. Several influential people contributed to making the village a great cultural community. People like W.H. Paulson, Dr. Sigurdur J. Johannesson, and Rev. Runolfur Fjelsted created a literary atmosphere, which spread well beyond the limits of the village, and Mrs. W.H. Paulson and Paul Magnusson were talented musicians who organized a band and a choir.[19] A mid-winter festival was established in Leslie, a mirror of a celebration held in Iceland, called Þorrablót,[20] which became such a success that people travelled to Leslie from different parts of the Saskatchewan Icelandic community to attend. By the end of 1910, the population of Icelanders in this community was eighty-three.

Two small settlements developed in the south of the region: Mt. Hecla and Holar. The former was named after the first school built in this community, and the latter was the name of a post office. Both settlements were characterized by their uneven land. The small, open patches between bluffs of poplars and brushwood made breaking land very difficult. Small sections were cleared, but the land was best suited for raising livestock. Mt. Hecla was straight south from Leslie and covered less than one township. The population in 1910 was around thirty. The Mt. Hecla School was built in 1908 and became the centre of all community activities.

Holar, which was south and slightly east of Elfros, centred around the Holar Post Office and the Walhalla School. Icelandic settlers, nine families and five single individuals, arrived in 1905 and, five years later, the Icelandic population was just under forty. It was a small community in size but very active in social and cultural activities. They established a Lutheran congregation with services at Walhalla School, which also was the place for concerts, dances, and other community entertainment. Both these settlements eventually became integrated with the Foam Lake, Leslie, and Elfros communities. The railway reached Elfros in 1908 but already numerous Icelandic families were in the vicinity. The first five arrived in 1903, fifteen arrived a year later, and more settlers moved to the Elfros district over the next two years. Once the railway was built, the village of Elfros sprang up and several Icelanders took advantage of business opportunities. A lumberyard and a general store opened, and John Goodmundsson, who partly owned the general store, became the first postmaster.

The Rural Municipality of Elfros was incorporated in 1909. After a strenuous campaign against a pioneer of non-Icelandic heritage, Thordur Arnason was elected reeve. The new municipality covered a much larger area than Elfros, and Arnason actually came from Mozart, another Icelandic community nearby. The population of Icelanders in 1910 was just above seventy.

The first Icelander to choose the vicinity of Mozart, which is west of Elfros, was John S. Laxdal. Originally a homesteader in the Morden settlement of Manitoba, Laxdal moved west after hearing favourable reports. He purchased land just west of Birch Creek and filed for homestead rights for four other people still in Morden: Jonas Thomasson, Johann Palsson, and the brothers John Egill and Axel G. Jonasson. Thomasson and the Jonasson brothers left Morden in the spring of 1904, taking with them four oxen. During the next few years, more settlers moved into the community and, with the arrival of the railway in 1908, a station and village were built at Mozart. Thorsteinn Laxdal and John K. Johnson opened a general store they called Johnson & Laxdal, and Peter N. Johnson started a lumberyard as well as some livestock marketing.

Nearly all the settlers came from other Icelandic settlements where community life had been active. A ladies' association was soon organized and a Good Templars chapter established, and together these two built a community hall, which later came under full control of the ladies' association. By 1910 the total population was over 100.[21]

Wynyard is still further west. The first settlers, a group consisting of four families from different, distant Icelandic communities, prepared themselves there for the winter of 1904-1905. Olafur Stephansson had emigrated from Iceland in 1898 and, after residing in North Dakota for six years, moved to this Canadian district. Magnus G. Isfeld brought his large family all the way from Brazil, and Gudmundur Thorarinsson and John Johnson, who brought his son with him, came from Winnipeg. All built huts and made some hay. None of them expected to see yet another family arrive, especially not in the beginning of November. However, Jon Jonsson Westdal, his wife, Anna, and four children had arrived from Iceland that summer, and after some deliberation in Winnipeg and Argyle, decided to head west. He managed, with the help of his compatriots, to build a sod house before the first snow. Olafur O. Magnusson wrote in *Almanak* in 1950 of the remarkable arrival of the Westdals:

> It requires daring and courage to settle on uninhabited land in a strange country
> with a family without a roof over one's head just before the attack of a Canadian
> winter. Fortunately some of the children were grown up and others in their teens.
> The first task was to put up a shelter. That was done on the Icelandic pattern—

sod was dug and rails used for rafters. But the main supports for the building had to be carried quite a distance, as there were no animals.[22]

The original settlers must have thought the Westdals would be the last arrivals in the fall of 1904. However, an additional five single men from North Dakota also appeared unexpectedly. They had been to their chosen site earlier in the fall to make hay. Hastily, they built a shelter for the livestock—a small herd of cattle and a few horses—before making a dugout for themselves. It probably was the most incomplete dwelling any Icelandic settlers in North America had hitherto made: using picks and shovels they dug into a slope and covered it with canvas and snow, and there they spent their first winter in Saskatchewan.

In the late 1890s, Icelanders in North Dakota had begun to look elsewhere for a settlement site, as their region was not large enough to sustain the population and possibilities for expansion were few. It is ironic that young people now had little choice but to look outside the Icelandic colony in North Dakota. They were forced, like their parents in Iceland before them, to look for opportunities away from their home soil. By the turn of the century, this problem had become serious and interest grew in Icelandic settlements in western Canada. A meeting held in 1904 sent a delegation of five to explore these new regions.[23] Halldor J. Halldorsson, Oli J. Halldorsson, Olafur O. Magnusson, Asgeir Gudjonsson, and Bjarni F. Bjarnason travelled to Foam Lake to meet with Thomas Paulson. He proposed a site further west by Big Quill Lake and, after thorough examination, the delegates selected an area south of Little Quill Lake and east of Big Quill Lake. Before returning to North Dakota, the delegation stopped at Yorkton to file on homesteads for a number of people.

In North Dakota, their favourable report encouraged many people to move to Canada. The group was divided into two, one to emigrate from North Dakota in 1905 and the other a year later. This was a necessary arrangement because not only were there many people who wanted to move, but most settlers brought livestock, and the train could not accommodate everyone. The settlers also agreed that there would not be time for such a large number of settlers to establish themselves all at once.

A special train was prepared for the transportation. Thirty boxcars and five passenger cabins carried more than 100 people in the first party. The train arrived in Wadena, the closest station to the new settlement site. The fifty-six-kilometre journey from the town was strenuous both for people and animals, as no roads had been built in the area and the terrain was moist in places. Many settlers required at least two journeys in order to carry all their belongings from Wadena. Most lived in tents initially while more adequate dwellings were constructed.

During the previous winter, Halldor J. Halldorsson had informed Canadian government authorities in Ottawa of the large number of settlers due to arrive from North Dakota. He also urged that a post office be established and, ultimately, his homestead became the first post office in the colony.[24] He called it Sleipnir. In the fall of 1905 he opened a small general store in his home, and then built a store a short distance away in the following spring. In 1906 it was transported to the present Wynyard townsite. Seventeen oxen were needed to pull the building over the frozen ground and snow.

While temporary homes were built, the settlers gathered fodder for the stock. There was plenty of grass and men even had time in the fall to clear and break some land in preparation for the seeding the following year. The soil was good, most necessary implements had been brought along, and this new colony was established.

The second group from North Dakota arrived in the following spring (1906). Although trains still did not reach the colony, people continued to flood in from different Icelandic communities both in Canada and the United States. The railroad reached Wynyard in 1908, after which the town developed quickly. The Wayne Hotel was built by a German immigrant, and a lumberyard, pharmacy, and a store soon followed. The first Icelander to build his home in Wynyard was Simon Sveinsson, who was a carpenter and later responsible for the construction of numerous houses in the area.[25]

Wynyard attracted people of different nationalities and never became a predominantly Icelandic town, although the Icelanders were influential. For example, H.J. Halldorsson soon began to advocate for a school division, because the large number of youth in the region meant that both an elementary and high school were needed. Many settlers opposed him at first, especially single and childless inhabitants, who fought against a possible school tax, but eventually a school district was established and schools built. Congregations were established early and two Icelandic churches were built in Wynyard, a Lutheran and a Federated church. Organizations, including a reading society and ladies' associations, were established, and functioned in the same way as similar organizations in other Icelandic communities.

The Kandahar-Dafoe region is furthest west in the Lakes Settlement. The first Icelanders moved into the region in 1905. A few, however, had filed on homesteads the year before—among them four Bjornson brothers from North Dakota—but most of the settlers in this open prairie area came from Argyle. This region was ideal for growing grain; there were no trees or bushes and on many homesteads every acre could be broken. Thomas Paulson had objected to this choice of land because he thought the region ill-suited for mixed farming. The experience in Argyle undoubtedly had its effect on these settlers as they welcomed the flat, open, unprotected prairie. And in due course, once their land began to yield, it was clear that these farmers had made an excellent choice.

The Lakes Settlement became the largest Icelandic rural community in North America, not only in area but also in population. Fridrik Gudmundsson wrote that there were 866 homesteads and 334 additional farms in a 768-square-kilometre settlement.[26] He expected the regular population of the community to be around 3600, excluding the numerous labourers. This Icelandic community grew in size and developed faster than any other Icelandic colony during the Icelandic immigration period of 1870 to 1914. An interesting combination of settlers from 1891 to 1908 witnessed prosperity hitherto unknown among Icelandic immigrants in North America. There were newcomers from Iceland, grain growers from Argyle, and farmers accustomed to mixed farming from Lake Manitoba and North Dakota. From the beginning of the settlement, most of the settlers knew what they wanted from their homesteads and how to achieve it; a grain grower in the Kandahar region immediately cleared acres next to his farm and a year later had a good harvest. Cattle raising and dairy production also had a good start in the eastern sections of the settlement.

A predominantly Icelandic community but certainly not an exclusive one, the Lakes Settlement also experienced at this time the primary steps of the transition from first generation to second. A segment of the population consisted of young people who had either arrived very young in America, or had been born there. Many of them had grown up with children of other ethnic backgrounds and now, as young farmers, were eager to participate in the emerging Canadian cultural mosaic. A sense of Canadianism was developing. Their parents had taken the huge step of emigrating to North America without understanding the creation of both the American and Canadian nations. The second generation, young businessmen in Wynyard or Yorkton, or farmers in the rural communities, paid much closer attention not only to developments in their own province, but also to politics in Ottawa. These young farmers had selected land on which they proposed to produce, and were determined to take part in any decision that affected their livelihood. Above all, they wanted the Icelandic characteristics they had inherited to become a visible contribution to the Canadian scene.

Two smaller Saskatchewan settlements were established on the Grand Trunk Pacific Railway, one in the Gerald region and the other at Spy Hill. The Gerald settlers, most of whom arrived in 1902 (six families and five individuals), came from different communities in North Dakota and Manitoba, and, in the case of two families, from Iceland. They established a Lutheran congregation in 1904, which they called Isafold, and almost every family of Icelandic origin in the community became a member. Too small to support a permanent pastor, the community used resident ministers of the Thingvalla-Lögberg settlements. A reading club was established in 1907. By 1910, about fifty Icelanders resided in the small community but only two years later, all but three families had left for the prosperity of the Wynyard and Kandahar regions.

Sixteen Icelanders settled at Spy Hill, east of Gerald. It remained a very small community, which never organized a congregation or Icelandic associations.[27]

As the major urban places developed, Icelanders became a part of Saskatchwan cities, including Saskatoon, Yorkton, and Prince Albert. Initially, only a few Icelanders settled in the capital city, Regina, probably because it was in the south whereas the largest Icelandic community was farther north. Generally, other than dealing with occasional cold springs or summer droughts, Icelandic settlements prospered in Saskatchewan.

There were three basic reasons for the emigration from the Icelandic communities in North Dakota into Canada. Most of the settlers in Dakota in the early 1880s had arrived, with little or no means, from New Iceland or directly from Iceland. In order to get started in the new community, they took out loans but the payments were difficult and the productivity of each farm was only moderate at first. Because circumstances in North Dakota were not favourable, many chose to sell. Another reason for out-migration was the increasing population. Nearly all the land had been claimed and new immigrants from Iceland and young North Dakotans who wanted to start their own farm had to look elsewhere. Finally, many could not adjust to the prairie climate. These people supported the idea of exploration on the Pacific coast in British Columbia. A meeting in North Dakota in March of 1888 resolved that one man, Sigurdur J. Bjornsson, should travel to the coast in order to obtain land for a future settlement. All present at the meeting and others in favour of the move agreed to support Bjornson financially, yet he left North Dakota with little more than a return ticket.[28]

He toured about 480 kilometres of coastline without finding anything suitable. On the way back home, in Calgary, he met Olafur Goodman, who suggested regions further north in the Red Deer River area. Goodman, or Olafur Gudmundsson, was the first Icelander known to have moved to Alberta. He and his family, and his father and brother, had arrived in Calgary late in 1887. Bjornson eventually secured Township 36, Range 1 and Range 2, for his compatriots in North Dakota. He returned to the Red Deer River area in early May. In his description of the region, he stated that he "liked the region north of the Red Deer River, the soil is fertile and grassy, can easily be divided into meadows and grain fields separated by belts of trees and bushes. Fishing in lakes and rivers is good and the winter there is shorter and considerably milder than in Manitoba."[29]

While Bjornson was away, many farmers in North Dakota had sold their land and stock and settled their accounts. They were dismayed when they learned that the land was in Alberta rather than on the coast, but had little choice but to join the group of 1888 that left North Dakota on 24 May. All their livestock had been sold because the law prohibited its transportation across the border into Canada, but they purchased twelve cows, $20.00 to $25.00 each, oxen, and a few horses on the Canadian side of the border at Gretna. The livestock and all their belongings were transported by boxcar, which had been rented for $85.00 for the trip to Calgary. One man tended the stock from Gretna to Calgary, and the others in the group went to Winnipeg, where they bought stoves, farming implements, and the train tickets ($17.50) to Calgary. They left Winnipeg 29 May and reached Calgary very early 1 June. The travellers were in a joyous mood; their long journey from North Dakota had gone smoothly. But ahead was more strenuous travel than any of them could have anticipated.

Their settlement site was about 128 kilometres north of Calgary, and had to be reached on foot or on wagons, as there was no railway. The spring and early summer of 1888 were unusually wet in Alberta and the only road north had become a sea of mud. Jonas J. Hunford described this leg of the journey: "Often the men had to carry the women and children over the worst low spots. . . . I shudder as I recall seeing the women and children on top of the supplies on the wagons, the children grabbing their mothers, all soaked and chilled. At night they had to lie down and rest and sleep on cold wet ground. The Red Deer River was reached after six days."[30] Due to heavy rain, the level of the river was high and crossing it on wagons was impossible. In the end, after some deliberation, two flat-bottomed boats were built to transport people and belongings. Horses and cattle swam.

This trip to the new settlement site in Alberta was, in one respect, similar to the 1875 expedition in that people travelled through fertile prairie regions into a region considerably less attractive. While pushing through the mud towards the Red Deer River, the Icelanders crossed over some of the best grain-growing regions of Alberta, the Big Bend of the Red Deer River. But mixed farming still was their preference, and land with no hay meadows or bluffs of trees was not what they wanted, even though the land they sought meant harder work, because uprooting willows and poplar trees was hard, and breaking such land much slower.

Fifty people arrived on 27 June 1888. The wet summer of 1888 was followed by several dry years, which were worse. Thus, farms in the new community started badly, a situation made worse by a shortage of equipment and horses. Several farmers received encouragement from an experienced settler who moved into the community from North Dakota in 1889. The poet Stephan G. Stephansson had been involved in establishing the Shawano settlement in Wisconsin of 1875 and the North Dakota community in the 1880s. He declared that "the harvest will come if people will not lose courage," and he was determined to succeed. His leadership and effort influenced several of the younger settlers who were considering options elsewhere. He was instrumental in establishing the first post office in the colony and suggested the name Tindastoll. It was later changed to Markerville.[31]

The first five years were difficult. There was no bridge across the Red Deer River until 1902. The railway, which the settlers believed was going to cross their community, arrived in 1890 about twenty kilometres east of their colony and Innisfail became the market centre for the Icelanders. Their settlement was isolated and temporary employment was not available nearby. Although the Athabaska Co. built a sawmill on the south side of the Red Deer River, it was of little economic help to those Icelanders needing work.

Most of the settlers were poor and struggled to establish their farms. Little time or money was available for the construction of a hall in those early years, but in 1892 the settlers decided to begin preparations for a school. Logs were cut in the spring and brought to a site opposite Stephansson's home. Many individuals contributed to the construction of the school house, which was given the name Holar or Hola-school. In 1904 it was rebuilt on the bank of the Medicine River and another school was built near the post office at Tindastoll.[32]

Poverty and too much hard work, as well as different religious persuasions, prevented the settlers in Alberta from establishing a congregation or building churches. They called in ministers of foreign background to baptize their children or bury the dead. A burial site was donated by one farmer, Josef Stefansson, who lived near the Tindastoll post office.

This arrangement appeared to suit the majority of the settlers, who were without a congregation or pastor until 1900. However, there were visits by Icelandic pastors, deacons, or theologians. For instance, in 1898, Runolfur Marteinsson, later ordained pastor at Gimli, Manitoba, visited the Markerville community for ten days. It was believed the Icelandic Lutheran Synod made the arrangements for his visit, which took everyone by surprise. Marteinsson held four religious services during his short visit, two at the Holar School and two at Tindastoll; both schools at that time also served as community halls. Marteinsson returned to the community just before Christmas of 1899 and remained in the settlement until 6 February 1900. He established Sunday schools both at Holar and Tindastoll. His presence convinced many settlers of the need for a permanent pastor, and on 21 January 1900, a meeting attended by twenty farmers, representing eighty people, agreed to establish a Lutheran congregation, which was given the name Alberta Congregation. Later that year, the congregation obtained the services of Rev. Marteinsson for a period of two months; he had been ordained by that time. He arrived in the beginning of November and upon his departure, 1 January 1901, membership in the congregation had risen to 130. At the annual conference of the Icelandic Lutheran Synod, held in Selkirk, Manitoba, in 1900, the Alberta congregation was welcomed as a new addition.

For the next four years, several pastors were hired for short periods of time but on 12 July 1905, Rev. Petur Hjalmsson became a permanent pastor for the community. He delivered his sermons in five different locations in the settlement, receiving an annual income of $600.00. Members were obviously responsible for the payment of his salary, but further contributions were made by non-congregational members as well as the ladies' association, Vonin ("The Hope"). A congregational meeting on 17 September 1906 resolved that a church should be built, and on 25 May 1907 it was completed.

A conflict between Rev. Hjalmsson and factions in the congregations resulted in the termination of his contract in 1909 and a lasting division in the community. Numerous members left the congregations and in 1910 the Alberta Congregation withdrew its membership from the Icelandic Lutheran Synod in North America. Rev. Hjalmsson continued to serve in the community, and Rev. Carl J. Olson from Gimli, Manitoba, also visited Markerville and held religious services.[33]

A cheese factory and a retail store were established by a small group at Tindastoll in 1897. Insufficient machinery and lack of funds caused the end of the operation of the first factory. However, a second attempt was more successful and in 1899, the Tindastoll Butter and Cheese Manufacturing Association was established with Stephan G. Stephansson as the first secretary-treasurer.[34] Other significant organizations were the Fensalir Construction Company, which built the first community hall in Markerville in 1903, and in 1905 the Canadian Order of the Woodsmen of the World, which established a chapter and offered life insurance ranging from $500.00 to $3000.00. A chapter of the Good Templars was organized in 1904.

The slow start of the Markerville community did not prevent a continuous flow of Icelandic settlers to Alberta. Gradually, they settled among immigrants of other nationalities in regions south and east of Markerville. Towns such as Innisfail, Red Deer, and, of course, Calgary and Edmonton, also attracted Icelanders very early. Jon Jonsson of Markerville, for instance, was the first Icelander to move to Edmonton in 1904. He had a successful real-estate business, and has been referred to as one of the fathers of Edmonton. Other early businessmen of Icelandic descent in Edmonton were Asgeir Thorsteinson and Sveinn Thorvardsson, who were partners in construction and real-estate businesses. The most significant building of theirs was one of the first playhouses, which seated more than 600 people. Benedict Olafsson moved from Winnipeg to Edmonton in 1907. He was a photographer and a first-rate cornet player, and was active in the musical community.[35]

Young Oliver Johnson came to Winnipeg from Iceland in 1882 and then continued westward to Victoria in 1883; he was the first Icelander known to have reached the Pacific coast. Working at odd jobs in the province for the next four years, Johnson was in Victoria when the Finnsson family arrived in 1887.

In the last years of the nineteenth century, Victoria was the main attraction for Icelanders destined for British Columbia. Einar and Sigridur Brandson also arrived in 1887 with a daughter, Margaret, who later married Dr. Richard Beck of North Dakota. Also that year, Sigurdur and Valgerdur Myrdal moved to Victoria from New Iceland. They had originally emigrated from Iceland in 1876. Sigurdur Myrdal, a religious man, arranged for prayer meetings every Sunday until he moved across the border to Point Roberts in 1894. The services were held at his house until Icelandic settlers built a Lutheran church in Victoria. This small Icelandic community grew slowly in the 1890s.

Vancouver attracted fewer Icelanders before the turn of the century but in 1904, twenty-one families had moved to the city. Provincial figures from 1902 showed that 177 settlers had reached British Columbia. The first known settler in Vancouver was Gudmundur Anderson. Only one group of Icelandic settlers is known to have travelled to BC for the purpose of establishing an Icelandic colony. Their destination had been the Queen Charlotte Islands but the group was directed instead to the Osland Settlement.[36]

It is difficult to understand the initial lack of Icelandic interest in the Pacific province, but its potential was never discussed in either of the two Icelandic weeklies published in Winnipeg. The reason for this may well be that the majority of Icelanders in North America resided in the three Canadian prairie provinces and in rural communities in North Dakota or Minnesota. The content of *Lögberg* and *Heimskringla* reflected these communities and offered very little about other urban sites where Icelanders were not involved. The North American Icelandic community was essentially a farming community.

The Vancouver Icelanders, although not a united community, nevertheless felt the need to communicate and promote Icelandic sentiment. For this purpose, an Icelandic organization was established in 1908 and given the name Ingolfur. Its immediate task was the creation of a library of Icelandic books. Several members donated their own collection, thus establishing the necessary foundation, and gradually books and magazines were bought and the library grew. Ingolfur also assumed responsibility for organizing social and cultural events such as dances and plays.

The same year Ingolfur was established in Vancouver, Thorsteinn J. Davidson, formerly of Markerville, Alberta, had crossed the Rockies with his family and reached Prince Rupert, and was supposedly the first Icelander to settle in the northern regions of British Columbia. Kristinn Kristinsson also brought his family. Also in 1908, a Canadian businessman bought some land on the east side of Smith Island, which faced the Skeena River, and hired the two Icelanders, Kristinsson and Davidson, to sell the land at a profit. Evidently they knew of the interest of a group of prairie Icelanders and offered the land to the settlers, who eventually reached the site in 1913. A small town later developed, called Osland. The first group to arrive consisted of two families and eight single men. Salmon fishing had attracted them but they also intended to grow fruit and vegetables.

Conditions in the settlement were initially primitive, because it was isolated and communication with other communities was difficult. Men used small rowboats to go to the nearest market, approximately thirty kilometres away, but they used sailboats for fishing. These had to be towed out to the fishing grounds, one boat fastened to the next.[37]

British Columbia offered a wider variety of occupations than did other provinces. The early settlers were fishermen, farmers, loggers, or salesmen, but they also became active in business ventures and in professions such as medicine, law, and teaching. They had come to a province already well established, and they consisted mostly of single men or women or individual families, not groups of settlers. However, this did not prevent them from establishing Icelandic societies in the following years and, as the number of Icelanders grew, these organizations became a permanent part of British Columbia society.

In 1893 four young Icelanders in Bellingham, Washington, decided to explore the Point Roberts region. Kristjan Benson, John Burns, Gudmundur Laxdal, and Sigurdur Haukdal had heard about Point Roberts from a French immigrant, Disotel, who was married to an Icelandic woman, Gudlaug Jonsdottir.[38]

Point Roberts is a peninsula in Whatcom County, Washington, about five kilometres long and two and a half kilometres wide. Although it is part of the United States, Point Roberts extends south from Canada into Boundary Bay. The closest market was at Ladner in Canada, which would have been the ideal location for the settlers to get their supplies, but customs regulations made this impossible. Instead, a boat had to cross the bay to Blaine, about twenty-two kilometres away. On land, the distance from Point Roberts to Blaine was about fifty-seven kilometres, mostly on the Canadian side of the border.

The southwest point of the peninsula was lowland, just above sea level. The ocean had made a natural projection in front, which protected the lowland from the waves. On the east side, the peninsula was high, with steep cliffs and rough terrain. During the pioneer era when roads had not been built, settlers travelled along the beach. Most of the peninsula was covered with tall trees and bluffs, which made travelling on land more difficult. From the highest part on this east side, the view in every direction was breathtaking—the snow-covered Rockies in the north, the Cascade Mountains to the east and southeast, and in the west the southernmost point of Vancouver Island was visible on clear days. The ocean was teeming with fish, mostly salmon, and in the evenings, late in summer and into fall, the ocean looked more like a city as all the boats lit their lights. There is little wonder these early explorers loved the natural beauty of the region as well as the fishing opportunities. In the next twenty years, between forty and fifty Icelandic settlers came to Point Roberts. The Icelandic population in 1914 was over 200.[39] Of these settlers, many came from the southern regions of Iceland, the Myrdalur, and surrounding regions.

Clearing the land and establishing farms took a long time, so men had to earn a living elsewhere, usually fishing. Soon two big companies moved into the territory: first, the Alaska Packers Association, or the APA, as it became known; and later George & Barker Salmon Packing Co. Gradually, individual fishing was terminated but both companies offered employment. Young women earned between $5.00 and $10.00 per day, but the men worked shifts, some at nights looking after nets while others transported the catch from the fishing vessels ashore to the factories. Employment was steady for eight to ten weeks for the women, but six to eight months for the men, and obviously helped the young settlement on its way to prosperity.[40]

The US government originally intended to build a military base on Point Roberts and the land claimed by the Icelanders was initially not available for settlement. A few Americans resided in huts here and there on the peninsula, and probably were aware of the plan, since very few of them cleared land or built homes. As the Icelanders offered to purchase their lots, they were informed that the land could not be bought, though the huts and improvements could be sold.

The Icelanders and other immigrants began to seek possession of their land and sent several petitions to Washington. Eventually, Ed C. Ellet, a special agent of the United States Land Office in Seattle, arrived. He was supportive of the

Icelandic settlers, and in his first report to the Commissioner at the General Land Office in Washington, DC, he remarked that "twenty-one out of the forty-five claimants on the Reservation are Icelanders, and they are the most frugal, industrious and altogether, the most desirable foreign settlers that I have found in the State of Washington."[41] On 26 August 1905, he wrote to the Commissioner at the General Land Office in Washington, DC:

> In view of the fact that Point Roberts Reservation has no value for Army or Navy purposes, and the further fact that for eighteen years last past Settlers have been allowed to take possession of the Reservation and build homes undisturbed by the Government, until the Reservation has a home and a claimant on almost every legal subdivision, I respectfully recommend that the Reservation be thrown open for settlement in legal subdivisions of not more than forty (40) acres to each claimant....
>
> I found a curious condition existing, especially among the Icelanders, to which I presume I should call the attention of the Department. Several of them, who have taken forty (40) acre tracts, have sold five (5) and ten (10) acre tracts off of it to other Icelanders, who are living upon the tracts they have bought. They have done this innocently and are entirely ignorant of that section of the Statute, No.2291, which would preclude the original claimant from proving it. Any legislation should include the waving of this Statute in these special cases.[42]

The settlers in Point Roberts awaited a solution and finally in the early spring of 1908 a bill came before the United States Senate:

> Be it enacted ... that the following described lands ... being in Whatcom County, State of Washington, and being a portion of the "Point Roberts Reserve," be, and the same are hereby, opened to settlement and entry under the homestead laws of the United States only, in such manner and at such time as the Secretary of the Interior may prescribe: Provided, That the actual bona fide settlers upon said lands on January 1, 1908, shall have sixty days from the opening of said lands and public notice thereof to make entry of the land settled upon and occupied by them, subject, however, to all the provisions of the homestead law.[43]

The Department of the Interior then acted swiftly on behalf of the settlers. Each settler received a letter in which their privileges were explained. Sigurdur Myrdal's read as follows:

Department of the Interior
General Land Office
Washington, D.C.
May 13,1908
Mr. S. Myrdal
Point Roberts, Washington

Sir:
        I have to advise you that instructions were issued on May 9, 1908, for the opening to settlement and entry under the general provisions of the public lands

laws of the lands in the Point Roberts Reserve on June 23, 1908. Actual bona
fide settlers on the lands have three months from said date to place their entries
of record.

Very respectfully,
Fred Dennett
Commissioner [44]

In her book, *Echoes from the Past,* Runa Thordarson described the reaction
to the good news:

> All the men went to Seattle to the land office. It was a happy time for everyone
> when they came back on the mail boat, which arrived shortly before noon. While
> the men were gone, the women planned a big community picnic to greet them.
> It was a beautiful sunny summer day at Tinkham's Grove. Daga (Thorsteinson)
> and her girls baked, and fried chicken and helped with the picnic. This was one
> of the happiest gatherings ever held at Point Roberts.
>
> Colonel Edward Tinkham, one of the early settlers who owned property on
> the west side of the Point suggested it would be appropriate to send a gift of
> some kind to President Roosevelt to show their appreciation. Helgi (Thorsteinson)
> butchered his largest sheep and donated the skin. This was expertly tanned and
> a rug made from it by Mr. Elsner who had learned the trade in Germany. It was
> then sent to President Roosevelt.
>
> A letter of thanks was received from the President saying the rug was being
> used in his bedroom in the White House. [45]

The fate of the rug is unknown, but Thordarson's reflection of the event is
interesting. Most noteworthy is the community spirit. Colonel Tinkham, probably British, suggested the present and Mr. Elsner, another non-Icelander, tanned
the skin. This type of cooperation was typical in the community.

On the western side of the point there was a store, a schoolhouse, and a community hall, which was operated by both Icelanders and other immigrants. An
Icelandic reading society and a Lutheran congregation were established early.
Gradually outnumbered by Icelanders, the other settlers began to frequent the
social and cultural functions arranged by the Icelanders and even attended Icelandic religious services. On occasion, to meet their demands, pastors gave services in English. [46] Due to the limited availability of land, the settlement could only
reach a certain size and even though riches were seldom spoken of in those times,
people lived in comfort.

The history of early Icelanders in the State of Washington centres on the towns of
Blaine and Bellingham, and the village of Marietta. All three are within reach of
one another and located on the coast of Bellingham Bay. Marietta was a small
village on the north side of Bellingham Bay. The first Icelanders to arrive in the
vicinity were two women married to Norwegian settlers. Thorunn Halldorsdottir

Lee had immigrated to Canada with her father in 1876,[47] but moved to Dakota, where she met and married Oli Lee, a Norwegian settler in the Grafton district. In 1883, Gudny Thorleifsdottir Lee emigrated from Iceland to North Dakota, where she found employment as a housemaid at the home of Thorunn and Oli Lee. Here she resided for five years, during which time she met and married Oli's cousin, Petur. Both families moved to the coast in 1888 and settled in Birch Bay, about sixteen kilometres from Blaine.[48] The first Icelander to move into Blaine, however, was Joel Steinsson, who brought his family to Birch Bay in 1888, then sold his property and moved into Blaine in 1889.

The district was settled quickly. The bay was teeming with fish and wealthy speculators bought all the land they could and resold at a profit. Thick forest stretched from the hills down to sea level and several sawmills were established, attracting labourers from afar. Numerous canneries were also established just before the turn of the century and, until around 1910, most of them were successful. There was plenty of work, and women, teenagers, and older children earned reasonable wages. In Blaine, at one point, there were seven large canneries. However, the boom did not last as machines replaced the human hand and eventually the stock of fish was threatened by over-fishing. One by one, the canneries disappeared.

Icelanders came to the district from different communities in the States and Canada. Most of these were families who either had been encouraged by friends or family already in Washington, or were drawn west by reports of the boom. Young men and women also arrived individually. The only organized group came from Selkirk, Manitoba.

All the settlers in Blaine had to buy their land. Because most of the land was covered with trees, it was a tremendous effort to clear it and start farming. It is interesting to note that, in Washington, Icelanders experimented with gardening and growing vegetables and fruit, items many of them had never seen in Iceland. Gardening in Iceland in the second half of the nineteenth century was very limited. Pall Thorsteinsson, for instance, arrived with a group of settlers from Myrdalur in Iceland in 1887 and went to Victoria. He moved to Point Roberts in 1894 and started farming in company with others on thirty hectares of land. He was the first to specialize in growing berries on a large scale.

Although the Icelanders in Washington were scattered, a sense of being part of an Icelandic community was evident very early. Larger communities like Point Roberts, Blaine, and Bellingham established organizations, such as the reading society Kari, founded in the home of Gudmundur E. Goodman in Bellingham. According to a settler, "A reading society, Kári was established March 14th 1914. The driving force was Mr. Goodman whose home was used for the occasion. There were 40 founding members."[49]

The west coast of the United States was settled quickly in the last decade of the nineteenth and the first decades of the twentieth centuries. The Icelanders were attracted to the milder climate of the Pacific coast and were soon part of various communities, especially in Washington. Seattle was about 154 kilometres south of Bellingham but Icelanders had reached the city as early as 1888. In 1890 the population of the city was 42,837. The Icelandic numbers continued to grow and young people became engaged in various professions. Einar Einarsson ("Grandy") and Fridbjorn Fridriksson managed the only Icelandic grocery store; both of them moved west from Gardar in North Dakota just after the turn of the century. In order to increase business, as traffic during the day was often slow, Fridriksson visited a number of regular customers every day and took their orders. He then tended the store and delivered the orders in the afternoon. Apparently, they ran a successful business.

The settlers in Washington had great difficulty in establishing congregations in the early years; the Icelandic communities were still small in size and somewhat scattered, and there were no available pastors. However, in 1904 an Icelandic congregation was established in Seattle through the efforts of Rev. Runolfur Runolfsson, Einar Einarsson, and a few others. For some time, Rev. Runolfsson had served an Icelandic Lutheran congregation in Utah. His tenure in Seattle was brief, as his congregation became disappointed with his work and his contract was terminated. As a replacement, the congregation called on Jonas A. Sigurdsson, who had served in North Dakota before moving to the coast. Retired as pastor and no longer a member of the synod, Sigurdsson agreed to maintain the Sunday school and hold service once a month.

The Icelanders operated a hall at which they held social and cultural events. The composer Helgi Sigurdur Helgason had moved to Winnipeg from Iceland in 1890, where he lived for four years. He then moved to the Akra settlement in North Dakota and, in the fall of 1900, went to Seattle. He had not been there long when his work was noticed. The *Seattle Times* said:

> The Icelanders in Ballard are making a name for themselves in choir music. The City can be proud of a choir conducted by H.S. Helgason, which recently was established in Ballard. Helgason also conducts the Scandinavian choir *Norden*. The Icelandic choir recently gave its first concert, which was an absolute treat.[50]

A reading society, Vestri ("West"), was also established. It organized regular meetings and cultural events. J.A. Sigurdsson was editor of a newsletter published by the reading society.

The pattern of the Icelandic community of Washington State is comparable to that of British Columbia. No large groups from other Icelandic communities organized a migration to either place but hundreds of individuals, families and single people, moved west after the late 1880s. Although many people looked for opportunities to farm, different professions awaited most of them. The majority ended up in the large urban regions, and, in both places, Washington and BC, there were opportunities for young people at the turn of the century.

14
Assimilation and Icelandic Festivals

The year 1905 is significant in the history of Icelandic settlers in North America because, by that time, all the Icelandic settlements of importance had been established. Communities in Canada from Ontario to the west coast had been formed. In the United States, new communities in Washington State supplemented those in some of the midwest cities, such as Chicago and Duluth. Rural communities existed in Minnesota and North Dakota, and the first and oldest Icelandic community at Washington Island was still flourishing. In addition, Icelandic immigrants individually had sought and found opportunities in other rural or urban communities throughout North America. Some were married to non-Icelanders. In those cases, their ties with Icelandic communities were often minimal as the people assimilated into North American society.

The number of mixed marriages is unknown, but in the late 1870s, the first occurred in Winnipeg, when young Icelandic women married Canadians. The pioneers in Manitoba had some reservations regarding such arrangements, perhaps understandably, because a few of the marriages ended early with unfortunate consequences. Those people promoting an exclusive Icelandic settlement obviously opposed such marriages, although their opposition was rarely expressed, and when the dream of establishing an exclusive settlement ended in the late 1870s, and settlers from New Iceland as well as new immigrants from Iceland began to spread out in groups, searching for new sites, mixed marriages were considered unfortunate. This attitude reflected the Icelanders' adherence to their heritage and their determination to preserve it. However, as the years went by, and Icelanders' daily involvement in Canadian or American matters increased, and as their children came of age, this attitude changed. By 1900 mixed marriages had become a common occurrence, especially in the urban areas.[1] In Winnipeg during the 1880s, not only was there an increase in such arrangements, but also in a tendency to assimilation, more than in any other Icelandic community at that time. Icelandic visitors to the city or new immigrants from Iceland frequently commented on the "Canadianized" Icelanders of Winnipeg, who not only eagerly absorbed anything Canadian, but also mixed their mother tongue with translations of English words.

This situation in Winnipeg disturbed Jon Olafsson (the same man who had gone to Alaska in 1874), who became editor of *Lögberg* in 1890. He compared Winnipeg Icelanders to Icelandic students at the University of Copenhagen, Denmark, where he had spent some time during the 1880s. The contrast was marked, as Icelandic students in Denmark were often highly critical of the intellectual and spiritual life of their compatriots in Iceland. They supported the struggle for independence, some becoming leaders of the independence movement when they returned to Iceland. In Olafsson's opinion, all Icelanders, wherever they resided, should be committed to fight for that cause. But instead, he discovered people who "think more of establishing businesses in Winnipeg than freeing Iceland from Danish oppression."[2]

In another article in *Lögberg*, entitled "Onward, Onward Icelanders," Olafsson stated that more than 3000 Icelanders lived in Winnipeg and more than 10,000 in Manitoba.

> People of Icelandic background form the largest non-English speaking group in the province yet not one holds an important position in the community. Two or three hundred Swedes run their own immigration office and have demanded the service of a native Swede at the main post office, which now has been granted. We publish two weeklies: they only one monthly. We outnumber other Scandinavian groups in Winnipeg by far yet we accomplish much less. What are the reasons? We should not be so totally dominated by the English majority; it is quality that counts not quantity.
>
> Ten Swedes, Danes or Norwegians are more noticeable than two or three thousand Icelanders; here in Winnipeg these make sure to have foreign dignitaries at their social and cultural events, which in turn always results in some coverage by the local press. We make no such efforts. If we want to be recognized in North America as Icelanders, our voices must be heard.[3]

Jon Olafsson clearly had failed to understand the situation in Winnipeg. He had left North America in 1875 and his only information on developments in Icelandic communities came from letters and articles published in Icelandic newspapers. Such news never discussed the assimilation taking place in Winnipeg as a positive step towards a better life. On the contrary, authors made every effort to describe in as positive a manner as possible the progress in Icelandic communities. It must be remembered that many of these people had been heavily criticized for migrating and wanted to justify their decision to leave. The adoption of "foreign" lifestyles in Winnipeg and other urban communities was rarely discussed. Olafsson's comparison of Icelandic students in Copenhagen and Icelandic citizens of Winnipeg was also unfair. The students, upon completion of their studies, returned to Iceland to become involved in their nation, while most of the immigrants in Canada were establishing their lives in a new, foreign community of which they fully intended to be a part as soon as possible. A step towards that achievement was, for many Icelanders in Winnipeg, to establish businesses in the city. Olafsson obviously still expected his compatriots, whom he had left in 1875, to be struggling to remain Icelanders in North America fifteen years later.

In his 4 June 1890 article in *Lögberg*, Olafsson pointed out that other ethnic groups in Winnipeg celebrated their own national day, Norwegians on 17 May, Danes on 25 June, and he suggested Icelanders should select 2 August for a similar purpose. The first Icelandic celebration in North America had taken place on that day in 1874 in Milwaukee and in Iceland a new constitution had been accepted. Early August would also suit farmers, as seeding was over but harvest not yet begun. He concluded his article by calling on at least 3000 Icelanders to parade through the streets of Winnipeg to a park where the actual celebration should take place: "We must unite in the effort to make this work. Forget our disagreements and make this a success. We at *Lögberg* challenge *Heimskringla* to support this project. Our leaders must work together and plans need to be made immediately."[4]

Jon Olafsson was not the first to suggest an Icelandic celebration. Eggert Johannsson, editor of *Heimskringla*, had also suggested such an event in an editorial: "Icelandic immigrants are now scattered throughout western Canada and Dakota. An annual event would serve as means to unite them. Icelandic heritage is in great danger on this continent and if we make no effort to preserve it, we might as well cease to call ourselves Icelandic." He thought Winnipeg was the ideal location for such an event because Manitoba had the largest number of Icelandic immigrants in North America. While he recognized that transportation to the celebration might be a problem, he urged his readers to give his suggestion serious thought and challenged "all good people to work in harmony towards such a worthy goal."[5]

Heimskringla agreed with *Lögberg*, and although preparation time was short, a committee was appointed to organize the first festival in Winnipeg. The committee chose Victoria Gardens as the location for the celebration and mapped a route from the First Lutheran Church. Sports events, such as track-and-field competitions and Icelandic wrestling, were organized and prizes purchased for the winners. The Icelandic Choir volunteered to sing in the park and the Infantry School Band was hired. Invitations were sent to guests of honour, such as the premier, cabinet ministers, consuls, and other dignitaries. The program was to include toasts to Iceland, to North America, to guests of honour, and to Icelandic immigrants. Addresses in reply would be delivered by the "foreigners." This program, which in many ways was based on the 1874 Milwaukee celebration, set a high standard for future celebrations. Both Icelandic weeklies in Winnipeg repeatedly encouraged people to attend and urged other Icelandic communities elsewhere in Canada and the United States to organize their own celebrations. Preparations had gone well, but on Friday, 1 August, a heavy rain fell in Winnipeg. The streets soon became a sea of mud. The planned parade and all outdoor activities were threatened. However, by Saturday morning the rain had stopped and the sun shone on those Icelanders gathered at Nena Street, south of the First Lutheran Church, shortly after 9 a.m. At 10:30, members of the festival committee began the parade. The Infantry School Band led the parade, followed by four men in traditional Icelandic costume, carrying flags. They were followed by other men, then teenagers and children. Due to the terrible street conditions, most of the women rode in rented carriages. The parade left the First Lutheran Church to travel east on Ross Street, south on Isabel, east on Notre Dame, north on Main Street, and east on Rupert Street into the park by 11:30. Games and sports events were underway shortly afterwards but the actual celebration began at 2:30 p.m.

The Infantry School Band opened the ceremony in the afternoon with "Lofsöngur," which later became the Icelandic national anthem. Toasts and Icelandic songs were presented and then the foreign guests of honour addressed the Icelanders. Among them were the Lieutenant-Governor, Sir John Schultz, Attorney-General Isaac Campell, and the American consul, Mr. Taylor. The premier of Manitoba was not in Winnipeg.

In their greetings, the guests of honour spoke highly of the Icelandic immigrants and complimented them for their accomplishments in both the province and the city of Winnipeg. Shortly after their speeches, rain fell in earnest and the festival committee was forced to cancel what remained of the celebration, including the finals in sports and the dance in the evening.[6]

Despite the limited time for preparations and the miserable conditions, those people in attendance were pleased with the celebration. Both weeklies gave favourable accounts of events—understandably, as both editors were on the committee. The celebration attracted local media attention, as was planned. Both the Manitoba *Daily Free Press* and *Winnipeg Daily Tribune* discussed the event. The former praised Icelandic culture and the achievements of the Icelandic nation; it complimented Icelandic immigrants for being able to assimilate so easily and for their general interest in Manitoba's public affairs. It concluded with these words: "These immigrants should also be complimented for being so proud of their ethnic background but their history is marked with endless hardships." The *Tribune* said that "many citizens, who are unfamiliar with the number and size of the many ethnic groups in Winnipeg, must have been amazed with the Icelandic parade. It surely must be the most remarkable parade ever seen on our streets...

Not only are the Icelanders important for this province as one of the largest ethnic groups, but they are among the best educated and most progressive."[7]

The recognition sought by Olafsson had been achieved but, as had been the case at Victoria Gardens on 2 August, a dark cloud lingered over the future of the celebration. Almost from the beginning of the planning, it had been apparent that Icelanders in Winnipeg would have difficulties in working together at future celebrations. A debate had occurred over which date to select for the annual event, 2 August or mid-June. Those opposed to 2 August, led by Sigtryggur Jonasson, argued that the constitution granted to Iceland that day in 1874 was incomplete. In an article in *Lögberg*, Jonasson said, "This constitution has brought the progress of the struggle for independence in Iceland to a stop."[8] He insisted that Icelanders back home would never select that day as an occasion for a national celebration.

Those in favour of 2 August, on the other hand, argued that the granting of the constitution had been celebrated both in Iceland and North America. The date was, therefore, significant in the history of Iceland as well as in the short history of Icelanders in North America. The debate continued and at one point in 1897, two festival committees had been appointed, one preparing a 2 August celebration, the other a mid-June festival. Jonasson's group also suggested 17 June, the birthday of Iceland's great political leader of the nineteenth century, Jon Sigurdsson. This date was later selected as the national holiday.

Although the planning of the Icelandic annual event in Winnipeg was marred by the debate, it still set an example for other communities. Festivals patterned after the Winnipeg celebration soon were organized in Icelandic communities throughout North America. Wherever such a celebration took place, emphasis was placed on the Icelandic content of official programs. Festival committees strove to publicize their celebration, and they were successful in bringing the presence of Icelandic settlers, and the Icelandic heritage, to the attention of the wider community. As transportation improved, entertainers such as musicians and poets travelled to various celebrations. Stephan G. Stephansson, for example, was often called on to read his poetry. Such visits brought the North American Icelanders closer together and it became increasingly common for people to travel great distances to take part in festivals with family or friends in different communities. It is doubtful if any other event or organization did more for the promotion of Icelandic sentiment in those years than the summer celebrations.

Jon Olafsson had arrived in Winnipeg from Iceland believing he would find his compatriots striving to promote their heritage and making every effort to remain Icelandic. Instead, he discovered them working harder at assimilating, adjusting to, and accepting North American ways. Even his friends who, in Milwaukee in 1874, were so determined to remain Icelanders in America, now accepted their position in the multicultural Canadian or American society.

Most of the Icelandic immigrants in North America had had very little political experience. They were accustomed to political matters being in the hands of a foreign power and, in the New World, they were unprepared to participate. In rural communities where they were the predominant nationality or a significant part of the population, they accepted the responsibilities of membership on school boards, municipalities or county councils, but it was not until the mid-1890s that anyone ran for provincial or state legislature. In the more heavily populated areas such as Winnipeg, lack of fluency in English was, at first, an obstacle. This resulted in what may have appeared to be lack of interest, but that was not the case. Individuals such as Sigtryggur Jonasson, Frimann B. Anderson, and, later, Baldvin L. Baldvinsson, were interested in political issues. The two Icelandic weeklies founded in Winnipeg in the second half of the 1880s were not politically involved at first. They were supposedly cultural papers aiming at promoting Icelandic sentiment. But *Heimskringla*, for instance, soon began to discuss the obvious lack of political awareness in the Icelandic community:

> Politics is just the rules made by society for itself and every individual. It is the forming of the laws by which we live and the managing of funds we contribute for public use. It is the responsibility of everyone to support the good but destroy the evils of politics as well as anywhere else. If we choose an organized society we need politics and as we Icelanders insist on being citizens of the province in which we live and as we do not consider ourselves inferior to others, we must play our parts in politics.[9]

The paper then offered lectures on politics in the next few issues, explaining, among other things, the function of each of the two major Canadian political parties. It is noteworthy that *Heimskringla* devoted considerable space to Canadian politics, mostly local, but ignored the American system. This is significant because, increasingly, both *Lögberg* and *Heimskringla* concentrated on local issues concerning Winnipeg or Manitoba, and thus served only a certain portion of the North American Icelandic community. *Lögberg*, for example, devoted fourteen editorials to Manitoba politics during the first year of publication. These included comments on railroad issues, the tariff, and natural resources questions. In the provincial election of 1886, *Heimskringla* was concerned with the election of representatives who would give more time and energy to immigration issues, including, for example, the reception of immigrants to the province. However, the alleged lack of Icelanders' interest in public affairs and politics had been thoroughly contradicted long before the turn of the century. Almost every settler in every community was caught up in political affairs, not only of his closest community, but also that of the entire country, Canada or the United States. With the second generation, among young people brought up in Canadian or American societies, political awareness was fully established.

A clear political division developed in Winnipeg and Manitoba. This, along with the frequent religious disputes, caused yet another division in the North American Icelandic community. It was threefold, actually, as there were factions in Winnipeg, rural Manitoba, and the remaining Icelandic communities. Icelanders outside Manitoba began to cancel subscriptions to both papers because they felt left out of their discussions. Many people in the United States, Saskatchewan, Alberta, or BC felt the papers had abandoned their original purpose of preserving Icelandic heritage and promoting Icelandic sentiment. In Gimli, attempts were made to launch new publications but, due to insufficient subscriptions and high costs, they failed. Hotly disputed issues probably hastened the development of political awareness. Assimilation to Canadian or American society became easier for those people actively engaged; to others less politically minded, such controversies prevented the healthy progress of the Icelandic community.

After the turn of the century, there was an unusually large number of young people in the rural Icelandic communities. They were the sons and daughters of the settlers but also students who homesteaded in one of the new settlements, working their farms in the summer. There were also young men who had homesteaded but needed the financial return from the sale of their homestead to sustain new businesses in the villages or towns. These young people helped broaden local horizons, as they brought to these smaller communities the multicultural trends they experienced in the cities. Most came from Winnipeg, as the University of Manitoba was then the only university on the Canadian prairie. It had been generally a degree-conferring institution, but once the university took over instruction in the sciences, new departments were established. Three denominational colleges, Wesley (Methodist), Manitoba (Presbyterian), and St. John's (Anglican), were established, and Wesley, especially, became significant to the Icelanders.[10]

In 1884, Frimann B. Anderson's plans for an Icelandic high school in Winnipeg had failed. Three years later, in 1887, Rev. Jon Bjarnason received the amount of $100.00 from the Lutheran Synod for his editorial work in *Sameiningin*, which he donated to a fund for the founding of a college to be associated with the Icelandic Lutheran Church in America. No one knew the standard of education in Icelandic communities better than Bjarnason, who had toured numerous settlements in the previous few years. Elementary education was adequate but higher education was not. In 1890, for example, fewer than ten Icelanders in North America had received college education. Bjarnason envisioned a school that would increase interest in higher education in the Icelandic communities, provide facilities for future theology students, and strengthen Icelandic heritage in North America.

The plan was for the school to commence in the fall of 1890 in rented quarters. However, when Bjarnason became seriously ill, the opening was postponed. His recovery was lengthy but a fundraising campaign for a school building continued. By the end of 1896, the account had risen to $3151.89. Bjarnason was able to continue his campaign, despite a lack of enthusiasm among some of his compatriots. At the 1896 annual conference of the synod, he persuaded his colleagues to make the school the synod's chief concern. The town of Crystal, North Dakota, donated $2000.00 to the project, and offered three hectares of land for the school. Rev. Jonas Sigurdsson was appointed to visit Icelandic communities to raise funds, and contributions began to flow in. In 1897 North Dakota communities had raised $589.50, Winnipeg $537.75, Argyle $420.75, and Minnesota $261.85.

The North Dakotans fought hard to have the school built south of the border. Crystal raised her donation to $3000.00 and four hectares of land. Both Winnipeg and Dakota wanted the school. Harsh words were spoken and, owing to this strong difference of opinion, little was done in the next while to raise more money, though by 1900 the fund had reached $6048.91.[11]

On 9 October 1901, the Board of Governors of the University of Manitoba agreed to begin instruction in Icelandic. Of foreign languages, Latin was a required subject but now the students at the university could choose any two of the following: Greek, French, German, and Icelandic. Wesley College in Winnipeg offered assistance in return for the assurance that the synod would pay the salary of an instructor in Icelandic subjects. In October 1901 classes began. This attracted most of the Icelandic arts students from the prairie provinces to Wesley College, and as a result even science students preferred to attend there. This led to Wesley's becoming the centre of all activities among the Icelandic students, whether they were at the Medical College or the Agricultural College. On 1 January 1901, the Icelandic Student Society was established. Its main objectives were to "provide financial assistance to students in need; assist in spreading knowledge of Icelandic Literature among Canadians; and encourage Icelandic students to become acquainted with non-Icelandic literature, particular that of Canada."[12]

The first president of the society, Ingvar Buason, who graduated in arts in 1900, offered a slightly different interpretation of the society's objective in December of 1902 when he stated that "the Student Society is sincere in its desire to help raise the reputation of the Icelandic nation in the eyes of the English-speaking people. It seeks, within its powers, to bring about that the Icelanders be given the recognition and honor they deserve."[13]

It is interesting to note the change in main objectives. By 1902, all the society's efforts were directed to maintaining Icelandic heritage. The students were Icelanders. Their society should, therefore, be used as a means to stimulate interest in Icelandic language and literature, not only just within the society but also among the Icelandic general public. It is unknown whether the society was effective in its aims. It remained active up to the First World War, and although activities were suspended during the war, they were resumed immediately after. The society was mostly concerned with the situation within Canada and made little effort to influence Icelandic compatriots south of the border. This was the second generation, young people born and brought up on Canadian soil, who looked upon themselves first and foremost as Canadians, not Icelandic immigrants to North America, as their parents had considered themselves.

Across the border, in North Dakota, another student society had been established in 1897 in Grand Forks by Icelandic students at the University of North Dakota. This American-Icelandic society functioned very much as did the one in Winnipeg. Meetings were held regularly at the home of Jon Jonsson and his wife, Gudny Eiriksdottir, in Grand Forks, where many students accepted a meal or an invitation for an overnight stay.[14]

Graduations from educational centres such as the University of Manitoba or University of North Dakota became an annual event after the turn of the century. The first Icelander to graduate from a Canadian university was Frimann Anderson in arts in 1884, recipient of an $80.00 scholarship.

One founding member of the Icelandic Student Society at the University of North Dakota excelled in his field to such a degree that he earned world-wide recognition. Vilhjalmur Stefansson, though born in Canada, was raised in North Dakota from the age of two and attended the elementary school at Mountain. An exceptional student, he studied at Grand Forks, Iowa, and Harvard. Upon graduation, he was in charge of three explorations to the Arctic. The first, in 1906 to 1907, was jointly sponsored by Harvard University and the University of Toronto. His second, from 1908 to 1912, was supervised and sponsored by the American Museum of Natural History and the Canadian government. A third, from 1913 to 1918, was financed by the government of Canada.[15] His achievements must be considered among the greatest of any second-generation North American of Icelandic background.

If Vilhjalmur Stefansson has the distinction of being the best-known North American Icelander in the first half of the twentieth century, Stephan G. Stephansson ranks as the greatest contributor to the promotion of Icelandic heritage and culture in the Icelandic North American community. Perhaps never a great farmer, Stephansson nonetheless earned his living on the farm, but it was his poetry that caught the attention of his countrymen. He is mostly remembered for his poems expressing fond memories of Iceland as well as his love for Canada. During his visit to Iceland in 1917, Gudmundur Finnbogason, the head librarian of the National Library in Reykjavík, said:

> Stephansson's descriptions appear to me to have the special merit that as soon as the words are thrust in place, just where they are intended, a word picture sparkles so that the whole world becomes alive—a complete image. It is just that which has through the ages been the mark of true poetry—to give life and heartbeat to everything, to attune the visible world to the soul of man, to be its own and its abode.[16]

In his book *Canadian Overtones*, an anthology of Canadian poetry written in languages other than English or French, Dr. Watson Kirkconnell stated: "I would like to venture the opinion, however, that Stephansson is beyond question the equal of any poet that Canada has yet produced in English or French and may ultimately be recognized as superior to all. That opinion is based upon prosodic technique, diction, imagination and intellectual scope."[17]

Another writer, Guttormur J. Guttormsson, was born 21 November 1878 in New Iceland, near the present Riverton. He lost both his parents at a young age and after he reached grade seven his formal schooling ended. Throughout his hard toil of pioneer work, however, young Guttormsson's sense of the value of his Icelandic heritage grew. At the same time, he valued what he saw about him and became a truly Icelandic-Canadian, one who treasured his ethnic background but whose love of his new motherland was equally strong. Guttormsson has the distinction of being the only leading Icelandic poet born in America who wrote in Icelandic. His poetry, like Stephansson's, was read and discussed in every Icelandic community by all people who so fervently wanted to preserve the Icelandic language and heritage.

These two poets were by no means the only ones. Other poets included Jakobina Johnson (born in Argyle) of Seattle, and Kristjan N. Julius, of Kainn, in North Dakota, who contributed to the Icelandic North American literary scene. Their poetry was published in the two weeklies and later in the other publications that emerged in the Icelandic community. Of several prose writers, Johann Magnus Bjarnason was perhaps the most versatile. He wrote poetry as well as short stories but is probably best known for two novels, *Eirikur Hanson* and *Braziliufararnir*, both dealing with Icelandic settlers in America. He was born in Iceland, 24 May 1866, and emigrated to Nova Scotia with his parents in 1875. He then moved to Winnipeg in 1882, where he became a qualified teacher. He taught school in the Icelandic communities in Manitoba for more than twenty-two years before retiring to Elfros, Saskatchewan. The early prose writers were mostly preoccupied with the North American experience of Icelandic immigrants. Gunnsteinn Eyjolfsson wrote *Elenora* in 1884, which describes an unfortunate city encounter of a New Iceland girl. Gudrun H. Finnsdottir wrote short stories that dealt with Canada as experienced by the Icelandic immigrant.

Publications of various works of literature became common after the turn of the century in Icelandic communities and many individuals contributed articles on various topics such as history, and poetry, short stories, and translations.[18] The most significant publication of this nature was the *Almanak*, an annual first published in Winnipeg in 1895. It was an important contribution to the settlers' efforts to promote Icelandic sentiment in North America, and it contributed significantly to what later developed as a distinctive North American Icelandic culture.

Another publication was *Freyja*, which was launched in Selkirk, Manitoba, in 1898 and was probably the only women's suffrage paper in Canada of the time. The publisher was Sigfus Benedictsson and his wife Margaret was editor. Her story is quite remarkable. She was born in Iceland in 1866 but, like the poet Guttormsson, was forced to look after herself in her early teens. She emigrated to North Dakota in 1887, where she lived for a few years before moving to Winnipeg.

She married her husband in 1892. They lived for a while in Winnipeg and moved to Hecla Island before setting up a printing press in Selkirk in 1898. In 1902 they moved back to Winnipeg.

During her difficult childhood and early adolescence, Margaret came to recognize inequality. She read much about oppressed people, unhappily married women, and unfortunate girls in the big cities. She became acquainted through correspondence with women's leaders such as Lucy Stone and Elizabeth Stanton. *Freyja* was a monthly, normally forty pages long, and was actually a literary magazine as well as a women's suffrage journal. It included poetry by Stephan G. Stephansson, literary reviews, and a children's corner, as well as regular contributions on women's suffrage. *Freyja* also published public lectures and letters. It continued publication until 1910. In the meantime Margaret had founded an Icelandic women's suffrage society in Winnipeg in 1908 and her co-workers later (1910) established another at Gimli, called Sigurvon ("Hope of Victory"). In 1916, the government of Manitoba endorsed the vote for women, the first province in Canada to do so, and there is little doubt that her work contributed to this achievement. Although she concentrated on reaching her own compatriots, she fought for the rights for all Canadian women. The Canadian Suffrage Association invited her to attend a convention of the International Women's Suffrage Alliance in Toronto in 1909.[19]

There were many other Icelanders writing letters or articles, and giving public lectures on matters concerning their municipality, village, town, or province. Both Icelandic weeklies were filled in those years with items of communal or provincial concerns and regular comments on them from the editors. Such issues were far from purely Icelandic in nature; they often had nothing to do with Icelandic heritage or culture but, rather, concerned the entire community. And Icelanders did not only express themselves in *Lögberg* or *Heimskringla*, but gave their opinions in the big Canadian dailies, along with others of different ethnic backgrounds.

Conclusion

A large portion of the Icelandic population, or more than 14,000 people, had immigrated to North America by the year 1914. The migrants from Iceland came from all ranks of society; they were poor farmers, farmhands, labourers, skilled workers, fishermen, or merchants. Their reasons for emigration were many; however, most emigrants left Iceland because their future there was bleak. They believed that in America they would have a better chance of improving their lives.

No one anticipated in the early 1870s that so many people would eventually leave Iceland. The majority of the pioneer settlers of those years agreed with a small group of leaders who hoped to establish an exclusive colony for all Icelanders already in America and also those who might follow in the next few years. Men like Sigtryggur Jonasson, Rev. Jon Bjarnason, Jon Olafsson, and Olafur Olafsson argued that the best way for Icelanders to achieve their goals in America, and to preserve Icelandic heritage, was to settle together, somewhat isolated, either in the US or Canada. Their adjustment to North America would be easier, they believed. Nevertheless, Icelandic settlers probably did not differ much from other ethnic groups in America in that they could not prepare themselves for the psychological and cultural shock that awaited them in the New World.

The idea of a homogeneous colony was first raised in Iceland, a very natural and practical ideal. Immigrants from the same country usually hope to settle together in their adopted country, where they can help each other and use their mother tongue and traditions in a foreign, sometimes hostile, environment. The Icelanders had not prepared themselves to establish an exclusive colony. They understood that the North American community offered them the freedom to manage most of their affairs independently, without interference of province or state, yet they had to learn what kind of organizations were needed for such a settlement to function properly. Christer Lennart Mossberg said of the Scandinavian experience in America:

> The immigrants could only conceptualize the attractions offered by America— the idea of property ownership, the idea of religious freedom, the idea of democracy and a classless society. Before they actually made the voyage to America, they could not define these ideas in terms of daily events of their experience. They could only understand these concepts in terms of the conditions they rejected in Scandinavia. But the immigrants' emotional and spiritual lives were rooted in concrete experiences in the home country.[1]

The leaders of the Icelanders in America anticipated that the preservation of Icelandic culture, language, and nationality would be the main attraction of the all-Icelandic settlement. After all, the nineteenth-century Icelanders were driven by national pride "linked to images of Viking ancestry with its ideals of courage, defiance of fate, and yearning for freedom and new horizons."[2] However, some vital ingredients were missing, which they never managed to find.

One settler wrote in New Iceland that a strong leadership was what really had been needed. However, it is doubtful if anyone could have provided strong enough leadership in the colony to motivate the settlers. Paradoxically, their energy, education, and desire for freedom were elements that, combined with natural disasters, prevented them from achieving their aims in New Iceland. In a remarkable article in *Framfari*, Rev. Jon Bjarnason wrote:

> I was one of the many Icelanders here, who wished for an exclusive, Icelandic colony but am now convinced that an Icelandic settlement as people in Iceland and here have from the beginning hoped for cannot succeed and will without doubt always struggle. The main goal and objectives of Icelanders here in this land should not be to preserve their nationality because, truthfully, men should come here to begin a new life, get new ideas, become a new nation and rid themselves of whatever prevented progress and general well-being back home. My compatriots will never accomplish this if they isolate themselves here just as many here already have began to admit.[3]

The settlement never materialized as the leaders had intended. However, the original purpose of the chosen site on the western bank of Lake Winnipeg has never been forgotten; it was the only place in all of North America during the entire settlement period where they planned and hoped for an exclusive Icelandic settlement. Consequently, New Iceland, in this respect, stands out as the most significant Icelandic settlement in North America.

The settlers from Iceland gradually found out that life in the US or Canada was not just the struggle for mere survival, but also a struggle to find a way to reconcile loyalty to their adopted land and love of their motherland. In his poem "Útlegðin" ("The Exile"), Stephan G. Stephansson probably echoed the sentiment of most of his compatriots in North America.

> Somehow it has come upon me,
> I've no fatherland;
> Though my heart with love is bounded
> With a lasting band
> To my native soil that blessed me
> As a growing boy,
> When the world its shining glory
> Gave me hope and joy.
>
> Never could my foster mother
> Take my mother's place;
> Always there was something lacking,
> She could not replace.
> I have yet to know the meaning
> Of her legacy,
> Always there's an awkward feeling
> 'Twixt herself and me.[4]

But what exactly was this heritage they strove so hard to protect? The answer lies in the strong literary tradition in Iceland that goes back centuries to the days of early settlement. The roots lie in the Eddic and scaldic poetry and, of course, the Sagas. Throughout the centuries, during hardship wrought by foreign rulers or brutal elements of the land, literary activity remained strong. Its strength was never as significant as in the nineteenth century when the nation rose to commence on the road to complete independence.

Their attempts in America to transplant their literary tradition are evident. As long as they spoke, wrote, and read Icelandic, they believed their heritage would be safe. They realized also that this could be accomplished even without an isolated, all-Icelandic settlement. There was a vast quantity of literature published during the settlement period. Almost every Icelandic community in North America established reading societies that organized the collection of books. Books were common items in the possession of many settlers upon arrival and quite remarkable collections were often found in pioneer huts; for example, in the woods of Shawano County or by Lake Winnipeg. During his visit to New Iceland in 1877, Lord Dufferin remarked, "I have not entered a single hut or cottage in the settlement which did not contain, no matter how bare its walls, or scanty its furniture, a library of twenty or thirty volumes."[5]

Written material published in the numerous periodicals, or in the two weeklies, *Lögberg* and *Heimskringla*, varied in content, ranging from poetry and drama to harvest reports or fishing catch. Such material was not only thoroughly read in the communities but also keenly discussed. Rögnvaldur Pétursson wrote about the importance of the weeklies:

> How important the papers were for the preservation of the Icelandic language in North America becomes clear when their contents and subject matter are examined. There is hardly an issue, concerning the Icelanders ... since they commenced publication which they have not discussed. Every week, they have carried items from all the Icelandic communities and in doing so, have bonded together people who live in the most faraway parts of the continent. If some significant event was planned, the papers have discussed the matter in order to unite people in the scattered communities. Recognized writers have continously contributed either poetry or prose. It will never be known whether this collection (the poetry and prose) would have been as extensive if the papers had not existed.[6]

Once they accepted the inevitability of assimilation, the Icelandic immigrants adopted from North American society what they needed. They no longer considered living next door to foreigners a threat to their heritage. On the contrary, it was in many ways beneficial. In the farming communities where most Icelanders lived, valuable knowledge was gained by observing and working with experienced farmers. In the west, where most of the Icelanders in North America resided, the primary sod houses or huts of the pioneers gave way to frame dwellings. Almost overnight, life on the Saskatchewan and Alberta plains was transformed from trapping and hunting in the wilderness to the complex enterprise of growing grain, not only for local use but for the world market. The settlement in western Canada advanced rapidly, and, at the same time, grain production increased, and the trading system between the east and west flourished. Roads and railways kept the farmers in touch with outside communities and aided them in organizing groups for social reasons or to market their products more effectively. Farmers actively brought pressure to bear in politics if a new road or a branch-line railway were needed.

During the period between 1896 and 1914, Canada experienced the greatest wave of immigration in her young history; well over two million people arrived at Canadian ports. The majority of new immigrants were English-speaking but a large number arrived from countries such as Germany, Scandinavia, from Russia, Poland, Ukraine, Austria, and Italy. Only a small portion of the population had been of non-English or non-French origin when Canada became a nation in 1867. By the First World War, these people represented nearly one-fifth of the population. While the largest group of settlers was of British origin, the second-largest set of immigrants came from the United States (actually close to half were returning Canadians). These were mostly farmers already trained in North American agriculture and were of particular value in bringing the west under cultivation. Not all went west; many chose the booming eastern towns or the new northern mining and lumbering developments.

The boom in North American agricultural production and export also brought about growth in other areas. Significant innovations in technology, production of new farm machinery, and discoveries in science and medicine contributed to the growth in every aspect of the North American society.

In these extraordinary circumstances, the second generation of Icelanders came of age. They never had to ask themselves how to become good citizens, as their parents had. It is natural for people to love their native land, their place of birth. Now, the second generation wondered how to remain loyal to their Icelandic heritage, not to their homeland. In the North-West Rebellion of 1885, twenty Icelanders enlisted and at least eighteen fought in the war. Coming from a land where military obligations were unknown, most of them undoubtedly enlisted because they saw it as their duty as new citizens of Canada. In the First World War, more than 1200 young, second-generation Icelanders from Canada and the United States were in the war service.[7] As they volunteered, the transformation from Icelandic-American or Icelandic-Canadian to American-Icelandic or Canadian-Icelandic was completed. The history of Icelanders in North America had entered a second phase: the pioneer days were gone.

Appendix
Constitution of New Iceland:
Selected Articles and Sections

Article 1 - Division of New-Iceland
The Icelandic settlement in New-Iceland is named "Lake-Region," "Vatnsðing" and shall be divided into four districts. The four districts are: Vidirnes-district, comprising Townships 18 and 19 in Ranges 3 and 4 east: Arnes-district, comprising Townships 20 and 21 in Ranges 3 and 4 east: River-district, comprising Townships 22 and 23 in Ranges 3 and 4 east: Big-Island-district, comprising the entire island Hecla.

Article ll – Election of district committees and conciliators
The inhabitants of each district shall, at a public meeting, which is to be held annually on the seventh day of January, or on the eighth day of January, when the seventh falls on a Sunday, elect five men to a committee called District Committee, two conciliators and one vice-conciliator. They who receive the largest number of votes are duly elected members of the District Committee, but only if there are present more than half the residents in the District who are eligible to vote in accordance with Article 111 of these Laws and regulations.

Article lll – Right to vote and eligibility for election
Every man shall have the right to vote for the election of a District Committee who is eighteen years of age, is a resident or owns real estate or who is a

householder or has steady employment in the district, and who has unblemished reputation. All those who have a right to vote are also eligible for election to District Committees, except those who are incumbent clergymen or permanent public school teachers, but no one shall be eligible for election who is not twenty-one years of age.

The eighteen-year limit was not copied from Iceland or Canada but was probably introduced here as so many immigrants in New Iceland were under twenty. Since 1873, 136 immigrants from Iceland in America belonged to the fifteen-to-nineteen age group and the age limit undoubtedly served the purpose of encouraging young people to remain in the settlement. A steady employment was sufficient to be eligible to vote, which gave young people yet to become homesteaders an opportunity to become actively involved in all matters concerning the colony. Such chances had not existed in Iceland for the youth.

The clause *"who has an unblemished reputation"* derives from Iceland. This qualification existed throughout all the Scandinavian countries in the late nineteenth century.

Article IV – Duties to the public

1. Meeting attendance: Residents in every district shall attend a public meeting in the period March 15th-April 15th on the date and at the place determined by each reeve, in order to discuss matters affecting the public welfare of the district.
    This was compulsory.

2. Roadwork and road fees: Every male twenty-one years old is compelled to work two days of road construction or he shall pay $2.00 to the road fund in which district he resides. Those who do not have a permanent residence shall do the same in which district they are employed at the time roadwork is expected. District Committees determine where and at what time of year such labor is performed.

3. Notice of deaths, births and marriages: Every householder shall inform the reeve of deaths or births in his home. Each male who gets married shall inform the reeve.

4. State of husbandry: All farmers and householders are obliged to provide the reeve every year with clear accounts of the state of their husbandry.

5. Support of widows and orphans: Residents of each district are obliged to support widows and orphans according to regulations approved by the inhabitants of each district. Those unable to work for whatever reason shall likewise be supported.

6. Meeting Halls: Residents in every district shall provide for a meeting hall.

7. Fee for public need: Every voter shall pay the sum of twenty-five cents annually to a fund for public needs. Payment due before end of September each year.

Article V – Election of District Reeve, Treasurer and Secretary

District Committees are to elect from among themselves a District Reeve, a Vice-Reeve, a Treasurer and a Secretary.

Article Vl – Duties of District Committees

1. Supervision of roads

2. Support of widows and orphans

3. Assistance to the poor and disabled

4. Arrangement of meeting halls

5. Election of Governor of the Regional Council: All members of committees of each district are duty bound to attend meetings to elect a Governor and a Vice-Governor of the Regional Council. The meeting for this purpose is to be held on the seventh day after the meeting for the election of District Committees, one year at Lundi (Icelandic River) and the other at Gimli.

6. Health Care: Committees to supervise the general well being of individuals in every district. In the event of an outburst of a contagious disease, committees to make proper precaution in order to prevent an epidemic.

7. Support of fellowship and enterprise

Article Vll – Functions of District Reeves, Treasurers and Secretaries

A. Duties of Reeve

1. Plans for general meetings

2. Arrangements for committee meetings

3. Records of meetings

4. Records of population and husbandry

5. Statutory labor

6. Records of deaths, births and marriages

7. Records of auctions, real estate transactions and administration of district funds

8. Attendance at Regional Council meetings

9. All records available for auditing by January 7th, each year

B. Duties of Treasurer

1. Collection of all fees

2. Bookkeeping

C. *Duties of Secretary*

1. Keep records of all public and committee meetings

2. Elections. Shall prepare list of eligible voters, receive and count votes in all elections

Article Vlll – Management of estates of deceased persons and revenue

This was necessary as New Iceland was in an unorganized territory. District reeves had similar powers to those of Surrogate Court Judges and fees were fixed on a percentage basis.

Article IX – Functions of conciliators and arbitrators

The duty of conciliators was to reach a settlement in all personal disputes. If only one party requested assistance, a conciliator was supposed to attempt to settle the dispute. In case of failure and if one party wanted, then the dispute was to be submitted to the arbitration of five neutral individuals. Each party was to select two and both chose a chair. In the event they could not agree on a chair, then the Governor or the Vice-Governor of the Regional Council was to be the chair.

The settlers realized that disputes would take place and decided that settlement should be by conciliation or arbitration. There were no provisions of fines for violations of any of the Laws and Regulations. People were expected to be more concerned with the developing of the colony than breaking the laws. Provisions for serious crimes were not made. In such cases, matters would be referred to Ottawa.

Article X – Drafting of by-laws

The district committees are to draft proposed by-laws, which must be submitted to the voters. To become law they must receive a majority of the votes of all the eligible voters.

These bylaws dealt with issues such as relief, fences and stray livestock.

Article Xl – The Regional Council – The Governor of the Council

Section 1: Formation of the Regional Council

Lake Region shall be governed by a committee of five, called the Regional Council. This Council shall be composed of the District Reeves of the four districts of the region, and a man who is to be elected in accordance with Article VI, Section 5, and who is called Governor of the Regional Council.

Section 2: Election of Governor

The Governor is elected at a meeting of all members of the district councils, who, as set out in Article VI, Section 5, are compelled to attend. If no one obtains a majority of the votes there shall be a second ballot, limited to the two candidates who received the largest number of votes.

Article Xll – Meetings of the Regional Council

One meeting is to be held each year, alternating between Lundi and Gimli.

Article Xlll– Functions of the Regional Council

1. The council to discuss all issues concerning the settlement as a whole. For example, colony boundary lines, settlement of non-Icelandic immigrants in the colony and investment of non-Icelanders in local businesses. Council is to draft by-laws for such matters, which will become law once a majority of council members has approved.

2. The council shall arrange and supervise the construction of a main highway through the entire settlement from north to south and all roads which cross the colony from east to west. Council is also responsible for the construction of all bridges across rivers, creeks and mash lands.

3. Auditing of records and accounts

4. Council shall mediate if differences arise between districts, or the matter may be submitted to compulsory arbitration, under Article IX.

Article XlV – Functions of the Regional Governor

1. Governor shall call all Regional meetings and chair them.

2. Keep records of meetings

3. Publish summary of records of the districts

4. Keep records of statutory labor

5. Shall refer to the Government of Canada all matters that concern the Region and are required to be referred; and shall notify the District Reeves of all directives of the Government in so far as they concern the Region.

The settlers were aware of their own powers in a reserve in an unorganized territory, but realized just as well that they were bound by legislation of the Parliament of Canada and by federal Order-in-Council binding upon all citizens of Canada.

6. Notify reeves of issues to be discussed at district meetings

7. Chair arbitration committees

8. Give annually an account of his work

Article XV – Validity of elections and voting

Elections are valid for only one year. The majority of votes decides the election. A man may seek re-election.

Article XVl – Payment for writing material and books

Payment of material needed by the Governor, Treasurer, or Secretary to keep records was by the regional treasury.

Article XVll – Coming into force of these laws and regulations

These laws and regulations came into force once they were published in *Framfari*, on 11 January 1878.

Article XVlll – Amendments to these laws and regulations

These laws and regulations may be amended upon motion passed at a main meeting of the Regional Council, and subsequently approved by a majority of all eligible voters of the region at District meetings which shall all be held on the same day.

Endnotes

Chapter One

1. Sources disagree on the date of their arrival in Utah. One states they reached Utah in the spring of 1856; another states they arrived in Salt Lake City in the fall of 1855. That is unlikely, as no means of transportation in 1855 could have carried them from Iceland to England, and thence to America and to Utah, in only two or three months. Those who made the trip in the next few years were up to nine months in transit, so it is likely that the first Icelanders to settle in North America did so in the spring of 1856.

2. Hjálmar Bjarnason, "Brot úr Ferðasögu Þórðar Diðrikssonar frá Íslandi til Utah," *Almanak* (1920): 70. Bjarnason's article is based on Didriksson's own account of events during his journey from Iceland to Utah in 1856. Bjarnason himself emigrated to Utah in 1885.

3. Þorsteinn Þ. Þorsteinsson, *Saga Íslendinga í Vesturheimi*, vol. ll (Winnipeg: Þjóðræknisfélag Íslendinga í Vesturheimi, 1943), 12.

4. Ibid.

5. In his article "Saga Íslendinga í Utah," *Almanak* (1915): 40-45, E.H. Johnson does not mention Mrs. Hansen or her daughter. However, LeRoy Whitehead includes her in his "Icelandic Converts Honored," *The Desert News,* Salt Lake City, 30 July 1938.

6. Þorsteinsson, *Saga Íslendinga,* 66.

7. Ibid., 68.

8. Ibid., 76.

9. Ibid., 86.

10. Ibid.

11. For more information on migration from Iceland to Brazil, see Þorsteinn Þ. Þorsteinsson, *Ævintýrið frá Íslandi til Brasilíu* (Reykjavík: Ísland, 1938).

12. Walter Lindal, *The Saskachewan Icelanders* (Winnipeg: Columbia Press, 1955), 153.

13. Júníus Kristinsson, *Vesturfaraskrá 1870-1914* (Reykjavík: Institute of History, University of Iceland, 1983), Table 7.

14. Árni Guðmundsson, "Landnám Íslendinga á Washingtoneyjunni," *Almanak* (1900): 28.
15. Ibid., 35.
16. Conan Bryant Eaton, *Washington Island* (Washington Island: Jackson Harbor Press, 1997), 55.
17. Guðmundsson, "Landnám Íslendinga," 33-35.
18. Kristinsson, *Vesturfaraskrá 1870-1914*, 101. Magnusson was forty-five and his wife forty-seven.
19. Ibid.,125. Bjarnason's daughter Kristen, travelling with him, was eighteen and his son Ágúst was fourteen.
20. *Norðanfari,* 8 March 1872.
21. Þorsteinsson, *Saga Íslendinga*, 118.
22. Guðmundsson, "Landnám Íslendinga," 31.

Chapter Two

1. *Lögberg*, 25 November 1897. Many Icelanders changed the spelling of their names after migration. Pall Thorlaksson never did.
2. Þorsteinn Þ. Þorsteinsson, *Saga Íslendinga í Vesturheimi,* vol. II (Winnipeg: Þjóðræknisfélag Íslendinga í Vesturheimi, 1943), 121.
3. Ibid., 122. This is borne out in Þorlákur Jónsson's personal records of the time and is the only source to mention it. His son did not mention in any of his letters a fianceé in Iceland, nor was he ever linked with a woman during his years in America. However, he stated in one letter that he had to travel back to Iceland to resolve a matter concerning a woman.
4. In Iceland in the early 1870s, young people from the northern regions faced harder times than those from the south. Overpopulated farms were more common in the north and there was less arable land. Yet, in the early days of emigration from Iceland to America, most immigrants came from the south. Perhaps Thorgrimsen's part in the immigration movement was large and his influence reached well beyond his store at Eyrarbakki. After 1872, however, most immigrants from Iceland came from the north and northeast regions.
5. Þorsteinsson, *Saga Íslendinga*, 125.
6. Jóhannes Arngrímsson, "Letter to the Editor," *Norðanfari,* 22 September 1872.
7. Ibid.
8. Þorsteinsson, *Saga Íslendinga*, 130.
9. Arngrímsson, "Letter to the Editor," *Norðanfari*, 22 September 1872.
10. Þorsteinsson, *Saga Íslendinga,* 133.
11. *Norðanfari,* February 1873.
12. Þorsteinsson, *Saga Íslendinga,*135-136. Minutes of meeting.
13. Ibid., 137.
14. Ibid., 142-143.
15. Thorstina Jackson, *Saga Íslendinga í Norður Dakota* (Winnipeg: The City Printing & Publishing Co., 1926), 359.
16. Þorsteinsson, *Saga Íslendinga,* 151.
17. Jón Bjarnason, "Apologia Pro Vita Sua,"*Áramót* (1909): 35.
18. Jónas Þór, *A Religious Controversy among Icelandic Immigrants in North America 1874-1880,* MA thesis, University of Manitoba, 1980, p. 21.

19. J.J. Bíldfell, ed., *Jón Bjarnason, Rit og Ræður* (Winnipeg: Columbia Press, 1946), 286.
20. Þorsteinsson, *Saga Íslendinga,* 157.
21. Björn K. Skagfjörð, *Norðanfari,* January 1874.
22. Þorsteinsson, *Saga Íslendinga,* 192.
23. Páll Þorláksson, *Norðanfari,* January 1874.
24. Jón Halldórsson, "Tildrög til íslenskrar nýlendustofnunar í Nebraska," *Almanak* (1914): 150-156.

Chapter Three

1. Thorleifur Jackson, *Frá Austri til Vesturs* (Winnipeg: Columbia Press, 1921), 63.
2. Jón Ólafsson, Letter to Rev. Jón Bjarnason, December 1873.
3. Bergsteinn Jónsson, "Aðdragandi og Upphaf Vesturferða af Íslandi á Nítjándu Öld," *Andvari* (1975): 18.
4. Sigfús Magnússon, "Kafli úr bréfi," *Norðanfari,* June 1874. This letter was written at Lancaster P.O., Nebraska, 14 June 1874.
5. Ibid.
6. Þorsteinn Þ. Þorsteinsson, *Saga Íslendinga í Vesturheimi,* vol. II (Winnipeg: Þjóðræknisfélag Íslendinga í Vesturheimi, 1943), 225-226.
7. Ibid., 226.
8. Hjörtur Pálsson, *Alaskaför Jóns Ólafssonar 1874* (Reykjavík: Sögufélagið, 1975), 41.
9. Pall Thorlaksson, letter, 9 October, 20 November 1874; 15 January 1875. Wisconsin State Historical Society: Rasmus B. Anderson papers. Thorlaksson wrote to his friend in Wisconsin in English, Danish, and Icelandic, switching from one language to another in the same letter.
10. Pálsson, *Alaskaför,* 41. See also Þorsteinsson, *Saga Íslendinga,* 239.
11. Jón Ólafsson, Letter to Bjarnason.
12. Jónas Þór and Terry Tergesen, *Saga Íslendingadagsins* (Gimli: The Icelandic Festival of Manitoba, 1989), 8.
13. Rögnvaldur Pétursson," Upphaf Vesturferða og Þjóðminningarhátíðin," *Tímarit Þjóðræknisfélags Íslendinga* (1933): 71. Also on the celebration see Thorlaksson, "Letter to the Editor," *Norðanfari,* October 1874; and Þorsteinsson, *Saga Íslendinga,* 231-235.
14. Jón Bjarnason, *Þjóðólfur,* October 1874.
15. Þór and Tergesen, *Saga Íslendingadagsins,* 10.
16. Ólafsson, Letter to Bjarnason, November 1874.
17. Þorsteinsson, *Saga Íslendinga,* 227.
18. Rögnvaldur Pétursson, "Landskoðunarferðin til Alaska, 1874," *Tímarit Þjóðræknisfélags Íslendinga* (1934): 14.
19. Ibid., 16-17.
20. Þorsteinsson, *Saga Íslendinga,* 230.
21. *New York Evening Post,* 22 December 1874.
22. Pétursson, "Landskoðunarferðin." Also see Hjörtur Pálsson, *Alaskaför Jóns Ólafssonar 1874* (Reykjavík: Sögufélagið, 1975).
23. Sigurður J. Jóhannesson, "Landnám Íslendinga í Minnesota," *Almanak* (1900): 57.
24. Ibid., 58.

25. Ibid.
26. Þorsteinsson, *Saga Íslendinga,* 229.
27. E.H. Johnson, "Saga Íslendinga í Utah," *Almanak* (1915): 62-66.
28. Jón Halldórsson, "Tildrög til íslenskrar nýlendustofnunar í Nebraska," *Almanak* (1914): 152-156.

Chapter Four

1. Jónasson's teacher, Tomas Davidsson, often nicknamed "Language-Tomas," had a reputation of not only knowing foreign languages but also having excellent ability to teach.
2. Þorsteinn Þ. Þorsteinsson, *Saga Íslendinga í Vesturheimi,* vol. II (Winnipeg: Þjóðræknisfélag Íslendinga í Vesturheimi 1943), 200.
3. Ibid., 199.
4. Thorleifur Jackson, *Frá Austri til Vesturs* (Winnipeg: Columbia Press, 1921), 42-43.
5. *Norðanfari,* 18 January 1874.
6. Ibid., 25 January 1875.
7. Ásgeir Baldvinsson, "Landnám Íslendinga í Muskoka og tildrög að því," *Almanak* (1900): 45.
8. Þorsteinsson, *Saga Íslendinga,* 204.
9. Ibid., 205.
10. Baldvinsson, "Landnám Íslendinga," 45.
11. Þorsteinsson, *Saga Íslendinga*, 208-209.
12. Ibid., 211.
13. Ibid., 213.
14. Sigtryggur Jónasson, "Letter to *Norðanfari,*" 1875. Written 1 February 1875 in Kinmount, Ontario.
15. Ibid.
16. Ibid.
17. Þorsteinsson, *Saga Íslendinga,* 287.
18. Sigtryggur Jónasson, "John Taylor og Elizabeth Taylor," *Syrpa* lV(1920): 99-101.
19. Sigurður J. Jóhannesson, "Þáttur Íslendinga í Nýja Skotlandi," *Almanak* (1900): 49.
20. Walter J. Lindal, *The Icelanders in Canada* (Winnipeg:Viking Printers, 1967), 104.
21. Jóhann Magnús Bjarnason, "Æskuminning um Magnús lögmann Bjarnason," *Eimreiðin* (1912): 133.
22. Thorleifur Jacksson, *Brot af Landnámssögu Nýja Íslands* (Winnipeg: Columbia Press, 1919), 14-15. Quotation from an article by Johann Briem, "Ferðasaga Ameríkufara frá Sauðárkróki til Nýja Íslands sumarið 1876," originally published in *Framfari.*

Chapter Five

1. This religious sect had a history dating back to the Middle Ages. Their name is taken from Menno Simons (1496-1561), a leader of the Anabaptists in Holland. In 1789 thousands of them fled to South Russia where they established German-speaking colonies in the Ukraine, which flourished. The first group of Mennonites to settle in America did so in the late seventeenth century in Germantown in Pennsylvania.

Their opposition to warfare often led to their persecution, and this was the reason many of them came to Canada from Russia in the late nineteenth century.

2. Þorsteinn Þ. Þorsteinsson, *Saga Íslendinga í Vesturheimi*, vol. II (Winnipeg: Þjóðræknisfélag Íslendinga í Vesturheimi, 1943), 325.

3. Wilhelm Kristjanson, *The Icelandic People in Manitoba: A Manitoba Saga* (Winnipeg: Wallingford Press, 1965), 23.

4. *Winnipeg Tribune*, 18 November 1839.

5. Þorsteinsson, *Saga Íslendinga*, 328-329.

6. Ibid., 329.

7. Walter Lindal, *The Icelanders in Canada* (Winnipeg: Viking Printers,1967), 138.

8. Þorsteinsson, *Saga Íslendinga*, 330.

9. Ibid., 332.

10. Lindal, *The Icelanders in Canada*, 115.

11. Ibid.

12. Þorsteinsson, *Saga Íslendinga*, 336.

13. Friðrik Bergmann, "Friðjón Friðriksson," *Almanak* (1908): 28-29.

14. Most records state that 285 Icelanders arrived in Winnipeg on 11 October. If that was the case and no one else came aboard the *International*, then perhaps two babies were born during the journey.

15. The account of the journey from Kinmount to New Iceland is largely based on Þorsteinsson's work, *Saga Íslendinga*, 334-337.

16. Thorleifur Jacksson, *Brot af Landnámssögu Nýja Íslands* (Winnipeg: Columbia Press, 1919), 10-11.

17. Þorsteinn Þ. Þorsteinsson, *Saga Íslendinga í Vesturheimi*, vol. III (Winnipeg: Þjóðræknisfélag Íslendinga í Vesturheimi, 1945), 3-11.

18. Jón J. Bildfell, "Early Historical Glimpses of the Icelandic People in Winnipeg," *Icelandic Canadian* (1947).

19. Þorsteinsson, *Saga Íslendinga*, 5. For more on the early years in New Iceland, see Skafti Arason, "Review of the period 1850-1889," published in Thorleifur Jacksson, *Frá Austri til Vesturs* (Winnipeg: Columbia Press, 1921), 69-81.

20. Þorsteinsson, ibid.

21. Ibid., 6.

22. Símon Símonarson, "Icelandic Pioneers of 1874," *Icelandic Canadian* (Winter 1946): 24-26. Also on early housing in New Iceland, see Þorsteinsson, *Saga Íslendinga*, 6-7.

23. Bergmann, "Friðjón Friðriksson," 30-31.

24. Þorsteinsson, *Saga Íslendinga*, 9.

25. Guðlaugur Magnússon, "Landnám Íslendinga í Nýja Íslandi," *Almanak* (1899): 28-29.

26. Þorsteinsson, *Saga Íslendinga*, 10.

27. *Heimskringla*, 16 August 1939.

28. Lindal, *The Icelanders in Canada*, 124.

29. Ibid., 125.

30. F.J. Fridriksson, Letters to Bjarnason, 29 December 1874. Special Collection Dafoe Library, University of Manitoba.

31. Jonas Þór, "A Religious Controversy among Icelandic Immigrants in North America," MA thesis, University of Manitoba, 1980, pp. 60-61.

32. For more information on these early times in New Iceland, consult the works of Nelson Gerrard, *Icelandic River Saga* (Arborg: n.p. 1985); Þorsteinsson, *Saga Íslendinga*; Sigtryggur Jónasson, "The Early Icelandic Settlements in Canada," *Historical and Scientific Society of Manitoba* 59, 22 (March 1901); and Magnús Sigurðsson, "Landnemar Geysisbygðar í Nýja Íslandi," *Almanak* (1932): 34-112; "Landnemar Víðirbygðar í Nýja Íslandi," *Almanak* (1933): 33-110; and "Landnemar Víðirbygðar og Geysisbygðar í Nýja Íslandi," *Almanak* (1934): 59-61.

Chapter Six

1. Edward M. Ledohowski and David K. Butterfield, *Architectural Heritage, the Eastern Interlake Planning District* (Winnipeg: Manitoba Department of Cultural and Historical Resources, 1983), 8.
2. For further accounts of poor soil in New Iceland, see George Houser, *Pioneer Icelandic Pastor: The Life of the Rev. Paul Thorlaksson* (Winnipeg: The Manitoba Historical Society, 1990).
3. Walter Lindal, *The Icelanders in Canada* (Winnipeg:Viking Printers, 1967), 127. Also Þorsteinn Þ. Þorsteinsson, *Saga Íslendinga í Vesturheimi,* vol. III (Winnipeg: Þjóðræknisfélag Íslendinga í Vesturheimi, 1945), 29.
4. Helgi Skúli Kjartansson, "The Onset of Emigration from Iceland," *American Studies in Scandinavia* 9 (1976): 94-100.
5. Þorsteinsson, *Saga Íslendinga*, 29.
6. Lindal, *The Icelanders in Canada,* 128.
7. Jóhann Briem's account was first published in *Framfari*. In 1919 it appeared in Thorleifur Jacksson, *Brot af Landnámssögu Nýja Íslands* (Winnipeg: Columbia Press, 1919), 14-15.
8. Lindal, *The Icelanders in Canada,* 31.
9. Jacksson, *Brot af Landnámssögu,* 16-19.
10. Ibid, 93.
11. Ibid.
12. Fridrik Sveinsson memoirs, entitled "Endurminningar frá Landnámstímum (Fyrsta viðkynning við Rauðskinna)," published in Jacksson, *Brot af Landnámssögu*, 33-37.
13. Þorsteinsson, *Saga Íslendinga,* 43.
14. Jónas Þór, *A Religious Controversy among Icelandic Immigrants in North America 1874-1880,* MA thesis, University of Manitoba, 1980, pp. 54-55.
15. Páll Þorlaksson and Þorlákur Jónsson, "Fyrstu ár Íslendinga í Dakota," *Almanak* (1901): 38. As he faced death due to illness in early 1882, Þorlaksson told his story to his father, Þorlákur Jónsson, who wrote it down. This article was eventually published in *Almanak* (1901).
16. Jacksson, *Brot af Landnámssögu,* 97.
17. Wilhelm Kristjanson, *The Icelandic People in Manitoba: A Manitoba Saga* (Winnipeg: Wallingford Press, 1965), 47-48.
18. W.L. Morton, *Manitoba: A History* (Toronto: University of Toronto Press, 1967), 177.
19. Þorsteinsson, *Saga Íslendinga,* 54.

20. Numerous sources discuss the smallpox epidemic. See Jacksson, *Brot af Landnámssögu,* and *Frá Austri til Vesturs; Almanak* (1900): 38-40; and Kristjanson, *The Icelandic People,* 47-52, 67.

21. Lindal, *The Icelanders in Canada,* 140-141.

22. Ibid.

23. *Framfari,* 22 December 1877.

24. See Appendix for the main articles and sections.

Chapter Seven

1. Þorsteinn Þ. Þorsteinsson, *Saga Íslendinga í Vesturheimi,* vol. III (Winnipeg: Þjóðræknisfélag Íslendinga í Vesturheimi, 1945), 128.

2. Guðlaugur Magnússon, "Landnám Íslendinga í Nýja Íslandi," *Almanak* (1899): 47.

3. Ibid.

4. Þorsteinsson, *Saga Íslendinga,* 130.

5. Ibid., 93.

6. Jónas Þór, *A Religious Controversy among Icelandic Immigrants in North America 1874-1880,* MA thesis, University of Manitoba, 1980, p. 63.

7. Ibid., 64.

8. Ibid., 67-69.

9. *Framfari,* 19 March 1878.

10. Ibid., 15 November 1877.

11. Ibid.

12. *Framfari,* 24 January 1878.

13. Jón Bjarnason, "Apologia Pro Vita Sua," *Áramót* (1909): 21.

14. *Framfari,* 12 February 1878; 20 February 1878.

15. Þór, *A Religious Controversy,* 97.

16. Ibid., 98-99.

17. Valdimar Eylands, *Íslensk Kristni í Vesturheimi* (Reykjavík: Edda, Þjóðkirkja Íslands, 1977), 68.

18. *Framfari,* 5 April 1878.

19. Thorleifur Jacksson, *Frá Austri til Vesturs* (Winnipeg: Columbia Press, 1921), 97-98.

20. On the government loans, see Wilhelm Kristjanson, *The Icelandic People in Manitoba: A Manitoba Saga* (Winnipeg: Wallingford Press, 1965), 110-112.

21. Jacksson, *Frá Austri til Vesturs,* 98.

22. *Framfari,* 25 July 1878.

23. Kristjanson, *The Icelandic people,* 112-113.

24. *Framfari,* 13 March 1879.

25. Þór, *A Religious Controversy,* 108.

Chapter Eight

1. *Framfari,* 9 July 1878.

2. Þorsteinn Þ. Þorsteinsson, *Saga Íslendinga í Vesturheimi,* vol. III (Winnipeg: Þjóðræknisfélag Íslendinga í Vesturheimi, 1945), 96.

3. Ibid., 49.

4. Ibid., 50.
5. Ibid., 58.
6. Ibid., 62.
7. Wilhelm Kristjanson, *The Icelandic People of Manitoba: A Manitoba Saga* (Winnipeg: Wallingford Press, 1965), 75-77.
8. Þorsteinsson, *Saga Íslendinga*, 116.
9. Thorstína Jackson, *Saga Íslendinga í Norður Dakóta* (Winnipeg: The City Printing & Publishing Co., 1926), 137.
10. *Framfari*, 7 January 1879.
11. Ibid., 24 July 1878.
12. Þorsteinsson, *Saga Íslendinga*,120.
13. On 4 February 1878, *Framfari* reported that the congregation in the southern part of the Vidirnes district was gathering material for their church, the first to be built in New Iceland. It was to be six metres wide and nine metres long. Its location was in the southernmost township in the district on the west side of the road. On 12 April, the same year, *Framfari* reported that a church was under construction at Breidavik in the River district. This one was expected to be about seven metres long, approximately six metres wide, and two and a half metres high. The foundation for yet another church was laid in 1877 in Vidirnes and a graveyard surveyed. This church was to be seven and a half by nine, and three metres high. In 1889 this abandoned church site was purchased by an Icelandic settler. He used the foundation and what still remained of the walls and built a house.
14. Thorleifur Jacksson, *Frá Austri til Vesturs* (Winnipeg: Columbia Press, 1921), 78. Also on churches (construction plans) in New Iceland, see Þorsteinsson, *Saga Íslendinga,* 112-113.
15. Framfari, 10 July 1878.
16. Ibid., 24 July 1878.
17. Þorsteinsson, *Saga Íslendinga,* 136.
18. Ibid., 137.
19. The translation appeared in *Framfari*, 7 January 1879.
20. Ibid., 30 November 1878.
21. Ibid., 10 December 1877.
22. Ibid., 4 January 1878.
23. Þorsteinsson, *Saga Íslendinga,* 143.
24. *Framfari*, 23 November 1878.
25. Þorsteinsson, *Saga Íslendinga*, 147.
26. Ibid., 148.
27. Ibid.
28. Ibid., 149.
29. *Framfari*, 10 December 1877.

Chapter Nine

1. Thorleifur Jacksson, *Frá Austri til Vesturs* (Winnipeg: Columbia Press, 1921), 97.
2. Wilhelm Kristjanson, *The Icelandic People in Manitoba: A Manitoba Saga* (Winnipeg: Wallingford Press, 1965), 90.
3. *Framfari,* 31 July 1878.

4. Ibid., August 1878.

5. Ibid., 11 December 1878.

6. Kristjanson, *The Icelandic People,* 85.

7. Ibid., 89.

8. For a more detailed account see "Debate of the House of Commons of the Dominion of Canada, 1878," vol. IV, Sessional Papers (Ottawa: Government Printing Bureau, 1878).

9. Kristjanson, *The Icelandic People,*102.

10. Ibid.

11. The following may explain the tone in the media in Iceland. The word *vesturheimskur* is a compound adjective. The first part, *vestur,* means "west," and *heimskur* is "foolish, ignorant." An individual labelled *vesturheimskur* was then someone "foolishly obsessed with the West." A headline of a report from Akureyri in an Icelandic periodical in July 1878 read: "*Allt fullt af vesturheimsku fólki.*" Loosely translated, this means "The place is packed with people foolishly obsessed with the West."

12. Sessional Papers, 1880.

13. *New York Star*, August 1879.

14. Kristjanson, *The Icelandic People,* 112.

15. *Framfari*, 8 February 1879.

16. For example, in the summer of 1878, Jonasson bought the first haymower and in the fall planted some Ontario winter wheat. In 1880, he and Friðjón Friðriksson bought the steamer *Victoria* in order to improve transportation to and from the colony.

17. Thorleifur Jacksson, *Brot af Landnámssögu Nýja Íslands* (Winnipeg: Columbia Press, 1919), 51-52.

18. *Framfari,* 19 June 1878.

19. Guðlaugur Magnússon, "Landnám Íslendinga í Nýja Íslandi," *Almanak* (1899): 47.

20. Kristjanson, *The Icelandic People,* 122.

21. These were men such as Sigtryggur Jonasson, Friðjón Friðriksson, and John Taylor.

22. Sigurður Kristofersson was in charge as postmaster and Everett Parsonage became letter carrier in the colony.

23. Kristjanson, *The Icelandic People,* 122.

24. Sessional Papers A, 1880.

25. *Framfari,* January 1880.

26. Áramót (1880).

27. Jacksson, *Frá Austri til Vesturs,* 77.

28. Magnusson, "Landnám Íslendinga," 41.

Chapter Ten

1. Thorleifur Jacksson, *Frá Austri til Vesturs* (Winnipeg: Columbia Press, 1921), 84.

2. Ibid., 85.

3. Friðrik J. Bergmann, "Landnám Íslendinga í Norður Dakota," *Almanak* (1902): 24.

4. Thorstína S. Jackson, *Saga Íslendinga í Norður Dakóta* (Winnipeg: The City Printing & Publishing Co., 1926), 26.

5. Bergmann, "Landnám Íslendinga," 24.

6. Jackson, *Saga Íslendinga í Norður Dakóta,* 29. Also Bergmann, "Landnám Íslendinga," 28.

7. Later, Pembina County was divided in two and the western part became Cavalier County. The main part of the Icelandic settlement was by the Pembina Mountains. Two rivers flow from the mountains, Tongue River and Park River, and the ravine through which each of them runs was noted for an exceptional growth of several types of trees and pretty vegetation.

The northern boundary of the settlement was next to rough sand hills, while the southern boundary reached the northern confluence of Park River. The settlement close to the river carried its name but the district between Gardar and Mountain was referred to as Eyford, named after the first post office clerk in the district, Jakob Sigurdson Eyford.

The district on the banks of of the Tongue River was named after the river at first but in 1881, a post office was established called Coulee, by which the district gradually was recognized. However, Coulee was abandoned in 1883 and a new post office, Hallson, was established on the land of Johann P. Hallson. As a result of this move, the name Tongue River district was replaced by Hallson district. The sand hills are located in the centre of the area between Hallson and Mountain and the district called Sandhills. A post office was established in the district in the pioneer days and called Akra.

8. Jackson, *Saga Íslendinga í Norður Dakóta,* 31.

9. Bergmann, "Landnám Íslendinga," 36.

10. Ibid., 37.

11. Ibid., 59.

12. Ibid., 73.

13. Jackson, *Saga Íslendinga í Norður Dakota,* 42.

14. Ibid., 135-137.

15. Bergmann, "Landnám Íslendinga," 47-50. Also, on church and congregations, see Jackson, *Saga Íslendinga í Norður Dakota,* 57-60.

16. Jackson, *Saga Íslendinga í Norður Dakóta,* 60.

17. Ibid., 61.

18. Ibid., 68.

19. *Sameiningin,* March 1888.

20. Jackson, *Saga Íslendinga í Norður Dakóta, 306.*

21. Sigurður J. Jóhannesson, "Landnám Íslendinga í Minnesota," *Almanak* (1900): 60.

22. Ibid., 61.

23. Ibid., 66.

24. Ibid.

25. R. Marteinsson, ed., *Minningarrit Séra Jón Bjarnason* (Winnipeg: Columbia Press, 1917), 42.

26. Ibid.

27. *Leifur,* 1884.

Chapter Eleven

1. Júníus Kristinsson, *Vesturfararskrá 1870-1914* (Reykjavík: Institute of History, University of Iceland, 1983), Table 3.
2. Gils Guðmundsson, ed., *Öldin sem leið* (Reykjavík: Forlagið Iðunn, 1956), 187.
3. *Fjallkona*, March 1887.
4. Þorsteinn Þ. Þorsteinsson, *Saga Íslendinga í Vesturheimi,* vol. I (Reykjavík: Þjóðræknisfélag Íslendinga í Vesturheimi, 1940), 132-133.
5. *Heimskringla*, 28 July 1887.
6. Þorsteinsson, *Saga Íslendinga,* 135.
7. Ibid., 137-138.
8. *Fjallkona*, 15 August 1893.
9. As the figure indicates, an exact number is not known. However, this estimate is based on immigration figures in Winnipeg and migration from the city to different Icelandic communities.
10. Walter Lindal, *The Icelanders in Canada* (Winnipeg: Viking Printers, 1967), 159.
11. Ibid.
12. Many Icelanders, among them Rev. Jón Bjarnason, had looked at such practices with some concern, maintaining that in changing one's Christian name a person abandoned his religion. However, in the North American community, it became clear that anyone called Gudridur (Icel. Guðríður) or Gudbrandur (Icel. Guðbrandur) would never hear his name properly pronounced or correctly spelled. A Sveinsson would become Swanson and an Einarsson, Anderson.
13. *Framfari,* 22 February 1879.
14. At one point, for example, Gimli Icelanders and those in Winnipeg bitterly contested which place was most deserving of the statue of Jón Sigurðsson, which eventually was placed in front of the Legislative Building in Winnipeg.
15. Jón J. Bildfell, "Early Historical Glimpses of the Icelandic People in Winnipeg," *Icelandic Canadian* (Autumn 1947): 16-23.
16. Ibid.
17. *Leifur*, June 1883.
18. Tryggvi Oleson, *Saga Íslendinga í Vesturheimi,* vol. IV (Reykjavík: Bókaútgáfa Menningarsjóðs, 1951), 336-338.
19. Wilhelm Kristjanson, *The Icelandic People in Manitoba: A Manitoba Saga* (Winnipeg: Wallingford Press, 1965), 197-199.
20. Ibid., 267.
21. Tryggvi Oleson, *Saga Íslendinga í Vesturheimi,* vol.V (Reykjavík: Bókaútgáfa Menningarsjóðs, 1953), 125-127.
22. Ibid., 368-369.
23. Ibid., 371.
24. Ibid., 389.
25. Winnipeg *Free Press*, 24 December 1887.
26. Ibid., 15 May 1888.
27. Kristjanson, *The Icelandic People,* 237.
28. Ibid., 238.
29. *Lögberg,* 1 March 1895.
30. Emil V. Gudmundson, *The Icelandic Unitarian Connection* (Winnipeg: Wheatfield Press, 1984), 29.
31. Ibid., 21-24.

32. *Sameiningin*, July 1890.
33. Kristjanson, *The Icelandic People*, 192-194.
34. *Leifur*, 5 May 1883.
35. Kristjanson, *The Icelandic People*, 187.
36. For more on Icelandic publications, see Oleson, *Saga Íslendinga í Vesturheimi*, vol.V, 3-48.
37. Kristjanson, *The Icelandic People*, 162-163.
38. Oleson, *Saga Íslendinga í Vesturheimi*, vol. IV, 350-352.

Chapter Twelve

1. Björn Jónsson, "Landnám Íslendinga í Argyle-bygð," *Almanak* (1902): 25.
2. Ibid., 26.
3. Ibid., 28.
4. Ibid., 32.
5. Jónsson, "Landnám Íslendinga," 33.
6. Tryggvi J. Oleson, *Saga Íslendinga í Vesturheimi*, vol. IV (Reykjavík: Bókaútgáfa Menningarsjóðs, 1951), 10. At the initial meeting ninety-six members were recorded but a year later the membership had dropped to eighty-three. At that time there were forty-one males and forty-two females listed, sixteen of whom were twenty years of age or younger. Although the society flourished for a few years, it did not last very long. A Temperance Society with more direct objectives replaced the Reform Society in 1885.
7. Jónsson, "Landnám Íslendinga," 34-35.
8. *Leifur*, 31 July 1885.
9. Oleson, *Saga Íslendinga í Vesturheimi*, vol. IV, 17.
10. Wilhelm Kristjanson, *The Icelandic People in Manitoba: A Manitoba Saga* (Winnipeg: Wallingford Press, 1965), 321.
11. Jónsson, "Landnám Íslendinga," 35.
12. Kristjanson, *The Icelandic People*, 143.
13. Ibid., 142.
14. Ibid., 145.
15. Ibid., 142.
16. *Heimskringla*, 21 June 1887.
17. Jonsson, "Landnám Íslendinga," 37.
18. Statutes of Manitoba, 1897, Chapter 26, Section 10.
19. Kristjanson, *The Icelandic People*, 145.
20. Emil V. Gudmundson, *The Icelandic Unitarian Connection* (Winnipeg: Wheatfield Press, 1984), 69-72.
21. Kristjanson, *The Icelandic People*, 320.
22. Runólfur Marteinsson, ed., *Minningarrit Séra Jón Bjarnason* (Winnipeg: Columbia Press, 1917), 85.
23. Oleson, *Saga Íslendinga í Vesturheimi*, vol. IV, 232.
24. Sessional Papers (Ottawa: Government Printing Bureau, 1893).
25. Helgi Einarsson, *A Manitoba Fisherman* (Winnipeg: Queenston House, 1982), 11-12.
26. Jón Jónsson, "Íslendingar austan við Manitobavatn," *Almanak* (1910): 77-80.
27. Ibid., 82.

28. Ibid., 82-84.
29. For more on Interlake schools, see Kristjanson, *The Icelandic People,* 299-320.
30. Kristjanson, *The Icelandic People,* 309.
31. George W. Langdon, ed., *A Tribute to Soldiers and Pioneers of the Langruth District* (Manitoba: Langruth Community, 1950), 107-108.
32. Kristjanson, *The Icelandic People,* 312.
33. Ibid., 313-314.
34. Ibid., 315-316.

Chapter Thirteen

1. Walter Lindal, *The Saskatchewan Icelanders* (Winnipeg: Columbia Press, 1955), 82.
2. Helgi Árnason, "Ágrip af sögu Þingvallabyggðar," *Almanak* (1918): 77.
3. Ibid., 79.
4. Lindal, *The Saskatchewan Icelanders,* 86.
5. Ibid., 88.
6. Ibid., 92.
7. Ibid., 94.
8. For more information about the Churchbridge settlement, see Árnason, "Ágrip af sögu," 77.
9. See Lindal, *The Saskatchewan Icelanders,* 89-104.
10. Tryggvi Þorsteinsson, "Frá stofnun Tantallon-byggðarinnar í Saskatchewan," *Almanak* (1951): 68-70.
11. Lindal, *The Saskatchewan Icelanders,* 112-115. Also see Richard Beck, "Drættir úr Sögu Tantallon-byggðar," *Almanak* (1952): 74-79; "Landnámsþættir Íslendinga í Spy Hill, Gerald og Tantallon-byggðum," *Almanak* (1953): 36-44, and (1954): 69-87.
12. Friðrik Guðmundsson, "Vatnabygðir," *Almanak* (1917): 53.
13. Ibid., 55.
14. Jón R. Hjálmarsson, *A Short History of Iceland* (Reykjavík: Almenna Bókafélagið, 1988), 122-125.
15. Gils Guðmundsson, ed., *Öldin sem leið* (Reykjavík: Forlagið Iðunn, 1956), 234.
16. Guðmundsson, "Vatnabygðir," 55.
17. Ibid., 54-55.
18. Ibid., 64.
19. Lindal, *The Saskatchewan Icelanders,* 142.
20. This annual celebration, still held in Iceland and Icelandic communities in North America, has its roots in Viking tradition.
21. For more information on the small Saskatchewan colonies, see Lindal, *The Saskatchewan Icelanders,* and Gudmundsson "Vatnabygðir," *Almanak* (1917): 53-112, and (1918): 60-74.
22. Ólafur O. Magnússon,"Landnám Íslendinga sunnan Quill vatnanna í Saskatchewan," *Almanak* (1950): 35.
23. Lindal, *The Saskatchewan Icelanders,* 157.
24. Ibid., 160.
25. Ibid.
26. Guðmundsson, "Vatnabygðir," 56-57.
27. Beck, "Landnámsþættir Íslendinga" (1953): 39.

28. Ibid., 34.

29. Ibid., 36.

30. Ibid., 39.

31. Lindal, *The Saskatchewan Icelanders*, 192.

32. Ibid., 195.

33. Jónas Hunfjord, "Saga Íslendinga í Albertahéraði," *Almanak* (1914): 116-121.

34. Ibid. For more details see pp. 121-124.

35. Walter Lindal, *The Icelanders in Canada* (Winnipeg: Viking Printers, 1967), 199.

36. Ibid., 206.

37. Ibid., 200-209.

38. Margrét Benedictsson, "Íslendingar á Kyrrahafsströndinni. I. Point Roberts," *Almanak* (1925): 28.

39. Ibid., 28-65.

40. Ibid., 24.

41. Richard E. Clark, *Point Roberts USA* (Bellingham: Textype Publishing, 1980), 55.

42. Ibid., 56.

43. Ibid., 57.

44. Ibid., 58.

45. Runa Thordarson, *Echoes from the Past* (Point Roberts: privately printed, 1975), 27.

46. Benedictsson, "Íslendingarnir," 27.

47. Margrét Benedictsson, "Íslendingarnir á Kyrrahafsströndinni. II. Blaine," *Almanak* (1926): 69-70.

48. Ibid.

49. Margrét Benedictsson, "Bellingham og Bellingham Íslendingar," *Almanak* (1941): 33.

50. *Seattle Times,* 17 October 1902. Sigurdur Helgason was instrumental in launching the first Scandinavian Song Festival in Seattle, which took place in 1903. His contribution to the musical scene on the Pacific Coast was considerable.

Chapter Fourteen

1. Wilhelm Kristjanson, *The Icelandic People in Manitoba: A Manitoba Saga* (Winnipeg:Wallingford Press, 1965), 505.

2. *Lögberg,* 4 June 1890.

3. Ibid.

4. Ibid.

5. *Heimskringla,* 19 July 1888.

6. Jónas Þór and Terry Tergesen, *Saga Íslendingadagsins* (Gimli: The Icelandic Festival Committee, 1989), 23.

7. Quoted in ibid., 24.

8. *Lögberg,* May 1895.

9. *Heimskringla,* 9 September 1886.

10. Kristjanson, *The Icelandic People,* 244-246.

11. Ibid., 245.

12. Walter Lindal, *The Icelanders in Canada* (Winnipeg: Viking Printers, 1967), 220.

13. Ibid.

14. Thorstina A. Jackson, *Saga Íslendinga í Norður Dakóta* (Winnipeg: The City Printing & Publishing Co., 1926), 291.

15. Ibid., 98.
16. *Almanak* (1918): 28.
17. Watson Kirkonnell, "Canada's Leading Poet: Stephan G. Stephansson (1853-1927)," *University of Toronto Quarterly* 5, 2 (1936): 263.
18. For more information on Icelandic immigrant literature, see D.L. Neijmann, *The Icelandic Voice in Canadian Letters* (Ontario: Carleton University Press, 1997), 99-198.
19. Kristjanson, *The Icelandic People,* 372-375.

Conclusion

1. Christer Lennart Mossberg, "Notes toward an Introduction to Scandinavian Literature on the Pioneer Experience," *Proceedings of the Pacific North West Council on Foreign Languages,* 28.1, ed. John T. Brewer (Corvalis: Oregon State University, 1976), 113.
2. Daisy L. Neijmann, *The Icelandic Voice* (Ontario: Carleton University Press, 1997), 81.
3. *Framfari,* July 1878.
4. Stephan G. Stephansson, *Selected Translations from Andvökur* (Edmonton: The Stephan G. Stephansson Homestead Restoration Committee, 1987), 6.
5. Wilhelm Kristjanson, *The Icelandic People in Manitoba: A Manitoba Saga* (Winnipeg: Wallingford Press, 1965), 74.
6. Rögnvaldur Pétursson, "Þjóðræknissamtök Íslendinga í Vesturheim," *Tímarit Þjóðræknisfélags Íslendinga í Vesturheimi,* 1 (1919): 36.
7. *Minningarrit Íslenzkra Hermanna* (Winnipeg:Viking Press, 1923).

Bibliography

Books

Allen, Richard. *A Region of the Mind: Interpreting the Western Canadian Plains*. Regina: Canadian Plains Studies Center, 1973.

Arnason, David, and Vincent Arnason, eds. *The New Icelanders*. Winnipeg: Turnstone Press, 1994.

Arnason, David, and Michael Olito. *The Icelanders*. Winnipeg: Turnstone Press, 1981.

Ahlstrom, S.E., ed. *Theology in America*. Indianapolis: The Bobbs-Merill Co., 1965.

Arngrímsson, Guðjón. *Nýja Ísland*. Reykjavík: Mál og Menning, 1997.

_____. *Annað Ísland*. Reykjavík: Mál og Menning, 1998.

Balan, Jars., ed. *Identifications: Ethnicity and the Writer in Canada*. Edmonton: Canadian Institute of Ukranian Studies, University of Alberta, 1982.

Barth, Fredrik. *Ethnic Groups and Boundaries: The Social Organization of Culture Difference*. Bergen/Oslo: Universitetsforlaget; London: George Allen & Unwin, 1969.

Bergmann, F.J. *Trú og Þekking*. Reykjavík, Iceland, 1917.

Bíldfell, J.J., ed. *Jón Bjarnason Rit og Ræður*. Winnipeg: Columbia Press, 1946.

Bjarnason, Jóhann Magnús. *Brazilíufararnir*. Akureyri: Bókaútgáfan Edda, 1872.

_____. *Eiríkur Hansson*. Akureyri: Bókaútgáfan Edda, 1973.

_____. *Í Rauðárdalnum*. Akureyri: Bókaútgáfan Edda, 1976.

_____. *Vornætur á Elgsheiðum*. Akureyri: Bókaútgáfan Edda, 1970.

Bjarnason, Jón. *Guðspjallarmál: Prédikanir*. Reykjavík: Ísafold Printing Press, 1900.

Careless, J.M.S. *Canada: A Story of Challenge*. Toronto: Macmillan of Canada, 1973.

Clark, Richard E. *Point Roberts, USA*. Bellingham: Textype Publishing, 1980.

Cleverden, C.L. *The Women's Suffrage Movement in Canada*. Toronto: University of Toronto Press, 1950.

Creighton, Donald. *Canada's First Century*. Toronto: Macmillan of Canada, 1976.

Dahlie, Hallvard. *Varieties of Exile: The Canadian Experience*. Vancouver: University of British Columbia Press, 1986.

Dawson, Carl A., and Eva R. Younge. *Pioneering in the Prairie Provinces: The Social Side of the Settlement Process*. Toronto: Macmillan, 1940.

Derry, T.K. *A History of Scandinavia*. London: George Allen & Unwin, 1979.

Eaton, Conan Bryant. *Washington Island*. Washington Island: Jackson Harbor Press, 1997.

Edwards, John. *Language, Society, Identity*. London/New York: Basil Blackwell, 1985.

Einarsson, Helgi. *A Manitoba Fisherman*, transl. Dr. George Houser. Winnipeg: Queenston House, 1982.

Elias, Peter Douglas. *The Dakota of the Canadian Northwest: Lessons in Survival*. Winnipeg: University of Manitoba Press, 1986.

Erlendsson, Guðbrandur. *Markland*. Winnipeg: n.p., 1916.

Eylands, Valdimar. *Íslensk Kristni í Vesturheimi*. Reykjavík: Edda, Þjóðkirkja Íslands, Iceland, 1977.

_____. *Lutherans in Canada*. Winnipeg: Columbia Press, 1945.

Finlay, J.L., and D.N. Sprague. *The Structure of Canadian History*. Scarborough: Prentice-Hall of Canada, Ltd., 1979.

Friesen, Gerald. *The Canadian Prairies: A History*. Toronto: University of Toronto Press, 1984.

_____. *River Road*. Winnipeg: University of Manitoba Press, 1996.

Gerrard, Nelson S. *Icelandic River Saga*. Arborg: n.p., 1985.

Gimli Saga. Gimli: Gimli Women's Institute, 1975.

Guðmundsson, Böðvar, ed. *Bréf Vestur-Íslendinga*. Reykjavík: Mál og Menning, 2001.

Guðmundsson, Finnbogi. *Foreldrar mínir*. Reykjavík:1956.

Guðmundsson, Gils., ed. *Öldin sem leið*. Reykjavík: Forlagið Iðunn, 1956.

Gudmundson, V. Emil. *The Icelandic Unitarian Connection*. Winnipeg: Wheatfield Press, 1984.

Hagskinna. Reykjavík: Icelandic Historical Statistics, 1997.

Helgason, Jón. *Kristinsaga Íslands*. Reykjavík: Félagsprentsmiðja, 1925.

Hill, Douglas. *The Opening of the Canadian West*. Longman bókafélagið, 1967.

Hjálmarsson, Jón R. *A Short History of Iceland*. Reykjavík: Almenna Bókafélagið, 1988.

Houser, George. *Pioneer Icelandic Pastor: The Life of the Rev. Paul Thorlaksson,* ed. Paul A. Sigurdsson. Winnipeg: The Manitoba Historical Society, 1990.

Jackson, Thorstina. *Saga Íslendinga í Norður Dakóta*. Winnipeg: The City Printing & Publishing Co., 1926.

Jacksson, Thorleifur. *Brot af Landnámssögu Nýja Íslands*. Winnipeg: Columbia Press, 1919.

_____. *Frá Austri til Vesturs*. Winnipeg: Columbia Press, 1921.

_____. *Framhald af Landnámssögu Nýja Íslands*. Winnipeg: Columbia Press, 1923.

Joakimson, Thorleifur. *Brot af Landnámssögu Nýja Íslands*. Winnipeg: Columbia Press, 1919.

Jónsson, Steingrímur. *Hugvitsmaðurinn Hjörtur Þórðarson*. Reykjavík: Almenna Bókafélagið, 1973.

Kirkconnell, Watson. "A Skald in Canada." *Transactions of the Royal Society of Canada*, 3rd ser., Sec. 2:33 (1939): 263-77.

_____. *Canadian Overtones*. Winnipeg: Columbia Press, 1937.

_____. "Four Decades of Icelandic Poetry in Canada 1922-62." *The Icelandic Canadian* 22, 2 (1963): 17-27.

Kovacs, M., ed. *Ethnic Canadians: Culture and Education*. Regina: Canadian Plains Research Center, 1878.

Kristinsson, Júníus. *Vesturfararskrá 1870-1914*. Reykjavík: Institute of History, University of Iceland, 1983.

Kristjánsson, Wilhelm. *The Icelandic People in Manitoba: A Manitoba Saga*. Winnipeg: Wallingford Press, 1965.

Kvaran, Einar, and Guðmundur Finnbogason. *Vestan um Haf*. Reykjavík: Gutenberg, 1930.

_____. *Vonir*. Reykjavík:1890.

_____. *Vesturför*. Reykjavík: 1929.

Langdon, George W., ed. *A Tribute to Soldiers and Pioneers of the Langruth District*. Langruth: Langruth Community, 1950.

Ledohowski, E.M., and David K. Butterfield. *Architectural Heritage, the Eastern Interlake Planning District*. Winnipeg: Department of Cultural and Historical Resources, Province of Manitoba, 1983.

Lindal, Walter J. *The Icelanders in Canada*. Canada Ethnica Series 2. Ottawa: National Publishers; Winnipeg: Viking Printers, 1967.

_____. *The Saskatchewan Icelanders*. Winnipeg: Columbia Press, 1955.

Lydecker, R., and L.J. Somner, eds. *Duluth: Sketches of the Past*. Duluth: American Revolution Bicentennial Commission, 1976.

Lysengen, Janet Daley, and Ann M. Rathke, eds. *The Centennial Anthology of North Dakota History*. Bismark: State Historical Society of North Dakota, 1996.

MacPherson, Ian, and David Jones, eds. *Building beyond the Homestead: Rural History on the Prairies*. Calgary: University of Calgary Press, 1985.

Marteinsson, R., ed. *Minningarrit Séra Jón Bjarnason*. Winnipeg: Columbia Press, 1917.

Mayer, F.E. *The Religious Bodies of America*. St. Louis: Concordia Publishing House, 1956.

Mayer, Carl Stamm. *Pioneers and Friends*. Minneapolis: Luther College Press, 1962.

_____. *Moving Frontiers*. St. Louis: Concordia Publishing House, 1965.

Minningarrit Hins Evl. Lútherska Kirkjufélags í Vesturheimi. Winnipeg, n.p., 1910.

Minningarrit um 50 ára landnám Íslendinga í Norður Dakóta. Winnipeg: Columbia Press Ltd., 1929.

Minningarrit Íslenzkra Hermanna. Winnipeg: Viking Press, 1923.

Morton, W.L. *Manitoba: A History*. Toronto: University of Toronto Press, 1961.

Neijmann, Daisy L. *The Icelandic Voice in Canadian Letters*. Ontario: Carleton University Press, 1997.

Norðal, Sigurður. *Stephan G. Stephansson. Maðurinn og skáldið*. Reykjavík: Helgafell, 1959.

Norlie, O.M. *History of The Norwegian People in America*. Minnesota: Augsburg Publishing House, 1925.

Norman, Hans, and Harald Runblom. *Transatlantic Connections: Nordic Migration to the New World after 1800*. Oxford: Oxford University Press, 1987.

Oleson, Tryggvi. *Saga Íslendinga í Vesturheimi*. Vol. IV. Reykjavík: Bókaútgáfa Menningarsjóðs, 1951.

_____. *Saga Íslendinga í Vesturheimi*. Vol. V. Reykjavík: Bókaútgáfa Menningarsjóðs, 1953.

Olson, S.B. *Pioneer Sketches*. Winnipeg: n.p., 1960.

Palmer, Howard, ed. *The Settlement of the West*. Calgary: Comprint, 1977.

Pálsson, Hjörtur. *Alaskaför Jóns Ólafssonar 1874*. Reykjavík: Sögufélagið, 1975.

Patterson ll, E. Palmer. *The Canadian Indian*. Ontario: Collier Macmillan Canada Ltd., 1972.

Rasmussen, Janet E., ed. *New Land New Lives: Scandinavian Immigrants to the Pacific Northwest*. Washington: The University of Washington Press/The Norwegian-American Historical Association, 1993.

Ray, Arthur J. *Indians in the Fur Trade*. Toronto: University of Toronto Press, 1974.

Ruth, Roy H. *Educational Echoes: A History of Education of the Icelandic Canadians In Manitoba*. Winnipeg: Roy H. Ruth/Columbia, 1964.

Sessional Papers, 1876-1879. Ottawa: Government Printing Bureau.

Simundsson, Elva. *Icelandic Settlers in America*. Winnipeg: Queenston House Publishing, 1981.

Stephansson, S.G. *Bréf og Ritgerðir l-ll*. Reykjavík: Gutenberg Press, 1938-1939.

_____. *Bréf og Ritgerðir lll-lV*. Reykjavík: Félagsprentsmiðjan h.f., 1947.

_____. *Selected Translations from Andvökur*. Edmonton: The Stephan G. Stephansson Restoration Committee, 1987.

Taylor, Jeffery. *Fashioning Farmers: Ideology, Agricultural Knowledge and the Manitoba Farm Movement, 1890-1925*. Regina: Canadian Plains Research Center, 1994.

Teitson, Björn. *Eignahald og Ábúð á Jörðum í Suður Þingeyjasýslu*. Reykjavík: Oddi Press, Iceland, 1973.

Thompson, S. *Riverton and the Icelandic Settlement*. Riverton, Manitoba: n.p., 1976.

Thorvaldson, Skapti O. *Sveinn Thorvaldson MBE. A Family Chronicle*. n.p. 1984.

A Tribute to Soldiers and Pioneers of the Langruth District. Langruth: Langruth Community, 1950.

Turville-Petre, Gabriel. *Origins of Icelandic Literature*. Oxford: Clarendon Press, 1953.

Þorsteinsson, Björn, and Bergsteinn Jónsson. *Íslands saga til vorra daga*. Reykjavík: Sögufélag, 1991.

Þorsteinsson, Þorsteinn Þ. *Saga Íslendinga í Vesturheimi*. Vol. I. Reykjavík: Þjóðræknisfélag Íslendinga í Vesturheimi, 1940.

_____. *Saga Íslendinga í Vesturheimi*. Vol. II. Winnipeg: Þjóðræknisfélag Íslendinga í Vesturheimi, 1943.

_____. *Saga Íslendinga í Vesturheimi*. Vol. III. Winnipeg: Þjóðræknisfélag Íslendinga í Vesturheimi, 1945.

_____. *Vestmenn*. Reykjavík: Ísafoldarprentsmiðja, 1935.

_____. *Ævintýrið frá Íslandi til Brasilíu*. Reykjavík: Ísafoldarprentsmiðja, 1938.

Þór, Jónas. *A Religious Controversy among Icelandic Immigrants in North America 1874-1880*. MA thesis, University of Manitoba. 1980.

_____, and Terry Tergesen. *Saga Íslendingadagsins*. Gimli: The Icelandic Festival of Manitoba, 1989.

Walz, Gene. *Cartoon Charlie*. Winnipeg: Great Plains Publications, 1998.

Wright, Jim F.C. *Saskatchewan, The History of a Province*. Toronto: McClelland and Stewart Ltd., 1955.

Zampel, Solveig, ed. and trans. *In Their Own Words: Letters from Norwegian Immigrants*. Minneapolis: University of Minnesota Press/The Norwegian-American Historical Association, 1991.

Articles, Newspapers, Periodicals

Aldamót. Winnipeg, 1891-1903

Almanak. Winnipeg, 1895-1954.

Áramót. Winnipeg, 1905-1909.

Árnason, G. " Þáttur Íslendinga í Álftárdal." *Almanak* (1923): 54-85.

Árnason, Helgi. "Sögurþættir íslenskra innflytjenda í Pembina, Norður-Dakota." *Almanak* (1920): 38-59; (1922): 55-75.

_____. "Ágrip af sögu Þingvallabyggðar." *Almanak* (1918): 77-81.

Arngrímsson, Jóhannes. "Letter to the Editor." *Norðanfari*, 22 September 1872.

Baldvinsson, Ásgeir V. "Landnám Íslendinga í Muskoka og tildrög að því." *Almanak* (1900): 40-48.

Baldvinsson, Sigurður. "Framhald landnámssögu Álptavatnsbygðar." *Almanak* (1944): 59-78.

Beck, Richard. "Drættir úr Sögu Tantallon-byggðar." *Almanak* (1952): 74-79.

_____. "Landnámsþættir Íslendinga í Spy Hill, Gerald og Tantallon-byggðum." *Almanak* (1953): 36-44; (1954): 69-87.

_____. "Sigurður Helgason Tónskáld." *Almanak* (1942): 50-55.

_____. "Jón K. Ólafsson." *Almanak* (1948): 41-48.

_____. "Bókmenntaiðja Íslendinga í Vesturheimi."*Eimreiðin* 34 (1928): 41-69, 321-40, 35; (1929): 49-62.

Benedictsson, Margrét. "Íslendingar á Kyrrahafsströndinni. 1. Point Roberts." *Almanak* (1925): 21-65.

_____. "Íslendingar á Kyrrahafsströndinni, ll. Blaine." *Almanak* (1926): 66-90; (1928): 63-94; (1929): 36-72; (1930): 122-137.

_____. "Bellingham og Bellingham Íslendingar." *Almanak* (1941): 31-53; (1942): 31-49.

_____. "Íslendingar í Marietta." *Almanak* (1943): 52-65.

Bergmann, F.J. "Landnám Íslendinga í Norður-Dakota." *Almanak* (1902): 17-87.

_____. "Saga íslensku nýlendunnar í bænum Winnipeg." *Almanak* (1903): 34-66; (1904): 48-103; (1905): 81-107; (1906): 52-86; (1907): 65-92.

_____. "Friðjón Friðriksson." *Almanak* (1908): 21-40.

Bildfell, Jón J. "Early Historical Glimpses of the Icelandic People in Winnipeg." *Icelandic Canadian* (Autumn, 1947): 16-23.

Bjarnason, Hjálmar. "Brot úr Ferðasögu Þórðar Diðrikssonar frá Íslandi til Utah." *Almanak* (1920): 65-71.

Bjarnason, Jóhann Magnús. "Æskuminning um Magnús lögmann Brynjólfsson."*Eimreiðin* (1912): 127-139.

Bjarnason, Jón. "Apologia Pro Vita Sua." *Áramót* (1909): 18-56; *Þjóðólfur* (October 1874).

Bjarnason, Þórhallur. "Frá Grænlandi til Brasilíu." *Almanak* (1916): 59-63.

Breiðablik. Winnipeg, 1906-1914.

Budistikken. Minneapolis, 1874-1877.

Daníelsson, Halldór. "Þáttur um landnám í Big Point bygð." *Almanak* (1924): 49-90; (1926): 44-90; (1927): 39-65.

The Desert News. Salt Lake City, 1938.

Einarsson, Stefán. "Íslendingar í Washington D.C." *Almanak* (1946): 29-43.

Elford, Jean. "The Icelanders: Their Ontario Year." *Beaver* 304 (1974): 53-58.

Framfari. New Iceland, 1877-1880.

Freyja. Selkirk and Winnipeg, 1898-1910.

Frjettir frá Íslandi 1871-1877. Iceland, 1871-1877.

Göngu-Hrólfur. Iceland, 1873.

Guðmundsson, Árni. "Landnám Íslendinga á Washingtoneyjunni." *Almanak* (1900): 28-43.

Guðmundsson, Friðrik. "Vatnabygðir." *Almanak* (1917): 53-112; (1918): 60-70.

Halldórsson, Halldór J., and Ólafur O. Magnússon. "Landnám Íslendinga sunnan Quill vatnanna í Saskatchewan." *Almanak* (1950): 35-70.

Halldórsson, Jón. "Tildrög til íslenskrar nýlendustofnunar í Nebraska." *Almanak* (1914): 150-156.

Heimskringla. Winnipeg, 1886-1950.

Hjálmarsson, Finnbogi. "Landnámssöguþættir frá Íslendingum í Winnipegosis." *Almanak* (1930): 56-121.

_____. "Tildrög að landnámi Íslendinga við Little Salt í Norður Dakóta." *Almanak* (1931): 112-123.

Hornafjörð, B.J. "Framnesbyggðin í norður Nýja Íslandi í Manitoba." *Almanak* (1947): 29-37.

Húnfjörð, Jóhannes H. "Söguþættir af landnámi Íslendinga við Brown, Manitoba." *Almanak* (1937): 21-44; (1938): 87-112; (1939): 62-85; (1940): 51-75.

Hunford, Jónas J. "Saga Íslendinga í Albertahéraði." *Almanak* (1909): 31-44; (1914): 116-149.

Icelandic Canadian. Winnipeg, 1942—.

Ísafold. Iceland, 1874-1883.

Jóhannesson, Sigurður J. "Þáttur Íslendinga í Nýja Skotlandi." *Almanak* (1900): 48-54.

_____. "Landnám Íslendinga í Minnesota." *Almanak* (1900): 54-67.

Jóhannsson, Gunnar. "Landnemar úr Norður Dakota er fluttust til Gerald (Vallarbyggða) – vatnabyggða." *Almanak* (1954): 88-95.

Johnson, E.H. "Saga Íslendinga í Utah." *Almanak* (1915): 39-66; (1917): 170-171.

Jónasson, Sigtryggur. "John Taylor og Elizabeth Taylor." *Syrpa* IV (1920): 98-102.

_____. "The Early Icelandic Settlements in Canada." *Historical and Scientific Society of Manitoba* 59, 22 (March 1901).

_____. Letter to *Norðanfari*. Kinmont, Ontario, 1 February 1875.

Jónsson, Bergsteinn. "Aðdragandi og Upphaf Vesturferða af Íslandi á nítjándu öld," *Andvari* (1975): 3-23.

Jónsson, Björn. "Landnám Íslendinga í Argyle-bygð." *Almanak* (1901): 23-36.

Jónsson, Guðmundur. "Drög til landnámssögu Íslendinga við norðurhluta Manitoba-Vatns." *Almanak* (1937): 45-66; (1938): 60-86; (1939): 86-95.

Jónsson, Jón. "Íslendingar austan við Manitobavatn." *Almanak* (1910): 37-88; (1914): 61-115.

_____. "Enn um Brasilíuferðir." *Almanak* (1917): 110-119.

_____. "Vatnabyggðir vestasti hlutinn." *Almanak* (1919): 31-81.

Jónsson, Þorlákur, and Páll Þorláksson. "Fyrstu ár Íslendinga í Dakota." *Almanak* (1901): 37-51.

Leifur. Winnipeg, 1883-1886.

Lögberg. Winnipeg, 1888-1950.

Kjartansson, Helgi Skúli. "Vesturfarir af Íslandi." PhD dissertation, University of Iceland, 1976.

_____. "The Onset of Emigration from Iceland." *American Studies in Scandinavia* 9 (1977): 87-93.

Magnússon, Guðlaugur. "Landnám Íslendinga í Nýja Íslandi." *Almanak* (1899): 24-52.

_____. "Íslenskur innflytjendahópur í Toronto, Ont., árið 1874." *Almanak* (1920): 60-64.

Magnússon, Sigurður J. "Íslendingar í Peneybygð." *Almanak* (1934): 21-55.

Manitoba Free Press.

Matthiasson, John S. "Adaption to an Ethnic Structure: The Urban Icelandic-Canadians of Winnipeg." In *The Anthropology of Iceland*, eds. E. Paul Durrenberger and Gísli Pálsson. Iowa City: University of Iowa Press, 1989.

_____. "The Icelandic Canadians: The Paradox of an Assimilated Ethnic Group." In *Two Nations, Many Cultures*, ed. Jean Leonard Elliott. Scarborough, Ontario: Prentice Hall, 1979.

_____. "Icelandic-Canadians in Central Canada: One Experiment in Multiculturalism." *The Western Canadian Journal of Anthropology* 4, 2 (1974): 49-61.

McCracken, Jane. "Stephan G. Stephansson: Icelandic-Canadian Poet and Freethinker." *Canadian Ethnic Studies* 15, 1 (1983): 33-52.

Mossberg, Christer Lennart. "Notes toward an Introduction to Scandinavian Literature on the Pioneer Experience." In *Proceedings of the Pacific North West Council on Foreign Languages*, 28, 1, ed. John T. Brewer. Corvallis: Oregon State University, 1976.

Norðanfari. Iceland, 1864-1855.

Norðlingur. Iceland, 1875-1882.

Myrdal, Arni, S. "Recollections." *Lögberg-Heimskringla*, February 1 and 22, 1986.

Palmer, Howard, and Douglas Francis, eds. *The Prairie West: Historical Readings,* second edition. Edmonton: University of Alberta Press, 1992.

Olesen, G.J. "Sögu-ágrip Íslendinga í Suður-Cypress sveitinni í Manitoba" *Almanak* (1935): 21-54; (1936): 37-56; (1937): 67-88; (1938): 42-86; (1939): 24-61; (1940): 25-31.

Pétursson, R. "Upphaf Vesturferða og Þjóðminningarhátíðin." *Tímariti Þjóðræknisfélags Íslendinga* (1933): 66-78.

_____. "Landskoðunarferðin til Alaska, 1874." *Tímariti Þjóðræknisfélags Íslendinga* (1934): 9-29.

Saga. Winnipeg, 1925-1931.

Sameiningin. Winnipeg, 1886-1965.

Seattle Times, 1902-1903.

Sigurðsson, Magnús. "Landnemar Geysisbygðar í Nýja Íslandi." *Almanak* (1932): 34-112.

_____. "Landnemar Víðirbygðar í Nýja Íslandi." *Almanak* (1933): 33-110.

_____. "Landnemar Víðirbygðar og Geysisbygðar í Nýja Íslandi." *Almanak* (1934): 59-61.

Símonarson, Símon. "Icelandic Pioneers of 1874." *Icelandic Candian* (Winter 1946): 24-26.

Skagfjörð, Björn K. Letter dated 1 September 1873 and written in Rosseau, Ontario. *Norðanfari,* January 1874.

Svava. Gimli, 1896-1904.

Sveinsson, Bjarni. "Söguþættir Íslendinga í Keewatin." *Almanak* (1936): 21-34.

Syrpa. Winnipeg, 1911-1922.

Tímarit Þjóðræknisfélags Íslendinga. Winnipeg, 1919-1940.

Thorgrimson, A. "Íslenskt þjóðerni vestan hafs." *Syrpa* Vlll-lX (1920): 232-243.

Valgardson, W.D. "The Icelandic Community and Its Literature." *The Icelandic Canadian* 60, 1 (1982): 35-36.

Welsted, John, John Everitt and Christoph Stadel, eds. *The Geography of Manitoba: Its Land and Its People*. Winnipeg: University of Manitoba Press,1996.

Whitehead, LeRoy. "Icelandic Converts Honored." *The Desert News*, Salt Lake City, 30 July 1938.

Þjóðólfur. Iceland, 1871-1884.

Þorláksson, Páll (ed. Þórlákur Jónsson, 1882). "Fyrstu ár Íslendinga í Dakota." *Almanak* (1901): 37-51.

_____. "Letter to the editor." *Norðanfari*, January 1874.

Þorsteinsson, Tryggvi. "Frá stofnun Tantallon-byggðarinnar í Saskatchewan." *Almanak* (1951): 68-70.

Winnipeg *Free Press*. Winnipeg, 1875-1880.

Winnipeg Tribune. Winnipeg, 1875-1880.

Unpublished Material

Unpublished material is from Special Collections, Dafoe Library, University of Manitoba.

Friðriksson, Friðjón. Letters to Rev. Jón Bjarnason, 1874-1881.

Rev. Jón Bjarnason Clipping File. A collection of letters, articles to and by Bjarnason.

Olafsson, Jón. Letters to Rev. Jón Bjarnason 1873-1875.

_____. Report on Alaska project. 1874.

Thordarson, Runa. *Echoes from the Past*. Point Roberts, Wa. Privately printed. 1975.

Thorlaksson, P. Letters to Rev. Jón Bjarnason.

Index